NORTH AMERICA

A Human Geography

.50
80P
PB

NORTH AMERICA

A Human Geography

Paul Guinness
Michael Bradshaw

BARNES & NOBLE BOOKS

TOTOWA, NEW JERSEY

Library of Congress Cataloging in Publication Data

Guinness, Paul.
   North America: A Human Geography.
   1. North America—Description and travel.
   I. Bradshaw, Michael.   II. Title.
   E41.G85   1985   970   84-28434

ISBN 0-389-20557-5 (PBK)

First published in the USA 1985 by
BARNES & NOBLE BOOKS
81 ADAMS DRIVE
TOTOWA, NEW JERSEY, 07512

Contents

Stream-eroded landscape in the Ozark plateau, Missouri

The cover photograph shows the Central Business District of Los Angeles and the photograph on the title page is of a moraine lake near Banff in Alberta

Preface

This book is a 'different' geography of North America (defined as Canada and the United States of America) from those available, and is related to changes in geographical thinking and teaching. It is designed to provide a geographical understanding of two developed nations written from the outsider's perspective of two British geographers who have specialised in their study. It also aims to provide a series of studies in aspects of human geography in a broader framework than a more traditional regional geography text, and yet with greater cohesion in its case studies than is found in a general human geography text. This approach will make the book of value in sixth form and college human geography courses, as well as in courses with this particular regional emphasis. In the more general context, the studies described here can be compared with situations in the UK and in developing countries.

The outline of the book is related to these aims. The countries are introduced by way of the theme of affluence, its origins and present problems. A historical view of geographical development is then taken, followed by reviews of aspects of the systematic human geography of Canada and the United States.

Readers are recommended to use an atlas to complement the wealth of diagrams, maps and photographs. They may also like to update the statistics via the annual *Canadian Year Book* and the *Statistical Abstract of the United States*, and, on a more detailed level, by the *United States County and City Data Book* (published every five years, 1967, 1972, 1977, 1982).

Paul Guinness
Michael Bradshaw   1984

Acknowledgments

A number of people and institutions have contributed to this book. Dr Roland Allison was instrumental in suggesting many of the ideas in the early days. Professor Allan Patmore has acted as adviser and his many helpful suggestions have been adopted. Much information has been furnished by the libraries at London School of Economics, at the Canadian High Commission and the United States Embassy in London, and at the Centre for North American Studies at the College of St Mark and St John in Plymouth.

Both authors are particularly grateful to their wives and families who have helped to provide environments conducive to work.

Photographs in the book are included by kind permission of: US Department of the Interior Geological Survey (6, 139, 311, 322), Tourism British Columbia (61, 62, 233, 249, 251), British Petroleum (122), ESSO Petroleum (124, 172), USDA Soil Conservation Service (129, 134, 136, 184, 213, 220, 222, 226, 265, 274, 301), Ontario Information Services (169, 209, 228), Ontario Hydro (175), Ontario Department of Mines (180), Canadian Pacific (194, 195), Nova Scotia Communications and Information Centre (230), Ontario Department of Agriculture (231), Port Authority of New York (295, 297), NASA (306, 345), Los Angeles City Planning Department (315), Ontario Government (330), Department of Planning, City of Chicago (339), Chicago Convention and Tourism Bureau (341), ACE Photo Agency (cover).

Introduction: North America, the Affluent Continent

The promised land

Canada and the United States of America have been regarded by many outsiders as 'the promised land' ever since the North American continent was discovered at the end of the fifteenth century. The Spaniards looked for gold, the French found beaver furs and the British began to settle the continent as a means of escape from their homeland or as an area which could produce crops for sale in London, Bristol or Liverpool. Later groups from northern and southern Europe escaped there from religious, political or economic oppression, and today there are substantial migrations from Asiatic and especially Latin American countries. These peoples from around the world have looked to the USA and Canada as a place of freedom and economic opportunity.

Few countries in the world exceed the Gross National Product per head of the USA and Canada. Apart from West Germany these are mostly small states around the Persian Gulf with high national incomes from oil sales, or small European states (Figure I.1). The presence of over 230 million people in the USA and 25 million in Canada with such a high average national production means that the economies of these countries contain the greatest concentration of wealth in the world.

The geographer begins by observing differences between countries and by attempting to explain these differences. A list can be made of the physical and human resources which have contributed to such a concentration of economic wealth in North America in the twentieth century (Figure I.2). This century has sometimes been called 'The American century'.

Many would argue that the wealth of physical resources has been a major factor in the advancement of these two countries. Both were settled as largely untouched areas; the previous occupation by Indians and Eskimoes had done little to alter or use up the natural resources. The vast areas of rich soils, together with the deposits of minerals provided the basis for the world's most productive farm sector. The wealth from the gold discoveries of the mid-nineteenth century provided part of the capital for developing the transcontinental railroads and manufacturing industries of the late nineteenth century, and the wealth from oil and natural gas has been the basis for economic growth in the twentieth century, with the increased mobility provided by the automobile, truck and airplane. Minerals not available in the USA have often been found in Canada. The vast size of these

Fig. I.1 The leading nations in the world GNP league

Country	Population (millions) 1981	2000 (projected)	GNP per head (US $) 1979
Kuwait	1.4	2.8	17 270
Qatar	0.2	0.2	16 590
United Arab Emirates	1.0	1.6	15 590
Switzerland	6.3	6.9	14 240
Denmark	5.1	5.4	11 900
West Germany	61.3	65.6	11 730
Sweden	8.3	9.2	10 920
Belgium	9.9	10.7	10 890
USA	229.8	260.4	10 820
Norway	4.1	4.5	10 710
Iceland	0.2	0.3	10 490
Netherlands	14.2	16.0	10 240
Canada	24.1	31.3	9 650
Compare: Japan	117.8	132.1	8 800
UK	55.9	61.6	6 340
USSR	268.0	290.0	4 110

two countries (Canada 9 250 000 km²; USA 9 173 913 km²) meant an open frontier with plentiful unoccupied land in the early days. The USA still has 7 hectares per person, compared with 0.4 hectares in the UK (67 in Canada). The two countries extend from 25 degrees to 80 degrees north, a range of latitude that produces a variety of climates (Figure I.3), which in turn allows a multitude of different crops and tree species to be grown. The timber resources include hardwoods in the humid areas of the south-east and softwoods on the west coast and in the cold north. Most commercial timber comes from the fir and spruce forests of Canada and the west coast, and from the pine woods of the south-east. The crops range from temperate cereals, vegetables and fruits to subtropical sugar cane, rice, citrus fruits, tobacco and cotton. Although the tundra of the north and the desert of the south-west have provided difficult regions for settlement (Chapter 7), the wealth accumulated elsewhere has been used to irrigate sections of the desert. The position of the continent in the world has proved another important factor. From a beginning on the edge of the known world, North America went through a period lasting into the twentieth century when it avoided large-scale external wars. Since the bloody and destructive American Civil War in the 1860s there has been no fighting on the American or Canadian mainland. Even the involvement in World War I (1914–18) and World War II (1939–45) had positive results since it led to the increased growth of manufacturing after a period of economic depression in the 1930s, and did not involve destruction by bombing or ground fighting. By the end of World War II the centre of world economic power had shifted from Europe to the USA, which found itself in a central world position for trade with Europe, Asia, Africa and South America. Canada was drawn into the American economic empire increasingly as American money was used to develop Canadian mineral resources.

But it would be wrong to suggest that the physical environment and its resources had exercised a deterministic effect on the growth and eventual pre-eminence of the USA and Canada. For one thing, the peoples paid little attention to husbanding and conserving the resources they dug from the ground. Tobacco and cotton farmers plundered the soils of the south-east so that soil erosion became a major problem, highlighted again by the 'Dust Bowl' of the western high plains in the 1930s. By 1890 the Bureau of Census in the USA announced that the frontier of plentiful new

Fig. 1.2 *US growth factors*

	1776 INDEPENDENCE	1850	1900	TODAY
VIRGIN CONTINENT	Rich soils............	Soil erosion...........		Dust Bowl........ Better management
VAST SPACE	Land purchases...............	Open frontier...........	End of land frontier 1890 / Competition for space........	Still 7 hectares per head (U.K. 0.2 hectares)
STORES OF MINERALS AND FOSSIL FUELS		Coal........... Gold...........	Oil........... Copper...........	Gas........... Cheap fuels } Cheap worldwide sources } 1973 energy price rise crisis
WORLD POSITION	'Edge of Europe'	100 years of cheap defence (low taxes)	1917 World War I involvement and central world position	
VARIED CLIMATES		Range of crops: temperate to sub tropical..........	Areas of water shortage supplied – at increasing cost.........	Frostbelt v Sunbelt
ORIGINAL PEOPLES	Indians fought and removed...........		ignored........ greater political involvement and friction	
RELIGIOUS HERITAGE	Puritan in north........ 'Protestant work ethic'...........		WASP significance........	continuing factor
IMMIGRANT SKILLS	British...... German........ Irish.....	Italians....... Russian Jews.......	Immigration slowed..... Large Spanish speaking influx	
RACIAL EXPLOITATION	Slavery.........	Slavery ended.........	Blacks, Puerto Ricans etc at disadvantage..Friction	
ECONOMIC POLICIES AND POLITICAL DOCTRINES	State government dominant........	Little government interference with business and wealth accumulation	Beginnings of regulation........	NEW DEAL...... Increasing Federal involvement.........
SOCIAL MOBILITY	Get ahead' for immigrants: money = success............		High GNP.........	Attitudes questioned...
EDUCATION	Early free schools.........	Vocational programmes.........		Overextended in 1960s
AGRICULTURAL TECHNOLOGY		Focus of effort: Land Grant Colleges.....		High productivity... Cheap food... Overproduction... Increasing expertise
TRANSPORT	Water transport........	Railroad dominance........	Automobile and airline culture... (Rapid and efficient movement)	Urban development affected.........
TECHNOLOGY AND MANUFACTURING			MAJOR WORLD MANUFACTURER: mass production Science/technology mix: telephone, electric light,.........	Apollo.......
MASS MARKET	No internal tariffs........		Economies of scale........ Advertizing............	Extravagant use natural resources........... Vast government R and D expenditure Credit card systems............ Increasing female employment (more production and larger market)

Fig. I.3 *The major climatic regions of North America*

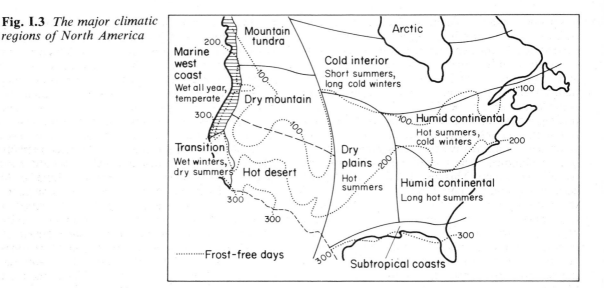

land was closed and that the USA would have to make do with the land it had. Since that time there has been increasing competition for the land available, and this has led eventually to a more careful approach to its use. The easy access to so many rich mineral resources meant that they were used up rapidly and that other resources were drawn in from around the world.

The dominance of world oil production by American companies kept world prices low until the OPEC price rises of 1973 and since, and this reliance on cheap energy and raw materials led to economic crisis and recession in the late 1970s and early 1980s as basic costs rose. The supply of water to the desert areas has resulted in a change in the balance of the economy in the USA, and some areas have been set back in competition with subsidised irrigation, while many irrigated areas like central Arizona are reaching the limits of water resources. Large and important question marks thus hang over the continuing supply of material resources to the gigantic maws of the American economy.

It is also important to realise, with George Perkins Marsh the nineteenth-century American conservationist, that whilst some 'think that the earth made man, man in fact made the earth'. This statement referred to the unfortunate impacts of human beings on the environment, but it also emphasises the importance of human resources in the development of the USA and Canada. The original inhabitants have not shared in the econ-

omic advances in the two countries until recently, and today many Indians and Eskimoes see their culture dying as the trappings of American economic life reach their isolated reservations. The new Americans brought attitudes and ideas with them as they immigrated from the seventeenth century onwards. Many were intent on getting ahead and making money unfettered by too much government interference. This was a major issue in the War of Independence (1776–83) and throughout the nineteenth century the free market-place economics of William Smith ('Wealth of Nations') predominated. Eventually the federal, state and provincial governments had to introduce laws so that the enthusiasm of the money-making businessmen was not allowed to result in great gains for themselves at the expense of their workers or customers. Thus railroad regulation arose in the late nineteenth century when a number of companies had made money on the transfer of stock and had allowed the condition of their lines and rolling stock to become dangerous.

In the twentieth century the role of the government has increased, but this is still accepted reluctantly by people and politicians. It was realised at an early stage that education was important for those who wished to get ahead, and free schools were established at the beginning of the nineteenth century. Vocational programmes always played an important part, and there was a special focus on education in agriculture. Special colleges were established after an 1872 Act making government grants of land in each state so that training and research in agriculture could be carried out. In combination with the development of production-line manufacturing of machinery and of chemical fertilizers, this has resulted in a highly technological and commercial agriculture which provides sixty per cent of the food in world trade as well as most of the home needs. All aspects of manufacturing benefited from the local development of innovative technology and management techniques. The United States became the world's workshop. This was aided greatly by the continuing supply of cheap immigrant labour until this was regulated in the 1920s. By then there was a large pool of black labour anxious to leave the repressive American South and move into the northern cities. Immigrants not only provided cheap labour, but also many of the ideas. This was particularly the case as scientists left Nazi Germany.

A further aspect of the industrial society was the development of the transport system from the continental railroads of the late nineteenth century to the improved waterways, roads, pipelines and air routes of the late twentieth century. These have provided the most mobile society in history with the means of rapid movement for people and freight. The growing wealth of the increasing population also provided a huge home market and encouraged the economies of scale which enabled the factories to produce, for instance, large, gas-guzzling automobiles at very low prices. (In the late 1970s it still cost less to buy a large American car with most of the trimmings in the USA than to buy a small British car in the UK.)

The increasing involvement of women in the labour force in the mid-twentieth century not only resulted in a further expansion of production, but also in an increased family budget and expenditure on goods, homes and automobiles. By the late 1970s items bought in American shops were cheaper than those in the UK (food and clothes a little cheaper, consumer goods and cars half the price), and American family incomes were well above the British average.

Many other indicators of American affluence could be cited. The Canadians kept pace with this to an extent, and became a part of the same economic system, financed from Boston, New York and Chicago.

As with the physical resources, not all the results have been positive. In addition to the conflict with the Indians, there was the institution of slavery and the subsequent penalisation and impoverishment of the Blacks and other ethnic groups: their chances of getting up the social and economic ladders and even getting ordinary jobs, are smaller than for whites. This has resulted in friction in the past and more is promised for the future. The dominant ethos of personal economic freedom is favoured by the successful majority, but raises questions about large sections of American society which do not see the benefits of the great affluence in their own homes. For many the whole set of values and attitudes which focus on general economic criteria, GNP and the nature of technical-industrial-urban society in the USA are now under question. Canadians have asked such questions publicly for a longer period of time, and Canada is often able to show the way ahead to the Americans. It was once said that 'a Canadian is a person who has not been offered a job in the USA'. More recently the flow of people from Canada to the USA has been reversed, and many Americans working in the Detroit or Buffalo areas prefer to live or spend weekends on the Canadian side of the border. American city planning departments look to Toronto as an ideal, and Canadians experience a greater spread of economic and social opportunity. The confidence in unending social and economic progress, often called 'The American Dream' and sometimes assuming the level of a secular religion, has been dwindling due to the problems of overseas involvement, government and economic mismanagement which have faced the country since the 1970s together with the increasing voices of the oppressed within the USA.

Quality of life

The obsession with the 'quantity of life' is giving way to a concern about the *quality of life*. The GNP is no longer seen as the only measure of well-being. An alternative measure derived in the 1970s is the Physical Quality of Life Index (PQLI), which originated in the Overseas Development Council in 1977. It is based on three measures (Figure I.4) which focus on the direct outputs of life expectancy, infant mortality and literacy, rather than on indirect inputs such as doctors per head, calorie intakes or years of schooling. It was

Fig. I.4 The Physical Quality of Life Index for selected countries. (After J W Sewell 1977)

Country	GNP per head 1974	Life expectancy at birth	Infant mortality per 1 000	Literacy %	PQLI (Sweden = 100)
USA	6 670	71	17	99	96
Sweden	7 240	75	9	99	100
USSR	2 600	70	28	100	94
Taiwan	810	69	26	85	88
Costa Rica	840	69	45	89	87
Sri Lanka	130	68	45	81	83
India	140	50	139	34	41
Haiti	170	50	150	10	31
Ghana	430	44	156	25	31
Zambia	520	44	160	15–20	28
Angola	710	38	203	10–15	15
Niger	120	39	200	5	14

designed for application to developing countries, but also shows that the USA has some weaknesses. This was pointed out by Vernon Jordan, the black leader and Director of the National Urban League, when it was released in 1977. The USA lagged behind countries like Sweden and the Netherlands when seen as a whole, but the blacks and some states have PQLI levels on a par with countries like Sri Lanka, Taiwan and Costa Rica.

The PQLI is a simple measure which allows a crude comparison to be made. The *Social Well-Being Index* is a more complex approach developed by David Smith. He saw the American way of life as an inconsistent mixture of public statements about freedom, justice and equality and the reality of inequality often engendered by unrestrained capitalism. In many parts of the USA the people are able to enjoy a very pleasant, affluent life, but in others there is poverty and inequality. He set out to measure these differences by looking at seven major aspects which affect a person's well-being or quality of life. The seven aspects are:

(a) Income, wealth and employment
(b) Living environment, including housing quality
(c) Health and access to health care
(d) Education length and level attained
(e) Social order as reflected in crime, family breakdown, drug addiction.

(f) Social belonging as demonstrated by electoral participation or racial segregation.
(g) Recreation and leisure opportunities

Smith produced a composite map based on over 100 components within the first six categories, since he found difficulty in obtaining good measures for (g). This map shows how the states varied in 1970 (Figure I.5). The approach can also be used for smaller areas, where greater extremes emerge, as in the Census tracts of cities (divisions of cities akin to the British ward). Others have attempted to compile a similar index in relation to national goals set for the USA. These goals tend to focus more on general economic factors than on areas of social or racial equality. The conclusions of all these approaches are similar – that the American South lags behind the rest of the country and that California and the north-east still (in 1970) were better places to live.

Geographers are thus involved in considerations beyond simple description of spatial variations. They wish to explain these, and many would also involve themselves in the issues. Some may suggest solutions which would be operated within the present structure of society and government. Others are more radical and see the inequalities and poverty as a result of the capitalist system which only a revolutionary solution will change.

Another aspect of considering the standards of living in the USA and Canada is the idea of *development*. In the past this has been confused

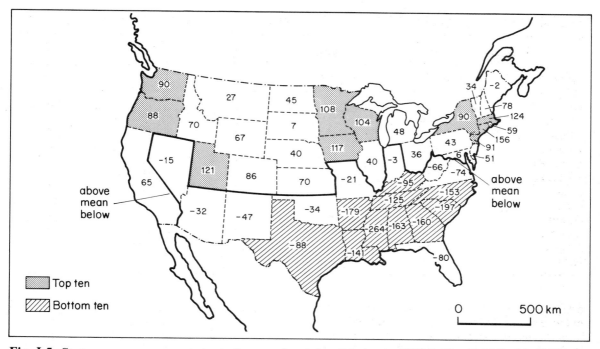

Fig. I.5 *State scores on a composite indicator of social well-being in 1970 (After DM Smith 1973)*

with economic growth, but it is now being thought of differently in relation to the well-being of a whole country. In developing countries one of the main tensions is in the local disparity between rich and poor and imposition from without of economic systems and processes which conflict with the local resources and cultural trends. Even the USA has been termed a developing country since it has such a range of incomes within its borders. Poverty exists in the inner cities, in the isolated mountain valleys of the Appalachians, on farms in the southeast, on Indian reservations and amongst the Mexican farm labourers in the south-west. Each region has its pockets of poverty. An indication of the variations within the country can be given by comparing seven of the richest with seven of the poorest counties in the USA (Figure I.6). There are over 3000 counties in the USA, with up to 150 in each state. The seven richest all have large populations, so that wealth is widespread within these counties. They are suburban counties on the outskirts of Washington DC (Montgomery, Fairfax), New York (Westchester, Nassau), Chicago (Du Page), San Francisco (Marin) and Detroit (Oakland). The seven poorest are in the deep south (Holmes, Greene, Jefferson, Tunica)

and in the Appalachian backwoods of Tennessee and eastern Kentucky. The median family income for Montgomery county is seven times that of Owsley county, and many other aspects in these contrasting groups of counties are related to that difference in income.

Other features of political and economic life also resemble the situation in developing countries. In the poor areas like eastern Kentucky the natural resources of coal and timber have been bought up and exploited by companies from outside the region and little of the wealth gained has been retained in the region itself. Many of the poorer southern states have a history of one party politics, another feature of many developing countries. Whilst it is clear that many of us would find difficulty in identifying the US economy with that of Zaire or Bangladesh, this discussion causes us to reconsider the nature of 'development' and the fact that even in the world's most affluent country there are many major pockets of poverty. Canada has some similar problems, especially in the rather isolated eastern Maritime Provinces and amongst the rural French in Quebec and the Indians and Eskimoes in the north. These are all on a smaller scale in comparison with the USA, and there is a

Fig. I.6 Characteristics of the seven richest and seven poorest USA counties in 1970 in relation to median family income

	RICHEST SEVEN							POOREST SEVEN						
	Montgomery, Maryland	Fairfax, Virginia	Nassau, New York	Dupage, Illinois	Marin, California	Oakland, Michigan	Westchester, New York	Holmes, Mississippi	Greene, Alabama	Jefferson, Mississippi	Tunica, Mississippi	Wolfe, Kentucky	Hancock, Tennessee	Owsley, Kentucky
Median family income ($) 1969	16 708	15 697	14 625	14 457	13 931	13 823	13 774	3 089	3 032	3 025	2 896	2 694	2 683	3 407
POPULATION														
Total	571 558	512 915	1 403 289	553 670	220 424	966 625	879 241	22 835	10 435	8 695	10 940	6 148	6 486	5 189
Density (per square mile)	1 555	1 286	4 856	1 673	424	1 115	1 985	30	17	17	24	27	28	26
% over 65	6.8	3.2	9.0	6.4	8.1	7.8	11.8	14.1	14.8	13.9	11.2	12.7	12.8	14.5
% urban	89.2	89.1	99.7	95.3	92.4	90.0	93.8	23.8	26.3	0	0	0	0	0
% black	4.1	3.5	4.6	0.3	2.4	3.1	9.5	68.1	75.4	75.3	72.7	0	1.2	0.3
% change 1960–70	53.3	78.9	9.9	56.5	42.1	31.5	10.6	−14.7	−21.7	−8.4	−29.5	−13.2	−13.4	−6.4
% net migration 1960–70	37.0	56.6	1.5	39.6	28.2	15.4	2.4	−26.3	−32.3	−17.0	−49.0	−23.2	−21.4	−16.7
% change 1970–75	7.9	13.2	−3.2	10.5	3.5	6.6	−1.9	−0.6	−3.4	−7.6	−9.0	7.2	−3.5	3.8
% net migration 1970–75	4.1	7.6	−4.3	5.4	1.0	2.1	−3.3	−5.0	−6.0	−11.6	−15.2	3.7	−5.2	0.4
birth rate (per 1 000) 1975	11.4	11.8	9.0	14.2	9.7	13.0	10.5	21.5	20.6	21.6	24.0	19.8	13.7	14.3
death rate (per 1 000) 1975	5.7	3.9	8.0	5.6	6.6	6.6	9.0	11.8	13.6	10.9	10.4	12.0	11.4	10.4
EDUCATION														
% over 4 years high school	79.5	78.8	65.8	72.0	55.5	63.9	64.5	28.0	26.8	22.0	19.8	16.6	16.0	31.2
LABOUR														
% unemployed	2.0	2.1	2.8	2.1	4.7	5.3	2.6	7.2	4.7	11.7	10.3	7.9	6.3	8.5
HEALTH														
doctors per 100 000 1975	321.6	137.6	265.1	157.0	366.1	245.7	353.9	21.9	38.3	92.0	27.4	16.3	30.8	38.5
INCOME														
% families below poverty line	3.0	3.5	3.5	2.3	3.5	3.8	4.5	53.0	53.7	59.0	55.4	59.0	55.5	61.6
% families 1969 over $15 000	56.1	52.7	47.9	46.2	44.1	43.3	44.1	3.2	5.3	2.4	4.6	1.9	1.7	2.5
Public assistance to families per month (1976) ($)	223	226	382	249	219	287	384	50	100	45	50	189	105	188
HOUSING														
% lacking plumbing	1.1	1.2	1.0	0.7	0.8	1.1	2.0	47.1	56.9	54.3	56.0	63.1	60.6	70.1
LOCAL GOVERNMENT FINANCE														
Property taxes per head (1970–71)	256	217	484	183	375	282	470	51	36	43	48	20	23	21
Expenditure per head (education, highways, welfare)	577	460	812	395	609	466	780	276	368	294	263	216	204	184
CRIME (1976)														
Known serious per 100 000	4 528	5 025	3 565	4 314	5 784	6 526	4 312	346	–	196	347	992	–	752

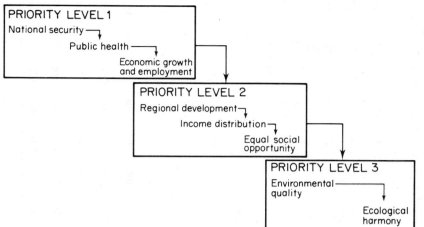

Fig. I.7 *Different levels of government preoccupation in relation to development (After T O'Riordan 1977)*

broader spread of income across the country's population.

In another indicator of development, the major preoccupation of government (Figure I.7), it is clear that the USA and Canada have advanced from the stage where national goals are related only to national security, public health and national income. The lobbies for a more equal distribution of wealth, regional development and environmental concern take them to a much higher level. This progress has been rapid in the 1960s and 1970s, but began much earlier with the problems of soil erosion and the preservation of wilderness lands in the National Parks movement. The large-scale affluence in North America has placed enormous pressures on the resources of energy and materials available. This was realised as a series of publications such as 'Limits to Growth' were produced in the early 1970s and emphasised the problems of such intensive use of earth resources without concern for the future. The Cuyahoga River in Cleveland burst into flame along its oil-covered surface, and Lake Erie lost its fish due to pollution by industrial effluent, fertilizers and washing powder residues. American society was termed 'the effluent society' and laws were passed in the early 1970s to impose strict anti-pollution laws. These have led to greatly increased costs for manufacturing instead of passing on the costs of such activity in an invisible form to society as a whole. The reliance on cheap energy resources has given way to a new era of expensive energy which has resulted in inflation. American society has to cope with major changes as a result of this new situation, in addition to attempting to spread the fruits of economic well-being throughout its society.

All of these developments are of immense interest to geographers, since their concern is with the real world. Charting progress in the world's most affluent society should alert us to problems we must face as well, and also to some of the pitfalls to avoid and the paths to follow.

Images of America

If the study of an area such as North America involves the identification and exploration of differences in economic opportunity and social well-being, together with an involvement in suggesting ways ahead for the future, it also necessitates (especially for the outsider) an attempt to understand what makes the local tick. As Wreford Watson has written (1979) 'The geography of any country is what people see in it, want from it and do with it'. This again emphasises the point that man makes the land, but also looks deeper than that theme to seek reasons which explain the ordering of the landscapes. David Lowenthal has studied approaches by different peoples to the world in which they live in terms of their set of values and vision of what life is for. Actions arise from these and affect the institutions which decide how land is used. The American scene has resulted from events over two or three centuries (compared with the much longer period in western Europe). Those involved in its evolution have been dominated by the basic necessity of getting a living and any aesthetic considerations have been reserved for special and unusual areas. This results in the dominance of the stark functional nature of much American building development, especially in the industrial growth period of the late nineteenth and early twentieth centuries, and the lack of permanence and continual rebuilding in city centres. Magnificent office blocks are constructed amidst derelict older buildings and extensive car parking lots and give the impression that individual features are more important than the whole. The remote and special are of interest rather than the nearby and typical, and the landscape has the unfinished appearance of one in the process of 'building for the future'. These are some of the features which Lowenthal – an American – sees as resulting from a particularly American approach to the design (conscious or unconscious) of its landscapes and enshrined in seemingly mundane areas such as planning laws. Canadians tend to take a different view, although it is often coloured by American attitudes. Their approach is often a combination of British or French values and a desire for orderliness and completeness.

This book

These ideas are basic to the development of this book. It is not just another regional geography of the USA and Canada, but attempts to develop a view of geography within this context. The real world is examined in relation to theoretical ideas. The major issues in American and Canadian society with a spatial aspect are studied from a geographical point of view, and an attempt is made to see the processes of change through American and Canadian eyes.

The emphasis on the historical evolution of the two countries is thus basic to the developing themes and to the use of geographical process models which have to be seen in a historical context. This leads to a consideration of the evolution of regional differences in the late nineteenth and twentieth centuries. The second major section is a geographical analysis of resource development in the US and Canadian economies. This begins with the basic question of energy and then takes the individual sectors of the economy. The final section brings together the studies of regional and economic geography in a consideration of urban America. This includes a study of the changing face of American and Canadian cities, the changing locations of manufacturing, retail and office industries in them, mass transit and the social problems of ghettos.

Part 1
The Development of Regional Differences

1

The Original Americans

The Indians and other groups, who inhabited North America before the European takeover from the sixteenth century onwards, included a wide variety of peoples living simply in close relationships with the different natural environments of the continent. There were between 5 and 10 millions of them. Whilst they can be categorized as being of stone age culture, the designation suggests a lower view than is justified. Many groups did live extremely simple lives, but others achieved much in social organization and in farming technology.

When the Europeans arrived they learnt much from the Indians, and could have profited to an even greater extent by attention to Indian habits. European occupation of the continent soon brought about the painful ejection of the Indians from desirable areas and this resulted in almost continuous warfare from the sixteenth to the end of the nineteenth century. The Indians, although decimated by European diseases, tricked and deceived into giving up their lands in exchange for paltry trinkets, and shifted from their ancient lands, had to be almost exterminated before the European conquest was complete. There seemed to be no way in which the two cultures could mix.

The eastern woodland Indians

As a group the Indians of the wooded areas east of the Mississippi River were the most highly de-veloped in culture, and supported the highest population densities. A large proportion of the peoples were essentially peaceful farmers living in towns and villages in a variety of house styles and with good government and highly-sophisticated social controls and class divisions. They accepted a belief that all living things had a spiritual unity. They revered the earth, but regarded possession of land as a trust for the benefit of all the tribe: there was little private ownership of land and it was divided only for use. This made it very difficult for the Indians to understand the land-grabbing ways of Europeans.

The eastern area of North America, being humid, temperate and of moderate relief, was covered almost entirely by woodland – in contrast to the drier western areas (Figure 1.1). This environment provided deep soils made fertile by long ages of recycling nutrients through leaf litter, and, especially in the southern parts, the long growing season encouraged the development of complex farming methods. There was also plentiful protein in the form of woodland wildlife and fish along the coasts and in the streams.

One group of peoples lived on the coastal plain: they were mostly smaller nations, but exhibited great variety (Figure 1.2). In the far north (present Maine, eastern Canada) they subsisted on fish and game with some primitive farming and maple sugar gathering on the southern margins. In the New England and Hudson Valley area, and in some other distinctive areas to the south (present New Jersey to Virginia; Georgia, Florida) there

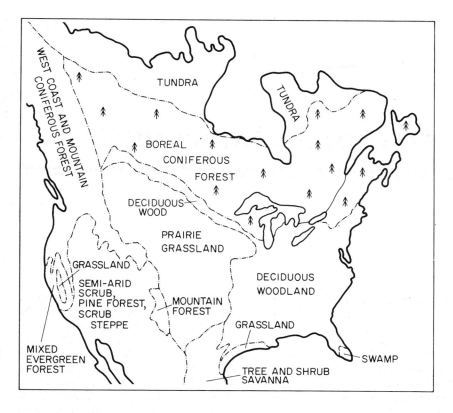

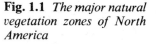

Fig. 1.1 *The major natural vegetation zones of North America*

was increasing reliance on farming to diversify the fishing and hunting along the swampy coastlands. The Indians cleared patches of forest by removing bark around the trees and letting them die, and then burning the undergrowth. They would then grow corn and beans. By the time of the main British occupation of these areas in the seventeenth century, however, European diseases (introduced since the early sixteenth century) had caused a major decline in the coastal Indian population, and the new occupiers were able to establish their early colonies more easily than otherwise might have been the case.

Inland, however, there were larger and more powerful peoples, who were to provide a greater barrier to the incoming Europeans. Many were grouped in confederations of tribes for mutual peace-keeping. Once again, there was a transition from north to south. The Hurons in Ontario, for instance, lived largely by hunting, but inhabited stockaded villages, holding 4000–6000 people. The Hurons linked up with the Algonquins of present Quebec, and the two had a long-lasting feud with the Iroquois League of Five (later Six)

Nations to the south of Lake Erie and the St Lawrence Valley. This League existed primarily to maintain peace amongst a group of peoples, and has been described as more advanced than many European institutions of the time. The Iroquois lived in villages of 600–700 people: a palisade enclosed a group of long houses, each with apartments for 10–20 families and a meeting room. The palisade was surrounded by fields of corn, beans and squashes (vegetables rather like marrows, but with many varieties, sizes and shapes), and they used up to fifteen varieties of hybridized corn, eight varieties of squashes and sixty of beans. These Indians hunted and fished, but also gathered up to fifty varieties of edible roots and thirty-four varieties of fruit. They burnt off the fields each year after harvest, thus returning nutrients to the soil, and by this means the same field could be used for up to twelve years. They also realised that beans grown with corn would concentrate important nutrients in the soil (although they did not know about nitrates as such). Their horticulture was thus as advanced as any in Europe in the seventeenth century.

Fig. 1.2 *Indians in North America prior to European incursion*

South and west of the Iroquois were groups of less powerful tribes with looser federations, but also largely sedentary farmers living in villages and growing corn, beans and squash. They lived in a variety of dwellings from long houses to wigwams constructed of saplings covered by strips of birch bark. All were self-sufficient and independent, and some nations like the Ottawa acted as traders amongst others like the Shawnee, Miami and Susquehanna.

The most advanced culture of all seems to have developed in the Lower Mississippi Valley and thrived from Illinois to Natchez between AD 700 and 1600. It was based on an agricultural revolution involving new implements and techniques, as well as the hybridizing of corn. This led to a population and cultural explosion, and major centres of several thousand inhabitants were characterized by ceremonial and administrative buildings on large mound structures. Little is known of this culture in its finest development, since the entry and rapid spread of European diseases led to epidemics and scattering in the sixteenth century. Some of the mound structures still exist, and

colonists found the Natchez centre in the final stages of disintegration. On moving out of the Mississippi Valley these Indians regrouped into several tribes, which still retained many of the advanced cultural features: most re-located in south-eastern parts of the continent where the environment was most similar to the one from which they had come. Thus the Muskogis (called Creeks by the English) included a loose confederation of over fifty towns in present Georgia and Alabama, and each settlement often had a specific function in relation to others. The Chickasaws, Choctaws and Cherokees occupied sixty large villages in the hills to the north of the Muskogis (in present Tennessee and North Carolina), and other Indian nations moved into Florida, replacing peoples exterminated by the Spaniards in the sixteenth century (the Seminole group was formed by interbreeding of Indians and runaway slaves). Many of these southern peoples lived in stockaded towns with over a hundred buildings around a central square. Buildings were often made of grass and plaster over a pole framework. Farming was the main occupation, producing corn, beans, squash and tobacco. Further remnants of the Mississippi culture were preserved in cooking skills, and clothing was often colourful and medicinal knowledge practical.

The western Indians

The more varied natural environments west of the Mississippi resulted in a fragmentation and isolation of many groups, and the dominance of arid conditions allowed lower densities to exist. There was thus a greater variety of lifestyles.

The plains between the Mississippi and the Rockies encouraged the development of a nomadic way of life; food and most other resources, in the shape of the buffalo, were available widely and in mobile form. Horses were used only after their introduction by the Spaniards, but provided increased mobility and were in widespread use by AD 1800. In the High Plains nations such as the Blackfoot, Crow, Arapaho, Cheyenne and Comanche were entirely nomadic and had no permanent villages. The more humid area to the east was the home of 'prairie Indians' (Iowa, Kansa, Missouri, Omaha, Pawnee), who planted corn around permanent villages and made summer/autumn excursions to hunt buffalo. The foothills of the Rockies were occupied by smaller peoples (Nez Perce, Ute, Shoslin), who also hunted buffalo in summer, but returned to winter camps in the uplands to gather roots and berries. All their material cultures were similar, using stone knives, bows and arrows, and stone-tipped lances. They lived in villages of buffalo-hide tipis — easily folded and moved. Social organisation was based on groups of 300–500 under a chief, and governed by a council. Each band included several 'soldier societies' and provided a practical group size for hunting buffalo. The bands were united loosely in tribal groups, which had occasional assemblies to re-state common aims.

The Rocky Mountains and often arid intermontane plateaus to the west provided even harsher environments. The scattered peoples were dominated by the quest for food, and overall numbers of Indians were small. The richest natural resources were in the north, around the Columbia River, where fish, bear, elk and jack rabbit provided a living above bare subsistence. But in the south, in the semi-desert of Nevada, the small nomadic groups were reduced to eating anything they could find. The family group was the basic social unit here, since larger groups could not be supported. Some groups were able to overcome the difficulties of the arid environment under special circumstances. Thus the Hopi and Zuni pueblo dwellers (present eastern Arizona, western New Mexico) constructed communal adobe houses in inaccessible cliffside cracks, and gained a living by hunting and growing corn. They developed weaving and pottery skills, and were highly cultured and peaceful. Along the Gila and Lower Colorado Rivers village-dwelling Indians operated a system of irrigation by spreading water over an area for crop-growing, and they also produced baskets and mats. There were also camp-dwellers such as the Navajo and Apache, who moved into this area from the Great Plains in the thirteenth and fourteenth centuries, blending that culture with local institutions. They carried on some farming to supplement the game and the Navajo took up sheep-breeding, but they dressed in grassland buckskins and colourful coats, and produced silver-turquoise ornaments.

The Pacific coastal Indians provided a contrast between north and south. The southern part of present California was not a good environment due to the lack of water, and small groups occupied isolated valleys with a low material culture (living in brush shelters and lean-tos). Northern California and the coastal region stretching north to southern Alaska was characterized by abundant game and salmon and some of the world's most splendid forests. The Indians here developed another advanced culture, with plank houses, large canoes and decorated totem-poles. Some tribes specialized, as in the Nootka whaling tribe on Vancouver Island using cedar dugout canoes.

The northern native Americans

To the north of the eastern woodlands, the Great Plains and the rich coastal forests of the northwest the environment again becomes restrictive: the growing season gets shorter and shorter, and resources for human subsistence are few. Thus the Indians in a belt from subarctic Canada to central

Alaska were few in number and spread out through the coniferous forests. Nations such as the Cree were mainly nomadic hunters and fishermen, since they did not possess the crops which would ripen under these conditions. They were also affected by European diseases: the Chipewayans, one of the most numerous Cree groups, lost ninety per cent of their numbers in a 1791 smallpox epidemic.

The northernmost areas were occupied by Aleuts and Eskimos, two non-Indian groups with ways of life adapted to limiting and demanding environments. Both appear to have migrated from Asia after the main Indian movements. The Aleuts have an Eskimo-like language, and hunt sea mammals from the Aleutian islands and western Alaska. They have developed a close knowledge of mammalian anatomy and medicine, but estimated numbers of 20 000 in the eighteenth century have fallen to 6000 today. The Eskimos (or Inuits) live in small bands hunting seal, whale and caribou along the northern coasts of Alaska and Canada. Theirs is an extremely specialised way of life, related closely to the changing seasons and limited resources available, but today few of them follow the traditional ways, and it seems that another of the indigenous peoples will go the way of the rest.

Summary

The original inhabitants of North America included a variety of peoples with different ways of life. All were dependent on local natural resources, and their lives were related to the changing seasons, length of growing season, availability of water, and supply of game or fish. In comparison with modern industrial society they were primitive in organisation and achievements, but in comparison with the intruders from Europe in the sixteenth and early seventeenth centuries the most advanced nations were often more than a match in farming, craft techniques and political organisation. Both the Indians and Europeans were restricted in terms of movement on land; both relied for longer distances on water-borne transport. The Europeans could cross the ocean, but, once on land, had to travel by foot, or had to have goods moved by pack animal. The European was more aware of commercial trading, but the Indians soon organized themselves to become a part of the system and to barter successfully.

2

European Colonies: Early Development

North America was effectively discovered by Europeans at the end of the fifteenth century. It may have been reached earlier by the Irish Celts or by Norsemen, but the combination of landfall in an inhospitable area (Labrador for the Norsemen) and the lack of back-up supplies prevented permanent settlement.

Environments of settlement

The Spanish conquistadors

In the same year that the Moors were pushed out of Spain Columbus sailed westwards to find a route to the Orient which was different from that opened by the rival Portuguese. He reached islands off the coast of North America in 1492 and within twenty years much of the Caribbean area had been settled by Spaniards looking for the wealth which Spain itself could not supply. They then turned to exploration of the eastern and southern coasts of North America. Juan Ponce de Leon named Florida in 1513, and from then until the 1550s a series of expeditions landed and ventured into the interior. Groups of Spaniards wandered through south-eastern North America (Figure 2.1), but found no gold, and succeeded

only in leaving a trail of death from the European diseases to which the Indians were not immune.

In 1559 the Spaniards attempted to colonize Florida, but this and later attempts were unsuccessful; their policy of using local natives as slaves did not work, since the Indians were too independent, and the Spanish soldiers would not lower themselves to do the menial ground-breaking and construction which was needed. The threat of French and piratè occupation of the strategic Florida peninsula made the Spanish authorities make several further attempts at colonization, but all failed until mission stations were planted after 1580. By 1650 the Franciscans controlled 26 000 Indians, but after that date there was a decline in recruitment from Spain and missions were abandoned in the face of an English takeover from the north.

In the west the Spanish occupation was longer-lived. It began with attempts to discover mineral wealth, but these soon petered out in failure. One of the most notable journeys was by de Coronado in 1540–2, who underwent many hardships in the arid region. When no riches were found the Spaniards developed the northern frontier area of New Spain as a buffer zone for the main part of the country, and reacted to threats (real or imagined) from outside. Thus Drake's piratical raids into the Pacific in the 1570s led to a movement to occupy the upper Rio Grande valley at San Juan (1598)

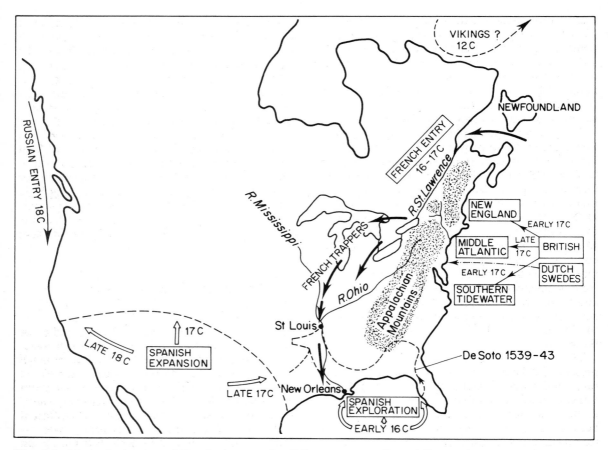

Fig. 2.1 *The colonization of North America by different groups from different directions. The place of landfall, and the differing intensions of the various groups played a major part in the later geography of the continent*

and Santa Fe (1609), and to set up farming amongst the local Indians. A century later French forays into the Mississippi valley from the north after 1687 caused a further alert. Missionaries were encouraged to move into Texas to try to convert the Indians. In 1718 the villa of San Antonio was founded and acted as a point of retreat during Indian attacks. However, when the Louisiana Territory became Spanish after 1763, little advantage was taken of this area and even Texas was neglected.

A third supposed threat loomed in the mid-eighteenth century as Russians moved their trading activities down the north-west coast of the continent, and this led the Spaniards to occupy California after 1767. An expedition under Portola reached San Francisco and reputedly

discovered the Bay for the first time after several sea expeditions had missed it. Missions were set up all along the southern Californian coast, including San Francisco (1775), San José (1777) and the town of Los Angeles (1781).

Although the Spaniards occupied a considerable part of what is now the USA, they were not successful in settling it, and their interest was half-hearted once they decided gold would not be found there.

The French in the north

Whilst Portugal and Spain led the initial phase of exploration from Europe in the sixteenth century, France and England were not far behind. Jacques

Cartier was sent across the Atlantic by Francis I in 1534, exploring the Gulf of St Lawrence and penetrating up that river in a series of voyages to 1541, when an attempt to plant a colony was unsuccessful. Cartier returned to France with news of the fishing grounds around Newfoundland, and this stimulated a wave of seasonal expeditions from western Europe.

Contact with Indians brought access to beaver furs, which were to provide a major trading item for the next 300 years. In 1603 the area of the lower St Lawrence was declared a French royal province, and a group led by Champlain was given monopoly rights in the fur trade for a short period. He and others explored deeply into the interior of the continent and eventually reached the Mississippi River. Champlain also established colonies at Port Royal in Acadia (1605) and Quebec (1608). The French, however, formed trading alliances with the Montagnais, Algonquin and Huron Indians and became embroiled in the running feuds between these tribes living north of the St Lawrence and the Iroquois Federation to the south.

The fur trade remained the basis for French presence in the area during the seventeenth century, and traders extended through the Great Lakes area to the Mississippi in the west and south to the Ohio River. The strategic portage points became the sites of forts to protect the French trading interests and formed the initial settlements which grew into modern Detroit and Chicago.

Numbers of permanent settlers grew slowly until Louis XIV made New France a royal province in 1661. This move led to formal possession of the interior lands and extension down the Mississippi with the setting up of the port of New Orleans as the base for the new colony of Louisiana. The move also encouraged further settlement, mainly along the St Lawrence from Montreal to the sea. Settlements lined the river banks to have access to the main means of transport, and blocks of land were sold to seigneurs who organized them into strips for settlement (Figure 2.2) with a short river frontage, but a long strip of land extending back across arable land and into woodland. This pattern also characterized the Louisiana settlements around New Orleans and is still found in these areas today.

The British southern tidewater plantations

Although it had been visited by a number of explorers, the central section of the eastern coastline was unsettled before 1600. Sir Walter Raleigh had attempted to set up trading colonies on Roanoke island in the 1580s, but they were not successful and it was clear that the only way ahead would be to set up permanent, self-sufficient settlements. The Jamestown settlement was established in 1607 and began what became a great tide of immigration from Europe.

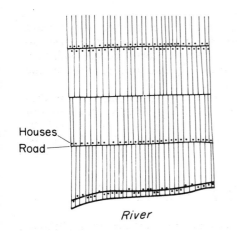

GENERAL PATTERN

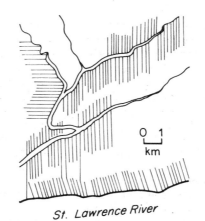

RIVER – ORIENTED PATTERN AT ST SULPICE

Fig. 2.2 *The features of long-lot land-use patterns, typical of the former French areas of North America, such as the lower St Lawrence valley and the Mississippi delta*

The southern tidewater area consisted of low-lying and swampy coasts and inlets extending over 100 kilometres inland, especially around Chesapeake and Delaware bays. The soils in the valley floors were fertile, but those on the hills were thinner and acidic. The plentiful annual rainfall of 1000-1500 millimetres was matched by long, warm summers. Indian burnings had removed much of the underbrush and so the land was easy to clear. Game and fish were plentiful. And yet many of the first settlers nearly starved to death due to disease and the planting of wheat in the soils with such a low nutrient content. Fortunately the Indians demonstrated that the burning of vegetation increased the soil fertility and provided seeds of their main crop, corn (maize). Then John Rolfe grew tobacco experimentally in 1612 and realised that he had found the staple crop which would provide cash and trade with England. Virginia became a Crown Colony in 1624, although life was still far from certain; while 3500 immigrants arrived between 1618 and 1624, the total population grew by only 1000 due to disease and the start of Indian attacks after 1622.

In 1630 the area north of the Potomac was granted to Lord Baltimore by Charles I as a place where Roman Catholics could live without prejudice. The first settlers of the Maryland colony in 1634 bought their land from Indians and immediately built a fortress on a high point. Both colonies (Virginia and Maryland) continued to expand by first occupying the land along the valley floors as far as the first waterfalls, and then spreading over the interfluves between. Settlers came in good numbers – Puritans driven out of England by the harsh policies of Charles I, and later Anglicans driven out by Cromwell (1649-60). Policies were again reversed after the restoration of Charles II in 1660.

The abundance of land and shortage of labour was a major factor of economic life in the colonies at this stage; poor people were brought over to work for 4–7 years for the cost of their passage, keep and 100 acres of land at the end. There was a constant need for such labour, although it was seldom of high quality.

Farther south there was more development in the Carolinas after a grant by the Crown of lands from Virginia to the 31st parallel in 1663. Two major centres developed – one on the southern border of Virginia, and the other at Charles Town, south of the Cape Hatteras sand bars.

Development was slower in these southern areas, since tobacco did not do so well in the swampy coastal area or the barren sandy soils behind. A fur trade was established by the 1680s and Savannah became a centre for this and the collection of naval stores (pitch from the pine trees). Rice was introduced in the 1690s.

The British in New England

The British colonies in New England were quite different in purpose and form from those in the southern tidewater lands. The first settlers landed from the Mayflower in 1620, and their success encouraged others to come to this area. The settlement of Boston set up by the Massachusetts Bay Company was the greatest draw and 24 500 settlers arrived between 1630 and 1640. Many of the puritans discovered that Boston was ruled in a restrictive manner and moved to Naragansett Bay where Providence was founded in 1636. They also moved westwards along the coast to the better soils of the Connecticut valley (Hartford 1636), or northwards into New Hampshire (Exeter 1638). Posts were established inland to attract the fur trade: these included Concord (1635), Chelmsford (1655), Northampton (1654) and Hadley (1665) – a series of very English names.

All this settlement was related to the distinctive New England system of land allocation. The dominantly puritan groups wished to see a commonwealth peopled by men and women of like faith; they abandoned the individual basis of land ownership and gave the colonial legislature control over settlement. Grants of land to individuals were relatively scarce (ministers, military veterans and school teachers were among the exceptions), and the large majority of the land went to groups planting new frontier towns (Figure 2.3). This method had the advantages of planned migration and communal defence against Indian attack, but created an elitist faction of conservative views, and some townships were slow to grow because they were regarded as unattractive. This pattern began to change by the late seventeenth century as the frontier advanced, and the earlier townships competed with each other and with newer centres for people and resources.

In the later part of the seventeenth century the conquest of the interior led to more frequent clashes with the Indians and a major war in 1675–

77, after which the Indian power in New England was largely broken, and they were removed from their lands or given menial tasks.

The Swedes, Dutch and English in the Middle Atlantic area

The lands between the Hudson River and Delaware Bay were occupied slightly later than the lands immediately to north and south, and had a more chequered start. The French had visited the Hudson earlier, but had not stayed. Henry Hudson sailed up the river in 1609, but Dutch fur traders were the first permanent settlers. Fort Orange on the site of Albany was set up in 1624, and Fort Amsterdam on the southern tip of Manhattan Island in 1626.

Meanwhile Swedes had set up a colony on the Delaware River and build Fort Christina in 1638 and Fort Gothenburg in 1644. New Englanders also attempted to settle there, but the Dutch removed both groups by 1655. Squabbles between traders in the Hudson valley eventually led Charles II of England to order the capture of New Amsterdam and the Dutch lands. This was carried out in 1664, and there was a rapid phase of British settlement in the area. New Amsterdam was changed to New York after being granted to the King's brother, the Duke of York. In 1681 William Penn received the Delaware lands as a payment of debt. He arrived in 1682 and selected the site for his main centre at Philadelphia. His colony was marked by liberty of religious expression and the granting of cheap lands. It became the main focus of settlement from England, Wales and Germany in the late seventeenth century: 10 000 immigrants arrived in four years and soon the fertile lands west of the Delaware were producing good crops of wheat.

By 1700 all 13 colonies (except Georgia, which had not been established, and Delaware, which had not been separated) were set up and expanding inland. The predominant subsistence farming outside the Chesapeake tobacco area was beginning to develop greater specialisations near the coast. At the same time the British West Indies had been occupied and developed for sugar plantations; their needs for food, horses and lumber could be supplied from the American colonies.

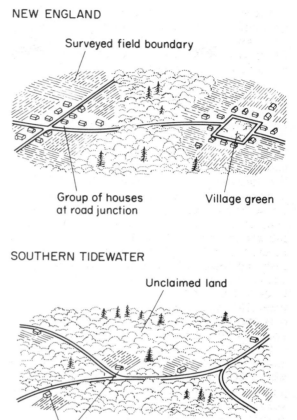

Fig. 2.3 *The typical features of New England townships and southern tidewater settlements in the seventeenth century. Such features had a major impact on the future development of land-use and settlement geography in these regions*

The expanding colonies: The first 'West'

After the initial settlement and consolidation came the process of expansion into the interior of the new continent. The years 1700–75 saw a major incursion westwards of the British colonies so that conflict with Indians, French and Spaniards became a major feature of the period. The tensions of this initial era of expansion also led to the revolution which established the United States of America as an independent nation.

The 'West' is a term which had a changing meaning in terms of the actual area involved from the late seventeenth century to the end of the nineteenth. The earliest phase of westward expansion was concentrated in the highland sectors of New England and New York and in the hilly piedmont and Appalachian valley areas of the central and southern colonies.

The north-eastern lands were the poorest, but were occupied from the coastal lowlands as the growth of population led to overcrowding, while others wished to escape the restrictive form of township organisation. Wealthy merchants bought up the best lands ahead of settlement, hoping to make money as the prices rose. At first the Boston and Salem merchants bought plots from township proprietors, but by the 1740s whole townsites were sold until the last Massachusetts land was disposed of in 1762. In Connecticut sales of land began in 1715 and the area west of the Connecticut River was largely auctioned off in the 1720s. The Governor of New Hampshire granted 129 townsites to such speculators in 1764, who then cashed in by attracting settlers to their newly acquired lands. This process resulted in rapid settlement in the valleys leading north into the hill country, but it also changed the character of New England. Settlements became more scattered and exposed as townships were created more rapidly than could be filled with people. Many of the new settlers came from the older parts of New England, but they also included new Scotch-Irish immigrants, settling especially around Worcester in central Massachusetts in 1718. The group settling west of the Connecticut River spilled over into the Hudson valley, causing tenant wars and leading to the establishment of the New York-Massachusetts boundary 20 miles east of the Hudson River.

The southern piedmont had been settled from the 1650s onwards as expeditions moved out from the Virginia forts. Fur traders based themselves on these forts and also found their way through gaps in the Blue Ridge to the valleys beyond, and even to the Ohio River before 1700. There was also a major move westwards by farmers into the rolling hills of the piedmont area, with its rich, residual red soils, in the early eighteenth century as the coastal plantations expanded in size to use slaves more economically. Many smaller plantations were crowded out. Immigrant Germans also joined this movement and by 1750 the entire Virginia and Carolina piedmont was settled.

The regulation of land sales became impossible; coastal plantations held large grants of 10 000 to 40 000 acres and smaller farmers had to take second-best land or buy land from the planters with few improvements. Agents in Europe attempted to sell the land as well, so that there was a steady advance to the west. Indians hampered the advance in the southern Carolinas. In 1730 a new corporation was created for the settlement of Georgia by debtors and others who wished to make a new life, but progress of settlement became slower after a good initial response. The land grants of 50 acres were too small, the coastal climate was unhealthy and there was conflict with Indians and with the Spaniards to the south.

The major development of this period, however, took place through Pennsylvania, where the tolerant Quakers opened their lands cheaply to anyone who would come. They also maintained good relations with the Indians, and William Penn bought large areas of land from them in the Susquehanna Valley. This was a contrast to the areas north and south; in New York, for instance, settlement in the Hudson Valley was discouraged first by fur traders and then by Indian troubles, and the colony placed many difficulties in the way of land acquisition.

The early eighteenth century saw the influx of two major groups of settlers, mainly to Pennsylvania. The Palatine Germans, after enduring numerous hardships, arrived first in New York in 1708, but soon moved to land along the Hudson and Schoharie Rivers. Various problems caused them to move to Pennsylvania and from 1710 groups moved from Germany via England direct to Pennsylvania and on to the Susquehanna valley. In 1726 there were 100 000 squatters in addition to those who had bought land. These became known as the Pennsylvania 'Dutch' by mistake, but soon dominated the fertile lands around Lancaster. Settlers moved into the lands of the Great Valley to the south-east, entering Virginia and the Carolinas by the 1750s. Some moved back east through gaps in the Blue Ridge to fill in unsettled piedmont lands.

The second major migration was by the Scotch-Irish from the northern part of Ireland, where they had been 'planted' by Cromwell in the mid-seventeenth century. Apart from having to clear land and fight off Irish tribes, they had been treated badly by the English, who had restricted imports of their meat, grain and wool. They left in large numbers when their leases came up for renewal in 1717–18, and again in the depression of 1740–41. Over 300 000 left for the colonies and most went to Pennsylvania to seek isolated areas where they could squat.

As settlement expanded, the British colonists came into conflict with the French or Spanish, or were plagued by running skirmishes with the Indians whom they sought to dispossess. Through much of the eighteenth century the main battles occurred where the French or British persuaded the Indians to fight with them against the other. There was fighting in northern New England, along the Mohawk valley, through central Pennsylvania and the Ohio valley, and southwards. Major outbreaks occurred during the periods of Anglo-French conflict in Europe (1702–13 and 1744–8), but issues of controlling the continental interior were undecided until the Seven Years War (1754–61) when Britain under Pitt put sufficient military resources into the field to contain French attacks and then mount a three-pronged attack on the French centres of Quebec (captured in 1759) and Montreal (1760) in the St Lawrence valley.

These wars were a time of great difficulties for those on the frontier, with Indian attacks forcing settlers to retreat. Once the wars were over there was an immediate push forward to settle the lands formerly occupied by the French and hostile Indians. The various attempts to take Fort Duquesne on the Ohio had involved the clearing of roads for the movement of military personnel and supplies. Once taken, the renamed Fort Pitt (later Pittsburgh) served as the main gateway to the west, and a number of companies were formed to speculate in the western lands.

The British government in London, however, held up this advance while it deliberated on the use of the newly-won lands. The Indian allies would not like to lose their lands, which many had helped to win from the French, and there were other interests who agreed with leaving these lands to the Indians – principally the fur traders backed by powerful groups of London merchants, and also less powerful humanitarian groups who wished to see an end to the slaughter and disruption of Indian life. Ranged against these were the land speculators, both in Britain and America, who demanded that the lands between the Appalachians and the Mississippi should be opened to settlement.

Whatever political arrangements were made in the period between the Seven Years War and its 1763 treaty (which effectively ended French rule in Canada, the Ohio and Mississippi valleys) and the War of Independence (1776–83), the settlers continued to move west into the Ohio lowlands, the Kentucky Bluegrass area and the upper Tennessee valleys. The main migration continued to thrust forward from Virginia and Pennsylvania, where the major routeways began. The area around Fort Pitt was settled rapidly, especially after the re-drawing of the Indian Boundary Line in 1768. When the Pennsylvania Land Office opened in April 1769 there were 2790 purchasers on the first day and 10 000 families in the area by 1771. Daniel Boone and various partners had explored the Kentucky area across the Cumberland Gap from 1767, and had built the Wilderness Road through this gap in 1774. This led to a rapid influx of settlers in 1775 and 1776, but the Transylvania Company, which employed Boone to build the road, was not able to control the situation and the State of Virginia annexed the territory as Kentucky county in 1777.

The period between 1763 and 1776 saw a worsening of relations between Britain and the American colonies. There were two major economic reasons for the rift between colonies and mother country, but they united north and south in rebellion. The English mercantile policy viewed colonies as providers of raw materials and markets for manufactured products, and trade was restricted to British ships. This irked the New England and Middle Atlantic merchants who wished to trade more widely. The restrictions on movement beyond the Appalachians annoyed the southern frontiersmen and the speculators, and the Quebec Act of 1774 (extending the Quebec frontier to the Ohio River) was a source of irritation to those pushing forward along the Ohio. Various taxes instituted to help pay Britain's heavy military bills in the Seven Years War and in maintaining protection against Indian attacks also resulted in strong anti-British feelings. The combination of interests brought together those who signed the Declaration of Independence in 1776.

The War of Independence which followed was fought on several fronts, and the British, armed with better gifts, set the Indians to attack the frontier areas beyond the Appalachians and also northern New England. Gradually the colonists came to terms with the Indians and reduced the Loyalists and British military forces to ineffectiveness, but only after much bloodshed. In 1783 a treaty was signed between the USA and Britain, giving the new nation all the lands to the Mississippi and opening the way for a new phase of expansion.

The colonial economy: spatial considerations

Each of the British group of colonies in America produced items in demand in England, in other colonies, and in southern Europe. A complex pattern of trade grew up across the Atlantic (Figure 2.4). This focused on the major ports of Boston, Providence, New York, Philadelphia, Baltimore and Charleston. Planters also loaded tobacco at plantation wharves in the Chesapeake Bay area. By the mid-seventeenth century the resident merchants in these ports had become the richest men in the American colonies, dominating social, economic and political life.

The mercantilistic system, based on trade with the mother country, restricted local diversification and affected development within the colonies. Two of the other main features of colonial conditions were the existence of plentiful land and a shortage of labour (especially skilled labour) and capital goods. Inland transport was slow and of small capacity unless a river was available. All of these factors gave rise to a distinctive economy and spatial patterns.

Throughout the period most people were dependent on the land and its resources for their livelihood; over ninety per cent lived at least partly from farming activities and sales of farm products. In addition, the commercial crops of the South and Middle colonies formed the main goods entering trade from the American colonies.

Fig. 2.4 *The pattern of trade across the north Atlantic between the American colonies, Britain, southern Europe and west Africa in the early eighteenth century*

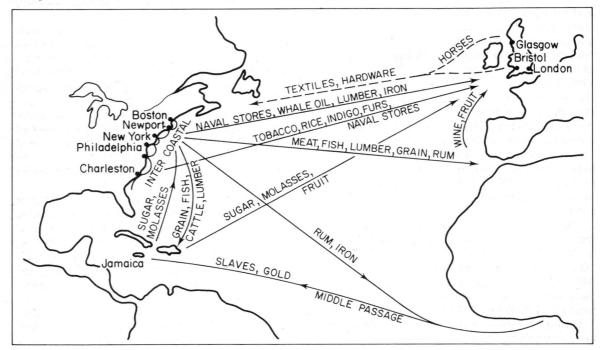

The southern colonies dominated the pattern of colonial trade. They were able to take advantage of the new lands and long growing season to produce tobacco (Virginia, Maryland and North Carolina), and later rice and indigo in the far south. The tobacco was introduced to Virginia in 1612 and soon became the main crop. Rice was grown first in the Charleston area in 1695 in the swampy coastal areas; later these were dammed and the tidal flow used to flood the fields. The introduction of indigo in 1743 provided an extra source of work and wealth. These southern plantations also grew their own food supply of corn (maize), wheat, fruit and vegetables, plus hay and animal products.

The middle colonies did not develop until later, but the Pennsylvania and New Jersey area became the chief wheat-growing sector, and other grains were also grown for export. In New England the poor soils and short summers allowed only subsistence-style farming with corn as the main crop along with wheat, vegetables, cattle and sheep. By 1770 the area was already a net importer of food.

Most colonies depended on bringing indentured servants from Europe: they would work for a period of years and then be free with land to set up on their own. Most of these workers were poor and unskilled, and south of New England they made up over fifty per cent of the total settlers. The alternative to indentured labour was slavery. This became important after 1650 and was established as the norm in the southern plantation colonies by 1700. Some were introduced to New England and the Middle Atlantic colonies, but they were never important there. It seems that the climate of areas north of Maryland did not allow field work for six months or more, whereas the investment in slaves was worthwhile only if they could be worked as long as possible. Also the commercial staple crops of the South − tobacco, rice and indigo − required much hand labour and could stand the costs of such investment.

The population of the British colonies grew from 25 000 Europeans in 1640 to 80 000 (mainly in Virginia, Maryland and Massachusetts) by 1660. By 1690 there were 200 000 and by 1710 340 000, but the eighteenth century saw much more rapid growth and the colonies contained a total of 2 250 000 by 1775.

Inland transport was very rudimentary. The main cities were on the coast or on a river and it was usually best to travel between them by water. Land transport became increasingly necessary due to military activity in the eighteenth century and a pattern of roads, often following old Indian trails, emerged. Most, however, were adequate only for single horses to pass and little more than a quagmire for much of the time. By 1760 roads connected Boston−Providence−New York−Philadelphia−Charleston; the Forbes road from Philadelphia to Pittsburgh and the Wilderness road into Kentucky were also improved for travel as long as the weather remained dry. It was not until late in the eighteenth century that stage coaches were in use for passengers, and the Conestoga wagon, developed in Pennsylvania, was available for freight. Postal services were also restricted and by 1750 a letter from Boston to Philadelphia would take 6 days; by 1760 there were 8 mails per year to parts south of the Potomac − and costs were high.

At a time when the Atlantic crossing took 4–6 weeks, the slowness and small scale of inland transport meant that beyond the busy plantation and city-port wharves society was very restricted in terms of spatial movement. Most domestic needs had to be met in the vicinity and there was little internal trade except around small market towns. Any extractive or manufacturing industry was likewise local and small in scale.

In an 'age of wood' it was necessary that supplies were available to provide fuel, construction materials and charcoal. There was commercial use of timber in ship-building along the New England coast, and by the early eighteenth century a third of British merchant ships were being built in New England. Fishing was also developed in the northern colonies, where fishing and whaling had begun in the sixteenth century before permanent settlement. There were good markets in southern Catholic Europe and the West Indies for salted dried cod.

The only mineral used was iron, and charcoal was employed to produce wrought iron or cast iron. Furnaces were distributed widely, and had small outputs, since both the ores and charcoal could be obtained in most regions. By the mid-eighteenth century the manufacture of iron in the colonies was probably equal to the total production of iron in England at the time.

Apart from the iron furnaces and forges there was little manufacturing industry in colonial America. Mills for grinding wheat and sawing wood used the power of falling water to drive wheels and simple machinery. The largest flour mills were built along the Delaware and around Chesapeake Bay near the grain-growing areas.

Thus economic activity in colonial times, apart from the commercial farming of the South and the shipbuilding and fishing of New England, was small-scale, widely dispersed and owned by individuals. This reflected the high 'friction of distance' (that is, high costs per mile and time taken in transport) of inland communication. Although there was no real factory production, the demand for it was becoming clear as urban centres grew. Some industries began to congregate into more localised groups; thus flour mills were particularly common on the Delaware around Wilmington; iron forges and furnaces near Lancaster in Pennsylvania; and shoes and textiles in New England. The British, however, resisted the development of large business concerns which would compete with those at home.

Urban growth: The east coast ports

Towns were basic to colonial life. They did not arise from a farming base providing an excess for marketing at local centres which somehow grew into towns, or from the need for trading posts to collect furs, but were set up in the initial stages of occupation and acted as centres for the extension of farming and trading to supply needs. By the early eighteenth century several centres were developing. The largest were all seaports engaged in the mercantilistic pattern of trade. Boston was the largest with a population of 13 000 (1730), followed by Philadelphia with 11 000 and New York with 8 000; other major centres included Providence, Norfolk and Charleston. The mercantilistic trade, however, did not supply sufficient occupation for these cities and their rapid growth. Many turned to other types of trade, although this was smuggling by the standards laid down in Britain. It grew to great proportions by 1750, providing many merchants with wealth and even greater ambitions. In addition there was an increasing interest in the interior of the colonies, where speculation in land became another source of wealth for the city-port merchants. It was thus in the coastal cities, set up to control British interests, where the main agitation and moves towards independence took place.

Even at this early stage many cities had begun to develop a particular character. Thus Boston was the focus of Massachusetts Bay with its busy shipbuilding and fishing industries, and had wide trading connections with the West Indies and Europe. New York became British in 1664 and its merchants were prominent in channelling the interior fur trade down the Hudson valley, and in flour-milling. During the War of Independence it was occupied by the British and thus became the main source of hard money; this gave it a start in trading enterprise after independence despite having to lose many of its loyalist connections and personnel. Baltimore was a late starter, but became a 'boom town' for a while. Chartered in 1729, it attracted few settlers and by 1750 had only 25 houses on the site in an area of dispersed tobacco farming and local wharves. The Stevenson brothers then saw possibilities for wheat farming in the area, set up a flour mill and arranged for a ship to call and collect the product. This led to a major shift of emphasis amongst local farmers and by 1790 the town had 13 000 people living in it.

As these coastal cities grew, there was a need for further development and internal organization. Many services such as fire-fighting and the police began as volunteer groups and developed to companies employing men (for example, Boston had its paid fire company in 1717, and this was kept busy in an era of wooden housing). Management of the poverty problem became an increasing drain on local resources, but average standards of living in the colonies were as much as three times better than those in Britain due to the shortage of labour which pushed up wages. The growing numbers of newspapers in the eighteenth century (Boston had 5 by 1715, Philadelphia 7 by 1776) reflected the advance of education and general culture; Boston was the second publishing centre (after London) in the British Empire in 1770.

The urban centres which had developed in the colonial era laid foundations for future development. Once the 'Big Four' (Boston, New York, Philadelphia and Baltimore) had been established and become prominent within their colonies it was unlikely that any other local centres would outgrow them. They had become the focus for trade, both trans-Atlantic and internal, had formed the largest concentrations of population, and had important sources of capital for local investment at later stages.

Other settlements in the colonial era were small (no more than a few hundred people) in the predominantly farming and hunting economy of the time. Some were set up as defensive points, and centres such as Detroit, Pittsburgh, Albany, Quebec, Montreal and Minneapolis (Fort Anthony) began in this way with British or French origins. New Orleans and St Louis were also in existence, but controlled by Spain and France at the time of independence.

Summary: *A spatially restricted society*

Despite the distance travelled on initial migration to America, the lot of most colonists was to travel little after arrival. Their horizons were limited to their own farm, plantation, village or market town, and it was a rare event to move beyond these. Such an existence affected location and behaviour in space. The geography of colonial America was typical of a spatially restricted society.

1. Patterns of land-use and movement were repetitive: each village had similar patterns of field arrangements and of daily movements to and from the fields; each had a range of crops to satisfy local needs with a small proportion for sale in towns. The more commercial plantations of the southern tidewater area still had to grow most of their food. Local mills and forges also repeated the small-scale patterns again and again.

2. Environmental controls were strong: the river bottomlands were the best lands and the earliest settled, followed by the poorer lands on the interfluves. The differences between farming in New England and the South were a direct reflection of the two natural environments.

3. Distance was a strong barrier due to limited technology: waterways were the only means of moving larger quantities of goods.

4. The cramping and conservative role of tradition and semi-feudal organisation in so many modern spatially restricted societies was not such a force in the American colonies, although the British mercantilistic policies did hold back some developments. In general the colonists adapted well to new conditions and soon adopted the superior Indian crops.

5. A major feature of all spatially restricted societies and their economies is the reliance on human and animal labour, rather than on mechanisation; this affects the scale of operations and the transport system.

6. Per capita productivity is low under such circumstances and standards of living increase slowly, if at all. There is little surplus and large families combined with restricted travel prevent the formation of larger enterprises.

7. In modern societies of this type a semifeudal economic system also stifles change and advance. In colonial America the mercantilistic system, the plantation system and at times the New England township system had a similar effect. The fragmentation of holdings became a particular problem in New England.

3

The Frontier Advances: 1783–1920

The period from independence to the early years of the twentieth century saw a series of major changes in the USA which provided the foundation for many of the present geographical distributions and movements and also for many of the present social and economic problems.

There was a steady increase in land available for settlement, as new areas were bought or won by treaty or battle. The Indians were eventually removed from all but a small part of the lands that had been theirs. Settlers came in their thousands to occupy these newly acquired and emptied lands, assisted by the agreed process for transferring land from federal to individual ownership. This process was aided further by new forms of transport – especially canal and railroad – which reduced the friction of distance and enabled growing groups of people to move to the new lands of the west. The 'West' itself moved from the piedmont and Appalachian valleys (1750s) to the lands between the Appalachians and the Mississippi River (1785–1840), then on to lands beyond the Mississippi and across to the Pacific coast.

Throughout the process of western migration the planting of towns was as important as farming settlement. Towns provided protection and markets, as well as a site for wealth which could be gained from speculation. The early towns grew up alongside the major waterways; beyond the Mississippi the railroads were basic to their suc-

cess due to the sheer scale of the continent. Later in the nineteenth century many American towns of the New England, Middle Atlantic and Midwestern areas became major manufacturing centres in addition to their commercial functions, and this resulted in rapid growth. At the same time developments in farming technology led to increasing specialisation and regional distinctiveness of products. The United States moved from a spatially restricted society to one of great mobility and interdependence, with product specialisation in the different regions which emerged. Canada followed similar trends, but some years behind throughout the nineteenth century.

Acquiring new lands

The thirteen original colonies which formed the new nation could scarcely visualise the extension of their lands to the Pacific coast within less than seventy years of independence. They began by owning the land from the Atlantic coast to the Mississippi River (apart from Florida), although much was still occupied by Indians, and the British in Canada trespassed over large areas in the north until the 1812 War settled that issue and confirmed the earlier accepted limits. Many of the thirteen colonies claimed areas west of the Appalachians, since they had been set up with sea-to-sea charters. By 1790 all except Georgia (which followed in 1802) ceded their western lands apart from certain sections used for settling military veterans. The ceded lands were to be used by the federal government to bring in revenue to cover debts incurred during the War of Independence. This was the first large area of 'public domain', or land owned by the federal government (Figure 3.1).

The public domain was enlarged in 1803 by the Louisiana Purchase, which added a large area west of the Mississippi just regained by France after 40 years of Spanish rule. France, occupied in Europe with the Napoleonic Wars, sold this huge area for $15 million ($27 million with interest, or approximately $200 million at 1975 prices), or 5 cents per acre. All or parts of thirteen new states were created from this land later in the century.

Florida was the next area to be purchased – from Spain in 1819. Spain also occupied Texas as a part of the territories it had settled as a buffer to its New Spain empire. This became part of the new Republic of Mexico when it achieved independence in 1821. Many Americans went to settle there, but increasing dissatisfaction with the vacillating government in Mexico City led to armed rebellion in 1836. A few Americans tried to halt the Mexican army at the Alamo in San Antonio, but were all killed. They succeeded, however, in killing many of the Mexicans, and the reduced army was beaten by a Texan force under Sam Houston later in the year. General Santa Ana, the Mexican President, was captured and released only when he promised Texan independence. Texas was an independent nation from 1837–45,'when it was accepted as a new state in the USA. Texas retained all the lands not in private hands, so there was no public domain there. The United States also bought a section of land to the north-west claimed by Texas.

The lands on the west coast south of 42 degrees also belonged to New Spain and then Mexico. Americans had been moving into California, at first with Mexican encouragement to expand the cattle industry in the central and southern sectors. When American settlers became dominant, the

Fig. 3.1 *The acquisition of new lands by the United States of America (After Clawson)*

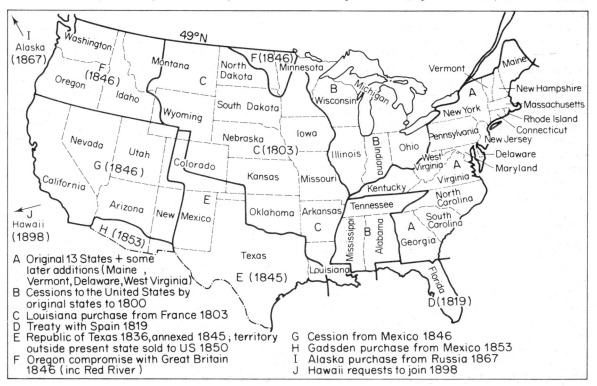

A Original 13 States + some later additions (Maine, Vermont, Delaware, West Virginia)
B Cessions to the United States by original states to 1800
C Louisiana purchase from France 1803
D Treaty with Spain 1819
E Republic of Texas 1836, annexed 1845; territory outside present state sold to US 1850
F Oregon compromise with Great Britain 1846 (inc Red River)
G Cession from Mexico 1846
H Gadsden purchase from Mexico 1853
I Alaska purchase from Russia 1867
J Hawaii requests to join 1898

USA offered to buy these lands, but in 1846 war erupted. This was one-sided and the American forces took over California with scarcely a shot fired. They went on to take Mexico City, but gave up many of the possible gains in the ensuing treaty. In 1893 the Gadsden Purchase added another strip of land to Arizona and New Mexico. North of 42 degrees the west coast lands were claimed by the British government due to dominance of the area to the 1820s by the Hudsons Bay Company. Once again, American settlers moved into the area over the Oregon Trail and another 1846 treaty set the national boundary at the 49th parallel.

The final major addition to the USA was Alaska, which was purchased from Russia in 1867. Later still, war with Spain in 1905 brought the dependencies of Puerto Rico (now a 'commonwealth') and Guam. Hawaii joined the United States in 1898 at its own request.

The story of Canadian expansion is really one of accepting what was left after claims by the USA following the War of Independence, the War of 1812 and the 1846 agreement. Canada became a self-governing dominion in 1867. It still has a larger total territory than the USA, but much of this is boreal forest and tundra.

Removing the Indians

The Indian 'problem' began during colonial days, when it was soon discovered that each new area had to be won for settlement by conquest and clearance. Although a policy of purchasing land from the Indians was pursued from time to time throughout this period, they were often paid with small sums or worthless trinkets and could not understand that they had given over possession of the land for all time. Even when an agreement between the federal government and Indians looked like being kept by the Indians, explorers, trappers, miners or farmers would violate it. As soon as the Indians retaliated, however, the army came back with sledge-hammer blows to humiliate or even exterminate whole nations. There were only short periods (in the early colonial days or in the first stages of settling the Great Plains) when the Indians had an even chance. It is significant that the Bureau of Indian Affairs was under the War Department until late in the nineteenth century, when any threat they had once posed was removed and humanitarian concern led to at-tempts to educate and incorporate the Indians in the mainstream of American life. This has affected some, but many Indians prefer to live on their reservations in simple fashion – even though they may be trained as doctors or lawyers and though their land may contain valuable mineral resources.

The first Indian problems after independence came when there was an attempt to remove them from the Ohio country; some peoples ceded their lands at conferences in 1783 and 1785, but others attacked the early settlers, encouraged by British forces holding on to a line of forts from Lake Champlain through Niagara and Detroit to Mackinac. War broke out in 1789 and the Indians were defeated at the Battle of Fallen Timbers in 1794. In the South speculators and traders at-tempted to move the Creek Indians by treaty, but the latter allied themselves to the Spaniards in Florida and went to war in 1785. Other attempts to move west into Kentucky came up against Indians as well, but the worst conflicts were in the War of 1812 against Britain. The British realised that they could use Indian grievances, smouldering after the loss of the Battle of Tippecanoe (1811) in central Indiana. At each turn however, the Indians were defeated and gave up their lands to move west.

In the 1820s such movements were formalised. The process of piecemeal removal of the Cherokee in the South began with a series of treaties from 1816–21, and started the idea of providing land farther west for the Indians. When President Jackson was elected in 1828 he changed the role of Indians from 'other nations' to United States subjects who did not have rights to the extensive lands they inhabited. The Cherokee protested that they were well-adjusted and assimilated (they had textile looms and cotton gins, schools, a written language and newspaper – and even had slaves like the Whites!), but to no avail. Persuasion eventually caused many of the south-east nations (Creeks, Cherokees, Choctaws, Chickasaws), to-gether with the Seminoles, to move out of lands in Georgia, Alabama, Mississippi and Florida to a large area prepared for them west of the Mississippi River. Some still remained on their old lands in 1838, refusing to move, but these were driven out at the end of the year and twenty-five per cent of them perished on the winter journey which became known as the 'Trail of Tears'. The new lands took up much of present Oklahoma and Kansas (Figure 3.2), but the moved peoples found it difficult to come to terms with the new environ-

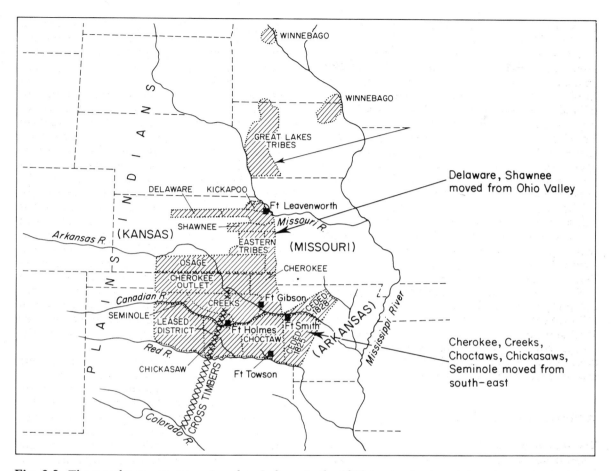

Fig. 3.2 *The new large reserve assigned to Indians in the 1930s*

ment and with the hostile plains Indians who resented their intrusion and despised them as farmers. The Shawnee and Delaware nations from the north-east joined the five southern nations, but they kept largely to the wooded eastern section of Indian Territory. Thus the policy of 'one large reserve' was implemented on land that was regarded as unfit for white settlement, and many hoped that the end of Indian troubles had been reached.

Then the push to settle lands north-west of the Great Lakes in the 1840s led to an ousting of tribes from Iowa, but resistance from the Sioux until a second large reservation was created in the Black Hills area of Dakota. There were also troubles as mining developed in the mountainous west after 1850, with large groups of miners tramping into

Indian lands. A pattern had been established in the California Gold Rush of 1848, where local legislation removed all protection from the Indians and the miners were able simply to turn them off land or shoot them. Whenever federal forces arrived most of the Indians were dead. Similar events occurred throughout the mining areas.

The last major Indian resistance took place in the area occupied by the strong, mobile plains Indians when the transcontinental railroads extended their lines across their lands, dividing up the 'one large reserve'. Indians raided mining camps in Colorado in the early 1860s and the Sioux made trouble farther north in 1865–7, whilst the Apaches farther south were not subdued until the early 1870s. A new policy was implemented during this phase of demand for the previously unwanted plains lands; the Indians were 'concentrated' into reservations instead of having free access to the plains. Meanwhile the plains Indians' main staff of life, the buffalo, was virtually exterminated between 1867 and 1883. At first it was shot for 'sport', but when a Pennsylvania tannery discovered in 1871 that buffalo hides could be used for commercial leather the destruction of the buffalo became an industry. As many as three million animals a year were killed, and by 1883 a special survey could discover only 200 (out of an estimated original population of 13 million) buffalo in the western lands. After 1868 there was a further stage in the restriction of Indian lands as the 'small reservation' policy was extended to all new areas being settled. Many Indians did not accept this at once, since it meant further retreat and it led to more wars with inevitable results. The final debacle at Wounded Knee in Dakota in 1890 was a massacre of several hundred unarmed Indians by mistake, but still in fear.

The United States had succeeded in removing the Indians from almost all the lands they had occupied in 1600; they were only left a few small areas, often in the least habitable parts of the country, and the numbers of Indians had been decimated by disease and war.

Land policy and the settlement of the new lands

Among the earliest problems of the new American republic were the questions of how to dispose of the public domain lands, and how the new lands should be governed. The federal government wished to make land available for sale, and it was decided that survey before sale would be the best approach. A law of 1785 set the basis; government surveyors would establish east-west 'base lines' and north-south 'principal meridians' for each state or groups of states (Figure 3.3). There would then be divisions into townships of 36 square miles (each square mile of 640 acres would be one section), but the lands would be sold to individuals. This approach combined the major features of land systems from the south and New England – rather as the Middle Atlantic colonies had acted in practice. Today the results of this

Fig. 3.3 *The United States Land Survey System. The map shows the way in which base lines and principal meridians were established, and the diagram illustrates the details of the division of land into sections*

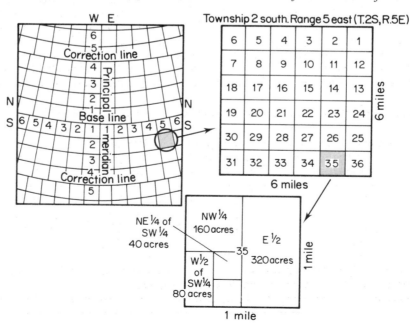

process of land survey and sale dominate the landscapes of all but the thirteen original states. The original thirteen states have a much less regimented appearance than the grid patterns of the later-settled states. Ohio was partly settled on the old system and partly on the new.

There was also controversy over the sizes of lots for sale and the prices to be asked. The more conservative east coast merchants wanted land to be sold in large tracts at relatively high prices so that they could have the main chance to acquire it and resell later at even higher prices. This type of speculation became one of the main features of westward-moving new settlement. Another group, however, wished to dispose of the land in small parcels at reasonable prices and with credit facilities, so that the ordinary citizens could buy their own land. They believed that all had a right to land ownership when it was so plentiful. Pressure of opinion for smaller and cheaper holdings led to gradual reductions of both the minimum area and price per acre (Figure 3.4).

Thus by 1812 anyone with $50 could buy a 40 acre lot (if he could obtain the land at minimum prices). This happened extensively; whereas the earlier lands in Ohio were sold in large blocks, the 'infill' after 1820 and 1832 was in 80 and 40 acre holdings.

A further problem was that in many places the first pioneers entered an area before the surveyors (and thus before the land sales). These 'squatters' often took up the best land, and it was difficult for the army to remove them since groups formed protective associations to resist eviction and to enable their members to obtain the lands at low prices when the auctions came. By 1820 these squatters had gained recognition, and the Pre-emption Act of 1841 allowed anyone settled on unsurveyed land to buy 160 acres at the minimum price.

Thus the progression of events was in the direction of encouraging more and more people to settle land in the west, and in the 1840s there was further pressure for the next step – to give land to new settlers. This idea was opposed by the southern states at a time when there was increasing friction over the slavery issue; the 160 acre unit was too small for the use of slaves and the new lands of the west would be filled with antislavery people. The matter was held up until 1862, when all the southerners walked out of the United States Congress. At this time the Homestead Act was passed, allowing any head of family over twenty-one years to have 160 acres of public domain lands for a small payment; this would be his if he lived on it, and cultivated the lands, over 5 years. By the time this measure was passed, however, most of the best lands as far as the tier of states west of the Mississippi had been taken, and the new lands beyond were so dry that 160 acres was too small for extensive cattle ranching or dry farming and too large for intensive irrigation. Even in these areas the transcontinental railroads built from the 1860s on the basis of sales of land granted by the federal government, took the best lands and speculators bought up much of the rest – either directly from Land Office sales, or indirectly from land grant awards to agricultural colleges. A homesteader often had to take land distant from communication lines and on poor soil. Nevertheless the Homestead Act still enabled many to obtain land, and others added land

Fig. 3.4 The changing bases for the disposal of public domain lands in the USA

Date	Minimum area to be purchased (acres)	Minimum price per acre (dollars)	Minimum farm price (dollars)	Credit
1796	640	2	1 280	50%, 1 year
1800	320	2	640	50%, 25% in 2 years
1804	160	2	320	25% in 4 years
1820	80	1.25	100	None
1832	40	1.25	50	None
1841	Squatters Rights (Pre-emption Act – could buy 160 acres at minimum price)			
1854	Land unsold for 30 years available at 12½c per acre			
1862	Homestead Act (160 acres for head of family; to be lived on and cultivated for 5 years)			

Fig. 3.5 Transport changes and USA geography

Phase	Local transport to 1825	Interior penetration 1820–60	Railroad dominance 1860–1910	Competing modes 1915 onwards
Major transport modes: goods and people	River, sea, Packhorse	Canal, River, Sea, Railroad, Wagon	Railroad, Canal, River, Sea, Wagon	Railroad, Truck, Pipeline, Canal, Airline, River, Sea
people	Foot, Horse, River, Sea	Foot, Horse, Coach, Canal, River, Sea, Railroad	Railroad, Foot, Horse, Coach, Canal, Sea, Electric Streetcar	Automobile, Airline, Bus, Railroad, Mass Transit
Settlement of USA and Internal migration	Mainly east of Appalachia: Ports in N.E. and middle Atlantic	Across Appalachia to Mississippi: settlement from rivers, lakes	Mississippi to Pacific: settlement from wagon trains, railroads	Internal migration to west coast and 'sunbelt' from north-east and north centre
	Plantations in south on tidewater	Towns of midwest sited on rivers	Towns of west sited on railroads	Increased personal mobility, spread of suburbs
Changing economy	Local self-sufficient economy in north	Internal exchange begins: New England factory goods for midwest flour, wool, meat, southern cotton	Extensive internal trading leading to specialisation of farming regions and manufacturing belt (textiles, steel)	Development of light 'foot-loose' industry and post-industrial society.
	Ports and tidewater planters depend on commerce	Small-scale manufacturing and agricultural society	Large-scale manufacturing and mechanised farming	Increasing focus of economic activity in large metropolis
	Little internal exchange of goods except locally and along east coast			Decline of employment in farming and (later) manufacturing.

bought from speculators to make a worthwhile plot.

A final problem concerned the government of the new lands. This had to avoid the mistake of the British government, which had become too remote from its colonists and did not allow them sufficient self-rule. The new lands north-west of the Ohio river were soon divided into states, and a variety of plans were discussed, but the main provisions were in terms of the process of gaining statehood.

1. A Territory would be established in newly settled areas under the control of a Governor and Secretary with three judges, all appointed by Congress in Washington.

2. When the adult population passed 5000 the Territory could elect its own legislature, sharing its power with a Council of five including the Governor and members of Congress.

3. Once the total population reached 60 000, this legislature could frame a constitution and apply for admission to the Union as a new State on equal terms with the older States.

The formulations of new constitutions as new territories petitioned for statehood again raised the question of the relation of the Bill of Rights to slavery. The new territories north-west of the Ohio river prohibited slavery, but the southern states allowed it. For many years the balance of slave and non-slave states in Congress was maintained, with one of each being admitted at a time, but in the 1850s there was increasing difficulty in doing this as more western territories were opposed to slavery. In addition, the increasing alliance in personal connections, trade and investment between the north-eastern states and the western territories resulted in a massive majority against slavery, and the southern states left the Union after the election of Abraham Lincoln as President in 1860.

The mechanism for the formation of new states was a successful move in that it perpetuated the Union until the Civil War, and then afterwards, and prevented political fragmentation. This would have involved economic fragmentation and could have prevented the growth of such outstanding developments within the USA later in the nineteenth century. Although there was often some delay in reaching statehood, it was evidently worthwhile, except in the case of the southern states in the mid-nineteenth century, when they felt that the rest of the Union was coercing them over the slavery issue. The other states would not

allow them to leave the Union, however, and were willing to go to war over this issue (rather than slavery as such) in order to maintain the whole.

Improving accessibility: Changes in transport

Independence was gained in an era of medieval transport conditions but by the latter part of the nineteenth century the railroads had become a major form of inland transport enabling the new lands to be occupied by millions of people and farm animals. This resulted in enormous bulk movements of grain, coal, iron ore and other commodities.

In 1783 the western margin of occupation extended into the Appalachian valleys, little more than 250 miles from the east coast after 175 years of colonisation. It took nearly another 50 years (to 1830) for occupation – defined as six persons per square mile – to advance a further 500 miles to the Mississippi river. Then it was true only in Kentucky and Tennessee. The following 50 years (to 1880) witnessed a further advance of 1000 miles to the foot of the Rockies. But by this time many had leapfrogged the continuously advancing frontier to settle in California and the Oregon Territory of the north-west, and most states had been part of the Union for some years.

This process of accelerating settlement was made possible by more rapid forms of transport with greater carrying capacities. Passengers and freight could be carried more rapidly and cheaply overland. A number of phases in this developing process can be traced.

1. Independence to 1825

For a further forty years after independence the river routes (with small boats, often canoes) and the packhorse trails remained the only means of internal communication. Old Indian trails were used widely and some improved; by 1816 there was a road 8 feet 6 inches wide from Maine to Georgia, and there were other roads, built largely for military access in the first place. Some inland routes had been improved, such as the federal

National Road from Cumberland, Maryland to Wheeling on the Ohio (1818) and eventually to Vandalia, Illinois. This had a foundation of crushed stone and was 30 feet wide with a central macadamised strip. Turnpike companies also built roads from which tolls were collected. The Philadelphia-Lancaster turnpike (1789) was the first and 86 companies built over 2000 miles of these roads in Pennsylvania, whilst there were 135 similar companies in New York and 180 in New England building roads between 1790 and 1830. These roads were used mainly by stage coaches and migrants, since the costs were too great for freight. Other roads had a surface of wide, heavy wooden planks which cost less, and were used especially on short hauls (often to water transport), but the life of the planks was only seven years and upkeep costly.

The main form of transport was by water and most roads were built to carry on where water transport left off. Some canals were built in this phase, but were mostly short and of minor importance until after 1815. The great emphasis was on unimproved river transport. Riverboat service was established between New York and Albany on the Hudson River from 1807 (a regular service covered the 150 miles in 32 hours) while the Mississippi-Ohio system could be exploited after the 1803 Louisiana Purchase from France.

2. The first large-scale transport: canal and rail, 1825–60

At the end of the War of 1812 New York State invested heavily in the Erie Canal (Figure 3.6) from Albany to Buffalo, a distance of 364 miles. Begun in 1817, it was completed by 1825 at a cost of $7 million, but the tolls soon paid for it and money could then be spent on improvements and branches. Upon the opening of the canal goods and passenger movements were transferred from the Ohio Valley, which had been the main avenue of transport to that date, to the northern routeway via the Great Lakes. By 1833 a regular packet service connected Buffalo and Detroit for $3, making the total cost of passage from Massachusetts to Michigan only $10. The opening of the Erie Canal set off a wave of further canal construction: from 1815 to 1834 2185 miles were completed and $58.6 million invested.

Some of the other canals were built to retrieve a part of the trade lost to New York. The State of Pennsylvania built a canal westward from Philadelphia to Pittsburgh between 1826 and 1834. Other canals were built to extend the Erie Canal access and to link it with the Ohio river (for example, the Ohio and Erie Canal from Portsmouth to Cleveland; the Miami and Ohio Canal from Cincinnati to Toledo). The combination of these canals routed a large proportion of the trade via the northern routes, although many cargoes still took the more southerly routes. Canals continued to be built until 1860, with major peaks around 1840 and 1855. But after 1840 railroads soon equalled and then rapidly exceeded the canals in mileage, taking over the major traffic.

As the canals developed in the north, so commerce boomed in the south with the development of the Mississippi steamboats. These were first introduced to the river in 1811, but reached their fullest potential only after 1820. Problems of variations in river depth, ice, sunken vessels and boiler explosions were overcome by improved designs. By the 1850s up to 750 steamboats were at work on the Ohio and Mississippi and were competing with the early railroads in speed, capacity and regularity. They were a major influence on settlement and trade in the west. Thus costs from Louisville to New Orleans for 100 lb of freight were $5 before steamboats, $2 in 1820 and 25 cents in 1840.

Baltimore forged ahead with the construction of the first North American railroad, the Baltimore and Ohio, but it met great difficulties in crossing the Appalachians (the maximum height on the route being 2754 feet) and for a time was left uncompleted, eventually reaching Wheeling in 1853. By this time other cities had completed rail links to the interior: the Boston-Albany line was ready by 1842, although changes in gauge along the route required two transhipments of goods. New York merchants relied on the Erie Canal and left railroads to local promoters; one could travel by rail from Albany to Buffalo by 1842, but there were eight local sections needing transhipment and the payment of tolls to the canal company until 1848. These sections were consolidated and in 1851–2 the New York Central Railroad connected New York with Buffalo, while the New York and Erie Railroad built a line across the southern part of New York State. The Pennsylvania Railroad was built from

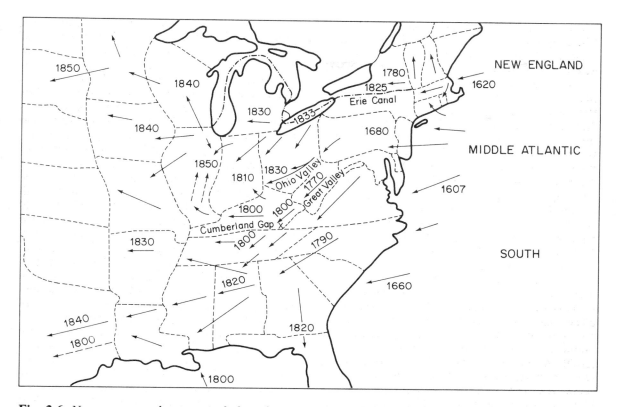

Fig. 3.6 *New routes to the west, including the Erie canal*

Philadelphia to Pittsburgh by 1852.

In the South also there was a phase of building railroads inland from the ports of Charleston and Savannah to Atlanta, Augusta and Chattanooga. In the 1840s 9000 miles of railroad track were added to the previous 1000, and the major framework of movement in the eastern part of the country established.

3. Railroad dominance, 1860–1910

Within a further 10 years another 30 000 miles of track were laid, leading to transcontinental rail links in the 1860s and a maximum rail network of 250 000 miles in the USA by 1910. There was a marked emphasis on east-west, rather than north-south routes as more and more produce from the interior flowed to the north-eastern seaboard (Figure 3.7). The railroads in the north gained by attracting lower insurance rates than the steam-boats, and the railroads took over most of the trade except for slow, bulky freight which the river system retained. The merchants of the east coast also had better connections in Europe for the sale of increasing grain surpluses. While the dominance of markets in the West Indies and South America before 1840 had favoured New Orleans, there was a new orientation of trends towards trade with England after the 1846 repeal of the Corn Laws which opened British markets to cheap foreign grain imports. The South became increasingly isolated from the close-knit North in terms of transport facilities, as well as in other ways.

Although less track was built in the 1860s due to the Civil War, technological developments made a great difference to the railroads during that decade and prepared the way for the subsequent boom. The new steel rails, although more costly than cast iron, were more durable and could take larger, more heavily-laden trucks. Steam locomotives were built with greater pulling power. By 1868

Fig. 3.7 *The growth of the rail net, bringing a closer trading interaction between the Midwest and the north-eastern seaboard. This map shows the 1860 situation, just before the Civil War*

Westinghouse air brakes made journeys safer and higher speeds possible, and after 1865 Pullman sleeping cars made long distance journeys more comfortable. Trains grew in size and costs fell, allowing a greater range of freight to be carried – especially bulky, low cost items such as coal, iron ore and grain. By 1861 the transcontinental telegraph service had dealt the high-cost mail service a fatal blow, and by 1869 the first transcontinental railroad was completed, relegating the Wells Fargo Stage company to a few other routes until they, too, were served by railroads. By 1883 there were four transcontinental routes from coast to coast. At this time the railroads owned 181 million acres of land as a subsidy from the federal government, but it was often held back for later sale. In general, however, this spurt of railroad construction opened up the western half of the USA rapidly, and it took some time for settlement to arrive and fill in the lands made accessible by the railroads.

In the already settled part of the country the second half of the nineteenth century also saw increased competition between the many privately-owned railroad companies, and several alternative routes served the main centres. There was also an increase in north-south lines, although the south-eastern and south-western areas lagged behind in through line combinations. The greatest proportion of track built from 1864 to 1900 was in the Great Plains states: many lines radiated west of Chicago in particular, but there were also lines running from St Louis, Kansas City, Minneapolis, Omaha and Denver. These first linked major centres and then formed spurs into farming lands. Two, three or four lines might enter the same town due to competition between railroads.

All this railroad building took up a large proportion of the money available for investment at the time. Government subsidies were augmented by municipal encouragement (guaranteeing railroad bonds and even providing fixed capital items such as terminals). The land grants from the federal government were the main sources of revenue during the major surge of building; at one time the railroads owned 25 per cent of Minnesota

Greely Fjord with Blackwelder Mountain Range in the background, North West Territories

and 20 per cent of Wisconsin, Iowa, Kansas and North Dakota. The railroad companies were also the first large corporations, leading the way in obtaining funds for their massive needs, and investment banks grew up to obtain money for them, mainly from Europe.

By 1870 users of the railroads were grumbling that the companies were abusing their positions and were not providing adequate or low cost services. High prices for short monopoly lines contrasted with low prices for competitive routes. Legislation was introduced to regulate activities and rates charged under the auspices of the Interstate Commerce Commission set up in 1887. The Commission had a chequered career of success and failure in the early days until further Acts in the twentieth century strengthened its powers.

As the railroads increased their dominant role, so many river and canal waterways languished, although major arteries such as the Mississippi and Great Lakes still maintained an important function. In fact the Mississippi below St Louis reached its high point of river freight traffic in 1880 and the Erie Canal in 1889. Total values fell markedly by 1900, and by 1915 50 per cent of all canal mileage was disused. Traffic on the Great Lakes increased at this time. When the canals were at the height of their use in the 1880s, the Great Lakes were just coming into their own, and between 1890 and 1915 the tonnage carried on them quintupled due to the use of larger vessels and the mechanised handling of iron, coal, copper and grain at the lake ports.

Immigration and internal migration

The availability of new lands and their increased accessibility led to massive migrations of millions of people during the nineteenth century. The movements involved those who had been living in the United States for some generations, many of whom moved westwards in stages. There were also many new immigrants – from Britain and northern Europe in the first half of the century, then from southern and eastern Europe towards the end (Figure 3.8). The major phases of migration can all be related to the 'push' factors of poor conditions in the source areas and to the 'pull' factor of new opportunities in terms of land or freedom in the receiving region.

The process was continuous. In some cases the 'push' factors were more important than the 'pull'. Reasons for migrations in general include the desire to increase prospects of wealth or land ownership (economic factors), but often the most important reasons for moving to the USA, or for moving within the country, included cultural and political factors. Some of the migrations led to people re-establishing their old ways in the new lands; others were innovative and led to a new way of life. At the level of *primitive migrations*, related to a low level of development and response to environmental changes, the best examples occurred amongst Indians before Europeans arrived. The plains Indians represent a group which migrated into new areas as drought made a source area hostile. They maintained their way of life, however, whereas the Indians of the eastern woodlands and the dry south-west developed sedentary farming and irrigation when they moved into these areas.

Forced migrations also occurred. The most notable internal migration of this type was the forced removal along the 'Trail of Tears' in the 1830s, when the tribes from the south-east were shifted to Oklahoma. Once there they kept to the familiar woodland environments as much as possible. The slave trade was a forced migration of blacks from Africa to a life in the United States which was completely different.

Another group of migrations were the result of '*push*' *factors*, but the people concerned had the option to migrate ('impelled migration') or stay and put up with the difficulty experienced in the source region. The farmers of the German Palatinate (the region at the junction of the Rhine, Main and Neckar) had experienced years of wars, destruction of homes, crops and lives, and folk migrated to the USA from the early eighteenth century onwards, especially to the farmlands of Lancaster county, Pennsylvania, to establish as much of their culture as possible. Similarly, the Scotch-Irish of north-east Ireland moved from one frontier situation to another. On the other hand, Russian Jews migrated from rural areas in their home country, but tended to re-establish their families in the late nineteenth-century cities of the USA. Many southern Irish also moved from poor rural areas to the innovative situation of large American cities.

Even within the United States, conditions in the eastern states led to strong push factors and extensive impelled migrations in the first half of the nineteenth century. This period saw an economic revolution in New England as small and largely self-sufficient farming communitites gave way to industrial centres: from 1810 to 1860 urban dwellers rose from 7 to 37 per cent of the New England population. Farmers began to change to new crops which were in demand in the factories and towns. The best soils in the Connecticut valley were used for tobacco growing, market gardening grew up around the new industrial centres, and, above all, the demand for wool in the textile mills led to a 'sheep craze' in the mid-1820s. Conversion to pasture took place all over Massachusetts,

Fig. **3.8** *The changing pattern of migration into the USA during the nineteenth century, with changing emphasis of source countries and areas*

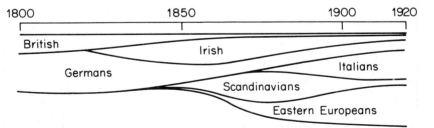

Vermont and Connecticut and the result was (as elsewhere) to release a large part of the agricultural population. Their lands were bought up by the owners of expanding sheep farms. Increasing quantities of cheaper grain from the west also reached the eastern areas in the 1830s and 1840s, putting many farmers out of business, not only in New England but in the former granary states of the Middle Atlantic, and thus releasing thousands more who made for the western frontier lands. Then in the 1840s the sheep craze reached Ohio, where wool could be produced more cheaply than on the New England hills, and the process of farm abandonment took over again in New England, where wool production was cut by half between 1840 and 1850. Whereas 60 per cent of the land in New England had been cleared for farming by 1830, large portions reverted to woodland after the middle of the century (and in 1970 83 per cent of the area was wooded). The release of people from New England and the Middle Atlantic states due to bad economic conditions in the source regions had a major effect on the new settlement of the frontier areas between the Appalachians and the Mississippi by the spread of Yankee values and ideals. At the same time many migrants moved freely for economic betterment or sheer adventure.

Immigration to the USA began to swell to a flood in the 1830s and continued to rise through the late nineteenth century, reaching 1.5 million at its height in 1914. After World War I, however, immigration was restricted, and in the 1930s many moved back to Europe in the time of economic depression. The main characteristics of population movements relating to the USA and Canada since 1914 were internal until the 1960s.

Urban growth and manufacturing industry

Just as the ports on the Atlantic coast controlled the economic life of the colonial phase, so the advance of settlement to the west was marked by an early growth of towns acting as commercial centres for newly settled areas.

Almost all American towns were set up on the major routes leading westwards. Pittsburgh was a good example of this. It had an important situation at the confluence of three rivers (Figure 3.9), where there was a small triangle of flat land. Pittsburgh became the centre of initial settlement in the Ohio valley, and later, when the Indians had been cleared from lands to the north-west, became the fitting-out point for intending settlers, who had not been able to bring much with them overland. Pittsburgh merchants attempted to provide for all needs: goods were brought in, or made on the spot in small workshops (especially heavy iron and glass goods which could not stand transport costs); credit was supplied by new banks, hotels were provided for the travellers; and the area was advertised back east by locally printed newspapers. Many other cities along the Mississippi-Ohio-Missouri system of waterways, and also along the shores of the Great Lakes (the

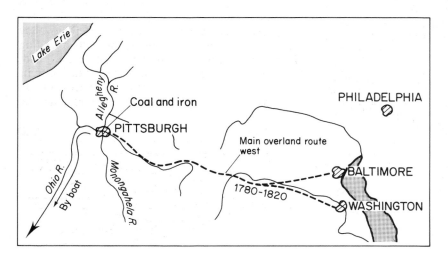

Fig. 3.9 *The site and situation of Pittsburgh in relation to its early growth*

main avenues of migration in the first half of the nineteenth century), grew up in similar ways. New Orleans was one of the largest American cities at this time, since trade to and from the new lands was funnelled through it. Even after the opening of the Erie Canal in 1825 (which led to the growth of Buffalo and other centres on the Great Lakes including Cleveland, Detroit, Chicago and Milwaukee) this trade was not affected greatly, since the lands along the Mississippi-Missouri were being opened up. There was a shift in trading, but the waterways, and the towns along their banks, maintained their dominance until most of the large towns in the east and middle west were established. Chicago grew up at a point where transfer between the Great Lakes and Mississippi waterway system was easy. It had been the site of a trading post and fort, and in 1819 it was suggested that a military canal should link the two systems. Congress granted Illinois state lands along the route to finance construction. The canal was not completed until 1849 but the lands were sold, especially in a number of planned towns, and a boom in land sales took place in the 1830s, bringing in speculators and businessmen who proceeded to promote the growth of the town.

In a similar way the building of railroads in the second half of the century was responsible for the siting and early growth of major settlements. Some places which began as small forts, trading or mining settlements, such as Kansas City, Los Angeles or Denver, grew only after the arrival of railroads gave them economic control over a larger hinterland; others, such as Atlanta, Dallas, Tacoma, Duluth, Cheyenne and Wichita were purely the result of railroad location and promotion. The lands granted to the railroads for financing construction of the permanent way made it very tempting for the companies to build new towns (for example, Tacoma), rather than route the lines through established centres (for example, Seattle) where the best and costliest sites had already been taken up. Established towns, however, were quick to see the advantage of railroad connections and many provided further grants to railroad companies or promoted their own railroads. Dallas, Texas, grew first as a railroad centre in the late nineteenth century (it had a population of under 10 000 before the railroads arrived): the Houston and Texas Central Railroad was planned to by-pass Dallas 8 miles to the east, but the citizens offered $5000, 115 acres of land and free right of way through their city to encourage the company to make the detour – which it did, and the first train arrived in July 1872. At least ten other lines were encouraged in similar ways to serve this city.

The initial growth of almost all American cities was thus related to commercial functions. It was not until the second half of the century – and especially in the last 25 years – that manufacturing industry increased in scale to become the major employer in urban areas (Figure 3.10).

Fig. 3.10 The growing importance of urban populations in the USA in the nineteenth century

	Number of places 5 000 +	Total population (millions)	Urban %
1800	21	5.3	5.2
1810	28	7.2	6.3
1820	35	9.6	6.2
1830	56	12.9	7.8
1840	85	17.0	9.8
1850	147	23.2	13.9
1860	229	31.4	17.9
1870	354	38.6	22.9
1880	472	50.2	24.9
1890	694	62.9	31.5
1900	905	75.9	35.9
(1970)	(4 140)	(203.2)	(69.2)
(1980)	(approx. 4200)	(226)	(73.0)

Pred has focused attention on this aspect of American growth in showing that once major centres of population were established they maintained their position – displaced in rank only by the emergence of newer centres in the west. In regional terms there has been little change from the earliest days; thus for the north-east New York, Philadelphia, Boston, Baltimore, Providence and Albany were the six largest urban complexes in 1970 and in 1810 they were ranked 1, 2, 4, 3, 7, 6 respectively. Pred explains this in terms of an early establishment of channels of interdependence between the major cities, a set of linkages which became self-reinforcing and led to further growth.

Between 1790 and 1840 Pred sees the gradual

mechanisation and extension of transport facilities in the pre-telegraph era as establishing the internal basis for intercity linkages. Before telecommunications information moved physically by mail, newspaper and human interaction, Newspapers were particularly important.

There was an improvement in the speed of information diffusion from the 1790s, when the new nation had little and slow exchange. News took 31 days to get from Philadelphia to Pittsburgh, 5 days from Philadelphia to New York and 15 days to Boston. There was a small zone, Philadelphia to Boston, where exchange of information was most rapid, but communication farther inland was in terms of months. By the 1840s, however, New York and Philadelphia could disperse information to the entire Ohio valley and Lakes area within 10 days through canal and steamboat services, together with express relays. Postal services also increased during this period, as did business travel. All developments consolidated New York's position at the top of the size-hierarchy.

The movement of information between large centres was paralleled by the increasing movement of goods. New cities situated on the Ohio and upper Mississippi and around the Great Lakes joined the 'big four'. As soon as such cities emerged they became exclusive centres of specialised economic information and transmitted it amongst themselves. They controlled the major bulk of trade, marketing and wholesaling. Further growth occurred due to feedbacks between trading functions and local manufacturing; each stage in growth led to new jobs and increases of population; this in turn led to further interdependence with other cities regionally and nationally. Such developments also resulted in an expansion of services and population, acting as a multiplier effect (Figure 3.11).

When modern industrialisation began it was concentrated in the large cities which already existed as commercial hubs. Manufacturing provided 32 per cent of total USA commodity output in 1860 and 53 per cent in 1900. The index of manufacturing production (1899 = 100) increased from 16 in 1860 to 25 in 1870, 71 in 1890 and 172 in 1910. Large American cities turned into industrial, as well as commercial centres, and manufacturing took over the role of growth-promoter. This meant that larger centres grew more rapidly than smaller. The pattern was reinforced by the concentration of railroad routes on the larger cities. Expansion of the network and the fall in freight rates between major cities by 70–75 per cent during the period 1860–1910 encouraged further concentration of activity in such centres where larger and larger market areas could be served.

Fig. 3.11 *The impact of a multiplier effect on the growth of a city*

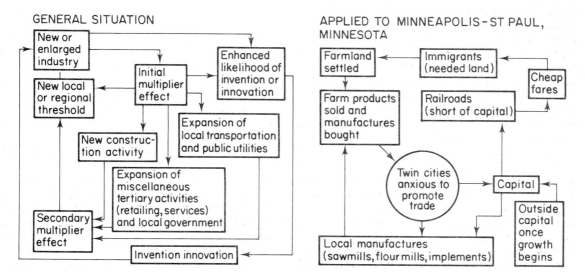

Thus the already-existing wholesale and trading facilities were added to by cheap transport and a growing pool of labour by migration from rural areas and immigration from Europe. This reduced costs and led to a further round of growth.

Manufacturing growth was the great development of the late nineteenth century, since it transformed not only cities, but every aspect of economic life, including transport and agriculture. By 1860 the USA was still an agricultural country with a growing number of small, factory-based manufacturing companies mainly in the textile field. Independence had enabled the country to develop its own manufactures, but for some time they were still dispersed in households, craft-shops or mills. Textiles were amongst the major products of the early nineteenth century, often associated with central gathering merchants who 'put out' the work (making textile goods, hats, shoes) and sold in quantity. Saw-mills, flour-mills, tanneries and iron forges were all highly decentralised and based on dispersed water power sites.

Factory production arose from the increasing use of machines in place of human labour. The English innovators in this field attempted to keep their ideas at home, but high labour costs in the United States encouraged early industrial espionage and construction of their own machinery. The Americans also contributed new aspects to this industrial revolution by making goods from interchangeable parts (as opposed to the one-off craftsman's product) and continuous process manufacture: these involved the use of machine tools to produce identical parts, and changes in power application. Both were used increasingly in producing metal goods such as firearms, clocks, sewing machines and farm implements, and by the 1850s this type of manufacturing was growing rapidly, especially in New England. Water wheel technology was improved, but by 1860 the use of steam-driven machinery was increasing in areas where water flow was unreliable.

Textile manufacture was the first to expand and was completely mechanised by 1860. Small metal goods were also being produced in the 1850s, but the iron industry was still relatively small-scale, although larger factories were developing around Pittsburgh and in eastern Pennsylvania.

The 1860 Census of Manufactures showed that flour and grain mill products were still those of greatest value ($248 million), but that the highest value added in manufacturing (the difference between the costs of raw materials plus labour and the price at which the goods were sold by the factory) was in cotton goods, woollen goods, boots and shoes, flour and meal, men's clothing and iron – in that order. The north-east (New England and Middle Atlantic States) produced $1270 million worth of goods (67 per cent of the national total), and accounted for $581 million of the value added in manufacture (68 per cent). The Ohio valley and Chicago regions were next in importance. Between 1810 and 1860 the total value of manufactures had increased from $200 million to $1885 million and capital invested in manufacturing from $50 million to $1000 million.

But this was only a beginning. In 1860 three major crops (wheat, hay, corn) still had a greater value added in production than the total manufactures; by 1900 the value of manufactures was twice that of all farm products and the United States had become the chief world industrial power. This acceleration of industrial development was due to a combination of technological developments and changing concepts of management. Technological changes affected every aspect of manufacturing. They continued in textiles with the introduction of ring spindles (1870) which could be operated by unskilled (non-union) labour and produced stronger yarn for automatic looms. After 1875 machinery was used for many of the operations in shoe-making and better quality hides were also available from the west. Many food industries developed in this period: flour-mills became mechanised and safe meat supplies became available with 1880 refrigerated rail cars, allowing western producers to compete in eastern markets and a few meat-packers to dominate the national market. Canning became increasingly important during and after the Civil War.

The most far-reaching developments were in the producer-goods industries and in sources of power. Producer-goods industries are those which manufacture major items of structural or motive machinery, including engineering materials (rails, bridge girders), locomotives or textile machinery (and stand in contrast to the consumer-goods industries which became prominent in the twentieth century). Steel was not available in large quantities until the Bessemer/Kelly method was introduced in 1864, but further improvements soon followed. The superior Siemens-Martin Open Hearth furnace gradually superceded the Bessemer furnace since it was also able to use scrap metal and be associated with coke ovens by using the hot gases from them. Developments in the later nineteenth century included increasing size (1860 blast furnaces produced 7–10 tons per day; by 1900 it was over 500 tons per day and less coke was required). Integration of plant produced great savings in heat by re-using hot gases and this led to the building of vast centralised plants with several blast furnaces, coke ovens, steel furnaces and rolling mills. This meant that iron and steel production became located at a small number of larger plants (Figure 3.12). Alloy and special steels were also developed: nickel steel was made by the Bethlehem Steel Company in 1890 for ship's plates.

Improvements in basic metals technology led to others in metalworking machinery: while Britain retained a lead in heavy machinery, the USA soon developed predominance in machine tools (which were to assume greater and greater importance in the twentieth century). Progress took place in accuracy, uniformity and simplicity of production, with the greatest concentration of machine tool manufacture in Pennsylvania until 1890, when Cincinnati took over the primary role.

Power sources saw a transition from reliance on animals, men, wind and water in 1860 to other sources by 1920. In 1850 75 per cent of power came from animals and man; by 1865 steam power had been introduced widely and in the 1870s outdistanced water power as the increasing efficiency of steam engines and the use of vast coal resources made it worthwhile. Electricity was added in the 1880s and brought new locational possibilities. Water power and coal-based steam power often determined the location of industry at the power source, but electricity could be transported to the user. By 1920 there was a trend towards utility companies, rather than the user-production of electricity, but although electricity at this date produced a third of the industrial power and half of the US domestic lighting, the main sources of energy were still water, coal, oil and gas.

Changes also took place in management which encouraged the concentration of large manufacturing units. 'Mass production', the continuous manufacturing of standardised goods, was prepared for by developments in mechanisation, applications of power, accurate machine tools and a greater uniformity in the materials used. The detailed planning and ordering of the assembly process was applied to railroad car (wagon) manufacture in the 1890s, but the first major exponent was Henry Ford with a stationary line for the production of his Model-T car in 1908 and the moving assembly line in 1913. This became a major feature of the twentieth-century factory organisation and resulted in dramatic increases in productivity together with greater agglomerations of factories linked to each other. Thus a series of component manufacturers would be linked to nearby assembly plants. Another development was the general increase in the size of industrial firms in the 1870s. Large size was seen to be more

Fig. 3.12 *The location of the US iron and steel industry about 1900, reflecting the process of concentration at a small number of points and the economics of raw material transportation*

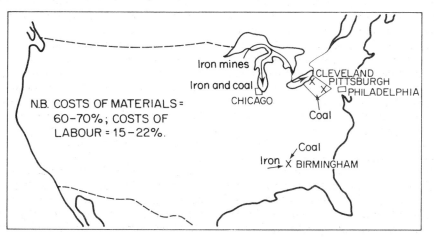

efficient in terms of lower costs for the increasing size of machinery and sequences of processes. Combinations of firms were 'horizontal' (acquiring firms producing the same product in order to control the market), or 'vertical' (acquiring the producers of raw materials or a sequence of different products which were later assembled). The consequent increase in firm size led to advantages in the hiring of better management, the establishment of a larger marketing department, the obtaining of cheaper finance and the negotiation of cheap railroad rates. In addition it was only the largest firms that could spare money for the increasingly important task of research and development.

These processes led at first to the monopoly control of markets, where firms became large enough to influence prices of their products and the period 1880–1905 saw major developments – beginning with 'gentlemen's agreements' on prices, then informal 'pools' and finally with more definite financial structures and mergers. The earlier phase (1879–93) was mainly a period of horizontal integration. This process involved the expansion of so many firms that there was overproduction, lowering of prices in competition and then mergers with the closing of less efficient and poorly located plants.

A second phase, 1898–1904, involved mainly vertical integration; the gap in activity (1893–8) was due to an economic recession, but over 3000 mergers occurred in the second phase and by 1905 large manufacturing companies were typical. Rapid urbanisation associated with the first phase of industrial growth in the 1870s to mid-1890s had led to demands for new ways of supplying goods. Swifts began the process of vertical integration by purchasing, processing and marketing meat products based on their Chicago office and soon dominated national production. The Duke family in North Carolina led in the production of machine-made cigarettes from 1884 and set up the American Tobacco Company in 1890 to cover all stages of the industry; by 1904 they had a virtual monopoly based on the piedmont area of the state. The extension of demand for water and sewer mains, gas piping and lighting, telegraph and power lines, street railways and skyscraper and

engineering constructional materials led to vertical integration in heavy industry. The Carnegie Steel Company of the 1890s owned coal and iron mines as well as iron and steel plant and constructional steel facilities, and in 1901 merged with Morgan's Federal Steel Company to form the

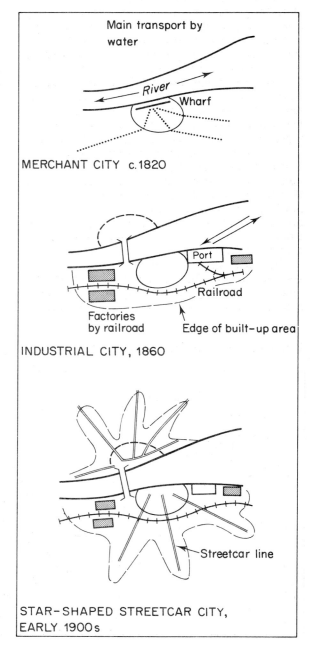

Fig. 3.13 *The star-shaped city of the early twentieth century, with its internal zones of commercial manufacturing and residential activity*

United States Steel Corporation, the largest in the world. In copper the Guggenheim Smelting and Refining Company of Philadelphia began the integrating process and in chemicals the Du Pont Company dominated explosives production by 1902. Similar concentration came in the manufacture of locomotives and farm equipment, and by 1905 forty per cent of national manufacturing capital was controlled by 300 large companies.

These various processes concerned with industrialisation led first to general distribution of small firms, then to consolidation and specialisation: Chicago, Cleveland, Pittsburgh and Birmingham became iron and steel centres; Cincinnati dominated machine tool manufacture; Philadelphia had copper and nonferrous metal manufacture together with chemicals; New York dominated the manufacture of clothing; Boston was still the centre for textile and shoe manufacture, although textiles were beginning to move south; and Winston-Salem dominated cigarette making. The north-eastern and midwest urban centres were outstanding at this time, and even as late as 1910 cities west of the Mississippi were still largely commercial in function.

The commercial functions of cities also changed and developed. During the early and middle nineteenth century wholesaling merchants had been the most powerful, taking the produce of manufacturers of consumer goods and selling to small-scale retailers. Transport developments in the later part of the century changed this: the ease of long-distance transport by rail and the development of intracity electric street railways in the 1890s meant that larger retail units could be set up in the centres of cities – bringing workers and shoppers from farther afield and gaining economies by buying direct from manufacturers. The manufacturers in turn began to advertise regionally and nationally. Wholesaling activity declined except in rural areas where units of retailing remained small. City centre department stores and specialist shops encouraged shoppers with delivery and credit facilities after the 1870s and extended this to most medium-sized cities by the 1920s. Chain stores such as F. W. Woolworth (1879) extended the benefits of mass production in low prices, and were followed by tobacco, hardware and drugstore chains by 1900. Thus the central shopping areas of cities developed and the growth of financial services resulted in the second major aspect of central business district concentration and employment. Another development in retailing, aided by the growth of transport and communications, and also hitting at the wholesale trade, was the growth of mail order firms. Two major concerns, Montgomery Ward and Sears-Roebuck, grew out of the late nineteenth century

Fig. 3.14 *Residential segregation in Boston, 1970 (After Conzen and Lewis)*

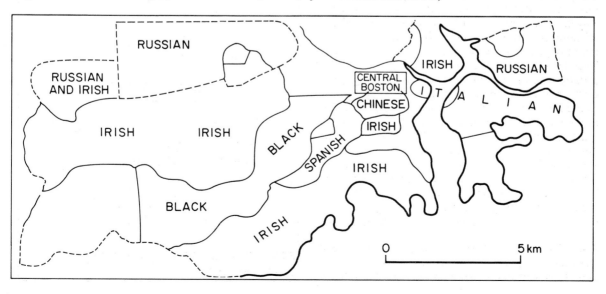

demand from rural and frontier America and became established in the Midwest for this reason – another factor adding to the centrality of the Chicago region.

City development was thus a major feature of the advance of settlement across the country. By 1920 there was a system of inter-related cities of different sizes providing a range of services in each region and across the nation. Within the major cities, each spreading outwards along a star-shaped pattern which reflected the development of residential suburbs along street railway lines (Figure 3.13), could be distinguished a central business district, a number of manufacturing zones close to railroad lines, and residential areas. Such differentiation had not been clear at the beginning of the nineteenth century, when the small urban centres had been very compact. In addition, by 1910 there was segregation within the residential areas: some were definitely for the wealthy and others for the poor; some were for Irish, Italian, Russian, Jew or other distinctive groups, since nearly 80 per cent of the late nineteenth-century immigrants stayed in the cities (Figure 3.14). Segregation also extended to regional groups within countries such as Italy: Neapolitans, Calabrians, Sicilians, Genoese, Milanese and Tyroleans did not mix, and seventeen distinct and different Italian neighbourhoods could be recognised in Chicago. Negroes had begun to move to the northern cities from the South as well. Immediately after the Civil War many moved into southern cities such as Atlanta, but from the 1880s most went straight from the rural south to northern cities and in 1910 New York had 92 000 blacks (1.9 per cent of the total population), Chicago 44 000 (2 per cent), Philadelphia 84 000 (5.5 per cent) and Washington D.C. 94 000 (28.5 per cent). Segregation was immediate: 60 500 of the New York blacks lived in Manhattan and 49 000 of these lived in a 23 block area of Harlem.

The growth of commercial agriculture

For much of the nineteenth century the United States remained an agricultural nation, but major changes took place within this sector as more lands were settled as transportation became easier and as the results of industrial and urban growth had their impact.

Before independence there had been some regional specialisation of products along the Atlantic coast with commercial production of staples (tobacco, rice, indigo) in the south and wheat in the Middle Atlantic area. Most farming outside these areas was eighty per cent subsistence. The last decade of the eighteenth century and the early part of the nineteenth saw the development of new farming areas in the south and the new 'north-west' (lands north of the river Ohio and east of the Mississippi). In the south cotton became 'king' and led to rapid expansion of the plantation system westwards; this was encouraged by the demand created in the British industrial revolution and the successful introduction of a gin to clean the short-stapled upland cotton. By the early 1800s production of cotton extended to the Georgia/South Carolina piedmont, and after the War of 1812 into the fertile lands of Alabama and Mississippi, then into the lower Mississippi bottomlands (leading producers by 1860) and eventually Arkansas and Texas. From 1800 to 1850 cotton contributed 50 per cent of the total value of United States exports and also provided materials for the textile industry of New England.

The use of slave labour was a feature of the cotton growing area in the south, and this became an increasing source of contention in the nation at large: the north-eastern and Middle Atlantic states prohibited its use from the start. After 1807 the slave trade from Africa was stopped, and slaves had to be smuggled in or bred locally: this led to soaring prices and to a growth in the size of plantations, since the minimum economic unit was 20 slaves on 800 acres, and the largest had 500 slaves on 40 000 acres. There has been a long debate on the economics of using slaves, but it seems clear that investment in slave labour could bring as good a return as other investments at the time. The wider consequences of using slaves were devastating to the whole southern area of the USA: the growth of large plantations was good for the small proportion of whites who owned them, but 5 million of the 8 million whites living in the south in 1860 were little better off than the slaves as smallholders on poor, exhausted soils. Soil erosion was a major relic of plantation farming, since the owners could move on to new areas farther west every decade or so. The investment in slaves also prevented the accumulation of real capital in the south and delayed industrialisation, while the plantation owners who dominated politics and business in the area were, on the whole, unfitted to take over managerial jobs after the Civil War. The south was thus at a disadvantage in management, finance, land, labour and communications and lagged behind the rest of the United States for a century.

The spread of settlement in the north led to commercial production of grain and livestock, sent east to markets at first via the Mississippi and New Orleans and then via the Erie Canal and its tributary links (Figure 3.6). This process also hastened the Civil War. Throughout the first half of the nineteenth century progress desired by the new West was hampered by the southern insistence on parity between slave and non-slave states in the Senate, since this allowed them to maintain their system. The latter part of the century saw major changes in agriculture as the western half of the USA was settled rapidly, encouraged by the federal and state governments. By 1910 the major farm regions which can still be recognised were in existence and production had multiplied out of all comparison with the pre-Civil War period. Improved transport, refrigeration and factory processing of food products increased demand and market areas. Scientific improvements included the use of chemical fertilizers and pesticides, and the development of new crop strains and animals suited to new conditions and bringing higher yields. American farming saw a period from 1830–80 when the machinery was being invented for ploughing and harvesting; a

Fig. 3.15 *The agricultural regions of the USA c1900*

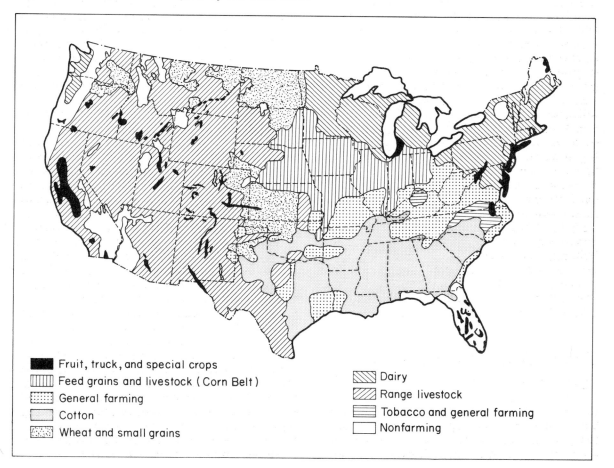

Fruit, truck, and special crops
Feed grains and livestock (Corn Belt)
General farming
Cotton
Wheat and small grains
Dairy
Range livestock
Tobacco and general farming
Nonfarming

period from 1860 to 1910 when machines were drawn by animal power; and after 1900 there was the increasing use of power-driven machinery with steam engines and tractors. These developments all led to rapid increases of production. The period from 1864 to 1896 was one of hardship, however, since continual gluts brought low prices before the major phase of industrial and urban growth and the opening up of foreign markets. Once these had caught up there was a period of farm prosperity in the years 1896–1920.

From a geographical point of view the most significant development in this later part of the nineteenth century was the differentiation of broad agricultural regions specialising in crops and animals which were best suited to environmental and economic conditions in the nation as a whole. The local scale of differentiation suggested by the von Thunen model had expanded in scale to become a national phenomenon (Figure 3.15). The midwest became the national granary and meatstock market with specialist regions for spring wheat, winter wheat, corn and dairying. In this area wheat production rose from 173 to over 1000 million bushels between 1860 and 1915, and corn from 800 to 3000 million bushels. The south maintained its emphasis on cotton and raised production despite the Civil War: from 1860 to 1914 the crops quadrupled to 16 million bales out of 35.5 million acres, although Texas became the main producer after 1905. Tobacco was reestablished as the main crop of the old south east of the Appalachians due largely to the Duke cigarette factory developments, and production recovered to 500 million lb in 1880 and 1000 million in 1910. Milk and milk products became a speciality in the Great Lakes area, the farms often associated with immigrants from Scandinavia or Germany. Fruit and vegetables were still grown on smallholdings around the major urban centres of the northeast and midwest, but the availablity of refrigerated transport, cheap railroad freight rates and the year-round warmth of Florida and California led to competition in eastern markets by 1920.

Summary: An interdependent society

Many further changes have occurred since the start of the twentieth century, especially in increased productivity, types of transport and manufacturing, and urban-rural links, but the nineteenth century laid the basis for the development of modern geographical conditions. By 1910–20 spatial organisation and distributions had changed from the independence situation of resticted mobility.

1. Patterns of movement and land-use were on a much larger scale and specialisation on a regional, and even a national, scale had become established.
2. Economic, rather than environmental, control had become strong in determining the location and concentration of human activities.
3. Distance was scarcely a barrier as transcontinental railroads enabled transport to take place to virtually anywhere in the continent. Intraurban transport had led to major changes in the internal geography of cities.
4. Innovation and speculation had resulted in rapid developments which took the American economy ahead of the rest of the world.
5. Reliance on animal and human muscle power had been replaced by machinery based on energy from fossil fuels in transport, in factories and on farms.
6. Per capita productivity had been raised greatly by this use of machines and the increases in the sizes of production units in factory, shop and farm.
7. The restrictive mercantilistic economic system of colonial times had given way to the free market system, increasingly assisted – and regulated – by government involvement in the interests of economic growth. The freedom of trading across state boundaries in the USA made a vast market available and encouraged the growth of production to satisfy the market's demands.

By the end of the period geographical space in North America was organised into a hierarchy of settlements with their manufacturing and service activities linked to each other, their food and raw material supplies and their markets by an extensive rail net. Manufacturing industry was concentrated in large units, especially in the north-east and north-centre (recognised as the 'manufacturing belt') and farming had differentiated into a series of specialist regions.

4
Complexity and Conflict in the Twentieth Century

The geography of Canada and the United States in the middle and later part of the twentieth century can be understood best if it is approached by the consideration of a number of trends and issues which have resulted in conflicts within different aspects of life in these countries. They illustrate the increasing complexity of relationships between economic, social and political factors, and the fact that geographical explanation itself has become a matter of multi-faceted approaches. The issues are listed here, each with a short introduction, and are taken up more fully in later chapters.

Varied energy sources

Energy is basic to all activity and human enterprise. At the beginning of the twentieth century it came largely from coal, with animal power still providing a major contribution and minor quantities from water power and oil. This century has seen the decline of coal as the major source and its replacement by oil and natural gas, the virtual eclipse of animal power, the engineering feats related to the large-scale development of hydroelectricity in both Canada and the US, and the modern technology associated with nuclear energy. The lack of an overall energy policy in the

United States has been responsible for much confusion and waste in the 1970s, and contrasts with the more consistent Canadian approach.

Varied transport modes

The railroad dominance of the early 1900s has given way to a multitude of transport modes – automobile, truck, airplane and pipeline – along with improved waterways. Competition between modes has been intense, and to the advantage of road and air transport which have been provided with most of their infrastructure in freeways and airports by wider public and government financing. The greatest effects have been in the rural areas, which have been glad of the greater mobility by road, and in the opening up of the southern and western parts of the USA and the western parts of Canada. The decline of the railroads was slower in Canada due to a combination of more efficient operation and less duplication by the largely government-owned rail lines, and the later building of motorway-standard roads. In the 1970s the development of container freight transport has provided a complementary, as opposed to conflicting, approach to the use of varied transport modes.

Town versus country

Most of this century to 1970 saw the growth of large metropolitan cities and groups of cities at the expense of small towns and rural areas. This growth has involved both people and wealth, leaving the rural areas lagging behind in economic and social well-being: areas such as the Appalachians, the rural American South, the Ozarks and the Atlantic Provinces demonstrate this effect. Grants from the federal government, especially in the United States, have tended to go to the cities, and the impact of the Interstate Highway programme after 1956 enhanced the trend. Since the 1970s, however, there has been a small, but distinct, reversal of this trend.

City centre versus suburbs

One impact of the development of the automobile and truck since the 1920s has been the concentration in, and growth of, the large metropolitan centres. Within these centres there has been a dramatic separation of older city centre, often isolated as a jurisdiction in its own right, from the new suburbs, which have attracted shops, factories and offices. This movement has created a gulf between the 'left behind' areas of older housing and abandoned buildings with their ageing, minority and low income inhabitants, and the growing affluent suburbs. Urban renewal programmes have led to a concentration of white collar office employment (mainly financial and government in emphasis) in the city centres and the construction of freeways to make the passage of commuters to these jobs easy has often displaced the poor from their housing. Public outcry has brought a widespread awareness of these problems, which lie at the heart of the geographical functioning of American cities. Canadian cities have fewer problems of this type and broader-based institutional arrangements for solving them.

Howe Sound photographed from Highway 99 in British Columbia

Segregation versus congregation

Allied to the previous issue is that of the separation within American cities of different groups of people having distinctive racial, ethnic, economic or social characteristics. 'Segregation' is the separation of these groups as the more affluent (that is, more mobile) avoid less acceptable neighbourhoods. This may involve a conscious movement from areas where the proportion of poorer groups is increasing (a process often described as 'white flight'), or a less conscious separating movement of the more affluent from older housing areas to more attractive suburbs. The result has been the production of 'ghettoes' containing a high percentage of poor with few job opportunities in the older city centres, and these areas become subject to a downward poverty spiral.

The element of 'congregation' is also often present, in which groups of similar racial/ethnic background and lifestyle choose to live near those of similar interest: such associations are often related to the provision of ethnic restaurants, cinemas and places of worship, or of recreation facilities patronised by particular socioeconomic groups. It is difficult to avoid the conclusion, however, that congregation is easier if you have the wealth or political power to choose your neighbours. Again, the social problems arising from these processes are more evident in American than Canadian cities, although the French-English division has some similar results in eastern Canada.

Employment changes

The twentieth century has witnessed a vast shift in occupational structure within both Canada and the USA. At the start of the century over half of their populations were involved in farming; by 1980 it was under 5 per cent. During the century manufacturing rose to the position of dominant employer, but has fallen behind the most recent growth sectors of retail, finance and services. In California these latter groups employ over 75 per cent of the working population. Everywhere white collar jobs, including a massive growth in the number of government jobs, are becoming dominant. Most of these jobs are based in cities, and this employment shift has also reinforced urban growth.

Population movements

The dominance of north-eastern USA and the Ontario-Quebec regions in the population distributions of the United States and Canada earlier in the twentieth century has given way to the growth of other regions during the course of the century. At first the advantages of the 'cores' were strong, and resulted, for instance, in the influx of black Americans from the poverty-stricken South when immigration from overseas was reduced from 1920. This particular movement rose to a climax in the 1950s, but has fallen away since, and during and after World War II there was a massive movement of both whites and blacks to California. The thrust shifted to Texas and the Old South, and overall has been dramatised as the 'Frostbelt v. Sunbelt' conflict, but involves a number of complexly-related elements: old industries moved to areas of cheap labour and energy; the warmer climate became an attractive factor as personal and corporate mobility increased; and the federal government sited new facilities (military, NASA) in these areas.

In the 1970s this regional conflict was becoming less important than one emerging between the east and west of the United States. The west is arid and contains much of the country's mineral wealth; it has received vast subsidies from the rest of the country for irrigation water, but resents the large remaining area of federally-administered lands and the 'colonialist' attitudes of large mining companies. The eastern states have seen the effects of irrigated crop competition on their own farming, and show resentment at the western attitudes. Such frictions may be inevitable in such a large country, but can be an important factor in geographical change.

In Canada there has been a similar shift of people towards the west and the growth of resource-rich provinces such as Alberta. This has produced tensions in relation to the lagging Atlantic Provinces and the aspirations of the Quebec population.

Conflicts between levels of government

The growth of continent-wide, and world-wide, economic relationships has necessarily involved government at all levels. In the United States there has been a growth of federal government and a relative decline of state-level interests, despite the voiced intentions of successive administrations in Washington in the 1970s. Federal income is so much greater than state income, that it has had a vast impact on geographical changes across the country from massive water resource projects and road-building to a multitude of smaller inputs for water, sewage, education and health facilities. The direct link between federal and urban government is a particular source of friction between federal and state government, since the latter is often ignored. This illustrates an important anomaly in the United States – the uncertain and variable position of local government. This is based on county divisions and municipalities (towns and cities), but is often polarised between rural and urban interests.

In Canada there is also a federal system, but the federal government based in Ottawa has fewer responsibilities than that in the USA, and the provinces administer resource development and have definite relations with local government units (and the power to reform them if necessary). The greater powers of the provinces (compared to the states in the US) makes it possible for them (for example, Quebec, Alberta) to consider pulling out of the federation.

Land-use conflicts

Even in two such large countries people have realised that land is a finite resource, and that conflicts are arising in specific zones. The demand for land in coastal zones, the impact of second homes, and the encroachment of urban areas on prime farmland, have provided important issues of public debate in the 1970s. Such issues find the Americans poorly-equipped, for their planning mechanisms have been slow to develop – a result of the attitude to the freedom of the private individual to develop his land as he wishes. There

is a gradual acknowledgement of the public responsibility to restrict certain land-uses, and to allocate land for public uses, but many are reluctant to cede that land is a resource for the community rather than merely a commodity to be used for private gain. Thus few effective means for combating urban sprawl have been devised.

Perhaps this is not such a vital issue for the United States as it is for Canada, where the proportion of good land in a climate suitable for farming is much smaller. Fortunately the Canadian provinces have evolved the necessary planning mechanisms to cope with the worst of the problem.

Growth versus non-growth

The unfettered economic growth of the mid-twentieth century has been subjected to increasing concern over environmental degradation and the usage of finite resources. This came to a head at the end of the 1960s, and although the 1970s have witnessed a swing from emotional environmentalism and the insistence by many on policies of strong growth restriction, towards a renewed emphasis on growth in a period of economic depression, much has been changed. The United States passed the National Environmental Protection Act in 1970 and a set of laws aimed at better control of water and air quality. There has also been an increased emphasis on the preservation of wilderness areas, focusing on the case of Alaska. Canada has also been active in these areas.

Canada, the USA and the world

While the internal changes and conflicts have been making the geography of Canada and the USA an increasingly complex study, both countries have become more involved with events in the rest of the world. Apart from some exports, both countries (especially the United States) maintained a degree of isolation until the end of the First World War and then through the interwar period, 1919–39. The Second World War, followed by the Korean and Vietnam involvements, brought the United States into the centre of the world political and economic stage, while Canada adopted a different set of international relationships during the same period. The United States has been associated with massive aid to war-stricken countries in Europe and Asia, with the rise of multinational corporations having worldwide interests, and with the growth of its agricultural exports. Its attitude to the poorer nations has often been determined by geopolitical views, with the anomalous support given to right-wing dictatorial regimes against suspiciously leftist groups. Its own economy has been hit in recent years by its free trade policy and the massive imports of cars and electronic and optical goods from Japan and Europe. Canada has developed careful exchange links with Japan and other Asian nations, and has often been perceived as a neutral by third world countries and other parties in conflict throughout the world. In both countries, these external relationships have affected internal geographies.

Some conclusions

These themes will emerge again and again in subsequent chapters. The listing here serves to emphasise the impact of growing population, growing affluence and demands for higher levels of services, growing mobility and the resultant growing complexity of interactions. The geographer at the beginning of the twentieth century was content to study the relationships between the physical and human environment, and especially the regional variations engendered by mountain ranges, lowlands, climates and soil types. By mid-century it was clear that economic considerations were as important as physical aspects in explanations of geographical distributions and changes. Today geographers must involve themselves in a study of social and political processes. This involves them in the analysis of attitudes and values which was emphasised in our Introduction. The path of geographical study has thus reflected the development of complexity in the world.

5

Regional Economic Variations

As the earth is not a uniform surface, and while human ability to exploit and develop resources characteristically varies over space, economic variations will persist both between and within nations. The economic history of the world to date supports such a hypothesis.

Although economists and governments alike have long been pre-occupied with the development of the national economic unit as a whole, they have, until recent decades, frequently ignored strident economic and social disparities between regions. This was particularly true of the US.

The post-war period since 1945 has witnessed a growing awareness of inter-regional contrasts by governments, due primarily to the heightened perception of economic variations by the general population and a new realisation of political power by disadvantaged areas or ethnic groups. This trend has to a significant extent been a consequence of the spread of advanced systems of transport and communications intensifying both the quality and quantity of information diffusion. Even the most capitalistic societies, epitomised by the United States, have come generally to recognise intense regional differences as being socially and politically unacceptable.

The era of regional planning developed first in western Europe but later spread to the rest of the developed world and in more recent times a number of nations in the less developed world have activated important and far reaching regional policies. In comparison to many European nations North America reacted slowly to its so-

called problem regions. Although previous policies can be recognised as having specific regional benefits it was not until the 1960s that both the United States and Canada introduced comprehensive systems of regional planning.

The identification of problem regions

Although many criteria have been used to identify area distress, most centre around levels of unemployment and per capita incomes. Government intervention in North America has been based primarily on these two factors.

Personal income data has the advantage of consistent reporting but does have certain limitations when used to compare prosperity between regions. It would be preferable to use a more comprehensive measure of income such as the Haig-Simons formula which takes account of fringe benefits and the cost of living which can vary significantly between regions. However the unavailability of such data on a national scale over a long time period necessitates the use here of personal income data with its limitations noted.

While significant income variations are apparent in both the United States and Canada the general trend in the two countries has been one of convergence. Disparities were much more pronounced in the United States than in Canada earlier in the century and the stronger recent convergence in the former country is a partial consequence of this fact.

Figure 5.1 illustrates the shifting income balance between the nine major divisions of the Unites States. The mean deviation between the regions narrowed from 28 per cent in 1940 to 9 per cent in 1980 but the regions registering incomes above the national average, New England, Middle Atlantic, East North Central and Pacific, remained the same. It must be noted however that this relative convergence of per capita incomes does tend to mask the large absolute income differences that still remain. In 1980 the per capita income gap between the highest and lowest ranking states in the coterminous United States was $4937 (Connecticut $11 445, Mississippi $6508).

A more detailed analysis of regional income variations is shown in Figure 5.2 where the 50 states are ranked according to quartiles (division into 4 groups according to rank). The position of the South as the country's focus of low incomes is most apparent.

Fig. 5.1 Per capita personal income by division 1900–1980

Division	Percentage of US Average			
	1900	1940	1970	1980
New England	135	127	108	105
Middle Atlantic	143	132	114	106
East North Central	107	112	105	103
West North Central	98	81	94	97
South Atlantic	51	77	90	93
East South Central	50	49	74	79
West South Central	61	64	85	95
Mountain	140	87	90	94
Pacific	163	135	111	113
Mean deviation (%)	37	28	12	9

Source: *Long term Economic Growth 1880–1965* (US Dept of Commerce) *Statistical Abstracts, Survey of Current Business.*

Recent per capita personal income trends for Canada are indicated by Figure 5.3. The most noticeable development has been the income improvement in the Atlantic provinces and Quebec. The fortunes of these two regions will be examined later in this chapter. The enhanced position of the Prairie provinces has been due mainly to the multiplier effect of growth in the mineral industries in Alberta and Saskatchewan, the forefront of a westward shift in the distribution of population and wealth currently underway in Canada.

Unemployment remains an important indicator of regional distress. However while there is a definite correlation between per capita incomes and unemployment it is far from conclusive, particularly in the United States. Many of the more affluent states suffer from high unemployment, often caused by contraction of key industries (structural unemployment) or by a level of inmigration considerably higher than the job opportunities available. New York and Pennsylvania are clear examples of the former while California characterises the latter. The car and steel industries have been major examples of structural unemployment since the late 1970s. In late 1981 in the United Auto Workers' region number 2, which straddles the depressed industrial area of northeastern Ohio and north-western Pennsylvania, 28 per cent of the union's 95 000 members were unemployed. The distribution of unemployment in the United States is indicated by Figure 5.4.

In Canada the relationship between income and unemployment is considerably stronger, with the highest unemployment rates in the 1970s recorded in the Atlantic provinces and Quebec, the two regions registering the lowest per capita incomes (Figure 5.5). British Columbia provides the main anomaly characterised by high personal incomes but also by periodic high unemployment. The attraction of the province to migrants is such that the labour inflow often precedes the creation of employment opportunities. The low unemployment of the Prairie provinces, the most important agricultural area in the country, is partly explained in terms of disguised unemployment on the land.

Benjamin Chinitz (1969) has provided an important contribution to the literature on regional distress. Using the eligibility criteria stated in the Public Works and Economic Development Act 1965, Chinitz identified seven types of regional distress. The criteria for federal assistance under

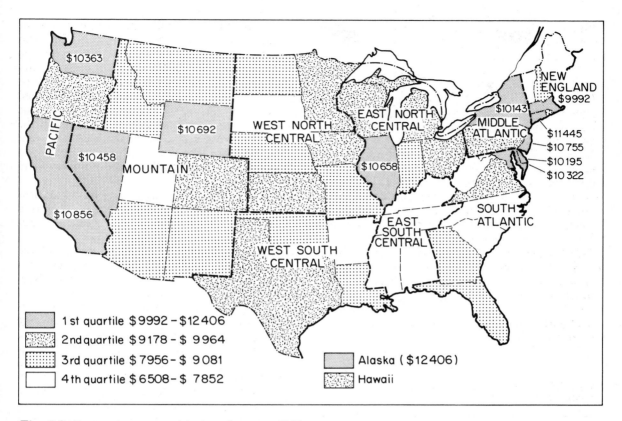

Fig. 5.2 *Per capita personal income by state 1980*

the Act, partly a result of political compromise, were (i) substantial unemployment (ii) persistent unemployment (iii) low median family income (iv) high out-migration (v) Indian reservations, (vi) prospect of a sudden rise in unemployment and (vii) at least one eligible area in every state.

The seven models of regional distress proposed by Chinitz are itemised in Figure 5.6 with a précis of the conditions applicable to each kind of region. It should be noted that by the early 1980s characteristics in some of the sample regions had changed to a certain extent.

The inclusion of model I is clearly a consequence of political compromise. Such areas lack the long term structural difficulties of the other model regions and inevitably fail to qualify for assistance in other countries. Chinitz argues that the difficulties suffered by the regional types are often so different that lasting solutions are only possible with the application of remedial plans specifically tailored to the problems evident in each region. However such flexibility is lacking under regional development in the United States.

The inclusion of model VI recognises the immense intra-urban contrasts that exist in many of the country's largest conurbations with the polarization of the nation's poor in the inner city. Pressure on the physical and social infrastructure of such areas has reached crisis point in many urban areas.

Model VII identifies the unique economic and social problems presented by Indian reservations. The distress suffered by reservations is of a different nature to the other types of problem regions and this requires individual planning considerations and policy goals. However, as the Indian communities claim, federal assistance to reservations has been limited in nature and extent. Indian conditions will be examined in more detail in the next chapter.

Fig. 5.3 Per capita personal income by province 1950–80

Province	Percentage of Canadian average			
	1950	1960	1970	1980
Newfoundland	51	56	63	64
Prince Edward Island	55	57	67	71
Nova Scotia	74	76	78	79
New Brunswick	70	68	72	72
Quebec	86	87	89	95
Ontario	121	118	118	107
Manitoba	101	99	93	90
Saskatchewan	83	89	72	91
Alberta	101	100	99	112
British Columbia	125	115	109	111
Yukon and N.W. Territories	n.a.	106	95	103
Mean deviation (%)	23	19	18	16

Source: *Statistics Canada.*

The causes of growth and the applicability of models of regional development

A full understanding of the factors generating regional economic development is vital if government funds are to be used in the most efficient manner. However in comparison to models of national economic development the art of regional growth theorising is still relatively primitive. H. W. Richardson (1973) describes it as 'A neglect of space, distance and location . . . . . compared with the vast literature on growth theory in general'.

Although a number of models have been proposed to identify changes in regional development and to explain the causal factors behind such transformations no one model has yet been generally adopted as the 'accepted' model of regional economic advancement.

Important milestones in the development of regional growth theory have been the development stages, export base, and cumulative causation (including the not dissimilar core-periphery model) theories. All have generated much debate among economists and geographers alike, achieving varying degrees of acceptability during different periods of time.

Development stage theory

Early theories have described a typical sequence of stages through which nations or regions move in the course of their economic development. Such ideas originated in the late nineteenth century with the German economists Hildebrand and List, culminating in more detailed descriptions such as those of E. M. Hoover and J. Fisher, and W. W. Rostow.

Rostow (1960) recognised five stages of economic development from the traditional society, characterised by limited technology and a static and hierarchical social structure, to an age of high mass consumption (Figure 5.7).

The crucial part of Rostow's model is the third or 'take-off' stage, the decade or two when economy and society are transformed in such a way that thereafter a steady rate of growth can be regularly sustained. Take-off is launched by an initial stimulus and characterised by a rise in the rate of productive investment to over 10 per cent of national income, the development of one or more substantial manufacturing sectors with a high rate of growth and the emergence of administrative systems which encourage development. After take-off follows the 'drive to maturity' when the impact of growth is transmitted to all parts of the economy with the transition to the age of high mass consumption following in a relatively short time period.

Rostow noted the United States reaching take-off, maturity and high mass consumption in 1860, 1910 and the early 1920s respectively. He saw Canada as rather an anomaly, showing the characteristics of high mass consumption by the mid-1920s after take-off a few years previously in 1920, with maturity following later around 1950. In the latter case, the inversion of the last two stages was made possible by the profitable export of staple commodities in demand on the world market.

However, while the model was initially postu-

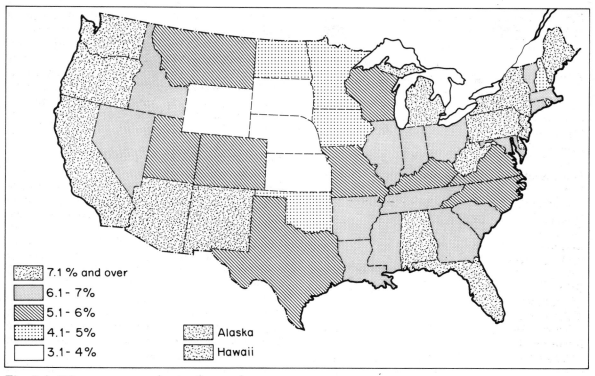

Fig. 5.4 *US average annual rate of unemployment 1976–80*

Fig. 5.5 *Canadian regional unemployment rates (Source: Statistics Canada)*

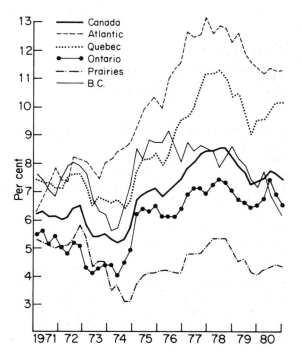

lated to describe the development of the national economic unit the growth of regional economies has frequently been compared to it.

Stage theory has been criticised on a number of counts particularly for its weak theoretical and empirical foundations and for its low level of explanation concerning the specific mechanisms which link the different stages.

It is possible to isolate various regions in North America and check their economic history against the model. A more valid comparison can perhaps be made if a slight adjustment is made by changing stage five to the age of high mass production. Such an adjustment allows clearer identification of previous and current economic variations.

However most authorities agree that when the sequence of stages is placed against the economic history of regions in the United States two basic discrepancies become apparent. Firstly that the stages bear only limited resemblance to economic development in the various regions and secondly it

Fig. 5.6 Models of regional distress

Classification	Title	Example	Characteristics
Model I	The rich and rapidly growing distress area	California	High unemployment. Rate of in-migration outstripping the creation of job opportunities. Contraction in defence – oriented manufacturing industries.
Model II	The well-to-do mature distress area	Pittsburgh	Per capita incomes close to national average but very slow growth or economic decline. Highly urbanised and industrialised. Over-specialisation in declining industries, i.e. steel. Poor capacity to diversify.
Model III	The not-so-poor depressed rural area	Upper Great Lakes	Incomes only moderately below the national average but high unemployment due mainly to declining job opportunities in primary industries. Heavy out-migration may lead to absolute decrease in population.
Model IV	The poor depressed rural area	The South	Very low per capita incomes. High dependence on agriculture and other primary industries. Limited number and variety of industries. Population relatively unskilled. Low educational achievement. Racial bias against large Black minority. High out-migration.
Model V	Special case of model IV	Appalachia	Again very low per capita incomes but unemployment rates significantly higher than model IV. Economic and environmental destruction due to earlier intense and indiscriminate primary activity.
Model VI	The large city ghetto	Chicago	Great increase in non-White population in inner city. High unemployment, low incomes, low educational achievement, deteriorating housing. Intense pressure on social infrastructure. Flight of Whites to suburbs.
Model VII	The Indian reservation	Navajo nation	Very low incomes, high unemployment. Poor agricultural land. Dependence on relatively primitive farming, timber, tourism. History of discrimination. Low level of accessibility–geographically, socially and politically.

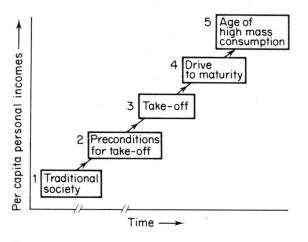

Fig. 5.7 *Rostow's stages of economic growth*

is misleading in the emphasis it places on the need for industrialisation. It is also restrictive as it lacks an inter-regional component.

Settlement and colonisation of new regions in North America was largely shaped by the search for, and exploitation of, goods in demand in national and world markets and thus a true subsistence economy is difficult to recognise in most regions after European settlement. Undoubtedly early settlement along the Atlantic seaboard was the nearest condition to such an economy.

Referring to the Pacific Northwest, D.C. North (1973) states 'There was no gradual evolution out of a subsistence economy. Instead the whole development of the region from the beginning was dependent on its success in producing exportable commodities'. If a subsistence economy existed in any other part of the United States it was solely because of a lack of transport, a condition which has never affected any American region for very long. One must conclude that stage theory has extremely limited relevance to regional economic development in North America.

The export base model

In place of the development stages theory North advocated the export base model which in its simplest form states that regional growth rates are a function of export performance.

The value of the export base model is that it emphasises the openness of regional economies and the role played by changing national demand patterns in regional growth. It certainly offers a partial explanation of the developing economic dominance of the north-east manufacturing belt in the nineteenth and early twentieth centuries. Export base theory borrows heavily on the concept of international trade and urges the finding of new exports to sustain regional development. In Appalachia the instability of export industries has been the apparent source of repetitive cycles of distress while 'booms' have been associated with high demand for the region's raw materials.

The export base model has also been frequently applied to the economic geography of Canada during the same period. J. Tait Davis (1980) states 'Broadly speaking, the distribution of economic activity among the provinces in the 1920s was the consequence of a historical development based on the exploitation of exportable commodities'. Davis stresses the multiplier effect as an important part of export base theory.

The theory can be criticised from a number of points of view. Undoubtedly its applicability to regional development in North America weakened with the increasing complexity of economic inter-relationships and certainly in the modern North American economy the export base model is much too feeble as a theory of regional growth. But as Richardson notes it has played an important role in the history of the subject and frequently recurs as one component in even the most sophisticated models of today.

Amongst other limitations regional economists have noted the relative neglect in the export base theory of the importance of autonomous investment, technical progress, capital accumulation and immigration.

Cumulative causation and the core-periphery model

Gunnar Myrdal's (1957) cumulative causation theory provides a more realistic theoretical basis for inter-regional economic change. Although originally framed in the context of lesser developed economies it can be used to understand, partially at least, development in more advanced nations. According to Myrdal, once growth has been initiated in a dominant region spatial flows of labour, capital and raw materials develop to support it and the growth region undergoes fur-

Fig. 5.8 *The process of cumulative causation (Source: Chorley, R. V. and Haggett, P. Socio-economic Models in Geography, Methuen, 1967)*

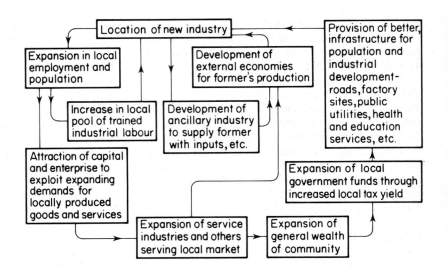

ther expansion by the cumulative causation process. Figure 5.8 illustrates how such a process operates.

A 'backwash effect' is transmitted to the less developed regions as skilled labour and locally generated capital is attracted away. Manufactured goods and services produced and operating under the scale economies of the economic heartland flood the market of peripheral regions, undercutting smaller scale enterprises in such areas.

However the cumulative causation theory also recognises that certain centrifugal 'spread effects' may benefit some regions outside the economic heartland or 'core region'.

Increasing demand for raw materials from such regions may stimulate growth in other sectors of the regional economy. If the impact is strong enough to overcome local backwash effects a process of cumulative causation may begin leading to the development of new centres of self-sustained economic growth. In this way sub-cores of economic development emerge. 'Spread effects' are most likely in regions which have a high level of raw material endowment and a reasonable industrial infrastructure.

Thus in an economy where backwash effects are dominant divergence of regional economies would be paramount, while in a situation where spread effects were emanating from the core region, convergence would characterise inter-regional economies.

The American economist Hirschman (1958) has produced similar conclusions to those of Myrdal although he adopts a different terminology, labelling the growth of the core as 'polarization' which is characterised by 'virtuous circles' (upward spirals of development) whereas the economy of the periphery is impeded by a 'vicious circle' (downward spiral) of its economy. Where inter-regional economic convergence is occurring Hirschman recognises a 'trickle-down' of growth from core to periphery. The major difference between the Myrdal and Hirschman approaches is that the latter stresses to a far greater extent the effect of counterbalancing forces overcoming polarization (backwash), eventually leading to econ-

Fig. 5.9 *A simple core-periphery model*

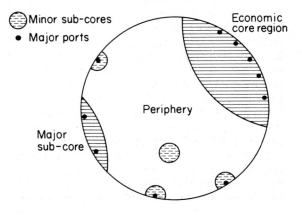

omic equilibrium being established.

Figure 5.9 indicates the general situation that has developed under the influence of considerable spread effects in North America.

The economic core, the manufacturing belt of the United States and Canada, developed rapidly throughout the nineteenth and early twentieth centuries at the expense of peripheral areas. National flows into the core were dominated by raw materials with much labour and capital coming from Europe.

It is noticeable that in both countries the major sub-cores, California and the Vancouver City Region respectively, developed at significant distances from the core region itself. Transport costs clearly insulated these regions to a certain extent from competition from the core region. In addition Pacific coastal location ensured increasing volumes of trade as the North American economy developed an Asian outlook.

Minor sub-cores such as Seattle, Houston, Dallas-Forth Worth, New Orleans and Atlanta in the United States and Edmonton, Calgary and Winnipeg in Canada also developed due to various factors including local resource endowment, key transportation functions and regional administrative importance.

Regional income patterns in the United States and Canada clearly illustrate a pattern of convergence and spread effects and in the United States sub-cores are now recognised as areas of considerable self-sustained growth. Development has been so rapid in recent decades that one might argue for the upgrading of some sub-cores from 'minor' to 'major' status.

However J. Tait Davis feels that the role of the Canadian heartland has often been overstressed in the country's economic development, 'At a national scale the operation of economic processes in Canada places the initial demand stimulus in the region of staple production. Development of the heartland economy is thus secondary, dependent upon and complementary to development of the periphery, not the other way around. In the present circumstances reference to a national-scale Canadian heartland is deceptive, exaggerating the importance of and distorting the role played by the centre in national economic development'.

Davis sees the recent shift in the economic centre of gravity westwards as steadily breaking down the heartland-hinterland concept which clearly had its greatest applicability between the 1920s and 1960s. A similar process is underway in the United States as centres of self-sustained growth have evolved in the south and west. The diffusion of wealth to these regions is strongly related to the decentralization of manufacturing industry from the northeastern manufacturing belt. The importance of the changing location of manufacturing industry is considered in more detail in Chapter Twelve.

Friedmann has related the work of Myrdal and Hirschman to a general theory of urbanization (Figure 5.10) and links regional income differences to the stage of development of city systems. In the North American context the economic dominance of the core region (the northeast manufacturing belt) has been dependent on the intense industrialization and urbanization of this area relative to the rest of the continent. The operation of agglomeration economies and economies of scale in the core region heightened regional contrasts in the nineteenth and early twentieth centuries.

According to Friedmann (1964) the process of convergence is only initiated when urbanization has progressed significantly to generate self-sustained growth. Such a relationship has undoubtedly applied to regional economic growth in the United States and Canada. The rapid development of urbanization in California paralleled the emergence of the state as the major sub-core in the US while the low level of urbanization in the south has been cited by many authorities as a major factor in explaining the persistence of low incomes in the region. In national terms, the situation in the United States and Canada approximates the third stage of the Friedmann model with the United States leading the way to the final stage.

Arguing that with greater urban size comes a tendency towards greater local self-sufficiency the American economist W. R. Thompson (1968) states 'The economic base of the larger metropolitan area is then, the creativity of its universities and research parks, the sophistication of its engineering firms and financial institutions, the persuasiveness of its public relations and advertising agencies, the flexibility of its transport networks and utility systems and all the other dimensions of infra-structure that facilitate the quick and orderly transfer from old dying bases to new growing ones'.

Fig. 5.10 *A model of urbanization and regional economic development (Source: Bradford, M. G. and Kent, W. A.,* Human Geography: Theories and Their Applications, *ODP, 1977)*

Stage 1. Relatively independent local centres; no hierarchy. Typical pre-industrial structure; each city lies at the centre of a small regional enclave.

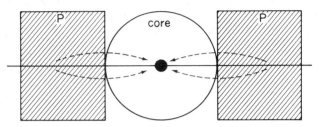

Stage 2. A single strong core. Typical of period of incipient industrialization; a periphery emerges; potential entrepreneurs and labour move to the core, national economy is virtually reduced to a single metropolitan region.

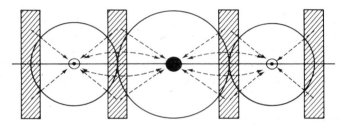

Stage 3. A single national core, strong peripheral sub-cores. During the period of industrial maturity, secondary cores form, thereby reducing the periphery on a national scale to smaller intermetropolitan peripheries.

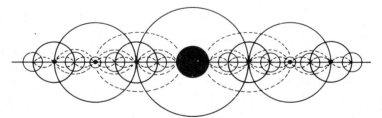

Stage 4. A functional interdependent system of cities. Organized complexity characterized by national integration, efficiency in location, maximum growth potential.

Regional growth models—a summary

All the models examined above have advanced the state of regional economic theory although individually none has provided a complete insight.

Many more complex mathematical models have been proposed to account for inter-regional economic variations but an analysis of such work is beyond the scope of this book. However, very limited conclusions have been drawn from such academic work and one must conclude that regional growth theory is still in its infancy, although the importance of such work is clearly recognised.

The economic geographer is faced with the problem of attempting to hold on to the inherent simplicity which is the hallmark of a good constructional model in a field which is becoming increasingly complex.

Government intervention and spread effects

A basic assumption of Myrdal's model is government non-intervention but he does suggest that in advanced economies spread effects may be induced by government policies aimed at assisting problem regions and that such action can be interpreted as only another aspect of cumulative causation.

While Myrdal is rather sceptical of government ability to promote significant spread effects Hirschman attaches much more importance to this factor. Friedmann also sees government action as crucial in helping to establish peripheral growth centres.

Before the Second World War economic growth in the various regions depended primarily on the private sector but in recent decades the impact of federal spending has greatly increased. Per capita federal spending has been significantly higher in extra-heartland regions in both the United States and Canada.

In the United States the sunbelt has in general been in receipt of a surplus of federal funds while the northeastern states have frequently complained that economic activity has been 'drained' from their region as a result of such action.

However there does seem to be general agreement that in North America spread effects were already operable before effective federal regional policies were underway and that the strong post-war development in the American sunbelt and the Canadian west would still have occurred in the absence of federal intervention although regional shifts would have proceeded more slowly.

Industry mix and innovation

Industry mix has been isolated by many regional economists as the most vital component of regional economic performance. Regions with a preponderance of high-growth industries are invariably perceived as dynamic and generate high per capita incomes. Conversely regions dominated by stagnant or slow growth industries are characterised by low wage rates and rank poorly by most other economic indicators.

Clearly when a key industry (one with major input and output linkages) raises its output it induces expansion in the output of other industries and thus is an important stimulus to the regional economy. Such industry is increasingly located in the sunbelt of the United States and in the western provinces of Canada.

A region's ability to maintain high growth industries is very dependent on its capacity to innovate and produce new or better products for which there is a high demand. In the nineteenth and early twentieth centuries innovative industries were largely confined to the northeastern manufacturing belt but in recent decades such industry has increasingly emerged in other regions and has undoubtedly been a central factor in the economic improvement of such areas.

Regional development policy in the United States

The first comprehensive federal programme to assist areas of economic distress was initiated by the 1961 Area Redevelopment Act but previous legislation can be identified as having specific regional effects. The most prominent of such actions was the establishment of the Tennessee Valley Authority in 1933 which, although a landmark in the history of regional assistance, was bitterly opposed by many politicians in the United States at the time and since.

The opposing arguments can be summarised under the theories of national demand and planned regional adjustment. The former states that problems of regional distress are temporary and that competitive market forces will result in optimal spatial distribution of economic activity. Short run regional unemployment and falling real incomes may result from declining regional competitiveness but in the long term the region will either attract new investment to take advantage of low cost factors of production or alternatively the unemployed will migrate to more prosperous areas and the declining region will adjust to a lower level of economic activity. Proponents of such an approach are sceptical about both the justification and the effects of financial assistance to distressed areas.

Conversely the theory of planned regional adjustment argues that market processes alone are unlikely to render optimal spatial distribution of economic activity. Unnecessary structural unemployment may be a consequence of factors such as failure to achieve economics of agglomeration and scale, immobility of factors of production, incomplete information and the ineffective use of private and public money. Essentially the theory states that assistance to stagnating and declining regions can be justified not only on the grounds of equity and redistribution but also because such aid, efficiently allocated, can improve national patterns of economic distribution and consequently increase total GNP.

These two extremes can be criticised on both theoretical and empirical grounds but do serve the purpose of summing up (simply) the arguments for and against comprehensive programmes of regional development in the United States.

In the 1950s the poorer regions became more vociferous in their demands for federal assistance and the balance of congressional opinion shifted slowly in favour of regional aid. The resultant policies have been heavily criticised both by those who regard them as lightweight and a consistent lobby which seeks the abandonment of such federal intervention.

The major legislation introducing federal assistance to distressed areas was passed in the early 1960s. The most important programmes were initiated by the Area Redevelopment Act 1961, the Public Works and Economic Development Act 1965 and the Appalachian Regional Development Act of the same year.

Fig. 5.11 *Economic Development Regions in the US (Source: Estall, R.,* Planning in Appalachia, *Transactions, Institute of British Geographers, Vol. 7, No. 1, 1982)*

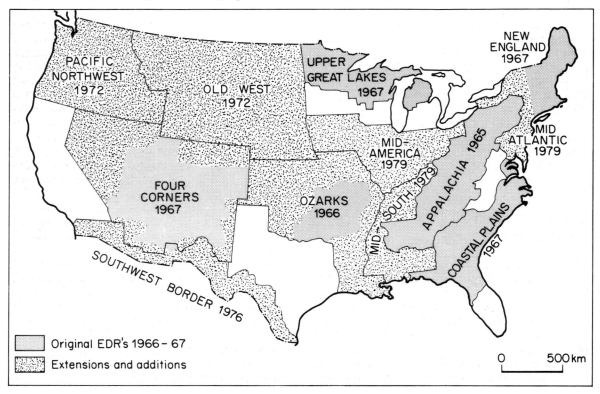

The Area Redevelopment Act 1961

Under the 1961 Act the Area Redevelopment Administration (ARA) was established to co-ordinate assistance to specified areas of intense poverty and unemployment. Such aid was primarily in the form of low interest, long term loans to extend local investment which had difficulty in obtaining the necessary extra finance from regular sources. Federal help was also directed towards infrastructure projects and retraining schemes, usually in the form of loans, as a means of increasing the attractiveness of recipient regions to new industry.

Localities which required assistance and qualified under the criteria established were designated Redevelopment Areas. The county formed the primary unit of organisation. Each Redevelopment Area was required to produce and submit an Overall Economic Development Programme to the ARA, highlighting sectors requiring new investment. By the end of the scheme in 1965 1120 Redevelopment Areas had been established, incorporating more than one-third of all the counties in the United States.

Political compromise to gain sufficient support for the scheme to get off the ground resulted in inadequate funds spread over far too large an area. The total investment in the four year period was just over $300 million. The ARA estimate that 71 000 new direct jobs were created by the programme which was replaced by the 1965 Public Works and Economic Development Act.

The main value of the 1961 Act was as a pilot scheme which provided valuable information and a basis for the more effective 1965 Act, although the former legislation did have reasonable success in certain regions.

The Public Works and Economic Development Act 1965

The new legislation created the Economic Development Administration (EDA), which replaced the ARA although its frame of reference was broadly similar. Low interest, long term loans remained an essential part of federal action, but increased funding allowed more help in the form of direct grants.

Eligible areas (the qualifying criteria are listed earlier in the chapter) were still required to submit an Overall Economic Development Programme which was to be revised annually. Experience from 1961–5 indicated that the average county unit was too small for effective economic planning and the generation of growth. Subsequently a new unit, the Economic Development District (EDD), was established to facilitate more efficient action.

An EDD had to contain at least two redevelopment areas (counties) and a 'growth centre'. Funds were to be focused on growth centres with the idea that, once the development process was established in such nodes, it would generate spread effects to the wider regions. The vast majority of EDD's contained between five and ten counties.

In an attempt to invest limited funds more effectively the number of redevelopment areas was reduced to approximately 900 in the early years of the new legislation. However in 1971 the eligibility criteria were relaxed because of political compromise and soon 1800 redevelopment areas covered land inhabited by over 100 million people. While redevelopment areas could be found in every state the most intense concentrations appeared in Appalachia, the South, the Upper Great Lakes region, the North West and the southern Mountain division.

A commensurate increase in funding was not forthcoming and this greatly limited the potential benefits of the programme. Lack of adequate investment and poor selection restricted many 'growth centres' to a role well below that envisaged when the legislation was initially passed. In a number of areas the provision of new jobs generated return migration or attracted new workers rather than reducing long term unemployment.

Public works schemes were an essential part of the 1965 Act but much debate ensued concerning the allocation of EDA funds, particularly between infrastructural and cultural projects. As B. Chinitz, R. Estall (1972) and other authorities have pointed out, much remains to be learned about the most effective way of tackling regional distress.

The Public Works and Economic Development Act also introduced an even larger planning unit, the Economic Development Region. The number of EDRs has steadily grown from the initial six areas established between 1965 and 1967 to cover most of the country.

It was felt that the regional commissions would allow for more co-ordinated planning over wider regions, irrespective of state boundaries, in a manner not dissimilar to the role played by the Appalachian Regional Commission.

The regional commissions (apart from Appalachia) have in fact had little impact as they are in control of very limited funds and tend to act mainly as a forum for states to get together and provide money for planning exercises or a few local projects.

The whole regional programme survived a number of concerted attempts by the powerful opposition lobby to ditch it, particularly under Republican administrations, but was finally terminated by the Reagan administration in 1981 (with the exception of the Appalachian 'finish-up' programme).

Appalachia—Contrasts in regional economic assistance

The Appalachian region has received by far the largest injection of federal funding through the two unrelated and contrasting programmes of the Tennessee Valley Authority established in 1933 and the Appalachian Regional Development Act of 1965. Both schemes are unique in the history of United States economic development.

The region

Appalachia can be recognised not only as a physical region based on the Appalachian mountains but also as a political (following the ARDA, 1965) and to some extent a cultural entity. However, with reference to the latter, a study of vernacular regions in the United States by Zelinsky (1980) did not identify Appalachia in its top seventy regions as evidenced by local usage of the term.

Delimitation of the region's boundaries depends upon the criteria selected but for the sake of simplicity the region referred to in this text is the planning area designated by the Appalachian Regional Development Act of 1965 (Figure 5.12).

The nature of Appalachia's economic problems stems from a combination of the region's physical landscape and man's previous inability or unwillingness to recognise the limitations of such an environment. A cross-section of Central

Appalachia (Figure 5.13) illustrates the basic physical sub-divisions. The Allegheny Plateau, an area of almost undisturbed and near horizontal rocks rising gradually eastwards to form the Allegheny mountains, comprises the western part of this highland region. The plateau is dissected by gorge-like valleys.

East from the steep 'front' of the Allegheny mountains is the ridge and valley province, a region of steep-sided wooded mountain ridges alternating with valleys trending in a northeast to southwest direction, and terminated to the east by a wide structural trough – the Great Appalachian Valley. This mountain zone is only about 24 km wide in Pennsylvania but over 160 km wide in North Carolina where the loftiest summit in the Great Smokey Mountains, Mt Mitchell (2037 m) is found. To the east of the Blue Ridge the Piedmont, a broad plateau averaging 80 km wide in Maryland and 160 km in Georgia and the Carolinas, slopes gradually down to the Fall Line

Fig. 5.12 *The Appalachia Region (Source: Appalachian Regional Commission)*

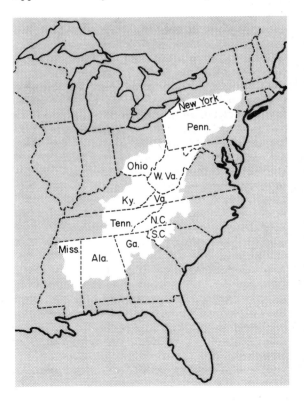

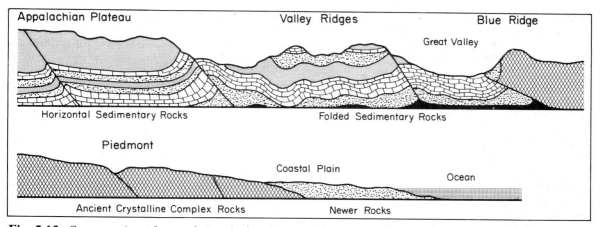

Fig. 5.13 *Cross-section of central Appalachia (Source: White, C. L., Foscue, E. J. and McKnight, T. L.,* Regional Geography of Anglo-America)

which marks the junction with the younger rocks of the coastplain. The general level of the Piedmont rises from approximately 150 metres in the east to 300 metres in the west.

The causes of economic distress

The economy of the region from the beginning has been heavily over-dependent on the primary activities of mining, forestry and agriculture and thus subject to the periodic fluctuations characteristic of the economic well-being of such occupations.

Although agricultural potential differs widely in a region with such a diversity of physical landscapes, in general modern agriculture is limited and there has been much abandonment of farmland. Indiscriminate and unscientific methods of farming by early settlers frequently resulted in appalling soil erosion. Appalachia remained well into the twentieth century a region of semi-subsistence agriculture within the most technically advanced and highly capitalised agricultural nation in the world.

Widespread timber clearance, both to make land available for agriculture and for direct commercial exploitation exacerbated the situation in this fragile highland ecosystem. In the latter part of the nineteenth century the region was penetrated by railroads and its luxuriant stands of hardwoods and softwoods were exploited by a multitude of timber companies with virtually no thought to the future regeneration of this most valuable resource.

Limited financial understanding led many early residents to sell valuable timber and mineral rights for relatively small sums and the exploiting companies did virtually nothing to enhance the well-being of local communities. In addition an apparent lack of concern for their own futures inhibited the development of education and other public services in the region. The unstable politics of Appalachia created by divided loyalties in the Civil War, the prohibition era and the coal union wars of the 1930s further hindered economic development.

From the 1870s to the early 1900s as the railway network was greatly extended, the coal companies moved into the region and remained to impart a devastating physical and social legacy. Although deep mines were at first dominant the location of much high quality coal at or very near to the surface encouraged strip mining after 1945 which laid bare huge tracts of land, ripping away topsoil and vegetation, disrupting drainage systems, polluting rivers, and uprooting and destroying animal life. The local rural population and poor European immigrants were brought together to work in the newly constructed mining camps and although conditions were frequently poor, mining did provide initially a huge source of employment. However this was only as long as the market for coal remained high.

The economic depression of the 1930s and the erosion of coal's traditional markets by new sources of energy proved catastrophic for many Appalachian communities. Mechanization and rationalisation of the industry in an attempt to increase competitiveness in the 1950s created further unemployment in a region where alternative job opportunities were virtually negligible. As the nation's major coal producing region, Appalachia bore the brunt of the industry's decline which was halted in the 1970s. Eight out of thirteen states in the region produce coal which amounted to about 60 per cent of total US production in 1980.

The role of the timber and coal companies in the region was predominantly one of exploitation with very low levels of investment in industrial and social infrastructure. Such a lack of investment has resulted in national economic expansion generally by-passing Appalachia. The region was relatively inaccessible and the people were characterised by poor health, low education and skill levels and low incomes.

W. Alonso and E. Medrich (1972) noted the lack of spontaneous growth centres (SGCs), identified on the basis of substantial in-migration, in Appalachia. Spontaneous growth centres are those which develop without benefit of special assistance, unlike induced growth centres which are in receipt of specific government funds. Between 1950 and 1965 Appalachia had only one SGC, Huntsville, Alabama, which owed its growth to NASA activities although more recently growth has been slowed by NASA cutbacks. Other than this the region had had only 10 SGCs since 1900 and none had managed to grow significantly for more than two decades. Alonso and Medrich conclude 'It is not surprising that a region defined by its economic difficulties should be rather light in spontaneous growth but the barrenness of this record is striking'.

Many economists have recognised the lack of urban centres in the region capable of providing the services, concentrated labour force and other external economies needed to support growth. Such a situation is particularly evident in central Appalachia. Various parts of the area have tended to fall into the spheres of influence of cities that have developed outside the region and such a lack of cohesiveness has made regional expansion difficult.

T. Klimasewski (1978) has shown that the in-migration of manufacturing firms does not necessarily result in considerable economic growth and the character of manufacturing activity in certain rural places works against long-lasting economic advancement. In Appalachia many manufacturing units are branch plants owned by large corporations established outside the region and as such generate little intra-regional exchange of revenue and resources. Location in such an area as Appalachia is mainly to take advantage of lower wage rates and the incentives offered by state and federal programmes.

The Tennessee Valley Authority (TVA)

The Tennessee Valley Authority, established in 1933, was the first attempt at regional development in the United States incorporating federal, state and local government. The TVA region (Figure 5.14) covers 104 000 sq. km in seven Appalachian states and has become a model for similar projects throughout the world.

The original objective of the TVA was to plan, conserve and develop the Tennessee River basin (the fifth largest in the US). The valley had become a focal point of poverty even by Appalachian standards due to a history of indiscriminate cultivation, poor farm management and totally uncoordinated and short-sighted timber harvesting. The following facts go some way to illustrate the poverty of the area in 1933:

(i) average income and average farm production per person was only two-fifths of the national average;

(ii) only three out of every hundred farms had electricity;

(iii) the basin suffered from a high incidence of malaria and vitamin deficiency diseases.

Farmers in the region were generally in debt and their families under-nourished. Manufacturing industry was negligible, as was other alternative employment. Problems of soil erosion were exacerbated by steep slopes and heavy rainfall resulting in very variable and usually declining yields. Unchecked runoff frequently choked the Tennessee River creating flooding and the low summer flows made navigation extremely difficult. The urban areas of the region with their limited size and lethargy characterised the general mood of depression emanating from their surroundings. In 1933 the Tennessee Valley had a population of over two million, one eighth of which were Black

Fig. 5.14 *The Tennessee valley region*   ▶

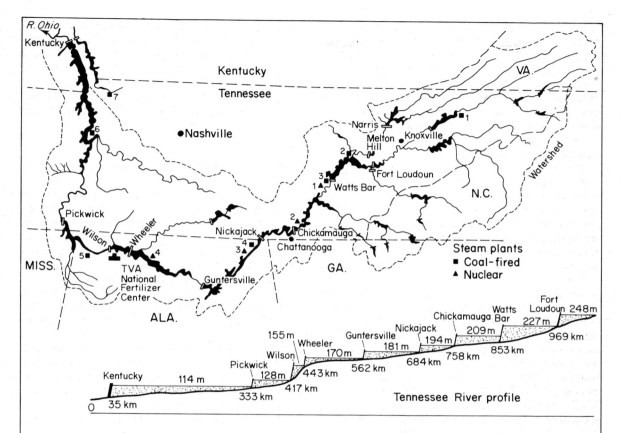

Tennessee River profile

Major TVA power supplies

	Generating capacity kw	Construction started	Placed in service
Hydro-electricity			
Pickwick	220 040	1934	1938
Wilson	629 840	1918	1924
Wheeler	356 400	1933	1936
Watts Bar	153 300	1939	1942
Fort Loudoun	135 590	1940	1943
Steam plants: Coal-fired			
1 John Sevier	823 250	1952	1955-57
2 Kingston	1 700 000	1951	1954-55
3 Watts Bar	240 000	1940	1942-45
4 Widows Creek	1 977 985	1950	1952-54, 1961-65
5 Colbert	1 396 500	1951	1955, 1965
6 Johnsonville	1 485 200	1949	1951-59
7 Cumberland	2 600 000	1968	1973
Steam plants: Nuclear			
1 Watts Bar	2 540 800	1973	1979-80
2 Sequoyah	2 442 160	1970	1978-79
3 Bellefonte	2 664 000	1974	1980-81
4 Browns Ferry	3 456 000	1967	1974-76

with most of the rest being 'poor Whites'.

The Tennessee Valley Act of 1933 assigned six important tasks to the Authority. These were (i) to control flooding, (ii) to improve navigation, (iii) to enhance the use of land in the basin, (iv) to develop electric power facilities (v) to reforest the basin where necessary and (vi) to upgrade the socio-economic conditions of the population.

The TVA has been generally recognised as a significant success although as one might expect of a scheme of such size it has not escaped criticism. However, much of the argument levelled against the TVA can be identified as politically rather than economically motivated as the concept of government intervention of this kind is the antithesis of many Americans' views on capitalism.

By the late 1960s the Tennessee Valley region had undergone a fundamental change. Employment was no longer dominated by agriculture and now had a larger ratio of manufacturing workers than the national average. Per capita incomes had risen to 70 per cent of the US level and the previous huge outmigration had been largely stemmed. An urban-industrial society had emerged in the Valley.

In 1980 TVA electricity generating capacity totalled 30 million kilowatts. TVA electric power is sold to local utilities and supplies a huge variety of new industries throughout the central South. As demand rapidly exceeded the capacity of the original hydro-electric system, high capacity coal-fired and nuclear plants were constructed in the valley (Figure 5.14). Approximately 80 per cent of TVA power is now generated at thermal plants, making the TVA the largest single consumer of coal in the United States at a rate of 30 to 35 million tonnes per year.

The river now has a 2.75 metre navigable channel as far upstream as Knoxville whereas prior to such improvements there were dangerous shallows on the Tennessee at Muscle Shoals and for long periods in the year there was only 1.2 metres of water to Chattanooga and only .45 metres above. Today the Tennessee has a series of elongated lakes with 33 major dams controlling its flow and that of its main tributaries. Controlling river flow was also the major factor in eradicating malaria which had brought so much ill health to the region.

Many of the impounded lakes are huge and present a distinctive watery landscape when viewed from the air. Farms, settlements and routeways were displaced in their construction and they have resulted in many new landscape features. Waterside location of industry, housing and recreation facilities are the most obvious and this inland area has become as much orientated to water sports as many coastal locations.

More than one and a quarter million acres of the Valley has been reforested and more than half of the total area is now covered by forest. The region's forests contain twice as much timber as they did in 1933 and they are growing three times as much wood as is being harvested.

Cheap TVA electricity, until the last few years when prices rose to near the US average, has attracted a wide range of industry into the Valley. Fertiliser production is of major importance along with aluminium, chemicals, petro-chemicals, food processing, paper mills and vehicle assembly.

The TVA has been largely responsible for the location of large projects such as the Oak Ridge atomic energy complex, the National Fertiliser Center at Muscle Shoals and the Redstone Arsenal and NASA rocket centre at Huntsville.

Chattanooga and Knoxville have functioned as the major growth centres of the region and along with other cities in the region such as Asheville and Huntsville reflect the changes that have occurred in recent decades in their greatly expanded suburban development.

The Appalachian Regional Development Act 1965

While the TVA did much to regenerate that part of Appalachia within its jurisdiction, socio-economic conditions in the rest of the region improved little. The immense poverty and structural problems of the area captured the attention of John F. Kennedy during his crucial West Virginia presidential-primary contest in 1960 and led to the establishment of the President's Appalachian Regional Commission to enquire into the problems in 1963. The Commission reported a year later, followed by the passage of the Appalachian Regional Development Act (ARDA) in 1965, just before the Public Works and Economic Development Act.

The Appalachian region as defined by the ARDA stretches from north-eastern Mississippi to southern New York. The concept of Appalachia had grown from the impoverished coal-mining and flood-prone counties of West Virginia, eastern Kentucky and six other states to include parts of 13 states, partly in response to a political necessity to produce enough support for the legislation. The region is primarily rural with 356 out of the 397 counties so classified. Containing about 10 per cent of the country's population Appalachia illustrates considerable economic diversity. In 1965 Maryland's designated counties had an average per capita income more than double that of Kentucky's.

The report of the President's Appalachian Regional Commission, which led to the 1965 legislation explained the region's demise primarily in terms of its historic inability to invest sufficiently in physical and social infrastructure and consequently ARDA funds were largely directed to improving these sectors.

The highway programme has been the focal point of ARDA investment, accounting for a massive 80 per cent of total funding in the earlier years of the scheme. However such a marked emphasis on highway construction has been criticised by many regional economists on the grounds that the economic activity encouraged by new roads is strictly limited and that investment in other sectors would be more beneficial. By 1975 funds allocated to other projects such as improving water and sewage facilities, access roads, housing loans, health schemes, vocational education, child development programmes and environmental improvement projects amounted to 45 per cent of total outlay. The early bias towards highway development shifted toward a much more balanced programme. Highway development has nevertheless had a major impact on the area and is still cited as first priority by local people.

In the 1970s, partly in response to criticism concerning its regional role, the ARC reorientated funding so that the poorest regions would benefit most. The major division used as a basis was into north, central and south. The region-wide discussions of needs and solutions which took place following the 1975 amendments to the ARDA focused on a series of 'Questions for Appalachia' related to these main divisions (Appalachian Regional Commission, 1976).

Northern Appalachia is characterized mainly as being part of the original 'industrial heartland', a region of coal mines and steel mills centred on Pittsburgh and with many medium-sized cities

often having a limited service role for the isolated areas between. The early railroad network and service had deteriorated and insufficient modern highways had been built. The area suffered from declining basic manufacturing, slow replacement by newer industries, unattractive cities and an abused environment. The major needs here were seen as providing replacement jobs in the short term and an improved environment in the longer term.

Central Appalachia had for long been a region dominated by coal-mining with the wealth taken out of the region. The decline of mining resulted in acute problems for a people who had always been poor and had not had access to average opportunities in education, health care and employment. Outmigration was massive between 1950 and 1970 and many counties lost more than half their population. This region required better internal communications for the delivery of basic services and access to more diversified employment, together with a massive effort in housing improvement. Much of the region required development from scratch, and was, on any count, the poorest section.

Southern Appalachia was undergoing rapid growth and industrialization, including the multiplier effects of TVA and suffered chiefly from poor access to services and poor housing, particularly in rural areas but also in some towns. It was also dominated by relatively low-wage industries and required diversification for more balanced growth, together with the provision of training for higher-level skills.

Figure 5.15 illustrates the state of progress of ARDA projects by August 1980. The plan for road building and improvement is based on 24 main corridors. Of the 5280 km designated 2499 km were complete, with a further 361 km under construction.

Undoubtedly Appalachia has been the major success story of recent legislation although it still lags behind the nation as a whole under most socio-economic criteria. Figure 5.16 indicates that the number of persons below the poverty level fell markedly from 31.2 per cent of household population in 1960 to 15 per cent in 1976 (compared with national totals of 22.1 per cent and 11.8 per cent respectively). The data also illustrates considerable differences between the three major sub-regions with the most dire poverty still concentrated in Central Appalachia.

Fig. 5.15 A summary of Appalachian projects approved as of August 1, 1980

Appalachian development highways *(Mileage)*	*Corridor System*	*Access Roads*
Construction completed	1 552.2	641.3
Under construction	223.8	67.8
Engineering and right-of-way in progress	584.5	77.0

Demonstration health programme	*Number*	*Amount ($ million)*
Planning grants	13	13.9
Operating health projects	739	203.2
Health construction projects	214	86.9
Child development	423	151.4

Land treatment and eroson control contracts	16 637	19.4

Mine area reclamation projects	96	53.2

Public facilities assisted	*Number*	*Amount ($ million)*
Health facilities	436	103.1
Higher education facilities	240	60.9
Vocational education facilities	1 085	353.2
Libraries	153	17.9
Water pollution control	976	239.7
Airports	148	17.5
NDEA grants to school systems	76	7.2
Other	319	69.1

Housing programme		
Project planning (loans)	101	3.9
Site and off-site development	123	7.0
State technical assistance	109	6.5
State housing agencies	35	21.1
Other	20	3.6

Source: Appalachian Regional Commission

The 1980 Census showed a total Appalachian population of 20.2 million, a gain of 2 million in the 1970s; nearly a million from natural increase and just over a million from net in-migration. This situation contrasts greatly with the 1960s when the entire population increase was just under 500 000, the consequence of a natural increase of 1.6 million and a net outmigration of 1.1 million. In the 1970s the population growth was 11.1 per cent, only slightly below the national average (11.4 per cent). However this figure tends to mask the differences between the three regions, registering 4 per cent (3.4 per cent natural increase, 0.6 per cent migration) in the north, 21.2 per cent (7.6 per cent natural increase, 13.6 per cent migration) in Central Appalachia and 18.7 per cent (7.1 per cent natural increase, 11.6 per cent migration) in the south.

Average per capita incomes have increased consistently from 78 per cent of the national average in 1965 to 84 per cent in 1979. In spite of the regional differences given above the disparity between subregions within Appalachia has been reduced more rapidly than the region has progressed in closing the gap with the country as a whole.

Many significant improvements have been recorded in the field of social infrastructure. For instance the ARC began a child development programme in 1971 primarily for pre-school children with the objectives of developing a system of comprehensive child development services. Considerable progress had been achieved by the end of the decade.

However in 1978 Appalachia still had five times as many families as the country as a whole with young children living in homes without adequate plumbing. Half of these families live in homes without modern heating. Also, in spite of general medical improvements 105 of the 397 counties are still underserved by doctors.

Thus while socio-economic conditions in the region have markedly improved much remains to be done to bring Appalachia into line with the national average. This is hardly likely to occur under the 'finish-up' programme with reduced

Fig. 5.16 Appalachia: unemployment, per capita incomes, poverty

Area	Percentage of labour force unemployed		Percentage of US per capita personal income		Percentage of population below poverty level
	1970	1980	1970	1979	1976
United States	4.9	7.1	100	100	11.8
Appalachian states	4.6	7.4	97	94	13.0
Appalachian region	5.4	8.4	81	84	15.0
Appalachian portion of					
Alabama	6.2	9.3	77	83	16.5
Georgia	3.3	7.0	74	76	15.0
Kentucky	7.5	9.8	57	68	29.0
Maryland	6.2	10.0	84	82	13.0
Mississippi	5.1	8.3	62	68	25.5
New York	5.1	7.2	91	82	9.5
North Carolina	4.5	6.4	80	83	16.0
Ohio	6.5	9.6	79	81	13.5
Pennsylvania	5.3	8.8	91	92	10.0
South Carolina	3.7	6.2	83	86	12.5
Tennessee	5.2	7.9	75	78	18.0
Virginia	5.4	7.2	67	77	18.0
West Virginia	6.1	9.4	78	85	16.0
Non-Appalachian portions	4.4	7.1	102	98	12.0

Source: US Statistical Abstract

funding for the period 1982 to 1987. The latter year will mark the termination of regional development funding in the US.

Regional development policy in Canada

Prior to the mid-1950s no explicit federal regional development policy was pursued in Canada although certain programmes such as the Prairie Farm Rehabilitation Act had firm regional implications. The first direct effort to compensate for regional economic disparities was the equalization programme established in 1957.

The Depression years blatantly exposed the fiscal weakness of the poorer provinces and led to the concept advocated by the Rowell-Sirois Commission in 1939 that the federal system should enable every province to provide services of average Canadian standards to its population without having to impose heavier than average tax burdens.

Equalization remains an integral part of the federal system. However it is not a regional development programme in the true sense, in that payments are not conditional on development uses of the funds. Nevertheless, in terms of simple expenditure impact, annual equalization payments, which in 1978–9 amounted to C$2.7 billion, have consistently been larger than those of the direct development programme enacted in the 1960s and 1970s.

While the equalization programme eased the financial burden on the poorer provinces it did nothing directly to tackle the structural weaknesses which caused regional imbalance. A number of individual measures were introduced in the 1960s to meet such needs.

The second phase of development policy was initiated by A New Products Programme for surplus manpower areas which commenced in 1960 to help areas of high unemployment and slow economic growth. The scheme permitted firms to obtain double the normal rate of capital cost allowances on most of the assets it acquired to produce products which were new to designated areas.

The Agriculture and Rural Development Act (ARDA) of 1961 was designed to alleviate the high incidence of low incomes in rural areas through federal-provincial programmes to increase small farmers' output and productivity. Annual expenditures under ARDA reached a maximum of C\$28.8 million in 1974–5.

In 1966 a Fund for Rural Economic Development (FRED) was set up to provide comprehensive rural development schemes in specifically designated areas characterised by widespread low incomes and major problems of adjustment but considered to have development potential. Under FRED, agreements were signed with four provinces, for five separate plans covering the Interlake region of Manitoba, the Gaspé in Québec, the Mactaquac and Northeast areas of New Brunswick and all of Prince Edward Island. The maximum annual expenditure under FRED was C\$60.2 million in 1973–4.

A totally area-specific scheme was established by the Atlantic Development Board (ADB) which was set up in 1962 with the objective of improving the economic structure of the Atlantic provinces.

The Area Development Incentives Act (ADIA) aimed to help areas of chronic high unemployment. The Act used accelerated capital cost allowances, income tax exemptions and cash grants as an inducement to manufacturing industry to locate in worst affected areas. The scheme, although achieving certain successes, has been generally criticised for lack of co-ordination and long-term planning.

In addition to some provisions in ARDA and FRED, during the 1960s the federal government focused attention on human resource development in lagging regions through a variety of manpower and mobility programmes which were being developed nationally, as well as the Newfoundland Resettlement Programme and the Canada New Start Programme.

The Establishment DREE

The third phase of regional development policy in Canada was initiated by the establishment of the Department of Regional Economic Expansion (DREE) in 1969 to assist the various regions to realise their economic and social potential. It was hoped that DREE would provide the national co-ordination frequently missing from earlier schemes.

While earlier efforts had characteristically concentrated on worst-affected regions, DREE proposed to centre activity on areas which had the potential for significant economic growth. As well as continuing the work of earlier schemes DREE embarked on two important projects, the 'Special Areas' programme and a new package of industrial incentives under the Regional Development Incentives Act (RDIA). The Special Areas scheme helped to upgrade the infrastructure of existing and potential growth centres, rendering them more attractive locations while RDIA provided a direct inducement to industry to locate in designated regions, particularly in the Special Areas.

General Development Agreements

A major policy review during 1972–3 witnessed the emergence of a new level of federal-provincial co-operation with the introduction of General Development Agreements (GDAs) and their subsidiary agreements. GDAs now provide the framework for the bulk of DREE initiatives.

This approach is designed to permit longer term cost-sharing incentives by the two levels of government. In 1974 DREE and nine provincial governments entered into ten-year GDAs. Each agreement outlines the broad objectives and opportunities for development in a particular province. Subsidiary agreements generally provide detailed plans and cost estimates relating to specific schemes agreed between federal and provincial authorities.

As a result of regional disparities the maximum federal share of costs for subsidiary agreements varies as follows:

Newfoundland, Prince Edward Island	90 per cent
Nova Scotia, New Brunswick, Saskatchewan	80 per cent
Yukon, Northwest Territories Quebec, Manitoba	60 per cent
Ontario, Alberta, British Columbia	50 per cent

From the start of the scheme to April 1980, 108 subsidiary agreements had been signed involving a total financial commitment of over C$5 billion, including a federal share of C$2.7 billion.

Figure 5.17 shows total DREE regional expenditure by year from 1969/70 to 1979/80 with the projection for the following year. The Atlantic provinces and Quebec, two contrasting regions in many ways, have dominated regional expenditure and are likely to do so for some time. The structural problems of these regions and the function of DREE funding in each area will be examined below. Ontario, Canada's industrial heartland and most populous province, has consistently received a relatively low level of funding.

Figure 5.18 indicates that in terms of per capita expenditures the position of the Atlantic provinces is even more dominant, at a level of approximately three times that of Quebec, again the second ranking region.

The Atlantic provinces and Quebec: Canada's problem regions

The Atlantic provinces, a land area of 285 000 sq km with 9.5 per cent of national popu-

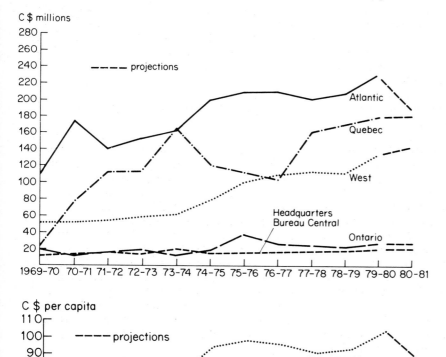

Fig. 5.17 *DREE regional expenditures by province 1969–81 (Source: Department of Regional Economic Expansion)*

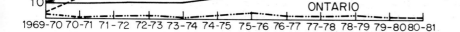

Fig. 5.18 *DREE regional per capita expenditures by province 1969–81 (Source: Department of Regional Economic Expansion)*

lation, have long been regarded as the major problem region in Canada, characterised by slow economic growth, strong reliance on primary industries, low per capita incomes and persistently high unemployment rates. In an attempt to rectify such inequality the provinces have figured prominently in Canadian regional development policies. Although this injection of federal funding has resulted in significant improvements covering many aspects of the regional economy, the Atlantic provinces still lag behind the rest of the nation according to virtually all accepted economic criteria.

In recent decades as the momentum of economic growth has shifted westwards Quebec's economic position has suffered, with per capita incomes well below the national average. Lacking the industrial diversity of Ontario and the attraction to new capital investment of the western provinces, Quebec's contracting staple industries have resulted in higher than average unemployment levels.

Eastern Canada then, identified as the combination of the Atlantic provinces and Quebec, presents the federal government with a nucleus of economic problems requiring sizeable inputs of financial assistance. While enormous contrasts exist between the structural difficulties of the two regions their common bond is a level of economic performance considerably below that of Ontario and the expanding western provinces.

Limited job opportunities have led to a general population drift away from the eastern region with all five provinces illustrating a post-1945 population growth below the national average. Figure 5.19 illustrates regional net migration for the period 1970–80 and shows a net loss for Quebec of nearly 200 000 persons.

The Atlantic provinces

Development in the Atlantic provinces has been hindered by a number of factors, particularly the paucity of natural resources, the low level of manufacturing industry and capital investment and the scattered nature of rural settlement. Although the provinces are the most rural of Canada's regions the generally infertile soils and cool summers have restricted agricultural im-

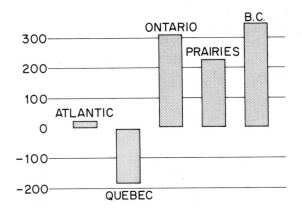

Fig. 5.19 *Canadian net migration (thousands) by province 1970–80 (Source:* Statistics Canada*)*

provement. A consequence of such a lack of agricultural potential is the highest percentage of rural non-farm population in the country.

The organising nuclei of the region are the ocean-facing seaports of St John in New Brunswick, Halifax in Nova Scotia and St John's in Newfoundland. However these major urban areas are of limited size in a region which has a total population of less than 2.2 million. The major population centres account for the lowest percentage of population for any region in the country. Such a low and dispersed population provides a very limited attraction for industries attempting to achieve a reasonable level of scale economies. Low capital intensity in the private sector and a relatively low level of public services have also been cited as disincentives to new industry.

With a resource based economy dependent on fishing, forestry and agriculture and with relatively little secondary manufacturing the provinces remain one of DREEs prime concerns. Current subsidiary agreements with the Atlantic provinces are aimed at stimulating resource industries, encouraging industrial diversification and improving infrastructure. Agreements also help agricultural improvement, tourist promotion and in the identification and evaluation of development opportunities.

1. Newfoundland To the end of March 1980, 18 subsidiary agreements had been signed under the GDA scheme. Details of the three largest programmes are as follows:

Fig. 5.20

Scheme	Duration	Costs shared by DREE	Province	Total
		(C$m)		
1. Highways 1976–81	4/76–3/81	88	13	101
2. St John's urban region	9/74–3/80	51	17	68
3. Forestry	6/73–3/83	58	8	66

Source: Department of Regional Economic Expansion.

Highway development has been vital in decreasing both the isolation of the province itself from central Canada and of many communities in the province from the main urban centres. In 1949 only 150 km of paved highways were in existence. Due to the wide scattering and intense isolation of many communities the provincial government introduced a resettlement scheme in 1953 by which payments were made to help families relocate in potential growth centres on the new highway network. In 1965 the federal government became a co-sponsor of the project. A primary aim of resettlement was to increase the scale of the large urban areas in order to provide a more viable basis for industrial development, particularly in relation to Newfoundland's offshore fishing industry.

Services to smaller communities were generally neglected and resentment grew as many people felt that they were being forced to move. Community evacuation became less of a policy priority after 1972 when resettlement funds were directed mainly to help workers move to available jobs. Overall the impact of the programme on the province's economy has been slight.

Under the GDA agreement upgrading and paving of a number of trunk roads, begun under earlier agreements, is continuing.

The St John's Urban Region agreement is tackling problems relating to water supply and transportation. The water supply system serving the region is being expanded to ensure adequate fresh water for future industrial use and residential expansion, and a direct road link between the city's harbour area and its chief industrial centre is being constructed.

The third major agreement was designed to improve the efficiency of the province's forest industry and to increase employment and income opportunities in this sector.

2. Nova Scotia As of the end of March 1980 twelve subsidiary agreements have been signed under the GDA. Figure 5.21 highlights the largest of these schemes.

The Halifax-Dartmouth project covers three broad development categories, metropolitan, port-related and industrial and includes development of the Halifax and Dartmouth waterfront area, new passenger ferries, a new water-supply system and construction of buildings by both public and private sectors.

Fig. 5.21

Scheme	Duration	Costs shared by DREE	Province	Total
		(C$m)		
Metropolitan Halifax-Dartmouth area development	3/75–3/82	80	30	110
Forestry	4/77–3/82	35	22	58*
Agriculture development	6/76–3/81	30	18	48

* Over C$1 m funded by the Employment and Immigration Department.

Source: Department of Regional Economic Expansion.

The agreement also recognises the need to encourage the local development of technology and ocean-related industries.

The objectives of the forestry agreement are to maintain the existing aggregate employment based mainly on the softwood species and to increase employment opportunities and incomes in harvesting and processing based mainly on the hardwood species.

The agricultural scheme aims to improve the viability and stability of agriculture. There are three elements of the agreement: expansion of the agricultural land base, livestock development and horticulture.

3. Prince Edward Island In 1969 Prince Edward Island and the federal government signed a fifteen year Comprehensive Development Plan under the authority of the Fund for Rural Economic Development. The purpose of the plan is to assist in the development of projects to increase employment and raise incomes while maintaining the unique island environment. Sectors of the plan cater for the development of agriculture, forestry, fisheries, industrial development, educational facilities, tourism, conservation, land adjustment, marketing and product development, and transportation. In fiscal 1979/80 DREE expenditives under the Plan amounted to C$29 765 000, by far the highest per capita funding in the country that year.

4. New Brunswick By the end of March 1980 seventeen subsidiary agreements had been signed under the GDA. Details of the three largest schemes are outlined in Figure 5.22. The Northeast New Brunswick project aims to improve the utilisation of human and physical resources to accelerate development. Under the forestry agreement a comprehensive province-wide forestry programme aims to increase timber production and expand the wood processing industry.

The highway programme is the fourth of its kind. Its purpose is to encourage through improved highway systems, broader community and area development and expansion of resource-based secondary manufacturing and service industries.

Fig. 5.22

Scheme	Duration	Costs shared by DREE	Province	Total
		(C$m)		
Northeast New Brunswick	6/77–3/82	67	28	95
Forestry*	10/74–3/82	57	15	74
Highways 1977–80	4/77–3/81	42	14	56

* C$2 M From Employment and Immigration Fund

Source: Department of Regional Economic Expansion.

Quebec

Quebec has been faced with mounting structural problems as the economic centre of gravity has moved westwards in the post-war period. Ample evidence of this regional shift is supplied by the large number of financial and commercial headquarters which have left Montreal to move west, mainly to Toronto.

The province's manufacturing base is heavily dependent on the so-called soft sectors, textiles, clothing, footwear and furniture with a considerable deficit in high technology growth industries compared to Ontario and the western provinces. About 60 per cent of job losses in Quebec in the latter part of the 1970s were in the 'soft' sector. The federal government has introduced quotas restricting the importation of certain articles of footwear and clothing but the provincial government and the industries concerned see these measures as being far too restricted and too late.

The objective of the provincial government is to attract high technology and export-oriented industries and to achieve greater self-sufficiency in many sectors such as food processing, steel and motor manufacture. A related aim is greatly to increase the amount of local processing of Quebec's raw materials thereby generating new jobs. The province is partly attempting to effect such a change by buying its way into a number of key industries. One such example is the asbestos industry where provincial control has increased considerably in recent years. At present only three per cent of the fibre mined in Quebec is processed there but the provincial government maintains that this level could reasonably be raised to 20–25 per cent. Such an increment would create 50–60 000 new jobs.

Quebec's abundant hydro resources supplying virtually the cheapest power in North America have become an even stronger locational factor in recent times of energy shortage. However the rising income levels in the west have created opportunities for substituting local production for goods and services formerly supplied from Ontario and Quebec with the latter suffering more heavily from this trend. Uncertainty about the political future of the province has also been detrimental to investment and has undoubtedly diverted many firms to locations further west.

In 1979/80 DREE expenditures totalled C$179 million, including C$118.6 million for subsidiary

Fig. 5.23 Quebec–General Development Agreements

Agreement	Duration	Costs shared by DREE (C$m)	Province	Description
Key highway networks	9/74–3/82	205.5	243.3	Improvement, repair and new construction of highways to provide rapid communication between urban centres and promote greater movement of industrial products.
Forest development	3/75–3/84	193.4	128.9	To develop an improved network of access roads to forests in northern Quebec.
Industrial infrastructure	3/75–3/83	82.6	55.1	Creating or expanding industrial parks in thirty urban centres. Upgrading facilities for fish processing.
Agricultural development	3/76–3/82	61.9	41.3	Land reclamation, soil improvement and land-use adjustment programmes.
Mineral development	3/76–3/81	17.2	11.4	Construction of access roads to the most promising geological areas; geoscientific mineral and petroleum studies. Improvements in processing technology.
Establishment of a bleached kraft pulp mill at Saint-Felicien	4/76–3/80	30	20	Private sector input of C$248 million. To utilise the Crown forest in the disadvantaged region of Roberval/Chibougamau/Saint-Felicien.
Airport industrial and commercial Park	6/76–3/82	7.9	5.3	To increase industrial development around Mirabel airport and encourage the estalishment of high-growth industries.
Water treatment facilities for the Montreal area	3/78–3/82	120	80	To ensure that the area will be supplied with water suitable for drinking and recreation.
Tourism development	4/78–3/83	45.6	30.4	To increase and diversify tourist attractions. Tourist promotion, creation of recreational parks, modernisation of facilities etc.
Public infrastructure	5/78–3/81	23	11.6	In seventeen municipalities with high unemployment. Projects include improvement of water and sewer systems, port facilities, recreation facilities.
Modernisation of the pulp and paper industry	5/79–3/84	90	60	To promote the modernisation of mills in order to make them more competitive internationally.

Source: Department of Regional Economic Expansion.

agreements and C$53.4 million for industrial incentives. While the Atlantic provinces are the main focal point of total DREE expenditures Quebec has been the major benefactor from industrial incentives granted under RDIA, accounting for 40.8 per cent of the total for projects completed by the end of 1978. Quebec remains the second-most important province in industrial terms after Ontario and unlike the Atlantic provinces has a strong industrial heritage. Industrial incentives have been channelled into the province in an attempt to modernise and diversify the province's industrial base.

As of the end of March 1980 thirteen subsidiary agreements had been signed under the GDA. Figure 5.23 gives a breakdown of the federal – provincial share of the eleven schemes which were still operative in fiscal 1979/80 along with a brief description of the nature of each project.

Bibliography

Alonso, W. and Medrich, E. (1972) 'Spontaneous growth centres in twentieth-century American urbanisation' in Hansen, N. (ed.) *Growth Centres in Regional Economic Development*.

Chinitz, B. (1969) 'The regional problem in the USA', in Robinson, E. A. G. (ed.) *Backward Areas in Advanced Countries*. London: Macmillan.

Estall, R. (1972) *A Modern Geography of the United States*. Harmondsworth: Penguin Books.

Friedmann, J. R. and Alonso, W. (1964) *Regional Development and Planning: A Reader*. Cambridge, Mass.: MIT Press.

Hirschman, A. O. (1958) *The Strategy of Economic Development*. New Haven: Yale University Press.

Klimasewski, T. (1978) 'Corporate dominance of manufacturing in Appalachia', *Geographical Review*, January, 68, 1, pp. 92–102.

Myrdal, G. (1957) *Economic Theory and Underdeveloped Regions*. London: Duckworth.

North, D. C. (1973) 'Location Theory and Regional Economic Growth' in Blunden, J. *et al.* Regional Analysis and Development. London: Open University Press, p. 78.

Richardson, H. W. (1973) *Regional Growth Theory*. London: Macmillan, p. 15.

Rostow, W. W. (1960) *The Stages of Economic Growth: A Non-Communist Manifesto*. Cambridge: Cambridge University Press.

Tait Davis, J. (1980) 'Some implications of recent trends in the Provisional distribution of income and industrial production in Canada', *Canadian Geographer*, XXIV, 3, pp. 221–36.

Thompson, W. R. (1968) 'Internal and external factors in the development of urban economics' in Perloff, H. S. and Wingo, L. Jr (eds) *Issue in Urban Economics*. Baltimore: Johns Hopkins University Press, pp. 43–62.

6

Regional Population and Social Variations

North America is a land which exhibits tremendous demographic and social contrasts, perhaps to a degree beyond even the perception of the average American or Canadian. The luxuriant superwealth of the affluent minority and the comfortable standards of mainstream middle-class North Americans seem light years away for many who, often because of their ethnic origins, have little hope of realising the 'American Dream'.

The Black Americans of the south and of the northern and western inner cities, the reservation Indians, the increasing numbers of Hispanics and the 'poor Whites' of the Atlantic Provinces of Canada and parts of Appalachia, all too frequently have a quality of life distinctly lower than that of North America as a whole.

The diversity that is inherent in North American culture, for so long seen as a source of strength, has in recent decades placed severe stress on the continent's social and political fabric. In Canada the position of French-speaking Quebec within the confederation has been a periodic source of instability yet again coming to the forefront of the country's politics in the 1970s, while in the United States Blacks and other minorities anger at the passing opportunities that accrue mainly to those of European origin.

In the past, geographers have mainly seen regional differences in economic terms but more recently have recognised that the overall quality of life which incorporates many non-economic factors is at least of equal importance in determining regional variations in human geography. Major studies such as those by D. M. Smith (1973), and R. Morrill and E. Wohlenberg (1971) have done much to advance geographical knowledge in this field.

Two basic forms of deprivation have become increasingly apparent. One is socially determined where, for instance, a group are discriminated against because of race or religion. The other is spatially determined, where the population of a region irrespective of ethnic or religious factors is deprived relative to other regions simply because of geographical location. The concept of 'territorial social justice' is now frequently used to refer to the latter.

The issues raised so far in the above paragraphs are numerous and often very complex. However there is scope in this text to examine only a relatively small number of factors which can be considered important indicators of population and social variations in North America.

1. Continental trends

At the dawning of the twentieth century the population of the United States and Canada stood

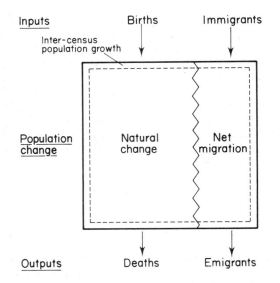

Fig. 6.1 *An input-output model of population growth*

declining fertility, a considerable and sustained net immigration and a major spatial redistribution of population.

A simple input-output model (Figure 6.1) can be used to illustrate the components of total population change. The role of net migration in North American population growth has always been extremely important and although the immigration rate has dropped substantially in the post-1930 period (with emigration remaining at a comparatively low level) the considerable lowering of natural increase from the early 1960s coupled with the restructuring of immigration laws in the US in the mid-1960s ensures the continuing significance of this factor.

The decline in fertility

Figure 6.2 shows the crude birth and death rates for the United States and Canada in the post-1940 period. Although longevity has continued to improve, the fact that both countries' populations are ageing has resulted in only a minor lowering of the crude death rates. In contrast the birth rate has oscillated markedly in the last four decades.

After a history of almost consistent fertility decline an extraordinary reversal of previous trends occurred from the late 1940s to the mid 1960s, referred to generally as the post-war 'baby-

at 76 million and 5.4 million respectively. By the beginning of the ninth decade the two nations' populations were approximately 226 million and 24 million, a continental increase in the 80-year period of almost 170 million. During this timespan the main demographic trends have been a high but

Fig. 6.2 *The US and Canada, birth and death rates 1940–80*

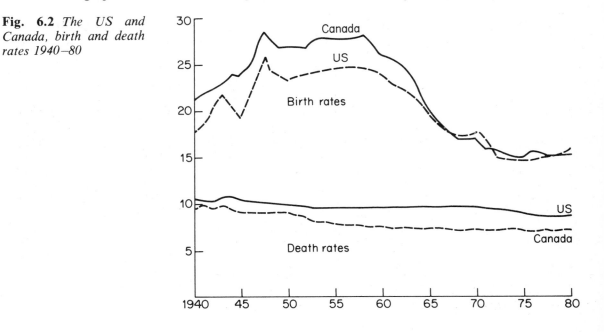

boom'. The only other countries that had baby-booms of similar duration and magnitude were Australia and New Zealand.

Of all four countries the Canadian boom was the most marked. During the first 50 years of the century the combination of a declining birth rate and a growing population produced an annual average of about 250 000 births with little variation from year to year. But from 1952 to 1965 the annual number of births was constantly in the range of 400 000 to 500 000. Now this oversized group make up one-third of Canada's total population.

W. P. Butz and M. P. Ward (1979) argue that the baby-boom of the 1950s can be explained as a response to rising male income whereas the 'baby-bust' of the 1960s was due primarily to increases in female wages and income. Although an increase in the wage of an employed woman also adds to family income it simultaneously increases the perceived price of children since the opportunity cost (the cost in terms of foregone alternatives) of having a child rises at the same time. The traditional argument has been that the decline in fertility has been due mainly to contraceptive improvement and while Butz and Ward acknowledge that achieved family size and desired family size are now much closer due to such developments they see the primary causal factor as the rise

in female income levels. In Canada women accounted for almost 40 per cent of the total labour force in 1980, up from 31 per cent in 1969. Female participation in the labour force may reach 45 per cent by 1990.

The birth rates of both countries fell below 25 per 1000 (p.a.) in 1965 and by 1980 had dropped with fluctuations, to about 16 per 1000. Fertility rates (the number of live births per 1000 women in the reproductive age range) have roughly paralleled the declining birth rate.

An ageing population

North America is steadily moving from an era with a large proportion of dependents in the pre-working age group (for a developed region) to one of progressive ageing. In 1900 when life expectancy was 47 years in the United States, persons over 65 years made up 4.1 per cent of the total population. By 1980 senior citizens were 11.3 per cent of the total with life expectancy at about 68 years for men and 75 years for women. It has been estimated that the over 65s will form over 20 per cent of the US population by 2030, a benchmark in a major demographic evolution.

Figure 6.3 illustrates the ageing of the US population where the median age is projected to

Fig. 6.3 Population and projected population by age (thousands), selected years: 1950–2010

Age	1950	1960	1970	1980	Projections 1990	2000	2010
All ages	152 271	180 671	204 878	227 020	243 513	260 378	275 335
Under 5 years	16 410	20 341	17 101	16 344	19 437	17 852	19 221
5–13 years	22 423	32 965	36 636	31 156	32 568	35 080	33 067
14–17 years	8 444	11 219	15 910	16 245	12 771	16 045	15 439
18–21 years	8 947	9 555	14 707	17 532	14 507	14 990	16 319
22–24 years	7 129	6 573	9 980	12 748	10 642	9 663	12 043
25–34 years	24 036	22 919	25 294	37 252	41 086	34 450	36 246
35–44 years	21 637	24 221	23 142	25 694	36 592	41 344	34 685
45–54 years	17 453	20 578	23 310	22 804	25 311	35 875	40 551
55–64 years	13 396	15 625	18 664	21 700	20 776	23 257	32 926
65 years and over	12 397	16 675	20 087	25 544	29 824	31 822	34 837
Median age	30.2	29.4	27.9	30.0	32.8	35.5	36.6

Source: US Statistical Abstract

rise from 30 years in 1979 to 35.5 years by 2000. Projections for Canada are broadly similar. Quite clearly a considerable reallocation of resources will be required to cater for the increasing numbers in the older age groups.

Immigration

Although the immigration into North America has reduced in the last half a century from its earlier very high levels, the United States and Canada both retain a considerable positive migration balance each year. Immigration has not only changed in terms of absolute numbers but also with respect to the countries of origin of arrivals in North America.

A simple migration model (Figure 6.4) can be used to help explain both of these trends. Every potential migrant is influenced by different factors at both origin and destination which may attract or repel. At origin close family ties may mean that the decision to migrate is made only in the light of the prospect of sustained unemployment. At destination the main attraction might be the opportunity of steady employment with good remuneration which is strong enough to overcome a distaste for the climate of that particular region. A factor such as culture may act as a significant 'push' or 'pull' factor for some individuals but may have little or no bearing at all in many migration decisions. The intervening obstacles will also figure in the migration decision as such factors as cost, time, potential dangers and legal barriers have to be considered. In addition, intervening opportunities may deflect the migrant from reaching his or her originally proposed destination.

Figure 6.5 illustrates the level of immigration into the United States from 1820 onwards and clearly shows the 1930s as a watershed. In the nineteenth century and the early decades of the twentieth century entry into the United States was generally unrestricted, particularly for Europeans. The general perception, that opportunities in the New World would provide a better quality of life, encouraged millions to cross the Atlantic, as detailed in Chapter 3. In the first 30 years of the present century alone an influx of approximately 18.5 million was recorded.

The intervening obstacles at the time were mainly emigration restrictions in certain European countries and the physical hardship and cost of the Atlantic crossing. The dangers of the crossing became negligible in the twentieth century compared to the desperate conditions which so many were forced to endure in the earlier period of migration. Undoubtedly the severity of the Atlantic crossing deterred many potential migrants when such conditions prevailed, with only the more enterprising and desperate making the journey.

While eastern European and a number of other countries still severely restrict emigration the main obstacle to the flow of migrants into the US in more recent times has been a tightening of immigration policy.

In 1924 a system of 'national origins quotas' was introduced. The new legislation, developed out of the US isolationist movement following the First World War, was designed greatly to reduce immigration and in particular to stem the influx of eastern and southern Europeans who poured into the US at the turn of the century. Anti-Chinese restrictions had already been in force for many years. The quota system openly favoured north-west Europe.

Fig. 6.4 *A simple migration model*

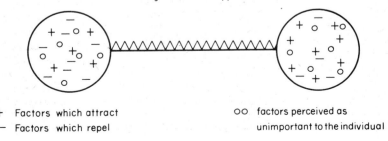

ORIGIN   DESTINATION

Intervening obstacles / opportunities

++   Factors which attract   oo   factors perceived as
——   Factors which repel   unimportant to the individual

Fig. 6.5 US immigration 1820–1979 (thousands)

Period	Total Number	Rate[1]	Period	Total Number	Rate[1]	
1820–1978	48 664	3.5	1911–1920	5 736	5.7	. . . .
			1921–1930	4 107	3.5	. . . .
1820–1830	152	1.2	1931–1940	528	.4	. . . .
1831–1840	599	3.9	1941–1950	1 035	.7	. . . .
1841–1850	1 713	8.4	1951–1960	2 515	1.5	. . . .
1851–1860	2 598	9.3	1961–1970	3 322	1.7	. . . .
1861–1870	2 315	6.4	1971–1979	3 962	2.1	. . . .
1971–1880	2 812	6.2	. . . .			. . . .
1881–1890	5 247	9.2	. . . .			. . . .
1891–1900	3 688	5.3	. . . .			. . . .
1901–1910	8 795	10.4	. . . .			. . . .

[1] Annual rate per 1 000 US population, 10-year rate computed by dividing sum of annual immigration totals by sum of annual US population totals for same 10 years.

Source: US Statistical Abstract

The racialist overtones of this system, resulting in considerable international and internal opposition, led to its abolition when new legislation was passed by the Johnson administration in 1965.

The 1965 Act, which became fully effective in July 1968, set an annual limitation of 120 000 immigrants from the Western Hemisphere (North and South America) and 170 000 from the Eastern Hemisphere. The legislation gives persons from every country within each hemisphere an equal chance of acceptance into the United States. Total annual immigration has generally been at a higher level than the sum of these limits because relatives of US citizens may be admitted without numerical limitation.

As the intervening obstacles to immigration into the US have been lowered for potential migrants in a number of world regions so the ethnic composition of new arrivals into the United States has changed significantly (Figure 6.6). Europe, the previous major source region, has been overtaken in the last two decades by the rest of North and South America and by Asia, a trend that is likely to continue in the future. The greater economic disparity between areas of the less developed world and the US (compared to that between Europe and the US) is clearly a more substantial inducement to attempt to enter the US.

As is invariably the case, immigration into the United States has been selective in terms of age and sex. In the 1971–9 period female immigration was 13.1 per cent higher than male due mainly to US citizens (frequently servicemen) choosing wives of another nationality. In terms of age selection during this period 26.1 per cent of arrivals were under 16, 59.2 per cent between 16 and 44 and only 14.7 per cent aged 45 years and over.

Immigration into Canada has followed a broadly similar pattern as changes in policy have altered the areas of origin of new arrivals. In the early 1950s over 90 per cent of immigrants came from Europe and the US but objections on the grounds of racial bias, particularly by the new Commonwealth nations, resulted in considerable legislative change. New regulations in 1962 and 1967 placed the emphasis on education and skills regardless of ethnicity. The aim here was not only to reduce racial bias but also to relate immigration more to labour market needs within Canada. Figure 6.7 summarises the changing origin of immigrants into Canada in the 1961–80 period.

Examination of annual unemployment levels and immigration totals in Canada indicates a significant inverse relationship. Undoubtedly during times of higher unemployment the potential immigrant's perception of opportunities in Canada will be downgraded, while immigration

Fig. 6.6 Immigrants by country of last permanent residence 1820–1979 (thousands)

Country*	1820–1979	% 1820–1979	% 1961–70	% 1971–79
Europe	**36 267**	**73.8**	**33.8**	**18.4**
Austria	4 316 }	8.8 }	0.6	0.2
Hungary			0.2	0.1
Germany	6 985 }	14.2	5.7	1.7
Great Britain	4 914	10.0	6.3	3.1
Greece	661	1.3	2.6	2.2
Ireland	4 724	9.6	1.1	0.3
Italy	5 300	10.8	6.4	3.1
Portugal	453	0.9	2.3	2.4
Spain	262	0.5	1.3	0.9
Sweden	1 273	2.6	0.5	0.1
USSR	3 376	6.9	0.1	0.7
Asia	**3 038**	**6.2**	**12.9**	**34.1**
China	540	1.1	1.0	2.4
Hong Kong	200	0.4	2.3	2.8
India	182	0.4	0.8	3.6
Japan	411	0.8	1.2	1.1
Korea	276	0.6	1.0	5.9
Philippines	431	0.9	3.0	7.9
Vietnam	133	0.3	0.1	3.3
The Americas	**9 248**	**18.6**	**51.7**	**44.9**
Canada	4 125	8.4	12.4	3.9
Columbia	156	0.3	2.2	1.7
Cuba	539	1.1	6.3	6.3
Dominican Rep.	235	0.5	2.8	3.3
Ecuador	91	0.2	1.1	1.1
Haiti	89	0.2	1.0	1.3
Mexico	2 177	4.4	13.7	14.7
West Indies	758	1.5	4.0	6.0
Africa	**142**	**0.3**	**0.9**	**1.7**
Total	49 124	49 124	3 321.7	3 962.5

* includes only nations contributing over 1 million migrants 1820–1979 or at least 1 per cent of total migrants 1971–79.

Source: US Statistical Abstract

officials are clearly aware of trends in their own labour market when interpreting entry criteria.

The United States and Canada have a good record for admitting refugees and waiving normal entry requirements, most recently illustrated by the numbers of Vietnamese, Cubans and Haitians allowed to settle in North America. However, illegal immigration, mainly from Mexico, has become a cause for concern in the US. Hispanics clearly form the fastest growing group in the United States and this trend is likely to continue in the near future. Because of its very nature, illegal immigration is very difficult to quantify but it is thought that there may well be as many as 6 million persons of such status currently in the United States.

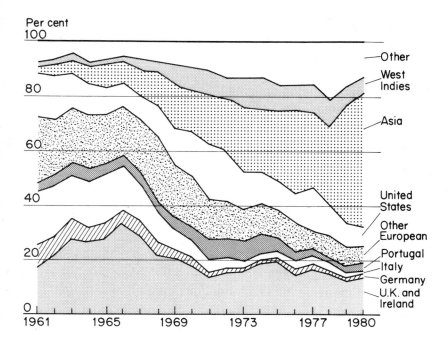

Fig. 6.7 *Canadian immigration by last country of residence 1961–80 (Source:* Statistics Canada*)*

2. Regional shifts

The westward movement of population has continued unabated in the twentieth century in both the United States and Canada to such an extent that the organisation of economic and political power in North America is in its greatest state of flux since the 1860s. In both countries the position of the traditional industrial heartland has been eroded as the new growth regions have expanded.

Figure 6.8 shows the divisional population changes that have occurred in the US since 1940 where the Pacific and Mountain regions followed by the South Atlantic registered by far the largest percentage increases during the period.

Every ten years the Census Bureau determines the centre of population as the point where the US would balance perfectly if it were a plane and each American on it had equal weight. In the first census in 1790 the centre was 23 miles east of Baltimore. Steadily moving westwards and more recently towards the south the centre reached Mascoutah, Illinois in 1970.

The 1980 census shows that the centre of population in the US has moved across the Mississippi River into southern Missouri (1.6 km west of the Desota City Hall in Jefferson County) and for the first time in US history most Americans live in the South and West.

Population change in the 1970–80 period on a state-to-state basis confirms the general post-war trend (Figure 6.9). The largest increases were registered by California (3.7 million), Texas (3.0 million), Florida (2.9 million), Arizona (.94 million), Georgia (.88 million), and North Carolina (.79 million). Two states actually lost population – New York (684 000) and Rhode Island (2500).

All the states in four divisions, the Pacific, Mountain, West South Central and East South Central had growth rates above the national average, joined almost by the South Atlantic where only Delaware and Maryland grew less rapidly than the national norm.

All states in the Middle Atlantic, East North Central and West North Central divisions were below the national average while the six New England states were equally divided above and below.

Economic factors encouraging internal migration have been the dominant influences responsible for such marked population changes, as

Fig. 6.8 United States population 1940, 1960, 1980

Division	1940	1960	Percentage change 1940–1960	1980	Percentage change 1960–80	Percentage change 1940–80
New England	8 437 290	10 546 000	25.0	12 348 493	17.1	46.4
Middle Atlantic	27 539 487	34 269 000	24.4	36 788 174	7.4	33.6
East North Central	26 626 342	36 340 000	36.5	41 669 738	14.7	56.5
West North Central	13 516 990	15 425 000	14.1	17 184 066	11.4	27.1
South Atlantic	17 823 151	26 066 000	46.2	36 943 139	39.3	107.3
East South Central	10 778 225	12 073 000	12.0	14 662 882	21.5	36.0
West South Central	13 064 525	17 008 000	30.2	23 743 134	39.6	81.7
Mountain	4 150 003	6 897 000	66.2	11 368 330	64.8	173.9
Pacific	9 733 262	21 352 000	119.4	31 796 869	48.9	226.7
Total	131 669 275	179 977 000	36.7	226 504 825	25.9	72.0

Source: US Bureau of Census

indicated in Chapter 5. Nevertheless not all of the shift can be attributed to movement out of the snowbelt. Large numbers of Hispanic immigrants have played a role and so did a higher birth rate in the south and west compared to the north-east.

The continuing movement to the sunbelt has been joined by a related but new phenomenon. Americans are not just moving to regions of expanding job opportunities but also to areas which are sparsely populated. For instance:

(i) The Rocky Mountain states combined had a growth rate of 37 per cent in the 1970–80 period in a huge region with only 5 per cent of the US population.

(ii) The three northern New England states recorded above average growth in contrast to the rest of the north-eastern region.

(iii) Among the individual states, Nevada and Arizona grew fastest of all, 63.5 per cent and 53.1 per cent respectively. Except for Florida and Texas the top ten in terms of population growth were composed of Western states with a combined population of 7.5 million and a density of about 3.5 per square kilometre.

(iv) The population of the top 50 cities fell by 4 per cent in the 1970s.

This trend is clearly supported by the case of California which grew much more slowly than the West as a whole. In the 1970s many people moved out of the state to other parts of the west to escape the stresses of intense urbanisation.

A similar westward movement is underway in Canada based primarily on the natural resource endowment of British Columbia and Alberta. However, Ontario and Quebec combined still account for 62 per cent of Canadian population (Figure 6.10). The causes and consequences of this movement are discussed in Chapters 5 and 12.

Political implications

The increasing population and affluence of the west and the south is having, and will continue to have in the future, strong implications for US politics and economics. One of the most obvious indicators is the distribution of state seats in the House of Representatives which is based on population. Reapportionment is effective with the congressional elections two years after the census. Figure 6.11 shows the changing divisional entitlement for the years 1940, 1960 and 1980 which indicates that the axis of political clout is slowly but assuredly moving in favour of the sunbelt. Analysis of the congressional districts which lost the highest percentage of population in the 1970s (Figure 6.12) shows that the heaviest reverses accrued to the large northeastern cities.

In Canada the western provinces are now wielding increasing political power as the hegemony of the Montreal-Toronto axis weakens. Many Albertans have voiced disagreement about

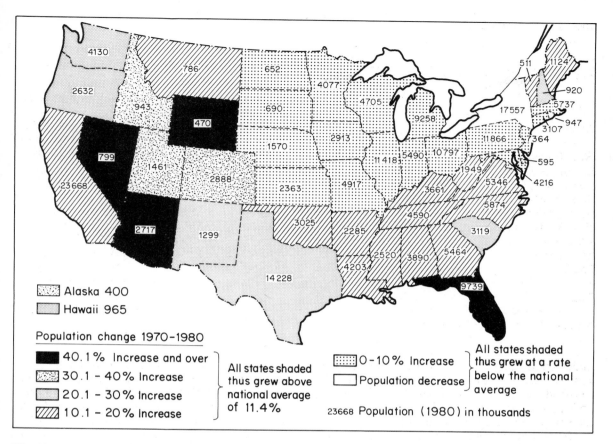

Fig. 6.9 *US population by state 1980 and rate of increase 1970–80*

Fig. 6.10 Population growth in Canada 1941–1981

Province	1941	1961	Percentage change 1941–61	1981	Percentage change 1961–81	Percentage change 1941–81
Newfoundland	303 300*	457 900	51.0	567 700	24.0	87.2
Prince Edward Island	95 000	104 600	10.0	122 500	17.1	28.9
Nova Scotia	578 000	737 000	27.5	847 400	15.0	46.6
New Brunswick	457 400	597 900	30.7	696 400	16.5	52.3
Quebec	3 331 900	5 259 200	57.8	6 438 200	22.4	93.2
Ontario	3 787 700	6 236 100	64.6	8 624 400	38.3	127.7
Manitoba	729 000	921 700	26.4	1 026 200	11.3	40.8
Saskatchewan	896 000	925 000	3.2	968 300	4.7	8.1
Alberta	796 200	1 332 000	67.3	2 237 300	68.0	181.0
British Columbia	817 800	1 629 100	99.2	2 744 200	68.4	235.6
Yukon Territory	5 000	14 600	192.0	23 200	58.9	364.0
N.W. Territories	12 000	23 000	91.7	45 700	99.0	280.8
Total	11 508 000	18 238 000	58.5	24 341 700	33.5	111.5

* Newfoundland not part of Canada until 1949.

Source: Statistics Canada

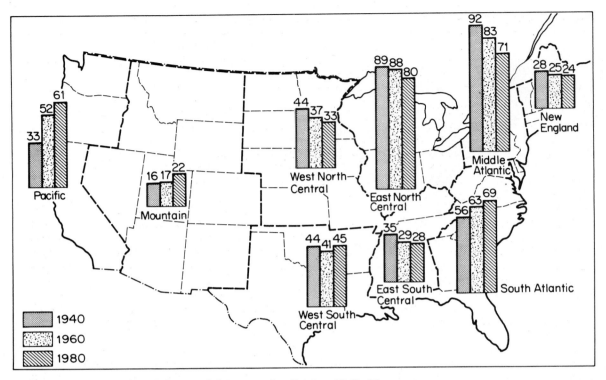

Fig. 6.11 *Changes in US House delegations by division 1940–80*

the state's financial contribution to the federation and a certain body of opinion (a small minority) feels that the province now has more in common with the states to her immediate south than with the central and eastern provinces.

3. Minority groups

A. The melting pot theory

Today approximately one in twenty Americans is foreign born, while native-born people of foreign parentage account for about 11 per cent of the total population. In general, Americans have regarded immigration as being advantageous to the socio-economic progress of the country in the belief that the United States would act as a melting pot to fuse together a diversity of cultures and create a typically American way of life.

Many authorities are however cynical about the validity of the melting-pot theory of majority-minority relations which has sometimes been expressed by the formula $A + B + C = A$, where A, B and C represent different ethnic groups, and A is the dominant one. Over time the other groups gradually conform to the attitudes, values and lifestyle of the dominant group, while A will change only marginally.

The melting pot theory may be applicable to white immigrants but beyond this it has obvious limitations. Clearly many people from minority groups do not regard full Americanization as either necessary or particularly desirable while many White Americans practice direct or indirect discrimination against minority groups which do not meet with their approval. The former is certainly true of many American Indians who seek to maintain, as far as possible, their traditional way of life, of a significant number of Blacks and more recently of Hispanics who want to preserve their language. In parts of the sunbelt the United States is becoming in effect a bi-lingual society.

The attitude of many French Canadians is diametrically opposed to the melting-pot theory and may eventually even bring about the withdrawal of Quebec from the federation.

Fig. 6.12 Congressional district populations–heaviest losses and gains 1970–1980

	Losses		Gains	
District	Percentage change	District		Percentage change
New York 21 (South Bronx)	−48.9	Florida 10 (Fort Pierce, Fort Myers)		+92.0
Michigan 13 (Downtown Detroit)	−38.6	Florida 5 (Clearwater, Orlando)		+90.5
New York 12 (Northeast Brooklyn)	−32.1	California 43 (San Diego area)		+86.4
Missouri 1 (North St Louis)	−25.0	Texas 7 (Northwest Harris County)		+86.0
Ohio 21 (Cleveland—East)	−24.7	Florida 11 (West Palm Beach)		+83.2
New York 37 (West—Buffalo)	−23.1	California 40 (Southern Orange		
New York 14 (Northern Brooklyn)	−22.6	County)		+67.0
New York 19 (Manhattan—Harlem)	−21.8	Arizona 4 (North Phoenix, Scottsdale)		+62.7
Illinois 7 (Chicago—West Side)	−21.5	Arizona 3 (Western Phoenix, Yuma)		+60.8
Illinois 1 (Chicago—South Side)	−21.1	Florida 4 (Daytona Beach)		+56.5
Ohio 20 (West and Central Cleveland)	−18.3	Texas 22 (Southern Harris County)		+51.3
Pennsylvania 14 (Pittsburgh)	−17.6	Colorado 4 (North—Fort Collins)		+49.8
Pennsylvania 3 (Central Philadelphia)	−17.3	Texas 3 (North Central Dallas)		+49.2
Pennsylvania 2 (West Philadelphia)	−17.2	Arizona 2 (South—Tucson)		+48.7
Michigan 1 (North Central Detroit)	−16.5	Colorado 5 (Colorado Springs)		+47.3
Pennsylvania 1 (Philadelphia—south)	−15.7	Texas 21 (South Central—San Antonio)		+45.1
Tennessee 8 (Memphis)	−15.5	Texas 2 (East—Orange)		+44.4
Michigan 16 (South Detroit, Dearborn)	−15.2	Georgia 9 (Northeast—Gainesville)		+42.9
Illinois 5 (Chicago—central)	−15.1	Colorado 2 (Denver suburbs, Boulder)		+42.7
Kentucky 3 (Louisville and suburbs)	−14.8	Florida 8 (Lakeland, Sarasota)		+41.8
Missouri 5 (Kansas City)	−14.5	Arizona 1 (Southern Phoenix, Mesa)		+40.3
Maryland 7 (Baltimore—west, central)	−14.0	California 1 (North—Chico)		+40.2
Minnesota 5 (Minneapolis)	−13.7	Hawaii 2 (Honolulu suburbs, Outer		
Missouri 3 (South St Louis, suburbs)	−13.2	Islands)		+40.0
Maryland 3 (Baltimore south and east,		Texas 15 (South—Brownsville)		+40.0
suburbs)	−12.8	Utah 1 (East—Ogden, Provo)		+39.7
		California 37 (San Bernardino,		
		Riverside counties		+39.1

Source: Congressional Quarterly

B. Black Americans

Blacks form by far the largest minority in the United States and their numbers continue to grow faster than the population as a whole. In the 1970 to 1980 period the Black population grew by 17 per cent and increased from 22.6 million to 26.5 million while the national population rose by only 11 per cent. During this period the Black proportion of the US population increased from 11.1 per cent to 11.7 per cent. The Census Bureau notes two reasons for this greater than average growth: a higher birth rate for Blacks and improved counting procedures in Black neighbourhoods. The latter point applies to all minorities who for a variety of reasons are usually undercounted by censuses. The better response in the 1980 census was also due to the fact that minority groups have increasingly appreciated the importance of political representation.

Figure 6.13 shows the divisional distribution of the Black population in 1960, 1970 and 1980. In general the trends follow those which began with the end of the Civil War and the abolition of slavery. From this time the movement of Blacks from the South to the industrial cities of the northeast gathered momentum to become one of the great migration streams of United States

Fig. 6.13 Distribution of Black population in the United States (%)

Division	1960	1970	1980
New England	1.3	1.7	1.8
Middle Atlantic	14.7	17.5	16.5
East North Central	15.3	17.2	17.2
West North Central	3.0	3.1	3.0
South Atlantic	31.0	28.3	28.9
East South Central	14.3	11.4	10.8
West South Central	14.7	13.3	13.3
Mountain	0.6	0.8	1.0
Pacific	5.1	6.7	7.5
Total	100.0	100.0	100.0

Source: US Statistical Abstract

Fig. 6.14 Estimated net intercensal migration of Blacks, by region: 1870–1980

Intercensal period	South	North			West
		North-east	North central	Total	
1870–1880	−60	+24	+36	+60	(na)
1880–1890	−70	+46	+24	+70	(na)
1890–1900	−168	+105	+63	+168	(na)
1900–1910	−170	+95	+56	+151	+20
1910–1920	−454	+182	+244	+426	+28
1920–1930	−749	+349	+364	+713	+36
1930–1940	−347	+171	+128	+299	+49
1940–1950	−1599	+463	+618	+1081	+339
1950–1960	−1473	+496	+541	+1037	+293
1960–1970	−1380	+612	+382	+994	+301
1970–1975	+14	−64	−52	−116	+102
1975–1980	+195	−175	−51	−226	+30

(Numbers in thousands. Plus sign (+) denotes net in-migration; minus sign (−) denotes out-migration.)

Source: US Statistical Abstract

history. Figure 6.14, showing the intercensal net migration of Blacks by region indicates that the heaviest outflow from the South occurred in the 1940–70 period. In the last decade the situation has been reversed and Blacks have started to return to the South as economic opportunities have improved in the region but also as a result of heavy unemployment in the northern industrial metropolises.

Nevertheless the South, which was the habitat of Blacks in 1960 (compared with over 80 per cent in 1880) retained only 53 per cent of that population in 1980. The fact that the East South Central was the only southern division to show a decrease in its share of the nation's Black population since 1970 is evidence that the era of high out-migration has come to an end.

The states with the largest numbers of the nation's Blacks in 1980 were New York (9.1 per cent), California (6.9 per cent), Illinois (6.3 per cent), Texas (6.5 per cent), Georgia (5.5 per cent) and Florida (5.1 per cent). Together these six states accounted for almost 40 per cent of the country's Black population. Only Georgia is in the traditional 'South'.

A distinctly different rank order emerges if the Black proportion of each state's total population is considered. Under this criterion the southern states clearly dominate, led by Mississippi, South Carolina, Louisiana, Georgia and Alabama.

An important contrast also exists in the intra-regional distributions of Blacks. In the South, while Black migration to the towns and cities of the region has been fairly intensive, many Blacks still remain on the land. However in the north and in the west the Black population is extremely concentrated in the inner city ghettos. Although there has been a greater degree of Black sub-urbanisation in recent years it operates on a very small scale and maintains segregation.

The influence of the Black population on the geography of the United States has been substantially greater than in either Canada or Mexico. In Mexico slavery was abolished much earlier than in the US and the Blacks dispersed, inter-married and gradually lost their separateness. In Canada Blacks form only a very small minority and for the most part have been absorbed into the wider community. It is the relative separateness and isolation of the Blacks in the United States that sets the country apart from its neighbours and which has been the course of so much internal conflict within the nation.

Under virtually all published socio-economic criteria the Black population is distinctly worse off than the nation as a whole and even though the reforms of the Kennedy and Johnson administrations did much to end active discrimination, passive or indirect discrimination, which is virtually impossible to prove in a court of law, is still very much a part of American society. The divide between Black and White remains an obstacle of huge dimensions in many areas and in the minds of millions of people of both major groups. The hostility that this divisiveness has provoked on numerous occasions is on a scale that has never been witnessed in European nations where Blacks form significant minorities.

A recent report by the Children's Defence Fund, a major social services lobby, entitled *Portrait of Inequality: Black and White Children in America* outlined the still enormous gap in health standards. Amongst many other inequalities the report noted that:

1. The infant mortality rate for Blacks is double that of the White community.
2. Black children suffer the effects of malnutrition at twice the rate of White children.
3. Black children and teenagers die from illnesses at rates at least 25 per cent higher than those for White children.
4. Black children are twice as likely to be admitted to in-patient psychiatric wards as White children.

Blacks have always been heavily over-represented amongst the unemployed, particularly in periods of economic recession. In the 1970s the Black labour force expanded much more rapidly than the labour force as a whole but Black employment failed to keep pace. As a result Black unemployment, which was 20.2 per cent of the total in 1969, rose to 23.2 per cent ten years later. Although opportunities in professional and managerial jobs have increased, Blacks are still very

Fig. 6.15 Median income of families, by race of head, selected years: 1959–1978

Category	1959	1969	1973	1978
Total (dollars)	5417	9433	12 051	17 640
White (dollars)	5893	9794	12 595	18 368
Black (dollars)	3047	5 999	7269	10 879
Black as percentage of White	51.7	61.2	57.7	59.2
Income gap (Black less White) (dollars)	−2846	−3795	−5326	−7489

Source: US Department of Commerce.

much under-represented in the higher socio-economic groups and much more likely to be in unskilled or semi-skilled employment.

Consequently family incomes are well below those for Whites, an alarming average gap of $7489 in 1978 (Figure 6.15). No progress at all was made in the convergence of Black and White median family incomes in the 1970s. As might be expected the percentage of Black families living below the poverty level is well above that of the nation as a whole.

C. The Indians

The Indians, the largest group belonging to the true indigenous population of North America, form a minority more unique and distinctive than any other in the continent. Their segregation is more intense and their socio-economic standing lower than all other ethnic groups. However in the 1970s Indian groups began to assert themselves more effectively in the political arena than ever before, particularly in the United States. Over 1.4 million Indians live in the United States, while a 1979 *Survey of Indian Conditions in Canada* noted a total Indian population of over 300 000. The latter report is the most recent comprehensive documentation of Indian life in North America.

In Canada, except in the North, Indian bands are located on reserve lands set aside through treaties and other agreements. In all there are 2242 separate parcels of reserve land with a total area of 25 965 square kilometres. About 65 per cent of the Indian population of the country is located in rural or remote communities compared to the national average of only 25 per cent.

The Indian population has been growing at a faster rate than the Canadian population as a whole in the last three decades, and increased from 180 000 in 1961 to 300 000 in 1979. Seventy per cent of Indians presently live in 573 bands on reservation land compared with over 84 per cent living on reservations in 1961. There are 10 different language groups speaking 58 dialects. Their distribution is shown by Figure 6.16.

Although the socio-economic conditions of the Indians have improved of late they remain well below the national average. Life expectancy, a clear reflection of health standards, is still ten years behind the Canadian norm. Less than 50 per cent of Indian homes are properly serviced compared to a national level of over 90 per cent, while one in three Indian families live in crowded conditions. Indian unemployment remains at about 35 per cent of the working age population, with between 50 per cent and 70 per cent of the Indian population in receipt of social assistance at any one time.

Violent deaths are three times the national level while suicides especially in the 15–24 age group, are more than six times the national rate. The Indian population is heavily over-represented in the country's jails and significantly under-represented in secondary and university education.

Government programmes, primarily under the auspices of DIAND (Department of Indian and Northern Development), have had a significant effect in Indian economic progress although Indian politicians still see the tribes very much as a forgotten section of the nation. An aggregate investment of over C$250 million into Indian economic development was made between 1970 and 1979, compared with less than C$50 million in the 1960s, resulting in more than 10 000 permanent jobs and at least 2000 continuing projects.

However, Indians are restricted under the Indian Act in the degree and manner in which they may develop and exploit reservation resources.

Fig. 6.16 *Canada; distribution of Indian population 1980 (Source: Department of Indian and Northern Affairs, Ottawa, Canada)*

Wolf Indians smoking moose meat, Moose Lake in British Colombia

Nevertheless the leasing of mineral rights has brought considerable wealth to some groups. Between 1970 and 1979 revenues from minerals increased roughly tenfold with almost all monies coming from oil and gas royalties. Such wealth is distributed very unevenly and the top five Alberta reservations currently account for in excess of 80 per cent of all Indian oil and gas revenue.

The American Indian Policy Review Commission in 1977 painted a bleak picture of reservation life in the United States, recording the lowest standards in the nation for health, education, housing and employment. Like their northern neighbours, American Indians want to share the benefits of modern society but are acutely fearful of what is frequently referred to as 'cultural genocide'.

The root of Indian poverty lies in the poor quality land of their reservations. As Figure 6.17 illustrates the geography of the American Indian today is very different to what it was before European colonisation.

As in Canada the Indian population has grown rapidly in recent decades, reaching over 1 400 000 in 1980. Figure 6.18 shows the divisional distribution.

Three states, Oklahoma, Arizona and California accounted for more than one third of the total Indian population.

With committed federal government help Indian tribes are making considerable progress in

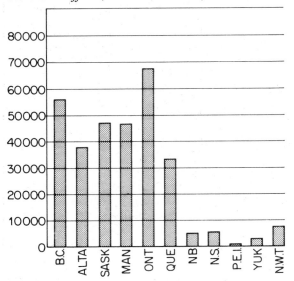

the management of their own affairs but are finding it difficult to gain maximum benefit from the new found resources of their reservations.

The federal government holds in trust approximately 21 million hectares for the benefit of and use by Indian tribes while other Indian land claims, which have been virtually ignored for two centuries, are now receiving serious consideration. The Sioux tribes in South Dakota and Indians in Maine have recently won Supreme Court or Congressional recognition of their land claims. The Maine Indians received both land and a financial settlement while the Sioux were awarded $105 million in 1979. However many Sioux would have preferred a land settlement instead.

Indian lands currently produce 15 per cent of the oil, 10 per cent of the natural gas and nearly all the uranium in the United States. In addition the reservations contain nearly one-third of strippable low-sulphur western coal.

A Council of Energy Resource Tribes (CERT) was formed in 1976 by 25 western tribes in an effort to establish a higher return from their assets. The Navajo nation, the largest Indian group in the country, has emerged as the leader of the organisation.

In 1978 the Navajo received over $15 million in coal royalties alone and in recent contracts the tribes have insisted that 75 per cent of the labour force be Navajo. However in spite of this increase in income 48 per cent of the Navajo still live below the poverty line with an unemployment rate of about 40 per cent.

In spite of the desperate need for greater investment on the reservations the Indians new-found wealth has been eyed covetously by the country as a whole. So far the federal government has never tried to tax the produce of the reservations but this policy is now being challenged by certain state and private interests.

Water resources are another source of controversy. Expanded mineral development has caused serious water pollution on some Indian lands while a concerted effort is under way by

Fig. 6.17 *The changing population distribution of the Indians in the US (Source: Wreford Watson, J.* Social Geography of the United States, *Longman, London, 1979)*

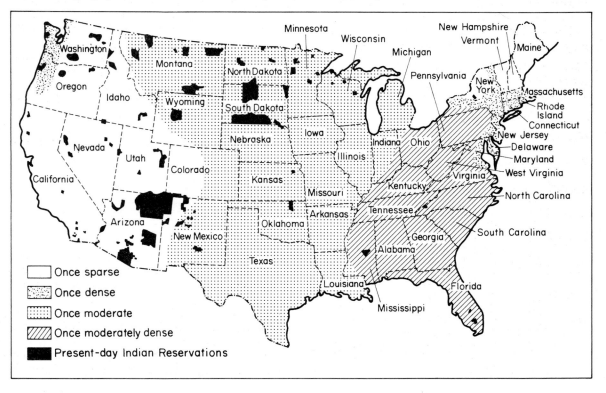

Fig. 6.18 Distribution of Indian population 1980

Division	Number	%
New England	21 600	1.5
Middle Atlantic	56 600	4.0
East North Central	105 900	7.5
West North Central	142 600	10.0
South Atlantic	118 700	8.4
East South Central	22 500	1.6
West South Central	231 000	16.3
Mountain	363 200	25.6
Pacific	356 200	25.1
United States	1 418 000	100.0

Source: US Statistical Abstract

other interested parties to limit Indian water rights to quantities in current use which would in effect prevent the intensification and expansion of Indian agriculture. Important projects are however underway. Of particular note is the Navajo Irrigation Project which will, when completed, pump water from the Navajo Reservoir northeast of Farmington, New Mexico, to irrigate more than 110 000 acres in the northwestern part of the state.

D. Hispanics

The 1980 census recorded 14.6 million people of Spanish origin (from Spanish speaking countries) or Hispanics as they are officially called (and this may be up to 20 million with illegal entrants). Now forming 6.4 per cent of the total population it is estimated that by the turn of the century, Hispanics, 80 per cent of whom are Mexican, will have displaced Blacks as the largest minority in the country.

Apart from Mexico, large numbers of Hispanics have also entered the United States from Puerto Rico and Cuba. Puerto Rican immigration has been overwhelmingly focussed on New York City while Florida has been the main point of entry and settlement for Cuban refugees from the Castro regime. The Puerto Ricans and Cubans are however generally distinct racially and politically from the Spanish-speaking Mexican Indians of the borderlands. The United States now has the fifth largest Spanish speaking population in the world.

Figure 6.19 shows the divisional distribution of this increasingly vociferous minority group. Four states, California (31.1 per cent), Texas (20.4 per cent), New York (11.4 per cent) and Florida (5.9 per cent) accounted for 68.8 per cent of all Hispanics in 1980. The great concentration of Hispanics in the sunbelt is not surprising considering that European colonisation of the US began in the southern borderlands when the Spanish established themselves in Florida in 1565 and later secured colonies in California, Texas, New Mexico and Arizona. The borderlands is one of the true cultural regions of the United States with the Spanish influence clearly evident in virtually all aspects of life. Hispanic residents are now a majority in San Antonio. In several cities including Los Angeles, San Diego, San Francisco, Phoenix, Denver and New York they outnumber American Blacks.

Hispanics are now growing more politically aware. In Florida pressure by the Cuban population has led Miami to become the first and only major American city to adopt an official policy of bilingualism. However, many other parts of the borderlands are in fact bilingual.

States such as California, Texas, Illinois, Massachusetts and New York have authorised bilingual education programmes while the federal government has recently funded a National Centre for Bilingual Research in Los Angeles. Thus the United States is making a distinct move towards vernacular language in primary and in some cases secondary education.

Fig. 6.19 Distribution of persons of Spanish origin 1980

Division	Number	%
New England	299 000	2.1
Middle Atlantic	2 305 000	15.8
East North Central	1 068 000	7.3
West North Central	209 000	1.4
South Atlantic	1 194 000	8.2
East South Central	119 000	0.8
West South Central	3 160 000	21.6
Mountain	1 441 000	9.9
Pacific	4 811 000	32.9
United States	14 606 000	100.0

Source: US Statistical Abstract

According to the Census Bureau there are between 3.5 and 6 million illegal aliens in the United States, most of them from Mexico. The heart of a recent report of the select commission on immigration and refugee policy was what to do about these illegal immigrants. The commission sees the influx as presently being out of control, thus threatening to create a large permanent group lacking the rights which are basic to 'official' residents.

Between 1971 and 1978 15.2 per cent of all legal immigrants into the United States came from Mexico, a total of 531 000 over the eight year period, and almost twice as large as the second major source region, the Philippines. Many Americans tend to think of Mexican immigrants as farm workers, an image that is now outdated. Today 80 per cent of Mexican immigrants find work in urban areas.

The majority of new arrivals have little choice but to take low paid jobs and consequently a high proportion of Hispanics live below the poverty level – 22.4 per cent in 1977 as opposed to the national average of 11.6 per cent.

E. French Canada – The challenge to the federal system

At no time since federation in 1867 has the Canadian system of government been under greater challenge than in recent years. The separatist movement which has vociferously surfaced from time to time in Quebec has been particularly active in the 1970s, culminating in the May 1980 referendum when the Quebec government asked the province's electorate for a mandate to negotiate a programme of sovereignty-association with the rest of Canada and withdraw from the federation.

The status quo has also been under attack elsewhere, particularly in western Canada where economic self-determination spurred on by natural resource prosperity is the prime motive for change. However while this relationship is in a state of flux the position of French Canada is undoubtedly the most prominent threat to the federal system.

French Canadians constitute about a quarter of the national population and are heavily concentrated in Quebec. Of all Canadians for whom French is the mother tongue 85 per cent live in Quebec while 82 per cent of the province's population speak French as their mother tongue. The French speaking population outside Quebec is particularly evident in adjacent parts of New Brunswick and Ontario (Fig. 6.20).

Of all New Brunswick residents who learned French as their first language 93 per cent live in the border counties while 69 per cent of Ontario's mother-tongue French population reside in contiguous regions. Together Quebec and the border counties account for 94 per cent of all Canadian's whose first language learned was French.

Quebec is the voice of French Canada and is distinct in North America by culture, language and politics. In the early years of settlement the French were numerically dominant in Canada with about three-quarters of the total Canadian population in the mid-eighteenth century, but a century later French representation was down to 30 per cent, remaining at that proportion until recently.

Conflict between a centralised federation which was the ideal of the English community and a decentralised confederation favoured by French Canadians was apparent from the establishment of the Constitution under the British North America Act of 1867. A trend towards greater centralisation has been evident since that date and has grown stronger in the post-war period. This has been viewed with alarm by many French Canadians who correlate increasing federal control with domination by the English community.

The fall in Quebec's birth rate below the national average in the 1960s, and the tendency of immigrants to assimilate into the English-speaking population (Anglo-conformity), have added to the concern of French Canadians for the survival of their language and culture.

Earlier French nationalist campaigns were aimed primarily at promoting the French language. For instance during the 1930s French nationalist elements in Quebec vigorously attempted to persuade the public to patronise French-speaking stores only. However since the 1960s economic emancipation has become a complimentary goal, initiated by the provincialisation of power companies in Quebec in 1963. Gradually a clearer view has emerged of the relationship between the economy and language in both Quebec and Canada as a whole.

In an attempt to preserve Canadian unity the federal government has legislated to acknowledge

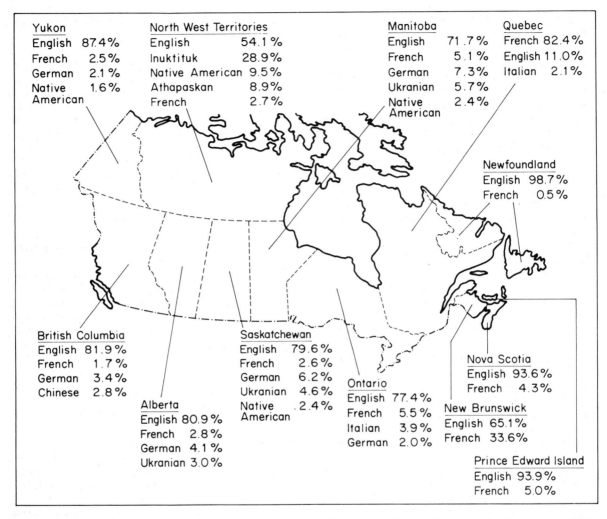

Fig. 6.20 *Canada; dominant mother tongue and significant minority mother tongues by region 1981* (*Source:* Statistics Canada)

the role of the French language in the country. The Official Languages Act of 1969 greatly increased the areas where the French language was to be used. Considerable progress was made towards the recognition of French as a language of administration and communication although the areas of financial and economic management in both the private and public sectors remained noticeably resistant to change. Nowhere has this been more apparent than in Montreal. The result has been a movement westward from Montreal of many corporate headquarters with which Quebec had

long been identified. Montreal's remaining English-speaking community has become increasingly isolated.

In 1977 the Quebec government passed Bill 101, 'The Charter of the French Language.' The Law required all firms with more than 50 employees to conduct its affairs in French (with certain time allowances) although discretionary measures could be applied to head offices and companies doing most of their business outside the province. The law also restricted the right to attend English state schools in Quebec to children with at least one parent who had attended English schools in Quebec. Immigrant children from abroad and elsewhere in Canada have generally to enrol in French schools.

The education provisions of the Act have been heavily criticised in many quarters but the Quebec government assert that there is wider provision for English schooling in Quebec than there is for French schooling in any other province.

An agreement reached in 1978 with the federal government gave Quebec greater control of immigration into the province.

However, such developments have failed to impress many French Canadians who advocate major constitutional reform. Perhaps the greatest effort to revise the Canadian constitution lasted from February 1968 to June 1971, ending in failure at the Victoria Conference. Quebec had wanted a new division of powers that would have given constitutional recognition to the Quebec nation.

Between October 1978 and February 1979 the federal government attempted to reach agreement on constitutional reform with Bill C-60 but a change in government brought this effort to an end.

The apparent failure to Quebec of such moves resulted in the May 1980 referendum whereby the Quebec government wanted, under its proposal of sovereignty-association, full legislative and taxing powers and the power to deal on the international scene, with an economic association with the rest of Canada based on a common currency. Justifying the province's economic viability the Quebec government noted that a sovereign Quebec would be the sixteenth largest country in the world in terms of area and the fourteenth in standard of living.

To the relief of the federal government 59.5 per cent of voters refused to support the provincial government's proposal. Quebec has decided to give federation another chance, but for how long? As the newspaper *Le Soleil* concluded after the referendum, 'nothing guarantees that English Canada wants to see the substantial changes Quebeckers envisage.' If Quebec eventually secedes from the federation such action could profoundly change the political and economic geography of North America.

Minority groups – the future

The foregoing sections illustrate the point that people who belong to clearly evident minorities in North America generally have substantially lower living standards than the population as a whole. This is particularly so in the United States where ethnic variation is far more intense.

However, the era of minority subservience is rapidly coming to an end as such groups are becoming politically more aware and determined to have a greater say in their own destiny along with a greater share of the continent's wealth. If progress towards real equality is not maintained in the remaining decades of the century then American democracy in particular could be placed under severe stress.

It is of course easy for the European to be scathing about the racial conflicts that exist in the United States without sometimes giving due credit to the progress that has been made to date. In many areas of legislation the United States and Canada are way ahead of European countries in attempting to ensure that racial discrimination is not practised. The difficulty is though that legislation can only go so far in the attempt to redress social injustice.

Social well-being and territorial social justice

The introduction to this book stresses that North Americans have become increasingly concerned with the overall quality of life as opposed solely to the quantity of life as measured by per capita income or other such narrow criteria. While income levels undoubtedly have a major effect upon social conditions the relationship is often a complex and far from perfect one. The classic example of the two diverging is one in which two middle-class White families, living in different regions have the same disposable income and face similar general costs of living but where other factors relating to the quality of their lives are markedly different. One family may live in a region where the infant mortality rate, the serious crime rate and the incidence of atmospheric pollution are considerably higher, while the provision of educational, medical and recreational facilities are significantly lower than in the home region of the other family. Thus while in crude economic terms their standard of living is very much the same, there is a great difference with respect to social conditions.

The term 'social well-being' has become increasingly used to describe the overall quality of life. Perhaps the best known work in this field is that of D. M. Smith who analysed a multitude of different variables to arrive at a score for each American state to indicate its degree of social well-being (Introduction, Fig. I.5). According to Smith, 'By many social criteria large parts of the rural South and the inner areas of many American cities belong to the underdeveloped world and not to the sophisticated modern industrial society that their inclusion in this nation's aggregate statistics implies'.

Smith's work reveals how some regions repeatedly rank at the bottom end of the social scale, most notably the South, northern New England, the southern Mountain states, and certain areas of the Great Lakes region and Western Plains. The highest scores were achieved by Connecticut (156), Massachusetts (124), Utah (121) and Iowa (117) while the worst off states were Mississippi (−264), South Carolina (−197), Alabama (−183) and Arkansas (−179).

Smith and others in this field such as D. Harvey, R. Morrill and J. Wreford Watson stress the geographical or territorial component of social justice, arguing that it is necessary to establish how far people may be disadvantaged on the basis of location alone.

The problem arises as to how social justice should be measured. While some would regard it as being equality of opportunity, others advocate the goal of absolute equality and of course the political structure that would be necessary to ensure such a condition. While recognising the problems involved and the embryonic state of the art, David Harvey suggests that we can arrive at the sense of territorial social justice as follows:

1. The distribution of income should be such that (*a*) the needs of the population within each territory are met, (*b*) resources are so allocated to maximise interterritorial multiplier effects, and (*c*) extra resources are allocated to help overcome special difficulties stemming from the physical and social environment.

2. The mechanisms (institutional, organizational, political and economic) should be such that the prospects of the least advantaged territory are as great as they possibly can be.

While these criteria are purposefully rather vague it is patently clear that North America is as far away from territorial social justice as it is from social justice with regard to ethnicity although concerted action has been taken on both counts as noted in this and the previous chapter. Of course many would argue that such an attitude is purely academic as territorial social justice is not a feasible national aim. The space is not available here to debate this point further but it is hoped that this section will make the reader aware of conflicting attitudes towards the subject as well as highlighting some of the more obvious social variations in the United and Canada.

People and poverty in the United States: real or imaginary?

Figure 6.21 shows by quintiles the percentage of persons by state classified as being below the poverty level according to the Census Bureau. All ten states in the bottom quintile are adjacently located in the south and south-east. The states in the top quintile registering the lowest incidence of poverty in order of least poverty first are Alaska, Connecticut, Massachusetts, Maryland, Wisconsin, New Hampshire, Hawaii, Iowa and Kansas. The percentage of persons below the poverty level in Alaska and Connecticut (6.7 per cent) contrasts markedly with the worst ranking state, Mississippi (26.1 per cent).

Poverty is relative and to a great extent self-perceptive. Many in the United States see themselves in poverty relative to the mainstream of the country and may be classified as such by the federal government but would be regarded very differently by third world standards.

There is deep disagreement within the United States as to how many people can be realistically classed as poor. The Census Bureau states 25.2 million or 11.6 per cent of the population in poverty in 1979. As the Bureau recorded 24.1 million poor ten years earlier the more recent figure is a serious indictment of the social efforts of the decade.

However some authorities have criticised the use of the poverty index, developed during the 1960s, arguing that it heavily over-estimates poverty in the United States. On the assumption that poor families spend one-third of their income on food, the poverty level was set at three times the cost of providing a minimum diet. Since 1969 the index has been adjusted to reflect changes in the Consumer Price Index. The most substantial criticism of the index is that, in considering only cash income, it completely ignores other assistance such as food stamps, medical care and housing aid which became relatively more important in the 1970s. Taking account of such transfers, economists have arrived at a multitude of poverty figures from eight million persons upwards but always almost invariably below the total set by the Census Bureau.

It must be noted that many Americans have what the average European might consider as a very hard attitude to poverty, frequently blaming the condition on the individuals so afflicted. Poverty has been regarded by some writers as a subculture whose attitudes and values are absorbed at an early age.

However, no matter how poverty is defined it is obvious that it does not occur haphazardly and clearly identifiable poverty regions can be recognised in both urban and rural areas. Urban poverty is concentrated mainly in cities of over one

million population, particularly in Black, Hispanic or Indian ghettos but also in the quarters of the poorer Europeans (Italian, Portuguese, Greek, Polish) and in Asian communities. Rural poverty is most frequently in isolated regions where there is an extremely narrow economic base and very limited job opportunities.

The 1979 data stresses that poverty is racially and sexually discriminating. Only 7.5 per cent of White households were poor and where the family had a male wage-earner the proportion was only 6.2 per cent. In contrast, for Blacks living in households headed by women the poverty rate was an alarming 52 per cent. However, due to the fact that the White population forms the overwhelming majority in the United States, Whites do dominate the absolute poverty totals with 16.7 million so classified against 7.8 million poor Blacks.

Infant mortality: a Black and White case

Health is a prime factor in any assessment of social

Fig. 6.21 *US population below the poverty line by state 1975*

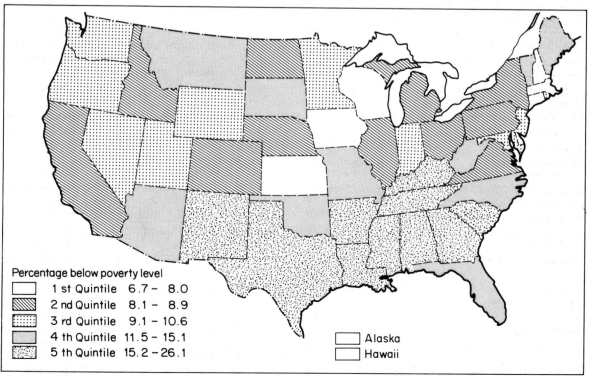

Percentage below poverty level

1 st Quintile	6.7 – 8.0
2 nd Quintile	8.1 – 8.9
3 rd Quintile	9.1 – 10.6
4 th Quintile	11.5 – 15.1
5 th Quintile	15.2 – 26.1

Alaska
Hawaii

well-being or territorial social justice. The difficulty arises, though, as to which criteria to use.
Which are the most relevant or significant
variables?

The data available are of two basic types which
may be referred to as indirect and direct social
indicators. The number of doctors per 100 000
state residents would be an indirect indicator as
one could only at best make very broad assump-
tions on the basis of such data. It does not provide
a direct indication of the health of the population
as does the infant mortality rate, the age-specific
death rate or the incidence of serious diseases.

The infant mortality rate has been selected here
to illustrate major ethnic and locational variations
in health conditions across the United States
because it is frequently cited by sociologists,
demographers and the medical profession as the
best single indicator of a country's or region's
social progress.

Figure 6.22 shows how the infant mortality rate
has declined for both the Black (and other) and
White populations from 1960 through 1970 to
1977 by division. The following points can also be
deduced from the map:

1. While the absolute gap has closed between
   Blacks (and others) and Whites the difference
   between the two groups has also declined on a
   relative basis in seven of the nine divisions, the
   two anomalies being the East North Central
   and New England.
2. The mean deviation between all the divisions
   for Whites declined steadily from 1.4 to 0.7 to
   0.5 for the three years noted. For Blacks and
   others the mean deviation is much larger and
   did not change between 1970 and 1977, the
   relevant figures being 5.1, 2.4 and 2.4 again.
3. While territorial differences across both groups
   have declined, sizeable differences can still be
   discerned. For Whites the most successful
   division in curtailing infant mortality, the
   Pacific, had a rate 1.7 per 1000 better than the
   East South Central, the highest infant mortality region. For Blacks and others the same
   regions were at the top and bottom of the scale
   but with a much wider gap of 9.1 per 1000.

Similar territorial variations in infant mortality
are evident in Canada as Fig. 6.23 shows.

Crime

Crime is a social factor which forms an important
part of the geography of a city, region or nation. It
can significantly affect the way that entity is
viewed from both within and outside. This can
have repercussions on economic well-being as a
high incidence of crime may appreciably
downgrade the image of a district, city or region
and thus figure as a negative determinant in the
location decision. In 1980 and 1981 the individual
murders of over twenty Black youths in Atlanta,
Georgia received worldwide publicity and certainly damaged the city's image which has been
carefully nurtured in the post-war period to bring
rising prosperity with the influx of a wide spectrum
of business activity.

Figure 6.24 illustrates the average annual
murder and non-negligent manslaughter rates in
the 1975–80 period for the states and provinces in
North America. Distinct regional differences are
immediately apparent with the South showing by
far the greatest concentration of crimes of this
category. California and Nevada form a separate
nucleus in the West while in the northeast New
York, Michigan and Illinois also registered high
rates. The lowest rates in the United States were
accumulated by northern New England and the
West North Central region. In Canada the overall
rate is very much lower apart from the anomalies
of the Yukon and North West Territories. As these
regions have a low population they have little
effect on the national totals but do highlight the
murder rates among the native peoples.

Homicide rates in the United States are well
above the levels recorded by other developed
countries and violence appears to be accepted as
part and parcel of American life to an extent that is
difficult for the European to comprehend.

Figure 6.25 shows divisional changes in four
major types of serious crime for the period 1950 to
1980. Overall the trend in serious crime in the
United States is rapidly upward.

Although there is a far from perfect relationship
between the graphs certain similarities do emerge.
In general the Pacific and the three southern
divisions, particularly the West South Central,
have the highest levels of serious crime, with New
England and the West North Central setting the
lowest rates in the country.

The reasons for such wide contrasts have been
the subject of much debate. It is certainly true that
many of the worst centres of violence are in regions
where strong racial, class and cultural differences
are in existence. It is also apparent that the

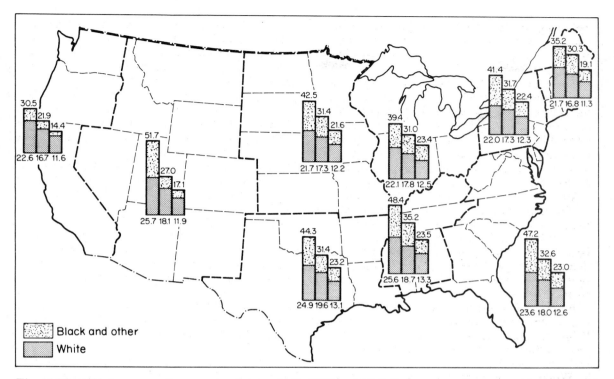

Fig. 6.22 *US infant mortality rates by division 1960, 1970 and 1977 (infant mortality rate = the number of deaths of children under 1 year of age per 1000 live births)*

Fig. 6.23 Infant mortality rates by province and territory

Province or Territory	1960	1970	1981
Newfoundland	35.9	21.8	9.7
Prince Edward Island	32.2	22.0	13.2
Nova Scotia	29.5	17.3	11.5
New Brunswick	29.9	19.7	10.9
Quebec	30.2	20.6	8.5
Ontario	23.5	16.9	8.8
Manitoba	30.0	18.9	11.9
Saskatchewan	26.4	22.4	11.8
Alberta	26.2	19.1	10.6
British Columbia	23.6	16.9	10.2
Yukon	48.3	35.5	14.9
N.W.T.	140.1	68.3	21.5
Canada	27.3	18.8	9.6

Source: Statistics Canada.

wealthiest states have some of the highest crime rates. Here authorities point to dualism, the existence of very rich and very poor side by side, as a prime causal factor.

Serious crime is escalating most rapidly in the large cities, indicating higher levels of anger and frustration than ever before as the aspirations of the least advantaged remain unfulfilled. Homicide is now the leading cause of death among Black men between 25 and 44 years old. The 1980 murder rates for the twenty largest cities in the United States are shown by Figure 6.26 which places Cleveland in an unenviable first place.

Recently Chief Justice Warren Burger stated at an American Bar Association meeting that 'crime and the fear of crime have permeated the fabric of American life'. On an intra-city basis the geography of crime has been shown to be an important influence on residential preference as well as on movement within the city, particularly after dark. The image of 'no-go' areas in the inner regions of many large US cities after dark has become an increasingly strong one. This is a phenomenon

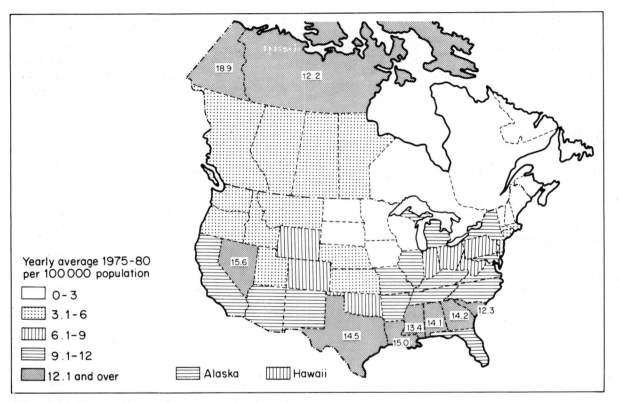

Fig. 6.24 *Homicide rates by state, province and territory*

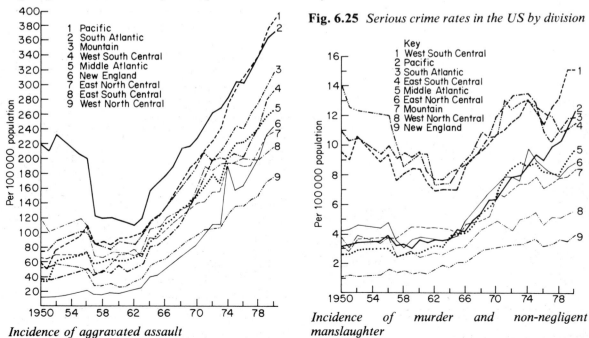

Fig. 6.25 *Serious crime rates in the US by division*

Incidence of aggravated assault

Incidence of murder and non-negligent manslaughter

with which European nations have only a very limited experience.

Crime has a distinct geographical distribution and as such has an effect on many other phenomena in the human landscape.

Bibliography

Butz, W. P. and Ward, M. P. (1979) 'The emergence of countercyclical US fertility', *American Economic Review*, June, 69, 3, pp. 318–28.

Harvey, D. (1973) *Social Justice and the City*. London: Edward Arnold.

Morrill, R. and Wohlenberg, E. (1981) *The Geography of Poverty in the United States*. New York: McGraw-Hill.

Smith, D. M. (1973) *The Geography of Social Well-being in the United States: An Introduction to Territorial Social Indicators*. New York: McGraw-Hill.

Fig. 6.26 Murder rates: how the 20 largest cities compare

	Popu-lation rank	Homicides during 1980	Homicides per 100 000 persons
1. Cleveland	18	280	48.9
2. Detroit	6	548	46.0
3. Houston	5	644	41.4
4. Dallas	7	322	35.7
5. Los Angeles	3	1 042	35.3
6. Washington, DC	15	202	31.7
7. Chicago	2	863	29.1
8. Baltimore	9	216	27.5
9. Philadelphia	4	437	26.0
10. Memphis	14	166	25.7
11. New York	1	1 790	25.5
12. San Francisco	13	110	16.3
13. Boston	19	91	16.2
14. Columbus, Ohio	20	91	16.2
15. Indianapolis	12	107	15.4
16. Phoenix	11	105	13.4
17. Milwaukee	16	80	12.6
18. San Diego	8	108	12.4
19. San Jose	17	62	9.9
20. San Antonio	10	69	8.8

Source: US Department of Commerce

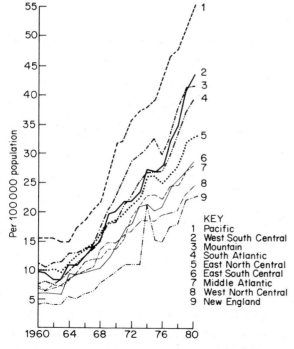

Incidence of forcible rape

KEY
1 Pacific
2 West South Central
3 Mountain
4 South Atlantic
5 East North Central
6 East South Central
7 Middle Atlantic
8 West North Central
9 New England

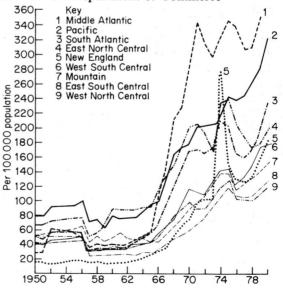

Key
1 Middle Atlantic
2 Pacific
3 South Atlantic
4 East North Central
5 New England
6 West South Central
7 Mountain
8 East South Central
9 West North Central

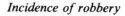

Incidence of robbery

7

The Challenge of the Physical Environment

Even for the most economically advanced continent in the world the physical environment remains a distinct and in some respects a growing challenge to the ingenuity of human beings. The purpose of this chapter is to assess the dual difficulties posed by the physical environment in terms of the settlement of areas of severe landscape, climate and soils and the problems associated with conserving the natural environment in the wake of unparalleled levels of economic activity. These issues are of course strongly related and encompass a myriad of individual and interdependent factors of which only the most prominent can be examined below.

The opening chapters of this book outlined the responses of the early settlers to the various physical environments encountered as the frontier moved west and north. Clearly the most formidable barriers were provided by mountainous terrain, infertile soils, aridity and low temperatures. In general, areas exhibiting these characteristics remain today sparsely populated although significant localised exceptions can be discerned, particularly in the arid lands of the south-western United States. Once adequate water supply has been secured, arid and semi-arid landscapes frequently provide an extremely pleasant residential environment and such areas have taken on the favoured 'sunbelt' image and have been focal points for high rates of in-migration in recent decades.

Mountainous terrain continues to be largely bypassed by settlement, the crucial factor being the establishment of transport routes either through or around the relevant barriers. Today most settlement in such areas is either linked to mineral development or tourism.

Cold climatic regions have historically been avoided by people in terms of permanent settlement when more hospitable, warmer alternatives have been seen to be available. A basic atlas population density map of North America is testimony to this fact. Harsh climatic environments significantly increase the difficulties, complexities and the cost of living and therefore act as a deterrent to permanent settlement. While cultural affinities are frequently strong enough to hold native groups such as the Aleuts and Inuits to their historic homelands, long-term in-migration of 'alien' cultures will rarely occur except in response to an extraordinary attraction such as a raw material in demand on the national or world market or for strategic purposes. Modern 'controlled indoor environments' however make such adjustments easier nowadays than in the past.

A combination of land above 400 metres, areas with annual precipitation below 400 mm and regions with a mean January temperature below −20°C occupies a sizeable proportion of the continent and should be compared with a map of settlement distribution. Such physical indicators are arbitrary rather than critical but do serve to illustrate the relationship between such 'problem regions' and population density.

When assessing the challenge of the physical environment a distinction must be made between generally stable environmental difficulties such as mountainous landscapes and very cold temperature and occasional, potentially catastrophic hazards such as hurricanes, earthquakes and volcanic eruptions–which merit coverage because of the large numbers of people who live in such potential danger areas and the long-term geographical effects such phenomena can have.

In an era of rising environmental awareness throughout the developed world, North America has undoubtedly been the focal point of the environmental debate. Although notable authorities dating from the middle of the last century have expressed concern about the ravages unleashed on the environment by urbanisation and economic activity it was not until the late 1960s and early 1970s that the issue of environmental protection became of major concern to a sizeable and vociferous section of the population.

The opening years of the present decade (the 1980s) have essentially been a period of reappraisal of the considerable body of environmental legislation that was passed in the 1970s. While significant progress has been made in this area certain legislative acts have attracted intense criticism from various quarters. The latter section of this chapter will examine the scope, and attempt to measure the success, of such legislation in the United States and Canada.

A. Cold climates– The Northlands

The Northlands of the United States and Canada illustrate numerous contrasting environments in terms of relief, climate, vegetation and soils. Some of the most prominent features will be introduced below to provide a background for the references to the Northlands (i.e. transportation, energy) which follow in later chapters. Alaska is taken as a case-study to analyse the basic problems and the economic activity associated with cold climatic regions.

While the term North or Northland is commonly used by both Canadians and Americans there is little agreement on its exact geographical definition. Apart from the various arbitrary latitudinal limits which have been used, the most popular of which are 55°N and 60°N, the more comprehensive efforts have involved the analysis of various physical and human criteria.

A frequently quoted classification is the one formulated by L. E. Hamelin (1968) whereby the

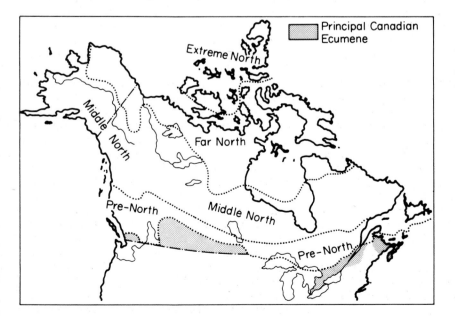

Fig. 7.1 *The Northlands (Source: Hamelin, L. E.* Un Indice Circumpolaire *Ann. Géographie, No. 422 (1968), pp 414–30)*

North is subdivided into the Middle North, Far North and Extreme North as illustrated by Figure 7.1. The remainder of Canada is classed as either the Pre-North or the Principal Ecumene, the latter region delimiting the major areas of population and settlement in Canada. Although Hamelin did not include Alaska in his analysis this can be done by simply extending the boundary line between the Middle North and the Far North westward. Thus the Arctic coastal plain and the Brooks Range would be included in the Far North and the rest of Alaska in the Middle North.

Hamelin analysed ten variables to obtain a total aggregate score of 'nordicite'. The factors considered were latitude, aggregate annual cold, types of freezing and icing, summer heat, total precipitation, vegetation cover, air service, accessibility other than by air, population density and degree of concentration, and degree of economic activity.

Overall Hamelin found that the density of population decreased steadily from 0.39 persons per square kilometre in the Middle North to 0.05 and 0.02 in the Far North and Extreme North respectively, resulting in a general population density of 0.16 per square kilometre for the Canadian North as a whole.

In a similar manner to Hamelin's analysis most authorities note the distinction between the Arctic in the central and eastern regions of the North, and the Northwest. The two differ in climate, topography, vegetation, settlement and economic activity. Climatically the whole of the Northland is bitterly cold in winter. In terms of relief, the Northwest is chiefly a region of mountains and linear valleys. The Arctic has a variety of topographic features ranging from ice-capped mountains which are the highest in eastern North America to extensive, lake covered, tundra plains. The vegetation line between the forested, subarctic Northwest and the treeless tundra of the Arctic provides the natural division between the two regions.

Due to its more equable environment the Northwest has a longer history of natural resource exploitation and settlement extension than the Arctic but this distinction has narrowed in recent times as huge energy and mineral resources have been identified in the latter.

Alaska—a resource frontier

Nowhere are the dual challenges of the physical environment more apparent than in Alaska, an area unique in American economic history because the eras of major exploitation and conservation have coincided. While the environmental lobby regard Alaska as 'the last wilderness', a fragile ecosystem to be protected from the ravages of development at all costs, the energy companies see the state as a vital domestic resource region.

Alaska provides the most prominent example in North America of an extension of the frontier of settlement in the twentieth century. Like other harsh environments around the world such as Northern Scandinavia, Siberia and the Sahara,

Fig. 7.2 *Boom periods in Alaska's economic development*

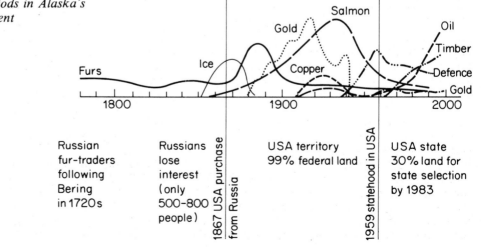

Abandoned gold mine, Carcross, Yukon

settlement and economic development have depended upon the discovery and exploitation of natural resources of high value and great abundance or on strategic considerations. The term 'resource frontier' has been applied to such regions. Resource frontiers are characteristically separated from more highly populated areas by apparent wilderness and wasteland and are thus non-contiguous unlike contiguous frontiers associated with the extension of agriculturally based settlements.

Early development Alaska has presented a formidable barrier to permanent settlement since it was 'discovered' in 1741 by Vitus Bering, a Dane in Russian employment. A fur boom was later followed by settlement pre-occupied with other natural resources. Settlement, such as at Kodiak was almost totally confined to the southern and western coastal zones. The population of such settlements was extremely transient accord-

ing to the demand and availability of exploitable commodities. The major economic booms which have affected the state are shown diagramatically in Figure 7.2.

In 1867 the United States acquired Alaska from Russia for $7 million and until the gold rush at the turn of the century the purchase was regarded by many Americans as an act of folly. Because of the harsh climatic conditions, the apparently impenetrable and inhospitable interior and the almost negligible economic base there seemed no way that this huge acquisition could be seen as an asset. A census taken in 1880 recorded only 430 White people and 33 000 natives of whom half were Eskimos.

Gold was the catalyst which brought large numbers of migrants to Alaska and into the interior for the first time. The first gold strike occurred in 1880. Juneau city was founded as a result of this strike to be followed in 1894 by Circle City on the banks of the Yukon after gold was

BP/Sohio Base Operations Centre, Prudhoe Bay, Alaska

discovered in streams nearby.

The Klondike gold rush began at the end of July 1896 after a discovery at Bonanza Creek. The main routeways to the area passed through Alaska, either up the Yukon River from the Bering Sea or inland from Skagway. Within three years big strikes at Nome and in the Tanana Valley resulted in the Alaska gold rush as opposed to earlier discoveries in the Canadian Yukon. Gold production reached a peak in 1906, the main mining area then being centred on Fairbanks on the Tanana River.

As gold production waned outmigration began to occur on a considerable scale. Between 1910 and 1920 10 000 people left Alaska, reducing the White population to about 28 000. In the latter year Fairbanks' population had reduced from its gold rush peak of 11 000 to only 2000. Skagway, the port of entry for the Klondike gold rush, reached a population of 20 000 which reduced rapidly as production decreased. The port has a population of only about 750 today. The ghost towns left in the old mining region are an enduring testimony to the short-lived gold boom.

Even during the early part of the century environmentalists expressed concern about the future development of Alaska and large areas of the territory were established as National Forests in the 1920s and 1930s. Alaska came to epitomise the wilderness which no longer existed elsewhere in the United States, a feeling which has never been lost.

The Alaska Railroad linking Fairbanks to the south coast followed the Matanuska Valley and as part of Roosevelt's 'New Deal' a scheme was initiated to develop the agricultural potential of the valley. However, of the 400 families who originally migrated to the valley only about a quarter remained due to the difficulties of agriculture and poor marketing opportunities in the state.

In the 1940s and early 1950s it was Alaska's strategic importance that was paramount in extending the frontier of settlement. Japan occupied some of the Aleutian islands in 1942, setting off a sizeable US investment in bases. The military presence reached 300 000 during the war and now averages about 35 000. Military activity has been largely responsible for the extension of the highway network from its previously skeletal framework and for the detailed charting of the coast.

In 1947 Alaska's population had stabilised, after the post-war military withdrawal, to 128 000 and then grew steadily to 226 000 (of which 43 000 were native) by 1959, the year of statehood. Alaska became the largest state in the union with the smallest population. The level of economic development was summed up by Siddall, writing in 1957, about the hierarchy of settlement in Alaska, 'Two anomalies are found: first that Alaska does not have any true regional capital within its own borders and second that the city which does serve as Alaska's regional capital is Seattle which lies from 620 (998 km) to over 2700 miles (4347 km) from the Territory'.

The impact of oil The discovery of oil was to alter radically the situation and to establish the state not only as an area of immense strategic importance but also as a prime economic resource region.

Alaska's first significant oil discovery was in July 1957 when the Atlantic Richfield company struck a large deposit on the banks of the Swanson River on the Kenai Peninsula in the south of the state. The Swanson River field came into production in 1960 at an initial 20 000 barrels a day. Most of the early drilling found only natural gas, sometimes in large quantities, but there was no

The Trans-Alaska pipeline, raised above ground to protect from permafrost

immediate market for it except in Anchorage.

In 1963 oil was struck in the Cook Inlet and by 1968 total state production had reached over 220 000 barrels a day, ranking Alaska eighth amongst the   producing states of America. From 1957 to 1968 the state collected $140 million from the oil industry, making petroleum Alaska's third most important industry after fishing and timber.

18 February 1968 undoubtedly ranks as the most important date in the history of Alaska. Drilling on the North Slope had proceeded since 1963 but all companies except one had given up due to lack of success. Prudhoe Bay State No. 1 was the only oil well left operating and for Atlantic Richfield it was virtually a last chance gamble. Contrary to all expectations the largest oilfield in the United States was discovered, bigger even than the East Texas field found in 1930.

In 1969 a winter road was constructed between Fairbanks and the North Slope and during April that year traffic to the North Slope was so great that Fairbanks airport handled more freight than any other air terminal in the world. The year witnessed an influx of over 9000 people into Fairbanks.

The discovery of oil in Prudhoe Bay heralded one of the greatest conflicts between developer and environmentalist. The various environmental groups such as the Sierra Club and the Wilderness Society have urged the federal and state government virtually to close off the state to mineral development.

Most Alaskans however favour a reasonable level of exploitation as oil is a huge source of income. Between 1969 and 1975 Alaska moved from twenty-sixth to joint first in the US in terms of the lowest proportion of persons below the poverty level. Revenue has been so high that in 1980 the state government waived income taxes and issued every Alaskan with $50 for each year spent in the state since 1959. In 1980 royalties and production taxes brought in a total of over $4 billion. However, although Alaska ranks first among the nation's fifty states in average incomes, it ranks only twentieth when both wages and prices are taken into account.

Income from oil will rise even further in the 1980s. Production in 1980 was 1.5 million barrels per day and only Texas (2.4 million barrels a day) produced more. New production from the nearby (to Prudhoe Bay) Kuparuk field will raise the region's output by nearly 250 000 barrels daily in the mid-1980s. The United States Geological Survey estimate recoverable reserves at 22–59 billion barrels while the state estimates reserves even higher at 68–138 billion barrels. Potentially recoverable gas reserves have been estimated at over 100 trillion cubic feet, a five year supply for the United States.

The hardest fought battle between the opposing lobbies was over the construction of the 1270km Trans-Alaskan pipeline from Prudhoe Bay to the ice-free port of Valdez on the south coast. The main environmental arguments against the pipeline concerned possible oil spillage due to earthquake damage and movement in the permafrost zone causing breakage. Disruption of the traditional migratory path of the caribou and disturbance of other wildlife was also of major concern. The Canadian government in turn is extremely worried about possible oil spillage off the coast of British Columbia.

Opposition halted construction for 4 years as $100 million worth of pipeline stockpiled at various points along the proposed route had to be treated with anti-corrosive material.

The pipeline consortium invested heavily in sophisticated ecological examinations to provide satisfactory evidence for the National Environmental Policy Act's requirements. After agreeing massive liability funds the pipeline was given the go-ahead by Congress in November 1973 due to the influence of the powerful oil lobby and the energy crisis brought about by turmoil in the Middle East. The project was completed in 1977.

Environmentalists mainly in the rest of the USA, argue strongly that Alaska has to be regarded as a unique environment because of its very fragile ecosystem. The permafrost of the north is an important component of this fragility. Under permafrost conditions the ground is permanently frozen except for the active zone, roughly the upper metre or two, which thaws in the summer. It is a delicately balanced system and disturbance of the surface tundra can lead to excessive summer melting and the development of a quagmire. Construction in such conditions demands firm foundation into the frozen ground below the active zone and an insulating passage of air beneath main buildings. The environmental costs of development are magnified in such an area where landscape scars can persist for a much longer period than in more temperate regions.

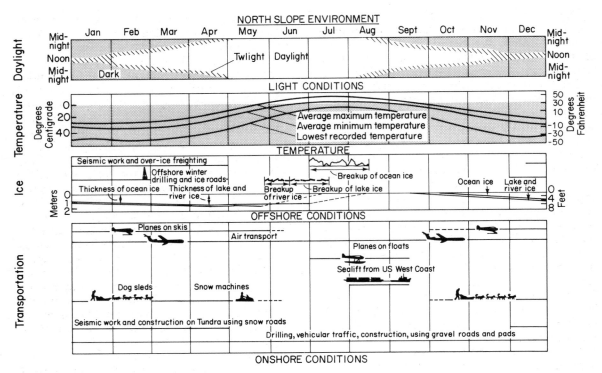

Fig. 7.3 *The North Slope environment (Source: Alaska Petroleum Company,* Prudhoe Bay and beyond, *June 1980)*

A moose passing under the Trans-Alaska pipeline near Atigun Pass

Methods of construction for the pipeline and for the Prudhoe Bay settlement have involved expensive techniques which ensure both the safety of the infrastructure and the preservation of the landscape in as natural a form as possible.

The Prudhoe Bay field encompasses approximately 1140 square kilometres but surface production facilities are contained in an area of 570 square kilometres, measuring about 16km north to south and 32km east to west. By agreement among the sixteen interest owners, the entire Prudhoe Bay field is being developed as one unit.

For 56 days in mid-winter the sun never rises above the horizon of the North Slope. Winter air temperatures drop as low as $-51°C$ but high winds can drive the wind chill factor to temperatures equivalent to $-79°C$. With annual average precipitation of less than 200mm the North Slope is considered an arctic desert. Figure 7.3 summarises the climatic conditions experienced on the North Slope and the implications for transportation. Because of Prudhoe Bay's remoteness a two-week supply of food is kept in reserve throughout the year.

The field's total permanent workforce numbers approximately 2100 (1980). During the next several years construction of facilities for the proposed oil recovery enhancement programme will mean an increase in the workforce which at its peak is expected to total between 4000 and 5000.

In spite of numerous regulations, land ownership remains the key to development or protection. The passage of the Alaska Native Claims Settlement Act in 1971 recognised that the natives aboriginal use of most of Alaska gave them rights to the land which had never been respected. Under the Act over 16 million hectares and almost $1 billion were ceded to the natives. This action has concerned the environmentalists as native groups are generally eager to gain income from their land.

Although over 32 million hectares were also set aside for national parks and refuges the ownership of much land and its eventual fate has yet to be decided. This situation will ensure that Alaska remains a focal point of the environmental debate for some time to come.

The economy and demography of Alaska show characteristics typical of a resource frontier region. Figure 7.4 shows the growth of the state's population from 1950 from which five periods of higher than average growth can be discerned. While migration is not the only component of population growth, analysis of Alaska's recent demographic history identifies it as the prime factor in each of these population surges.

The rapid growth of the early 1950s was due primarily to strategic development and the multiplier effect that such action established. The second and third surges marked were associated primarily with oil discoveries in the Swanson River and Cook Inlet areas. The sustained increase in the 1968 to 1972 period was due mainly to activity subsequent on the discovery of the Prudhoe Bay field. The final surge recorded was the result of the massive pipeline project, the decrease in population in 1978 marking the completion of the pipeline project in the previous year.

H. F. Lins Jr (1979) has examined the development of urbanisation in the Kenai-Nikiski region as a result of the Swanson River discovery. Figure 7.5 shows the results of his analysis. The urban-industrial complex established was resultant on the decision to run a 35km pipeline from the oilfield to the Cook Inlet shoreline when a marine terminal facility was constructed at Nikiski, about 16km north from the town of Kenai.

Prior to petroleum-induced expansion, Kenai, with a population of about 400, had a weak service function and was orientated towards self-sufficiency. Lins states that, 'With the exception of

Fig. 7.4 *Alaska's population growth 1950–80*

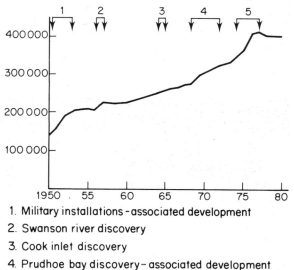

1. Military installations - associated development
2. Swanson river discovery
3. Cook inlet discovery
4. Prudhoe bay discovery - associated development
5. Pipeline construction

Fig. 7.5 *Urban-economic development in the Kenai-Nikiski region (Source: Lins JR, H. F. Early Development at Kenai, Alaska AAAG, June 1979)*

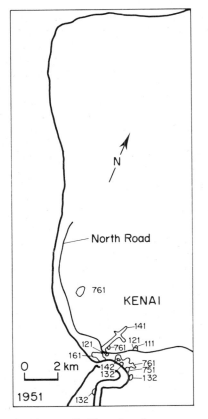

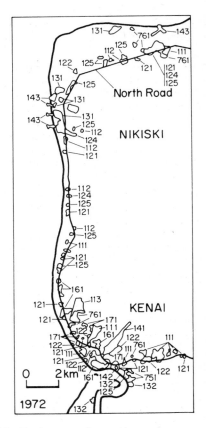

1 Urban or Built-up Land
  11 Residential
    111 Single-family
    112 Mobile home
    113 Multi-family
  12 Commercial and Services
    121 Retail
    122 Institutional (schools, churches, etc.)
    123 Military
    124 Pipe and equipment storage areas
    125 Industrial support
  13 Industrial
    131 Petrochemical and related activities

    132 Food processing and canning
  14 Transportation, Communications and Utilities
    141 Airfield and terminal facilities
    142 Communications facilities
    143 Marine terminal facilities
  15 Industrial and Commercial Complexes
  16 Mixed Urban or Built-up Land
    161 Same as 16
  17 Other Urban or Built-up Land
    171 Same as 17
    751 Quarrying activities
    761 Transitional areas

the airfield, Kenai was like a typical rural American town in 1850'. There were no sidewalks and paved streets, no municipal sewage and water supply system and only a few buildings with electricity or telephone. Most people burned wood for heat and used lanterns for light.

In the 15 years following the Swanson River discovery the area of developed land increased ten times. Nikiski has emerged as the industrial centre of the region and had developed its own commercial supply functions. Two core areas are now established, with extensive linear development between the two.

Sugden (1972) has compared the state's transport networks (Figure 7.6) with the Taafe, Morrill and Gould transport development model. He concludes that before the period of oil-associated activity the network was comparable to stage two and that recent developments have really accentuated this pattern making the contrast between the developed and the less developed parts of the state even more apparent.

It is unlikely that a major extension of the surface transportation network will occur as air transport will continue its dominant role in the state. One in forty Alaskans is a registered pilot and more private planes are owned per capita than anywhere else in the world—one for every hundred persons.

More than forty per cent of Alaska's labour force is in the armed services or in federal, state or local government, while manufacturing industry is noticeably weak.

Only three per cent of the state's population was

Fig. 7.6 *Transport development in Alaska (Source: Sugden, D. E.* Piping hot wealth in a sub-zero land. *Grographical Magazine, Jan 1972, pp 226–229)*

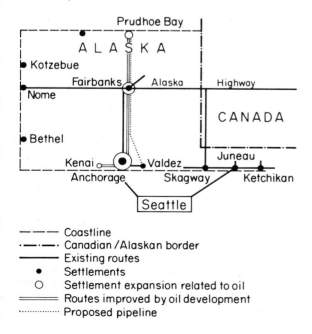

Coastline
Canadian/Alaskan border
Existing routes
• Settlements
○ Settlement expansion related to oil
Routes improved by oil development
Proposed pipeline

over 65 years old in 1980, the lowest figure in the United States (Florida registered the highest figure—17.3 per cent.) For the same year Alaska recorded a birth rate of 23 per thousand, the second highest after Utah, and the lowest death rate at 4.1 per thousand.

The future economic development of the state is far from certain and much depends on the land ownership issue. This was only partly settled by the 1980 Alaska National Interest Lands Conservation Act which set aside a large area of lands but allowed the possibility of their being re-opened for development after surveys of resources in the 1980s.

The environment will continue to present a strong challenge to settlement and economic activity and when the oil and gas of the North Slope eventually run out it is likely that the frontier of settlement will recede to its previous position on the Yukon. However, the interests of the mineral companies in Alaska extends beyond oil and gas. The industry claims that 33 of the 35 minerals of strategic importance to the US are present in the state and there have been a number of recent discoveries which could be commercially developed.

J. Wreford Watson (1976) sees Alaska as the testing ground for the American image of progress. In the past that image has been one of progress through exploitation of seemingly unlimited resources whereas now progress is viewed by many as conserving from today a heritage for future generations.

B. Water supply

1. Continental variations

Enormous contrasts exist in the availability of water over the continent of North America. As the most basic necessity for human life, water supply has been a dominant factor in establishing present day geographical patterns but while inadequate water provision has been a major constraint on settlement and economic activity the world over, the United States has led the battle to subjugate and integrate its drylands into the national economic system.

There is no absolute water shortage in North

America but rapidly increasing demand has caused localised problems. The Water Resources Council in the United States finds water shortages imminent in the Rio Grande and lower Colorado River basins and looming in other western regions, particularly in the Missouri basin. The delicate balance in many areas of the west is due primarily to the fact that the region with 60 per cent of the nation's land area receives only 25 per cent of annual precipitation.

While the south-west is undoubtedly the region where the most intense pressure on water supply is being experienced, other parts of the country especially the heavily urbanised and industrialised north-east have also indicated a developing awareness of the limitations posed by water delivery and availability. However, in such regions the problem is often more one of water quality rather than quantity.

Although total precipitation is much less in the western United States than in the east, daily withdrawals of water are virtually identical. Another dichotomy is apparent in the end-use of withdrawals with irrigation accounting for approximately 90 per cent of water used in the west whereas energy and manufacturing are prime users in the east (Figure 7.7).

Fig. 7.7 Water management in the USA

West		East
751 663	million litres/day withdrawn from resources for:	773 106
661 911	irrigated agriculture	49 792
34 704	domestic/commercial	93 325
20 703	manufacturing	210 398
10 492	energy	393 556
10 197	minerals	21 594
12 656	other uses	4 441

West: of total— 52 per cent not returned*
48 per cent used and returned.

East: of total— 12 per cent not returned
88 per cent used and returned.

* Lost in evaporation, transpiration, incorporation into products or crops, or consumed by humans/livestock.

Source: *National Geographic Magazine*, August 1980.

In spite of higher annual precipitation, water supply is causing concern in some parts of the east. The impermeable rocks of the eastern Appalachians absorb little groundwater, thus limiting the total number of available sources and for many communities the only accessible surface water is polluted to varying degrees by mine effluent and industrial waste. In recent years water supply has been generally recognised as the greatest single need of the rural poor.

In other regions suburbanisation has placed severe pressure on limited water resources. The extension of urban sprawl eastward along Long Island, New York is but one example. Here the growth of population in the counties of Nassau and Suffolk has exacerbated the water supply situation in three ways. The additional population has had a cumulative effect on demand while the extension of the built-up area has increased the amount of water running to waste from rainfall by surface runoff, thus reducing the water available to recharge groundwater. Contamination of supplies by sea water flowing into depleted aquifers has created further problems.

As in the west, interstate rivalries are evident. One of a number of disputes concerns the waters of the Delaware River, coveted by three states, New York, New Jersey and Pennsylvania.

Although water supply will present a considerable problem to many parts of the United States in future years a reassuring fact is that of the four trillion gallons of water that fall on the United States each day only one-tenth is used by people. Thus scope remains for advanced water management to combat deficiencies as they arise.

The danger of an overall shortage of water in Canada is remote. Local shortages do occur on occasions in various parts of the country but for the most part these are caused by lack of local facilities for the storage, purification and distribution of water. The area most susceptible to water shortages is the western Prairie region where low precipitation is coupled with relatively high evaporation rates.

As in the United States there is a basic imbalance between water supply and demand. 60 per cent of runoff is carried by rivers flowing northwards, away from 90 per cent of Canada's population which is concentrated within 200 km of the Canadian–United States southern boundary. Also about 36 per cent of the mean annual precipitation occurs as snow, most of which accumulates over several months before melting. At times therefore the rate of runoff is many times the average or there may be none if the rivers are frozen.

2. The drylands of the southwest: getting drier?

The attractiveness of the southwest region to both population and industry in the post-war period has placed a severe strain on water supply. Withdrawals from both surface and groundwater sources have reached critical levels while demand continues to rise at an alarming rate. Arizona claims that its supply of water already falls short of its needs by 2800 million cubic metres a year. California is said to have a shortage of 3700 million cubic metres and west Texas 5000 million cubic metres.

In many areas groundwater is being pumped out at a faster rate than it recharges, a process known as 'mining'. Increasing concern has been expressed about the Ogallala aquifer, an immense underground reservoir stretching 1300 km from South Dakota to Texas. 150 000 wells tap the Ogallala aquifer on the High Plains, irrigating an area of over 4 million hectares.

Some hydrologists have forecast economic decline for the region before the turn of the century with no feasible alternative supply to switch to as the aquifer's yields fall. West Texans have been mining the aquifer at a rate of about 6000 million cubic metres a year. Attention is now being focused on the southern High Plains in the vicinity of Lubbock, highlighted as the first critical area.

Arid lands of the southwest

Erosion in progress in the Badlands National Monument, approximately 20 miles southeast of Wall, South Dakota

The town is now a leader in the reclamation of waste water at a rate of about 70 000 cubic metres a day.

During California's worst drought in 1976 and 1977, 28 000 wells were sunk in a single year, lowering the water table significantly. With the resumption of normal rainfall the water table in many areas recharged fully but there were notable exceptions such as the San Joaquin valley where 50 years of mining groundwater has caused an area the size of Connecticut to subside, in places as much as 9 metres. In Orange County one local water district is spending around 15 cents per cubic metre to reclaim waste water which is then pumped into the ground to hold back the incursion of saline ocean water.

Figure 7.8 shows the present status of desertification in North America, highlighting its severity in the southwest. Desertification includes the impoverishment of ecosystems both within and outside natural deserts. It is characterised by the lowering of the water table, shortage of surface water, salinisation of existing water supplies and wind and water erosion. It is a developing and increasingly serious phenomenon in North America. For example the Sonoran Desert in the southwest is perhaps a million years old but has become distinctively more barren in the present century as economic development has progressed.

The exploitation of surface water resources has involved immense alterations to the landscape in the form of numerous dams and water transfer

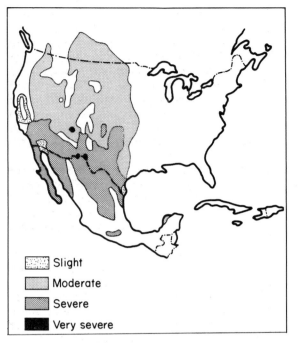

Slight

Moderate

Severe

Very severe

Fig. 7.8 *Desertification in North America (Source: Dregne, Harold.* **Desertification of arid lands.** *Economic Geography 53 (4); 325, 1977)*

schemes. California has been the focal point of such works where over 1200 dams are under state or federal jurisdiction.

3. The Colorado – A river under pressure

The 2333 km long Colorado River is an important source of water in the southwest. The Colorado rises in Rocky Mountains of northern Colorado state and flows generally southwest through Colorado, Utah, Arizona and between Nevada and Arizona, and Arizona and California before crossing the border into Mexico. The river drains an area of about 632 000 sq km. Centuries ago, American Indians used the Colorado and other rivers to irrigate their fields. Ruins of their old canals are still found in some parts of the desert.

Colorado water, which irrigates 1.2 million hectares of farmland and supplies major sunbelt metropolitan areas, is the subject of intense interstate and international rivalry. By the time the river reaches the Gulf of California it is reduced to

a trickle. Figure 7.9 indicates the water flow and withdrawals along the various sections of the system.

Salinity is high amongst the present problems of

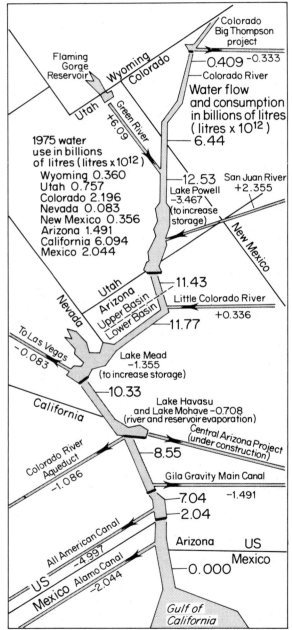

Fig. 7.9 *The demands on Colorado water (Source: National Geographic Magazine, Aug. 1980)*

the Colorado. The river carries about 9 million tonnes of salt a year, contributed both by tributaries flowing over salt beds and by irrigation water which dissolves about 4.5 tonnes of salt per hectare per year which filters back into the river. Thus by the time the Colorado crosses the United States – Mexican border it is highly saline.

As a result of strong Mexican protest various measures have been adopted to tackle this problem and the United States has built the world's largest desalination plant at Yuma, Arizona. The plant, with a capacity to desalt nearly 450 million litres of water a day uses the relatively new technique of reverse osmosis. This method of desalination is claimed to be much more cost effective than the traditional technique of distillation.

In spite of the current heavy demand on Colorado water a massive new withdrawal system, the Central Arizona Project, is under construction. The project was first suggested in 1947, agreed in 1968 and is scheduled for completion in 1987. When fully operational it will pump over 80 tonnes of water per second through a total height of 248 metres, carrying it by tunnel through the Buckskin Mountains over a total distance in excess of 480 km to bolster the depleted groundwater supplies of Phoenix and Tucson. The $2.2 billion project was about one-third completed in early 1981.

The scheme has been criticised on a number of points. Optimistic projections claim that the project will slow the rate of water table decline in the receiving region by two-thirds but even then depletion of groundwater resources will continue. Some hydrologists believe that when CAP is operational total Colorado water demand will frequently exceed supply and thus the scheme will be forced to operate below capacity. As upstream regions begin to exercise water rights more fully the problem of Colorado water allocation will become more pressing.

4. California—a question of balance

As the most populous state in the union California has exerted intense demands on the water resources of the west. Demand has only been satisfied by the construction of huge engineering projects to transfer water from surplus regions within the state.

A great imbalance exists between the distributions of precipitation and population as 70 per cent of runoff originates in the northern one-third of the state but 80 per cent of the demand for water is in the southern two-thirds. Low rainfall and high evaporation rates in the south produce runoff which averages less than 12.5 cm a year whereas in the north runoff figures are frequently in excess of 100 cm a year. Consequently the transfer of water from north to south has been a cornerstone of the state's water resources strategy.

While irrigation is the prime water user the sprawling urban areas have also greatly increased demand. The 3.5 million hectares of irrigated land in California are situated mainly in the Imperial, Coachella, San Joaquin and the lower Sacramento valleys.

Figure 7.10 shows the major component parts of water storage and transfer in the state which is based around two huge schemes.

The Central Valley Project (a federally funded project) was initiated by the State Water Plan of 1931. Water released by the Shasta Dam and other reservoirs flows down the Sacramento River, across the delta between the Sacramento and San Joaquin Rivers, to Tracy where it is raised 60 metres into the Delta-Mendota Canal. The canal carries the water 160 km south to Mendota where it is transferred into the San Joaquin River to replace water drawn from the San Joaquin behind the Friant Dam. The latter stores water for diversion to the Bakersfield area via the Friant Kern Canal. The Madera Canal irrigates an area north of Friant.

The Central Valley Project was completed in 1951. Apart from being vital to the state's water supply the Project has played an important role in expanding the hydro-electric capacity of the state, controlling winter flooding in the lower Sacramento and San Joaquin and improving navigation.

The other major scheme, the State Water Project, was designed primarily to supply water for non-agricultural use to the far south around Los Angeles. Scheduled for completion in 1990, water already flows the 965 km from behind Oroville Dam, the key storage reservoir, to the Perris reservoir southeast of Los Angeles. Water released from the Sacramento and Feather Rivers flows into and through the delta into the California aqueduct, the main component of the scheme. After being lifted 366 metres to the foot of the Tehachapi Mountains the water is then pumped 610 metres over the mountains and from there flows into the Perris and Castaic reservoirs. The Castaic reservoir began to supply the Metropolitan Water District in 1971 followed by the Perris reservoir in 1975.

The likelihood of eventual reductions in supply from the Colorado River prompted the state government in 1980 to set in motion the long-proposed $5 billion second phase of the State Water Project; the Peripheral Canal. The 68 km long canal will start at the Sacramento River, cut an arc southwards through the periphery of the delta, empty into a collection point called Clifton Court Forebay and feed into the California Aqueduct.

Although having separate origins, both projects are now subsumed, since 1957, under the California Water Plan.

Other transfer schemes also play an essential role. The Colorado River aqueduct, 400 km long,

carries water to the Metropolitan Water District from water impounded by the Parker Dam. In the extreme south of the state the Imperial and Coachella aqueducts transport irrigation water impounded behind the Imperial Dam.

The Owens Valley aqueduct, now 400 km long, functions to carry water from the Sierra Nevada to the Metropolitan Water District for urban use.

5. The future: various choices

Water supply is likely to be the prime limiting factor to future economic development in the southwest. As the demand for water continues to escalate, southern California and the water deficient areas of neighbouring states have covetously eyed the excess capacity of other regions. Figure 7.11 illustrates the major water transfer schemes which have been proposed in recent decades.

Fig. 7.10 *Major water transfer schemes in California (Source: Los Angeles Dept of Water and Power)*

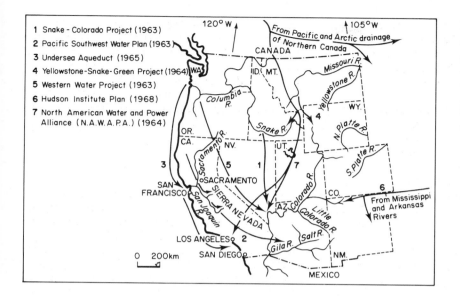

1 Snake - Colorado Project (1963)
2 Pacific Southwest Water Plan (1963)
3 Undersea Aqueduct (1965)
4 Yellowstone-Snake-Green Project (1964)
5 Western Water Project (1963)
6 Hudson Institute Plan (1968)
7 North American Water and Power Alliance (N.A.W.A.P.A.) (1964)

Fig. 7.11 *Major inter-state water transfer proposals (Source: Wilcock, D. N. et al.* Changing Attitudes to Water Resource Development in California, *Geography, July 1976, Vol. 61, No. 3)*

As yet there is no artificial transfer of water across state boundaries and in recent years the potential 'donor' states have hardened their attitudes against such schemes.

The north-western states strongly opposed the Colorado River Basin Project Bill of 1968 which amongst other suggestions proposed to transfer water from the Columbia-Snake river system into the Colorado. The transfer did not proceed and with the passage of a greatly amended Colorado River Basin Act the federal government prohibited for ten years all studies for water transfer to the Colorado from external states. The north-western states are fearful that, while they have surplus water now, the position may change in the future.

Undoubtedly the most ambitious of all the water transfer proposals was the North America Water and Power Alliance (NAWAPA) put forward in 1964. This huge proposal revolved around the transfer the Canadian water into the Snake and Columbia Rivers and the transfer of water to California and other southwestern states. While the scheme was technically and economically feasible the political obstacles proved critical. The Canadian government was, and still is, very wary about transferring vital resources to the United States which may eventually have the effect of hindering Canadian economic development.

Even intra-state water transfers are facing increasing difficulties. Hydrologists have suggested that the waters of the last of California's 'wild' rivers, the Klamath, Eel and Trinity, could be transferred south. However there is strong feeling against such proposals in northern California where the main economic argument against such developments is that these rivers represent the region's major natural amenity and could provide the economic base for future expansion in the area. In addition there is a growing awareness of the direct hydrological problems subsequent on water transfer.

Attention has focused more recently on the alternatives to water transfer. It has been argued in some quarters that the southwest is not so much short of water but only of cheap water and that conservation and a reform of water pricing would greatly reduce unnecessary demand.

Water obtained from surface sources in the southwest is generally heavily subsidised. While some surface water schemes are state funded, the major projects are under federal jurisdiction. When the Reclamation Act was passed at the turn of the century development of the southwest was dependent on huge federal spending which many authorities, especially in the eastern and central states where agriculture has been affected adversely by western irrigation projects, now believe should be curtailed.

In early 1981 it was estimated that water from new federal projects would cost at least 13 cents per cubic metre if the price covered construction of dams and canals together with operation and maintenance costs. In contrast, farmers in California's Central Valley paid about a fifth of a cent per cubic metre as the price is kept artificially low by a number of different laws. The current subsidy is about $1100 an acre per year in the Central Valley.

Clearly such subsidies encourage extravagant usage. Many farmers use poor quality land to grow low value crops such as alfalfa and sorghum which require large volumes of water. Contrary to the original aims of the Reclamation Act the main beneficiaries of current subsidies are large landowners.

Undoubtedly an increase in water pricing, which would be fiercely opposed in the southwest, would generate short term economic changes. Many marginal farms would be forced to close while a large number of farms would have to change to lower water consumption crops. Such transition would not necessarily obstruct the general economic development of the southwest but channel it towards a more efficient use of resources. However, in spite of mounting criticism of water subsidy the legal jumble of water rights will make water price reform a slow and complicated process.

Irrespective of water pricing reforms there remains much scope for conservation. The General Accounting Office estimated in a 1976 report that more than half of all the nation's irrigation water is wasted. Many farmers use relatively cheap open-ditch systems of irrigation which use about six times as much water as the most efficient sprinkler systems and one hundred times as much as drip irrigation which allocates measured quantities of water to each plant. Cheap water is obviously a disincentive to irrigation investment.

Canal construction could be modified in the interests of conservation. For instance, about one quarter of the 1500 million cubic metres of water transferred along California's unlined and uncovered Coachella Canal is lost by seepage and evaporation.

There is significant scope for the recycling of urban water. At present Los Angeles only cleans up about 74 million cubic metres a year of its potentially re-usable wastewater.

More extreme measures to supplement water supply which will also become more important are cloud seeding and desalination. The future strategy for water supply in the southwest should encompass all the feasible alternatives. Sensible resource management should ensure that the problems posed can be overcome.

C. Catastrophic hazards

1. Hurricanes and tornadoes

In the twentieth century hurricanes have killed more than 13 000 people in the United States and have caused immense damage to property in the eastern half of the country. Figure 7.12 shows the corridors of havoc created by the most catastrophic storms to attack the United States during this period.

The National Hurricane Centre in Miami and other research institutions carefully monitor by weather satellites these most destructive of atmospheric phenomena in order to learn more about their origin and to predict as early as possible the individual storm's likely pattern of behaviour. More accurate prediction, allowing evacuation of communities in the path of a killer hurricane, has helped to avoid the high casualty rates which were characteristic in the earlier decades of the century.

Ninety per cent of all fatalities have been due to drowning in the storm tides or walls of water that are swept ashore by high winds. The extreme low pressure in the eye of a hurricane causes the ocean surface to rise near the storm centre, forming a bulge up to two-thirds of a metre high. Driven by the wind, water piles on to the bulge as the storm follows a north-westerly path to the mainland. Forced against a sloping shoreline storm tides can hit the coast up to 8 metres above normal level

Flood damage from Hurricane Camille, 1969, in Nelson County, Virginia

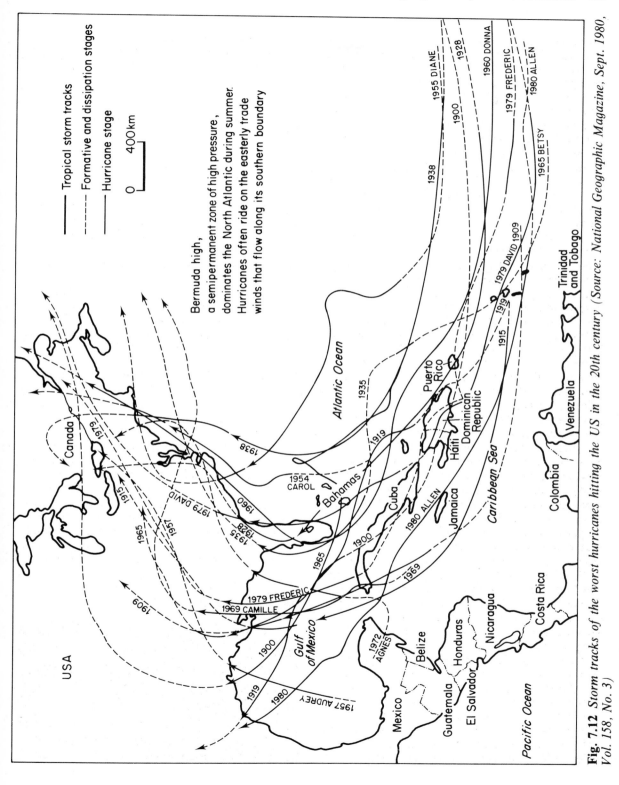

Fig. 7.12 *Storm tracks of the worst hurricanes hitting the US in the 20th century (Source: National Geographic Magazine, Sept. 1980, Vol. 158, No. 3)*

with devastating impact. Such a storm tide caused the death of 6000 people in Galveston in September 1900, the worst hurricane disaster in the history of the United States.

In an average year two or three hurricanes strike the US mainland, their course being set by the trade winds flowing along the southern edge of the Bermuda High. Hurricanes are classified according to the Saffir-Simpson scale. A storm ranked 1 is minimal; 2, moderate; 3, extensive; 4, extreme; 5, catastrophic. Three of the hurricanes shown on Figure 7.12 have fallen into the 'catastrophic' category. These are the 1935 storm which ravaged the Florida keys with winds of 240-320 km per hour killing 408 people; Hurricane Camille in August 1969 which devastated many communities particularly in the state of Mississippi, killing more than 300 people; and Hurricane Allen which left a trail of death and destruction in the Caribbean in August 1980 before hitting the coast of Texas.

The rising popularity of coastal residence has left an increasing number of people vulnerable to hurricane attack. For instance, off the south and west coasts of Florida more than 200 000 people live on offshore islands which are very susceptible to isolation in storm conditions which could seriously hinder evacuation. A related problem is that numerous coastal communities were constructed (and continue to expand) in unstable coastal zones before the transient nature of such areas was fully understood.

Flooding in Multnomah County, Oregon

A related atmospheric phenomenon but on a much smaller scale is the tornado, a violent cyclonic whirl generally about 100 metres in diameter and with an intense vertical current at the centre. The conditions required for the formation of a tornado are not precisely understood but involve great instability, high humidity and horizontal convergence of winds at low levels. Tornadoes form inland, particularly in the central plains of the Mississippi region where they originate in unstable tropical air and travel north or northeast. The path of a tornado can vary in length from a few hundred metres to hundreds of kilometres. The greatest frequency of occurrence is in a belt extending from Iowa through Kansas, Arkansas, Oklahoma to Mississippi. Iowa has the most, an average of 2.8 tornadoes per year.

Hurricanes and tornadoes occur with a much lower frequency in Canada but some have caused intense loss of life and damage, most notably Hurricane Hazel which left 100 dead and caused damage to the tune of $252 million.

2. Earthquakes

Earthquakes pose a continual threat to Pacific coastal communities particularly in California and Alaska but very limited efforts have been made by individual and corporate bodies to prepare for such potentially catastrophic occurrences.

The strongest earthquake ever recorded in North America was centred on Valdez in Alaska, measuring 8.6 on the Richter scale. 118 Alaskans died in this Easter 1964 disaster and violent earth tremors passed through Anchorage as its main street dropped 3 metres.

However the region of greatest concern is California, scene of the 1906 earthquake which devastated San Francisco. A great three-day fire completed the destruction which was initially triggered by movement along the San Andreas fault.

Figure 7.13 illustrates the position of the major fault lines in California and the location of earthquake epicentres since 1850. After a period of relative calm in recent decades the early 1980s have witnessed a resurgence of activity. Although from the late 1950s to 1980 California endured only two earthquakes of magnitude 6, five earthquakes in 1980 registered such an intensity, culminating in November of that year in a tremor of 7.4 degrees

off the coast of Eureka. The previous Californian earthquake to register 7 degrees was in 1951.

Each tremor is charted and studied intensely in the attempt to gain advance warning of an imminent major disaster. Seismologists regard the frequency of earthquake occurrence as an important predictive guide. In a broad region including western Nevada and northern Mexico, earthquakes of a 7 degree magnitude occurred every five or six years in the early part of the century, the longest lapse between them amounting to 18 years. However by 1980 the interval since a magnitude 7 earthquake had reached an abnormally long 25 years. Consequently seismologists believe that there is a 50/50 chance of an earthquake of serious proportions striking southern California during

Fig. 7.13 *Earthquake locations in California since 1850 (Source: The Economist Feb 14th 1981, p 27)*

the 1980s. Additional scientific evidence presented to confirm this view includes the increase detected in radioactive gases from wells, the increasing frequency of small and moderate tremors and the 'dramatic change' observed in the crustal strain pattern in the Los Angeles area, some two or three times as great as that previously observed.

A new agency has been established, sponsored jointly by the state and federal governments, to deal with earthquake emergency in southern

Fig. 7.14 *The eruption of Mt. St. Helens (Source: Geographical Magazine, August 1980)*

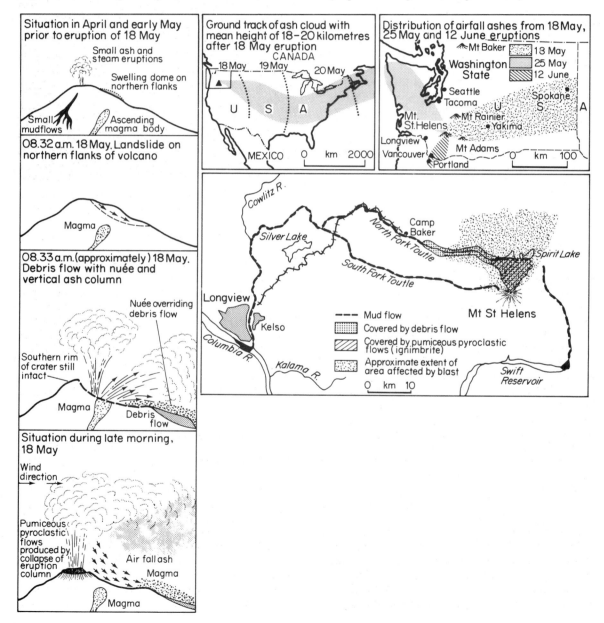

California. However, in general preventative action has been strictly limited.

As population densities have dramatically increased in the Pacific region in the post-war period so the possible loss of life from earthquake disaster becomes greater. Also as the complexity of infrastructural development continues to grow the environmental impact of such a disaster becomes potentially more hazardous.

In the 1970s a number of nuclear power plant siting applications were refused because of proximity to fault lines. Nevertheless California's operating nuclear plants are all in areas which have been affected at some time in the past by earthquake activity. While stringent regulations have been adhered to in construction it cannot be guaranteed that such plants could withstand a major earthquake.

Oil pipeline networks are also extremely vulnerable. Much of the opposition to the Trans-Alaskan pipeline centred on this issue. The fact that the southern terminus of the pipeline is at Valdez, epicentre of the major 1964 earthquake has not gone unnoticed.

3. Volcanic eruptions

The only active volcanoes in North America are located in the states of Washington, California, Alaska and Hawaii. Until the spectacular 1980 eruption of Mt St Helens in Washington state, research into volcanic activity was primarily centred on Hawaii which exhibits Kilauea with its fire pit called Halemaumau, and Mauna Loa with the active Mokuaweoweo on its summit.

The first evidence that Mt St Helens was once more becoming active occurred on 20 March 1980 when an earthquake of magnitude 4.1 was recorded. Seven days later the first eruption of ash occurred and similar small eruptions frequently took place in the following month. By the end of April a large bulge was rapidly swelling up on the northern flanks of the volcano.

On 18 May the whole northern side of the mountain began to move, followed immediately by a massive cloud of ash which mushroomed tens of thousands of metres into the atmosphere. The slumping of the northern side of the volcano exposed the hot rocks in the core which then reacted explosively. The eruption was thus a combination of a major landslide and subsequent

Aerial view from the southwest of erupting Mount St Helens Volcano, Washington, May 18, 1980

volcanic activity with the former being by far the largest product of the eruption in terms of volume. Figure 7.14 illustrates the sequence of events which occurred.

The eruption dramatically changed the topography of the volcano itself and of the surrounding area. A volume of well over one cubic kilometre departed from the mountain, ending up for the most part in the debris flow in the Toutle Valley. Figure 7.14 also shows the wider geographical area affected by the eruption. The eruption did not cease on 18 May. Renewed activity on 25 May and on 12 June sent ash clouds soaring into the atmosphere once more.

Virtually all the deaths attributed to the eruption were due to the searing hot gases emitted from the volcano moments after the landslide. This 'nuée ardente' ('glowing cloud'), a high speed avalanche of hot dust and rock buoyed up by incandescent gases was undoubtedly the most lethal component of the eruption.

The Toutle Valley is now filled to a maximum depth of 100 metres by volcanic debris. The damming of the river initiated huge mudflows which ultimately poured into the Columbia River.

While eruptions are relatively infrequent in North America their effects can cause major destruction and landscape changes. The west coast of the continent forms part of the Pacific 'ring of fire' and as such may well experience greater tectonic activity in the future. Careful monitoring of present conditions is essential if disruption and loss of life is to be kept to a minimum.

D. The environment: Perception and legislation

The development of environmental concern

The natural environment has been altered to a greater degree in a shorter time period in North America than anywhere else in the world. The rapid spread of settlement across the continent fostered a so-called 'frontier psychology' whereby the physical landscape was regarded as an obstacle to be subdued and put to commercial use. As environmental groups sadly lament, such an attitude is still prevalent among many North Americans today, particularly in the business world. However, recent years have witnessed a new awareness of the fragility of the natural environment by large sections of the population who have effectively translated their views into a wide spectrum of legislative action. In the 1970s environmental issues proved to be one of the major topics of national concern, particularly in the United States, where it rivalled issues such as racial strife and the Vietnam war.

While most legislation is of recent origin, concern about environmental destruction dates from the mid-eighteenth century when European nature-romanticism found acceptance in America's leisured classes. In the nineteenth century a growing number of strong-willed individuals advocated environmental protection and through their writings were instrumental in important legislative action dating from the latter part of the century. Such legislation contrasts markedly with that of recent years. Earlier government intervention was based on vetting commercial exploitation in areas of scenic beauty by designating outstanding areas as National Parks or National Forests while contemporary action has attempted to restrict the impact of economic activity on the environment by setting limits on the degree of environmental modification allowed.

Notable among the environmentalists of the last century were Ralph Waldo Emerson, Henry David Thoreau, George Perkins Marsh and John Muir. Emerson (1803–1882) in his first book *Nature*, published in 1836, expressed the view that wild nature was the ultimate source of life and culture. Thoreau's writings stirred many to a new appreciation of nature and his 1851 proclamation 'In wildness is the preservation of the world' is the motto of the Wilderness Society. Marsh (1801–1882), perhaps more than any other nineteenth-century writer, identified the extent to which economic activity was ravaging the landscape. Marsh believed that the destruction of the natural world would eventually damn civilisation unless there was a major change of attitudes to nature. John Muir (1834–1914), a renowned explorer and naturalist, founded the Sierra Club in 1892 and was instrumental in the establishment of the National Park system.

Campaigning by the environmentally conscious resulted in the historic 1864 Yosemite Park Act whereby California received the valley for 'public use, resort and recreation'. In 1872 Yellowstone became the first National Park in the United States and in fact in the world, and by the end of the century the west contained the framework of an extensive park system which was further developed in the twentieth century. The Forest Reservations Act of 1891 and the National Park Service Act of 1916 firmly established respectively the National Forest and National Park systems in the United States. Figure 7.15 illustrates both the special characteristics and the year of authorization of the present system of US National Parks. Most of the National Forests were set aside in the first decade of the twentieth century.

The retention of public lands for conservation purposes became a counter policy to the disposal of land for revenue and settlement. A number of authorities, notable among them Yi-Fu Tuan (1974), have recorded the changes in the general perception of the environment that occurred during this period. A similar movement was under way in Canada and in 1909 a North America Conservation Conference was convened by President Roosevelt who was himself strongly concerned with the relationship between people and their environment.

In Canada the first National Park, an area of 26 sq km protecting the mineral springs at Banff,

Fig. 7.15 The United States National Park System

Name	Location	Date authorised	Special characteristics
Acadia	S. Maine	1919	Mountain and coast scenery
Arches	E. Utah	1929	Giant arches formed by erosion
Big Bend	W. Texas	1935	Canyons and desert plain on the Rio Grande
Bryce Canyon	S.W. Utah	1923	Canyon with coloured walls and rock formations
Canyonlands	S.E. Utah	1964	Rocks, spires, and mesas; Indian petroglyphs
Capitol Reef	S. Utah	1937	Highly coloured sandstone cliffs dissected by gorges; named for a white, dome-shaped rock
Carlsbad Caverns	S.E. New Mexico	1923	Great limestone caverns
Crater Lake	S.W. Oregon	1902	Blue lake in a crater
Everglades	S. Florida	1934	Subtropical wilderness
Glacier	N.W. Montana	1910	Region of glaciers, forests, and lakes
Grand Canyon	N.W. Arizona	1908	Great gorge of the Colorado River
Grand Teton	N.W. Wyoming	1929	Scenic portion of the Teton Range
Great Smoky Mountains	Tennessee, N. Carolina	1926	Wild, beautiful area in the Great Smoky Mts
Guadalupe Mountains	W. Texas	1966	Mountain region; contains a limestone fossil reef
Haleakala	Hawaii, on Maui	1960	Largest inactive crater in the world
Hawaii Volcanoes	Hawaii, on Hawaii	1916	Volcanic region
Hot Springs	Central Arkansas	1921	Mineral springs
Isle Royale	N.W. Michigan	1931	Forested islands in Lake Superior
Kings Canyon	E. California	1890	Canyons, peaks, sequoias. See Sequoia National Park
Lassen Volcanic	N. California	1907	Volcanic peaks and lava formations
Mammoth Cave	Central Kentucky	1926	Extensive underground passages
Mesa Verde	S.W. Colorado	1906	Prehistoric cliff dwellings
Mount McKinley	Central Alaska	1917	Highest peak in North America
Mount Rainier	S.W. Washington	1899	Volcanic peak and glaciers
North Cascades	N. Washington	1968	Area of great alpine scenery in the Cascade Range; bisected by Ross Lake National Recreation Area
Olympic	N.W. Washington	1938	Rain forests and glaciers in the Olympic Mts
Petrified Forest	E. Arizona	1906	Petrified logs; part of the Painted Desert
Platt	S. Oklahoma	1906	Cold mineral springs in the Arbuckle Mts
Redwood	N.W. California	1968	Coast redwood forests
Rocky Mountain	Central Colorado	1915	Scenic Rocky Mts. region on the continental divide; many high snow-capped peaks
Sequoia	E. California	1890	Groves of giant sequoias
Shenandoah	N. Virginia	1926	Forested region of the Blue Ridge Mts

Continued overleaf

Fig. 7.15 Continued

Name	Location	Date authorised	Special characteristics
Virgin Islands	Virgin Islands, on St John	1956	Unusual scenery, marine life, coral gardens; ruins of the Danish colony
Voyageurs	N. Minnesota	1971	Scenic northern lakes region; interesting glacial features and history
Wind Cave	S.W. South Dakota	1903	Limestone caverns in the Black Hills
Yellowstone	Wyoming, Montana, Idaho	1872	Geysers, Yellowstone canyon, falls; first and largest U.S. national park
Yosemite	Central California	1890	Mountain region with Yosemite Valley
Zion	S.W. Utah	1909	Multicoloured canyon in a desert region

Source: The International Geographic Encyclopedia and Atlas.

was established in 1885. Today Canada has 28 National Parks covering an area of 129 500 sq km.

The development of environmental concern in the United States is also evident in a series of amendments to existing federal programmes in earlier decades. In 1935 the Federal Power Act was amended to require the licensing of any hydro-electric project to be contingent upon consideration of other beneficial uses. The Flood Control Act of 1936 required that cost-benefit analysis be used to assess the impact of a proposed project to 'whomsoever they may accrue'. More recently the Federal Aid Highway Act was amended in 1966 to protect public parks, conservation areas and historic sites from unnecessary intrusion by federally assisted roads.

The idea of preserving total wilderness areas also gained momentum during the century. In 1924 the first wilderness preserve was created when the US Forest Service set aside a portion of the Gila River watershed in New Mexico. The wilderness concept was greatly strengthened with the passage of the 1964 Wilderness Act when various federal agencies were authorised to designate potentially suitable areas for inclusion into the National Wilderness Preservation System. The 1980 Alaska National Interest Lands Conservation Act tripled the size of the Wilderness system by designating 22.8 million Alaska hectares as wilderness in National Parks, Wild Life Refuges and National Forests.

The huge current demand for recreational facilities is placing an ever increasing strain on such conservation areas and has resulted in considerable environmental damage in some locations. In addition the mineral industry has cast covetous eyes at many parts of the nation's wilderness. Under the Wilderness Act of 1964 all US non-park wilderness is open for gas and oil exploration until the end of 1983 although leases already granted can be developed indefinitely. In practice, however, only a very restricted number of leases have been granted in existing wilderness areas. To date the resource protection lobby has dominated congressional opinion but those in favour of a resource development policy have made a considerable comeback since the late 1970s, much to the consternation of the Wilderness Society and other environmental groups.

Recent environmental awareness

Perception has been recognised as being of fundamental importance to geographical understanding in recent years. Perception refers to an individual's (or group) evaluation or reaction when confronted with a reality. Environmental legislation can usually be termed 'corrective action' in that it is designed to improve environmental conditions which have been allowed to degenerate. The passage of such legislation in a democratic society normally requires considerable public pressure and/or support. This has generally been forthcoming in North America since the late 1960s because the state of the physical environment has become an issue of major importance to a larger and more vociferous proportion of the population than ever before. This national perception of environmental problems in both countries has consequently resulted in innovative legislation.

Environmental problems can be viewed as problems of externalities in that they are not dealt with in market transactions and inequities are clearly apparent over time and space. While pollution tends to disperse, economic benefits tend to concentrate. Inequalities develop between entrepreneurs who benefit from exploiting the environment as a free commodity and those who bear the cost.

Another kind of inequity is transgenerational, between those who create environmental costs now and those who will have to bear them in the future. In spite of much criticism recent legislation has gone some way to rectify such malpractice.

Broadly, environmental legislation can be seen in three categories with actions designed to improve the atmosphere, water bodies and the landscape.

Towards a cleaner atmosphere?

Atmospheric pollution is the most obvious of the environmental problems confronting North America in that all parts of the continent are affected to some degree and because its greatest concentration is invariably in the most heavily populated regions. The pervasiveness of air pollution has made it one of the major targets of the environmental lobby.

The United States Clear Air Act of 1970 and the Canadian Clean Air Act of 1970 form the basis of legislation designed to curb air pollution over the continent. While significant successes have been achieved during the lifetime of this legislation, opinion in many quarters demands a review of the practicality and efficiency of current methods with the likelihood of substantial future modifications.

In the United States the federal government through the Environmental Protection Agency (EPA) has established basic standards and the states are required to translate these into specific compliance programmes which in turn must receive EPA approval. For a number of major pollutants a maximum annual level of concentration and one or more standards for shorter periods are laid down. Regulations have focused on sulphur dioxide, soot, hydrocarbons, carbon monoxide, ozone, oxides of nitrogen and more recently lead.

However, by the beginning of 1981 over half of the population of the United States were resident in areas that still violated the national air pollution health standards. Criticism has mounted, both from manufacturers who have frequently incurred heavy costs in attempting to comply with legislation and from environmentalists who want new action to cater for pollution problems which were earlier overlooked. Figure 7.16 indicates the sectional breakdown of commercial expenditure on air and water pollution control in 1980.

Air pollution has been reduced in some areas by using methods which can only increase it in other regions. For instance, the concentration of sulphur dioxide in the air of American cities fell by 20 per cent in the 1970s but much of this reduction has been attributed to the construction of a new generation of very tall smokestacks which disperse pollution over a much wider area.

Instead of settling out quickly sulphur dioxide has been transported over great distances. In the atmosphere, both sulphur dioxide and nitrogen dioxide react with moisture and other compounds to form minute particles of sulphate and nitrate which many experts now believe are more hazardous than sulphur dioxide itself.

The first indication of this problem was the discovery of acid rain which was initially recognised in Scandinavia in the 1950s. Acid rain occurs when the sulphate and nitrate in the atmosphere combine with moisture to form acidic droplets which may eventually fall as precipitation of high acidity. Sulphates and nitrates may also float down to earth as 'acid dust' which may be inhaled.

Acid rain is threatening fish and plant life in thousands of lakes, injuring plant leaves, stunting the growth of trees, leaching nutrients from soils and interfering with photosynthesis. Ninety per cent of the lakes in New York's Adirondack Mountains now contain no fish and the problem is spreading rapidly although lakes in limestone areas are able to neutralise acid.

It is thought that the acid rain problem first appeared in Scandinavia and the northeastern USA – eastern Canada area because these regions were once glaciated and consequently have thin soils which cannot buffer the effects of the acid. The problem has only become apparent in recent decades because it results from the cumulative effect of sulphur building up over many decades of fossil fuel burning as the natural buffering capacity of rocks, soils and lakes is gradually eroded. Clean or normal rain has a pH of 5.6 and rain with a pH of less than 5.6 is considered to be acidic.

Fig. 7.16 U.S. Non governmental pollution control expenditures: air, water and solid waste 1980

Industry	Air $m	Water $m	Waste $m
Iron and steel	684	383	2
Non-ferrous metals	135	81	69
Electrical machinery	62	113	64
Machinery	65	123	8
Autos, trucks and parts	47	47	68
Aerospace	8	11	11
Fabricated metals	78	61	50
Instruments	48	53	45
Stone, clay and glass	69	37	21
Other durables	38	36	42
Total durables	1233	946	380
Chemicals	320	298	145
Paper and pulp	205	174	94
Rubber	101	58	42
Petroleum	875	619	131
Food and beverages	78	64	40
Textiles	32	44	34
Other durables	43	33	21
Total nondurables	1 653	1 289	508
All manufacturing	2886	2235	888
Mining	37	43	29
Railroads	17	30	6
Airlines	60	18	18
Electric utilities	2 349	937	328
Gas utilities	30	14	17
Communications and other transportation	27	49	17
All non-manufacturing	2 704	1 210	625
All business	5 590	3 445	1 513

Figure 7.17 illustrates the concentration of acid rain in the eastern part of the continent.

Acid rain is only part of the larger problem of the long-range transportation of airborne pollution (LRTAP) which seems virtually immune to present control strategies. The national standard for ozone, a by-product of photochemical smog is sporadically violated along the entire eastern seaboard from Washington DC to Maine.

In North America a total of over 30 million tonnes of sulphur dioxide is emitted into the atmosphere annually. About five-sixths originates from US sources, with some 5 million tonnes from Canada. The annual total for nitrogen oxide emission from the US and Canada is approximately 22 and 2 million tonnes respectively. Sulphur dioxide is generally a by-product of industrial processes. Its main source in the US is from fossil fuel power stations and in Canada from ore-smelting. About half of all nitrogen oxides are emitted from vehicle exhaust with the rest from electricity generation and other industrial processes.

In early 1981 the National Commission on Air Quality released a report ordered by Congress in the 1977 amendments to the Clean Air Act. This report contained 109 recommendations on how the Act should be amended. The Commission found that the nation's air was 'measurably better' than a decade earlier and was continuing to improve. However as Figure 7.18 indicates data from the Council on Environmental Quality for the 1970 to 1979 period shows that improvements have really been rather modest.

The most controversial recommendation of the Commission is that the 1982 and 1987 deadlines for states to comply with the national standards should be eliminated. Other suggestions abhorrent to the environmental lobby are to eliminate requirements that new plants in dirty-air areas install the highest possible emission controls and to give automatic approval to state air pollution control plans not reviewed by the EPA within 90 days of submission.

Canada has tackled air pollution in a similar manner although in general because the country has been faced with a more manageable problem a less complicated legislative response was initiated. However, although Canada is a more limited source region the eastern part of the country lies downwind from major US industrial areas. It is generally believed that about three to four times as

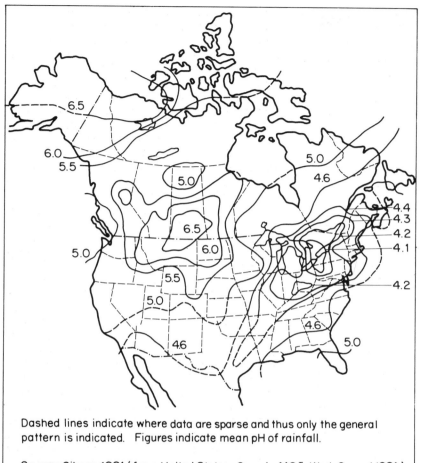

Fig. 7.17 *The regional incidence of acid rain in North America. (Source: Still waters: The Chilling Reality of Acid Rain. Ministry of supply and services, Ottawa, Ontario, 1981)*

Dashed lines indicate where data are sparse and thus only the general pattern is indicated. Figures indicate mean pH of rainfall.

Source: Gibson. 1981 (from United States – Canada. M.O.I., Work Group 1.1981)

much sulphur moves across the border from the United States to Canada each year than moves in the opposite direction. Recognising the extent of transboundary air pollution the two countries commenced formal negotiations concerning the problem in June 1981. A major worry for Canada is the determination of the United States to increase its utilisation of domestic coal, a major source of atmospheric pollution.

As in the US, acid rain is a considerable problem and it is now common in parts of Canada for rain to be ten times more acidic than normal. The Atlantic region is particularly vulnerable because the soils and aquatic systems in southwestern New Brunswick, Nova Scotia and Newfoundland have little natural buffering capacity.

The industrial regions of Ontario and Quebec are the greatest Canadian sources of air pollution and Sudbury is the site of the world's largest single point source of sulphur dioxide. The giant Inco plant is equipped with a 'superstack' 387 metres high, designed to disperse pollutants away from the area. The Atmospheric Environment Service has found that sulphur dioxide plumes from the plant can reach Toronto some 400 km away in a matter of only 17 hours.

A recent study by the Ontario Ministry of the Environment found precipitation in this part of Canada to have a mean pH between 3.95 and 4.38. South-central Ontario's precipitation is more acidic than in the Sudbury region and as acidic as in the northeastern US.

Fig. 7.18 US Air pollution – national emission estimates (millions of short tons)

Pollutant	1970	1975	1979
Particulates	23.1	12.8	10.5
Sulphur oxides	31.2	27.8	27.0
Nitrogen oxides	21.0	22.3	24.9
Hydrocarbons	30.5	25.8	27.1
Carbon monoxide	124.4	108.0	100.7

Source: US Statistical Abstract.

One problem is the absence of comprehensive data on air quality as monitoring is generally less sophisticated than in the US. The National Air Pollution Surveillance Network regularly collect data on ambient air concentrations of the most common contaminents on a continuing basis. The network is a co-operative effort of the federal, provincial and municipal governments. A number of significant improvements have recently been recorded as indicated by Figure 7.19. Amendments to the Clean Air Act have given the federal government additional powers to combat various aspects of air pollution.

The future of air pollution regulations is uncertain as public opinion seems to be tilting towards economic growth as opposed to increased investment in environmental protection. However

Fig. 7.19 Canada: Average of the annual means of NAPS stations for 1974 and 1979

Air contaminant	1974	1979
Sulphur dioxide (ppm)	1.6	1.2
Suspended particulates ($\mu g/m^3$)	78.6	66.0
Lead ($\mu g/m^3$)	0.68	0.39
Nitrogen dioxide (pphm)	2.80	2.6
Carbon monoxide (ppm)	2.44	1.7
Soiling Index (COH)	0.38	0.28

the environmentalists are campaigning vehemently for legislation to curb pollutants such as carbon dioxide and airborne carcinogens. Any such action would significantly increase industrial costs.

Dirty water

While the atmosphere contains the most obvious evidence of pollution, environmental concern has also developed over the continent's water resources, occasionally jolted by such alarming events as the ignition of Cleveland's Cuyahoga River in 1970 which was smothered in oil and floating debris, and the astonishing discovery in 1958 that Lake Erie was dying through a process known as eutrophication whereby pollutants stimulated the growth of algae, creating oxygen demands that eventually led to the suffocation of aquatic life.

Although a number of Acts relating to water pollution have been placed on the statute books of both countries the most important legislation has been the 1972 Federal Water Pollution Control Act Amendment in the United States and the 1970 Canadian Water Act.

Under the 1972 Act Congress set as a goal 'the elimination of discharge of all pollutants and the attainment of fishable, swimmable conditions in all the nation's waterways'. Up to 1980 EPA had pumped some $25 billion into the construction of municipal sewage plants as a major part of its pollution strategy. Such action has been sorely needed for pollution from sewage has led to the closure at least temporarily, of roughly one fifth of nearshore shellfish grounds in the United States.

In spite of notable improvements in some rivers the President's Council on Environmental Quality noted in 1981 that 'the quality of the nation's surface water has not changed much in the last five years'.

A major obstacle to pollution control is that high levels of water pollution come from 'non-point' sources, namely the runoff of contaminated water from fields and streets. Figure 7.20 shows the main characteristics of the major non-point sources of water pollution. 'Point' sources are those readily identifiable at a single location.

Increasing recognition is now being given to the crucial influence of land use on water resources. Controlling land use can help to diminish the impact of many non-point pollution problems and provide an alternative to expensive sewerage and treatment facilities.

The Canada Water Act of 1970 emphasises the need for consultation and co-operation with and among the provinces in comprehensive water resource management. This co-operation has recently been evident in the formation of special purpose boards, such as the Qu'Appelle River Basin Board in Saskatchewan to study critical problems in federal-provincial water use. Remedial action to combat water pollution will require a high level of capital investment. Nearly half of the population in Canadian cities of over 100 000 people is not served by primary treatment of sewage, Montreal being the most notable example.

Other important Canadian legislation includes the Ocean Dumping Control Act 1974, the Northern Inland Water Act 1970 and the Arctic Waters Pollution Prevention Act of 1970. The latter legislation was a response to the increasing development possibilities for oil and gas in the Northlands and established Canadian sovereignty over all waters up to 160 km from the coastline. Shipping using these waters now has to comply with strict pollution control regulations.

As a result of the Great Lakes Water Quality Control Agreement 1972, common water quality objectives were agreed between Canada and the United States. However the US response to the International Joint Commission which monitors the agreement has generally been lukewarm in contrast to much greater Canadian concern.

Fig. 7.20 Non-point sources of water pollution

Non-Point Source	Pollution-causing activities	Principal pollutants
Agriculture	Crop production, animal production, farm drainage	Sediment, nutrients from soil fertilisation, pesticides, organic materials, salts, animal wastes
Forestry	Access road construction and operation, harvesting systems, logging (esp. clear cutting), crop regeneration, other silvicultural processes	Sediment, nutrients, pesticides, organic pollutants, thermal
Mining	Exploration, construction of facilities, mine operation, mine abandonment	Sediment, nutrients, waters, dissolved minerals, salinity, sometimes radiation
Construction	Land development, transportation and communication networks, water resource facilities	Sediment, chemicals, biological materials
Urban runoff	Precipitation discharges containing pollutants, accelerated and concentrated by urban surfaces and collection systems	Organic materials, inorganic solids, coliform bacteria, pesticides, nutrients, heavy metals and sediment
Hydrologic modifications	Channel modifications, farm drainage, dams, resource recovery (especially sand and gravel) and related activities	Sediment, nutrients, pesticides, thermal, chemicals, micro-organisms
Residual Wastes	Foregoing categories create residual waste (solid, liquid, sludge) not discharged to water but conveyed to it by runoff and infiltration	As above, both hazardous and non-hazardous. Examples: sewage sludge, solids from air pollution control equipment, mine tailings, feed lot wastes, pesticide containers, radioactive wastes

Protecting the landscape

In the United States the move towards greater federal and state involvement in land use was primarily a result of wider public awareness of the 'negative externalities' that many land uses can create. The tremendous demand for land in the post-war period enticed many landowners to exercise property rights that had long lain dormant while local authorities were frequently attracted by extra revenue accruing from new development.

In many rural areas developers basked in a total absence of land use regulations as more and more individuals and communities became increasingly alarmed at the apparent lack of control over developers and speculators. The greater mobility of population was also making the use of land in one area the concern of a wider and wider population.

The cornerstone of land use control in the United States is the National Environmental Policy Act of 1969 which set clear environmental goals for federal agencies and required them to submit detailed Environmental Impact Statements (EISs) for all 'major federal actions significantly affecting the quality of the human environment'. For the first time federal planners and decision makers were required to prepare public reports which disclosed, along with other information, the unavoidable adverse environmental effects of the proposal and the alternatives available.

Opinions have differed markedly concerning the success of NEPA. The processes introduced by the Act have frequently resulted in lengthy judicial proceedings and of course, escalating costs. The Corps of Engineers is one of the few agencies which has made a systematic effort to assess the impact of NEPA on individual projects. Its analysis shows that as a result of NEPA between 1970 and 1978, 41 projects and studies were stopped or abandoned, 347 were modified and 102 were temporarily or indefinitely delayed.

Many environmentalists regard NEPA as a very limited and blunt instrument that can be circumvented by shrewd Congressional vote trading and the calling in of political favours. In the wake of critical federal reports about the environmental impact statement procedure, new regulations were adopted in 1978 with the goal of improving efficiency and reducing ambiguities.

Paralleling federal action has been a move towards greater state involvement in land use in the 1970s. Among the leading states in this process have been Hawaii, California, Vermont, Delaware, Maine, Oregon and Florida. In some cases the state's concern has been limited to 'critical areas', in others the state reviews all construction projects beyond a certain size.

The bulk of new state legislation was passed in the early 1970s and few states have adopted new land use control programmes since Congress rejected the National Land Use Policy Act in 1975. State coastal zone management has been the major exception. Programmes funded by the National Coastal Zone Management Act of 1972 are designed to protect coastal zones from over-development. Overall the record of coastal zone management, with a few notable exceptions, has not altogether been encouraging.

In the 1980s the procedures established in the previous decade will be severely scrutinised as the United States is faced with some difficult decisions concerning industrial development and resource use. Many Americans feel that there has been a tendency to over-regulate and thus favour a lightening of the legislative burden.

Various legal and administrative requirements for environmental impact assessment were introduced in Canada in 1973. The Environmental Assessment and Review Process for federal departments, crown agencies and private companies in receipt of government contracts, grants and loans was commenced in that year. Nine provincial governments have also adopted some form of environmental impact assessment.

Refineries, pulp mills, hydro-electric projects, highways, dams and airports have been the main target for formal environmental impact assessment in Canada.

Hazardous wastes

The land pollution problem, while clearly affected by the actual land use pattern in a locality, is also influenced by external factors. Ironically, the problem has been intensified, partly because of successes in air and water pollution programmes. Large volumes of toxic wastes accumulated because of air and water pollution regulations have been solidified and dumped on land. Numerous chemical dumps, many long since abandoned, threaten life, health, property and the continent's drinking water.

Estimates of the extent of the problem differ widely. Consultants hired by the EPA estimated that in 1979 there were between 32 000 and 50 000 chemical disposal dumps throughout the United States and that between 1 200 and 2 000 may be extremely dangerous. EPA project that total clean-up operations would cost between $22 billion and $44 billion whereas the Chemical Manufacturers Association see the problem as a more limited one and calculate total costs at between $247 million and $333 million.

The public have become increasingly alarmed at incidents highlighted by the national media. In 1978 more than 200 families were evacuated from a residential area constructed on an abandoned underground chemical dump at Love Canal near Niagara Falls, after seepage into homes. The site had been abandoned for more than 30 years before seepage occurred. E. C. Beck, a spokesman for EPA stated 'We have learned that Love Canal was merely the first detonation of a string of chemical time bombs literally strewn across the nation'.

Recent concern has also been voiced about the 9 hectares 'Valley of the Drums' in Bullitt County, Kentucky which contains more than 100 000 barrels of highly toxic chemicals.

The exact location of hazardous waste disposal sites is difficult to accurately ascertain but a useful state by state list was compiled by the House Commerce Oversight Subcommittee in 1979 after a survey of the 53 largest chemical manufacturers in the country. The states with the greatest number of disposal sites were Texas (319), Ohio (253), New Jersey (223). California (177) and Illinois (176). The lowest ranking states were South Dakota (2), Alaska (3), Arizona (3), Rhode Island (3) and Hawaii (4). While the report does not claim to be a comprehensive inventory it does highlight regions of intense chemical dumping.

To combat this far-reaching problem the Resource Conservation and Recovery Act went into effect in late 1980, more than four years after it was passed by Congress. Under this legislation all chemical manufacturers and movers will have to keep detailed records and make annual reports to the federal government. Dumping may only take place at EPA-approved locations. It remains to be seen if this action is enough to stop the poisoning of large areas of the United States. However with only one site approved in 1981 and up to 50 million tonnes of hazardous chemical wastes each year, some regions are experiencing a shortage of capacity.

Bibliography

Hamelin, L. E. (1968) 'Un indice circumpolaire', *Annales de Geographie*, 422, pp. 413–30.

Lins, H. F. Jr (1979) 'Early development at Kenai Alaska', *AAAG*, June, 69, 2.

Sugden, D. E. (1972) 'Piping hot wealth in a sub-zero land', *Geographical Magazine*, January, pp. 226–9.

Tuan, Yi-Fu (1974) *Topophilia: A Study of Environmental Perception, Attitudes and Values*. New Jersey: Prentice-Hall.

Watson, J. W. and O'Riordan, T. (1976) *The American Environment: Perceptions and Policies*. London: J. Wiley and Sons.

Part 2
Resource Development in the Twentieth Century

8

Energy and Minerals

The economic might of North America is in no small way related to the variety and abundance of minerals located beneath its eighteen million square kilometres. The availability of a myriad of resources combined with a ready supply of human capital in the form of industrial skills, entrepreneurial ability, investment and innovation has provided a firm basis for economic growth and development.

In comparison to most other nations the United States and Canada have in the past enjoyed a very priviledged position with seemingly unrestricted access to energy and minerals. Where domestic resources were insufficient to meet demand, easily obtainable and relatively cheap imports made up the deficit. Although the United States became steadily more reliant on mineral imports in the post Second World War period the situation in earlier years was not regarded as either serious or threatening to the economy.

However the period since 1973 has witnessed a drastic review of the situation. While the increasing dependence on foreign sources did not go unnoticed earlier, the use of the word 'crisis' was almost completely absent from North American mineral terminology until the last decade.

Declining reserves, falling levels of self-sufficiency, rapidly rising world prices and supply discontinuities from politically unstable regions, along with environmental difficulties have presented unprecedented problems, particularly for the United States.

While North America has proved to be in the past, and still is at present, a vast storehouse of mineral wealth, unparalleled levels of exploitation have seriously depleted reserves of many minerals. Such high levels of production have been necessary to meet the apparently insatiable demand from all sectors of the economy. For instance in the late 1970s Canada and the United States had the highest per capita consumption of energy in the world, using 8.77 and 8.48 tonnes of oil equivalent respectively. In contrast the levels for the USSR and western Europe were 4.2 and 3.42.

Although per capita consumption is at a uniformly high level there is a marked dichotomy between the United States and Canada in absolute terms due to the tremendous difference in population. In terms of total value, mineral production in the United States was approximately five times that of Canada in 1980. However, while the United States is now a very large net importer of minerals and fuels Canada remains a net exporter and a most sizeable one indeed in metallic minerals and more recently natural gas.

Until 1930 imports of minerals in short supply in the United States were roughly balanced by the export of surplus raw materials. Since that year this balance has not been maintained, with the deficit increasing sharply after 1945. In the 1970s the United States had to import on average 15–16 per cent of a huge and steadily rising total requirement.

Economic development elsewhere in the world has led to increasing competition for the world's mineral supplies and the United States now has far less influence on the world mineral markets than it had previously. In addition the geopolitical situation in a number of traditional source regions has changed to the detriment of the United States with repercussions such as the Arab oil embargo of 1973 and the Iran crisis of 1979. Along with other politically unstable regions, the situation in southern Africa, a source of a number of vital raw materials, has led to increasing concern.

The United States has become acutely aware of the vulnerability of many of its mineral supply arteries which now stretch to virtually all parts of the globe. Any deficiencies of raw materials caused by restriction or blockage of these vital supply lines are bound quickly to register adverse conditions for the economy as a whole. There can be little doubt that the security of adequate mineral and fuel supplies will become an even more dominant pre-occupation of United States domestic and foreign policy in the future.

Although energy and mineral supplies are essential to a developed country, domestic production directly contributes only 1 per cent of GNP in the United States as opposed to almost 9 per cent in

Fig. 8.1 *Total value of mineral production by state and province 1978*

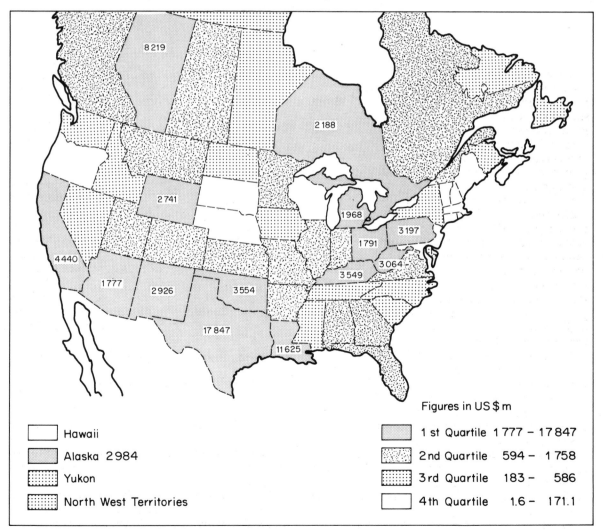

Canada. The industry is also a relatively greater employer in Canada with 3 per cent of the workforce against 1 per cent in the United States.

Environmental concern

Recently North America has shown a more enlightened attitude to the physical environment after a lengthy period in which it was largely neglected in the over-riding quest for increasing production.

As a result of increasing pressure from environmental groups, stringent controls have been introduced which have led to a significant rise in the cost of extraction and usage. Regulations have in some cases had a major effect in hindering the rates of exploration and production. The thesis of many environmentalists is that the traditional 'growth ethic' and materialistic values that have been so successful in creating economic prosperity in the past are not conducive to the future well-being of either North America itself or the world in general.

Fig. 8.2 *Total value of mineral production per square km by state and province 1978*

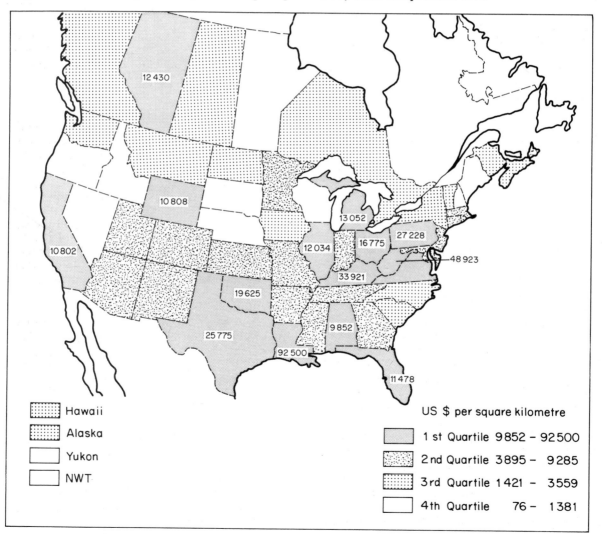

Spatial distribution

The location of total mineral production (including fuels) by value for American state and Canadian province is illustrated by Fig. 8.1 which shows the regions ranked by quartile. Absolute totals for the major regions are also indicated on the map.

The dominance of the American southwest is clearly evident. Texas is by far the premier region, with a value of production well above that of the second ranking region. The three other core regions shown by Figure 8.1 are central Appalachia, the Canadian Shield and western Canada.

However, the use of production figures in isolation can be misleading as no account is taken of area. Figure 8.2 indicates the value of mineral production per square kilometre with absolute values for the major regions inserted. While the American southwest maintains its strong position the placing of the north-eastern states is heavily reinforced. Using this criterion Louisiana overtakes Texas as the leading region, with West Virginia a clear second. Canadian production is seen in a totally new light with only Alberta remaining in the first quartile. Nevertheless eleven of the fifteen regions in the first quartile in Figure 8.1 remain in the first quartile when land area is taken into account.

Problems of definition

It is of vital importance to differentiate correctly between resources, reserves and supply. The resources which a country has of any mineral is the total amount of that mineral contained in the earth's crust within its borders. The reserve is that fraction of the total resources of the mineral that has been calculated to exist at commercially exploitable values under known technology. The supply of the mineral is the amount which can be produced and delivered to consumers.

The level of resources, reserves and supply can change very rapidly, each being partly dependent and partly independent of the other levels. Figure 8.3 shows the classification used by US Geological Survey. Resources are categorised into those which have been identified and those which are as yet undiscovered.

Identified resources which are not classified as

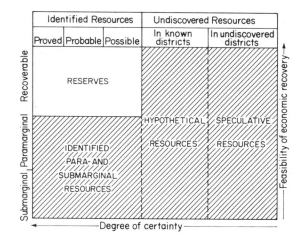

Fig. 8.3 *US geological survey classification of mineral resources (Source: Cameron, E. N. (ed) The Mineral Position of the United States 1975– 2000. 1973, University of Wisconsin Press, 69)*

reserves are classed as being either paramarginal or submarginal depending on the estimated cost of extraction. Paramarginal resources are those recoverable at costs as much as one and a half times those that can be borne now, with submarginal resources being more costly still to extract.

The position of a mineral deposit as to whether it is a reserve or a paramarginal or submarginal resource is dependent on a number of factors the most important of which are, the cost of extraction, the level of available technology, the market price and government intervention with regard to legislation, taxes and financial incentives.

As the level of supply is that volume of a mineral which can be produced by the industrial complex constructed on known reserves and transferred to the point of usage by the transport networks available it is consequently susceptible to the efficiency rates of these phenomena.

Energy: North America's number one problem?

The mainstay of a modern industrial nation is its ability to secure and utilise energy supplies. The world's most advanced economy has continually

Fig. 8.4   United States energy supply 1960–1990

Source	1960 (%)	1970 (%)	1980 (%)	1990 (% est.)
Hydro, geothermal, Solar	3.7	3.9	4.2	5.7
Nuclear	–	0.3	3.4	7.9
Coal	21.9	18.0	20.9	24.5
Gas	29.7	33.6	26.9	21.8*
Oil	44.7	44.2	44.6	40.1*
Total (Million barrels/day oil equivalent	21.9	33.3	37.9	40.4

* includes synthetics.
Source: Exxon Corporation, May 1981.

demanded greater energy inputs in its quest constantly to increase production to such an extent that with only 6 per cent of the world's population the United States now consumes over 30 per cent of the world's total energy product. The average American uses as much energy in a few days as half the world's people on a per capita basis consume in one year.

Falling domestic production and the need to import fossil fuels have heavily increased the cost of energy in the United States. Energy is now the economy's fastest growing burden. In 1967 the cost of end-use energy products amounted to 9.1 per cent of total GNP. By 1980 the cost had risen to 13 per cent of GNP. Importation also of course has an adverse effect on the balance of payments.

Although the United States possesses large coal reserves, the problem fuels are petroleum and natural gas because production of both has declined significantly. American petroleum production passed its peak in 1970 and natural gas in 1973 with imports filling the gap between supply and demand. The manipulation of these sources for political expediency is a prospect which has already indicated its potential in 1973 and 1979. To counter this trend the United States is anxious to develop to their full potential remaining oil and gas reserves, and alternative domestic sources of power.

As Fig. 8.4 shows, fossil fuels accounted for 92.7 per cent of total United States energy in 1980, a slight decrease from 96.3 per cent in 1960. By 1980 the only other contributing sources were nuclear, hydro and geothermal power.

The role of hydro-electric power is limited by the small number of viable sites remaining and the development of geothermal energy is still in an embryonic stage.

Recent studies estimate that the United States will not possess a practical system for the solar generation of electricity until the turn of the century. Bioconversion, tidal and wind power will probably never be able to contribute more than a small percentage to American energy needs.

However, many prominent environmental groups disagree vociferously with such conclusions, claiming that the alternative sources of energy could play a much more important role if sufficient levels of investment were directed to these means.

But on the projection of present trends the only domestic sources that can be made available in sufficient quantities to bridge the crucial period to the end of the century are coal and nuclear power. Yet the future of both energy sources will depend greatly on the severity of environmental opposition and government legislation.

The present energy situation in North America has been created primarily by a soaring level of demand which rose by 73 per cent in the United States between 1960 and 1980 and by approximately 100 per cent in Canada in the same period. Even the most optimistic projections point to very significant increases in the coming decades.

In comparison to the United States, Canada's energy economy exhibits both complementary and contrasting trends. Canadian petroleum production is also declining, having reached its peak in 1973, but deposits of natural gas, discovered in recent years, are being rapidly exploited. Much of this is destined for markets south of the border.

As in the United States, petroleum is the major source of energy in Canada contributing 39.2 per cent to the total in 1980. However the relative role of hydro-electric power at 25.7 per cent is much more important. Natural gas, coal and nuclear power contributed 22.0 per cent, 9.0 per cent and 4.1 per cent respectively.

In recent years the United States has floated the idea of a common energy market with Canada and Mexico. However, in spite of the potential economic advantage of such a scheme, political realities have led to a lukewarm response from America's immediate neighbours.

Petroleum: Rising prices— Uncertain supply

Petroleum supply more than any other factor has been the key to the North American energy situation in recent decades. The general perception of energy as being at crisis point in the 1970s was precipitated almost entirely by declining levels of domestic production coupled with the rapidly escalating price and increasingly intermittent nature of overseas petroleum supplies.

Production in both countries is falling, albeit with fluctuations, having reached a peak in the United States in 1970 followed closely by Canada in 1973. In 1980 the United States ranked third in world production (427.9 million tonnes) after the USSR (603 million tonnes) and Saudi Arabia (493 million tonnes). Canada ranked eleventh with a production level of 80.3 million tonnes. As demand had increased reserves have been depleted. 'Published Proved' reserves in the United States and Canada stood at 4100 and 900 million tonnes respectively in 1980. Together the two countries hold only 6.0 per cent of total world reserves compared to the massive 55.3 per cent contained in the Middle East.

Net imports of petroleum into the United States rose from 24.1 per cent to 45.9 per cent of total consumption between 1970 and 1977 but by 1980 had reduced to 38.9 per cent as higher prices and increasing coal consumption curtailed demand. In Canada net imports as a proportion of total consumption were 12.7 per cent, 8.9 per cent and 10.4 per cent for the three years respectively.

In an attempt to curb oil importation Canada is now diverting petroleum, previously exported to the United States, to her eastern provinces. Net exports of petroleum to the United States fell sharply from 42 million tonnes in 1975 to 13.4 million tonnes in 1980 following the eastward extension of the Canadian pipeline network from Sarnia to Montreal in 1976.

The location of currently producing and potential oilfields is shown by Figure 8.5. As Figure 8.6 indicates Texas, Louisiana and California remained dominant regions in the 1970s, although all three states suffered declining production be-

tween 1971 and 1980 reaching a massive −48.5 per cent in Louisiana. The only real encouragement to the petroleum industry in the United States has been the increasing flow from Alaska which will become even more important in the future.

Alberta, which produced 87 per cent of Canadian petroleum in 1980 is the only province which ranks significantly in North American terms, being the third most important region after Texas and Alaska.

Petroleum is most markedly the premier energy source in both the United States and Canada, contributing 44.6 per cent and 39.2 per cent respectively to primary energy consumption in 1980 and thus the continuance of sufficient supplies is of vital importance to economic stability. To this end both governments have found it necessary to intervene, at times heavily, in the functioning of the petroleum industry.

In 1959 the United States introduced an import quota system which functioned until 1973. The legislation was designed to stem the importation of relatively cheap foreign oil into regions remote from domestic oilfields. The objective was to maintain relatively high prices for domestic petroleum which at the time was more costly to produce and also to encourage exploration and development. The quota system was scrapped in 1973 when declining levels of domestic production coupled with the Arab oil embargo made it necessary to increase importation significantly.

W. J. Mead (1979) argues that United States import quotas distorted the pattern of oil production worldwide and led to excessive production from rapidly declining US resources contributing directly to the energy crisis of the 1970s.

In 1971 the Nixon administration introduced an intricate system of price controls to shield US consumers from the full brunt of world oil price increases. This scheme was gradually phased out between June 1979 and February 1981 in the hope that by allowing the price of US petroleum to float upward to the world market level, consumers will be forced to conserve energy and thus decrease national consumption levels. Petroleum is the main energy type consumed in all nine divisions except the West South Central where its consumption is exceeded by natural gas (Figure 8.7).

The Canadian government has also acted to keep down the price of petroleum since 1974 by a system of compensation payments to those re-

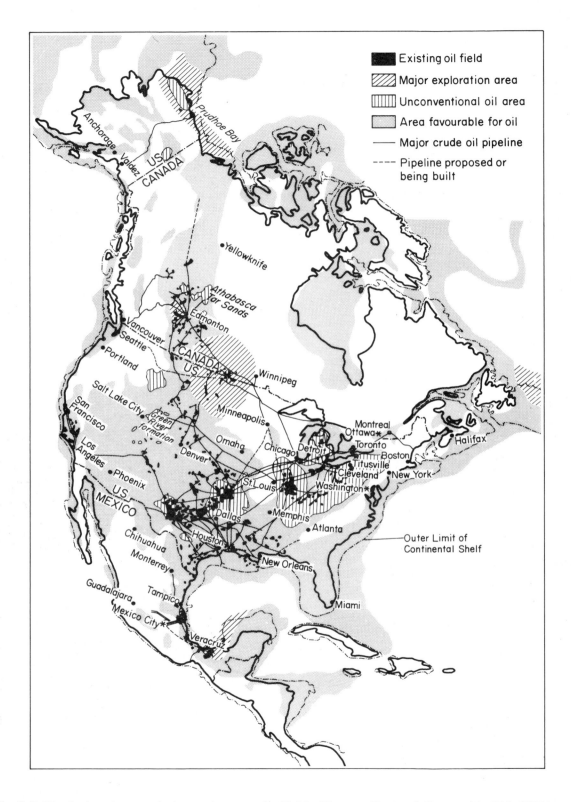

Fig. 8.5 *North America: producing and potential oilfields (Source: National Geographic, Feb 1981)*

Fig. 8.6 The USA: major petroleum production states

State	1971 (m tonnes)	1980 (m tonnes)	Percentage change 71–80	Total production 1859–1980 (000's tonnes)
Texas	166.9	134.3	−19.5	6 165 672
Alaska	10.9	81.5	+647.7	197 892
Louisiana	127.6	65.7	−48.5	2 551 614
California	48.9	47.8	−2.2	2 509 098
Oklahoma	29.1	20.0	−31.3	1 632 464
Wyoming	20.2	17.3	−14.4	623 201
New Mexico	16.1	10.6	−34.2	493 630
Kansas	10.7	8.0	−25.2	669 439
US Total	471.2	427.9	−9.2	16 975 510

Source: *Oil and Gas Journal.*

Fig. 8.7 *US energy consumption by division 1979*

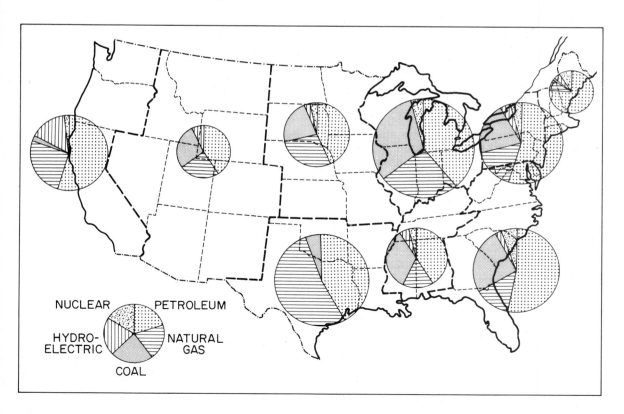

gions which have been forced to import higher priced foreign oil.

Undoubtedly North America's voluminous consumption has been heavily encouraged by the low consumer price which is largely a result of the minimal level of government taxation compared to other developed countries. The average price of a gallon of petrol in mid-1978 (with the appropriate taxation level in brackets) was $.94 (.34) in Canada, $.86 (.17) in the US, $2.23 (1.08) in West Germany and $1.63 (.81) in Britain.

While the US decontrolled oil prices in early 1981 Canadian policy was that oil prices should not exceed 85 per cent of the international price or the average price of oil in the United States, whichever was lower.

United States domestic proven oil reserves have been dwindling at a steady rate since the late 1950s when they stood at over 8000 million tonnes. Although the reserves were given a boost with the discovery of the Prudhoe Bay field in Alaska they have continued on the normal pattern of decline since then. Alaskan production will increase throughout the 1980s but in the time it will take to do so production from other states will steadily fall. The Prudhoe Bay field is unique in that it accounts for approximately a third of proven reserves. Similarly in Canada the rate of annual consumption has outstripped the identification of reserves.

Nevertheless research, exploration and development are progressing in a number of new directions and areas. With declining production from conventional resource zones, frontier and offshore locations are attracting most current interest.

The best prospects appear to be in the Beaufort Sea-Mackenzie Delta region where the United States and Canada are both actively engaged in exploration. Drilling ships have been used in the Beaufort Sea and new islands have been constructed by thickening sea ice in shallow water to support drilling rigs. This method of drilling on ice is unique to Canada.

Attention is also being focused on two other Alaskan offshore areas; the Cook Inlet and the Gulf of Alaska. Other promising offshore locations are the Sverdrup Basin in the northern Arctic Islands; the Labrador Shelf; the Baltimore Canyon 160 km off the coast of New Jersey; the Georges Bank off the Massachusetts coast; the Gulf of Mexico and the waters off southern California and Georgia.

Offshore Newfoundland witnessed a great exploration boom after oil was struck in autumn 1979, 320 km southeast of St John's. Preliminary estimates believe it to be the largest single find in North America since Prudhoe Bay in Alaska.

Unlike earlier wells which were largely drilled on private land, the new offshore and frontier regions lie in federal territory for which federal leases need to be obtained. In the past this has often been a slow process which the oil companies argue desperately needs to be speeded up. With development of frontier sources Canada aims to be self-sufficient again in oil by 1990.

The gigantic leap in oil prices from $3 to $32 a barrel between 1973 and 1980 has resulted in renewed interest in oil bearing formations which were previously considered marginal. An example of such an area is the Williston Basin, a vast petroleum reserve of 26 million hectares stretching across North and South Dakota, Montana and the provinces of Manitoba and Saskatchewan. The American sector has become the centre of renewed activity in recent years. The Basin has been the scene of drilling since 1950 but the easily recoverable crude, approximately 1.5 million barrels, has already been extracted. It is estimated 55 million barrels remain but most of what is left occurs in numerous small deposits leading to higher than average costs of extraction.

Recent interest has also developed around 'enhanced oil recovery' (EOR). Until recently it was uneconomical and technically very difficult to remove more than one-third of all the discovered oil. Much of the remaining oil is still inaccessible but it has been estimated by the Department of Energy that between 25–45 billion barrels can be extracted. Enhanced recovery is an elaborate form of washing more fuel from oil-bearing rocks. Not only does it dispense with exploratory drilling but it makes use of many existing wells and pipelines.

Unconventional oil sources

Oil shales and tar sands are attracting increasing investment. Oil shale is a fine-grained argillaceous rock containing hydrocarbons in the form of a waxy material known as kerogen. When distilled out the hydrocarbons produce crude petroleum which on further refining can be used as conventional crude oil. The world's largest deposits exist in the western US where significant volumes of oil are locked in shales in at least 13 states. Most of this is too diffuse (11–16 gallons of oil per tonne of rock) to be exploited economically but in a 44 000 square km area at the interesection of Colorado, Utah and Wyoming is an extensive deposit containing more than 27 gallons per tonne. These deposits, which are the most commercially exploitable in the US contain around 600 billion barrels of oil of which about one-third is recoverable. Production is projected to reach 500 000 barrels a day by 1990.

When shale oil production begins, it will not mark the birth of a new industry but the re-emergence of an old one. In the mid 1800s there were about 55 small plants making shale oil from shales in the eastern states. But the industry folded up when cheaper crude oil was discovered in Pennsylvania in 1859. Other oil-shale deposits attracting attention are the Devonian shale in the eastern United States (Fig. 8.5) and deposits in Alaska.

Tar sands are sedimentary formations of loose grained rocks bonded by heavy bituminous tar. Processing separates out the tar. As with oil shale extraction, the quantities of material to be mined and eventually disposed of are huge.

The world's largest deposits are the Alberta tar sands which are located in the north and northeast of the province and cover an area of 49 000 square km. The Athabasca deposit which is the largest accounts for 23 000 square km. It has been estimated that there are over 600 billion barrels of crude bitumen in the Athabasca area, 50 and 54 billion barrels respectively in the Peace River and Wabasca deposits and 164 billion barrels in the Cold Lake deposit. The total of about 900 billion barrels may ultimately yield about 250 billion barrels of synthetic crude oil. Modern development began in 1967 although small scale operation did take place in the 1930s and early 1940s. By 1980 production had reached 150 000 barrels a day.

Even with research and development extending in so many different directions the relative contribution of petroleum to the energy economy of North America will undoubtedly fall in the coming decades. The over-riding objective of the United States and Canada is to find enough petroleum in the intervening period until alternative sources can increase their contribution.

The United States, gravely concerned about the political leverage associated with imported oil, began in 1977 the construction of a Strategic Petroleum Reserve which will eventually be a one billion barrel underground store to be used if overeas supplies are again seriously discontinued. The oil is being stored in a string of salt domes and abandoned salt mines in southern Louisiana and Texas which can easily be linked up to pipelines and shipping routes. Delays have beset the programme and with considerable opposition there is some doubt if the project will meet its initial completion date in 1985.

Coal: A fuel in abundance

In North America as in the world as a whole, coal reserves are substantially in excess of those of oil and natural gas. However in comparison with the other fossil fuels the coal industry has had to contend with increasingly greater problems with respect to extraction, storage, transportation, air pollution and most importantly consumer preference. Consequently the relative contribution of coal to the energy economy of the United States and Canada declined steadily during the twentieth century until the late 1970s when critical shortages of oil and natural gas forced a re-evaluation of the role of coal.

The United States in particular is looking to coal to stem fossil fuel imports. In 1979 the federal government increased the target for coal to an annual production of 1.8 billion tonnes by the end of the 1980s. Although production has steadily increased in recent years many authorities believe such a target to be wildly optimistic in view of the growing array of environmental problems confronting the industry. Other projections see as a realistic target a production of 1–1.5 billion tonnes.

At the turn of the century coal provided 85 per cent of energy supply in the United States, falling in 1950 and 1974 to 36 per cent and 18 per cent respectively. The changing energy situation in the latter 1970s reversed this trend and by 1980 coal accounted for 20.9 per cent of total energy.

Canadian reliance on coal has always been at a much lower level due to the earlier dominance of hydro-electric power and in 1980 coal accounted for only 9 per cent of Canadian energy. Nevertheless the trend towards coal's use as a replacement for oil and gas has already begun and will greatly increase in the future.

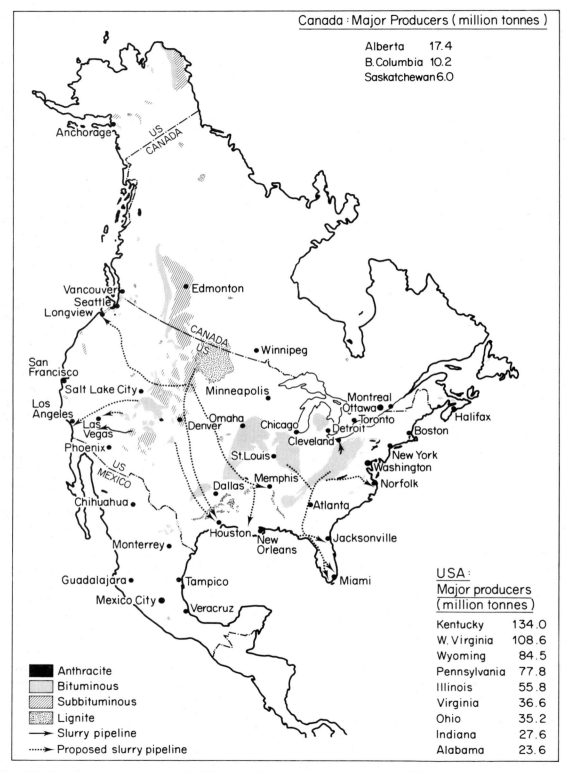

Fig. 8.8 *North American coalfields (Source: National Geographic, Feb 1981)*

The relative decline of coal has been primarily related to the changing technical requirements of fossil fuel consumers and the developing availability, at least until the early 1970s, of oil and natural gas. This situation has been evident to varying degrees in all sectors of the economy.

Petroleum products currently have a monopoly over the transport sector and the trend in North American refinery operations has been to upgrade domestic crude supplies to obtain increasing amounts of the high-value lighter products demanded by transport users. Coal has totally lost its market with the railways which in 1945 took 25 per cent of the then booming coal business while usage by the household and commercial sectors has declined drastically.

The major market for coal is electricity generation which accounted for 71.1 per cent of 1980 coal production. In the industrial sector coal is not only a source of energy but also for some industries a raw material. However even in this sector problems relating to transportation, storage and pollution have resulted in changes in consumer preference.

Although coal's relative position has suffered, absolute production has increased steadily in both nations. In 1980 the United States and Canada produced 757 and 36 million tonnes of coal respectively, contributing approximately 26 per cent and 1.2 per cent to total world production. The United States is the largest world producer and also has about 30 per cent of the world's proven reserves. US exports reached 65 million tonnes in 1980, and are expected to increase to 90 million tonnes by 1985. Major port improvements, particularly at Hampton Roads and Baltimore are under way to facilitate such large bulk movements.

The location of North America's coalfields is shown in Figure 8.8 which includes data for the ten major producing states in America and the three main coal producing provinces in Canada. A most noticeable distinction between the two countries is that while the overwhelming volume of US production is concentrated in or in close proximity to the manufacturing belt, Canadian coal is very distant from major markets. The distance between centres of production and consumption in Canada has resulted in the movement of US coal from the Appalachian and the Midwestern coalfields across the border to the industrial areas of eastern Canada. Alberta and British Columbia, which are the largest producers of Canadian coal, export the bulk of their production via the Pacific coast, with Japan being the main customer.

Although US coalmining is still heavily concentrated in the Appalachian and Midwestern coalfields the pattern of extraction is rapidly beginning to change with the recent development of the large strippable reserves in the western states.

Interest in western coal was limited and almost entirely local prior to the 1970 Clean Air Act. The Act has caused major problems with the use of eastern and midwestern coal, 80 per cent of which is classed as being of high sulphur content (2.8 per cent and over) but conversely has opened up a huge potential market for western coal which is dominantly low in sulphur content.

A number of other important contrasts must also be considered. In early 1979 eastern underground coal bought at the mine cost an average of $22-$24 per tonne while the average price at the large stripmine operations in the west was $9-$10 per tonne. Seventy five per cent of US strippable reserves are located in the western states. However, transport costs in moving the coal to the east and midwest sometimes exceed the minemouth cost of the coal, and eastern coal has advantages in the export markets.

Another disadvantage of western coal is its lower mean heat content and thus to fuel a large thermal plant as much as 24 per cent more western coal may be required compared to top quality eastern heating coal.

Mining costs are not confined to extraction alone. The Surface Mining and Control Reclamation Act of 1977 mandates that mine operations use effective techniques to restore stripped land to its original condition capable of supporting whatever function prevailed before mining. The Act clearly has strong financial implications for the western mine operators.

If the new United States targets for coal are to be fulfilled then further development of the western coalfields is an absolute necessity. All the principal coal-hauling railroads are investing heavily in new equipment to handle the anticipated increases in coal traffic. Electric utilities are working on major problems to accommodate the shift from oil/gas to coal burning in many existing and in all to-be-built fossil power plants. In some cases extensive plant modifications are necessary.

Although the US has extremely large reserves, estimated at more than 200 billion tonnes, the pace of development is dependent upon a number of crucial variables, the most important of which are, (i) the present absence of a realistic and firm federal energy policy, (ii) uncertainty about future Environmental Protection Agency emission requirements and (iii) uncertainty as to the date of new technological advance which might produce better alternatives to coal.

The environmental problems associated with the spectrum of coal-associated activities are formidable, as shown by Figure 8.9.

In Canada production is projected to rise to 64 million tonnes by 1985 but transportation to markets presents a major problem. Rail lines are being upgraded and special train systems are being built to carry western coal to Thunder Bay where a new coal terminal was opened in 1978 to facilitate the movement of coal by lake vessel to central and western Ontario. Major evaluation programmes are presently examining resources in Nova Scotia and north-eastern British Columbia.

Liquefaction and gasification

Both the United States and Canada have been engaged in the development of coal liquefaction and gasification. Alberta's large reserves include extensive deposits of low grade coal currently uneconomic to transport over significant distances. Federal and provincial authorities along with private companies are investigating the possibility of building gasification plants near the coalfields or gasifying the coal underground. In both cases the manufactured gas would be moved by pipeline.

The techniques required for gasification and liquefaction were developed some time ago and the major problem in North America with regard to these energy sources is cost. In 1980 synthetic oil equivalents from coal were $10-$25 per barrel more expensive than ordinary petroleum but this relationship should gradually change in favour of synthetic fuels if the world price of oil continues to rise at a faster rate than that of coal.

Fig. 8.9 *Environmental disturbances from coal-related activities (Source: American Gas Assocation and US Department of Energy)*

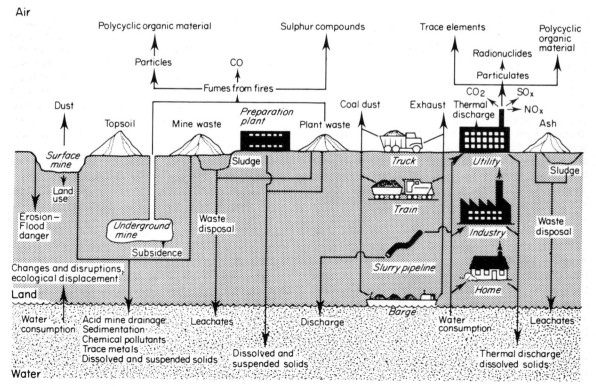

While a few small industrial plants are already in operation, the primary aim is to produce high BTU gas which can be fed directly into an existing gas pipeline system without diluting the BTU value of gas already flowing in it. A consortium led by America National hope to have such a plant in commercial operation by 1984.

Apart from the operational costs of the liquefaction and gasification processes other problems are apparent. According to the National Coal Association, to obtain 1.5 million barrels per day of coal synthetics, an additional 225 million tonnes of coal per year will have to be mined. In addition to the direct environmental impact of coalmining, serious environmental concerns remain unresolved about direct liquefaction.

The future contribution of synthetic fuels to the energy economy of North America is difficult to estimate with any degree of accuracy. The US government in 1979 set a target of 1 million– $1\frac{1}{2}$ million barrels a day by 1990 but many energy authorities regard a figure of 500 000 barrels as being more realistic.

Severance taxes: Conflict between energy-rich and energy-poor states

An increasing number of states have imposed taxes (severance taxes) on energy sources produced within their borders. Although this practice was initiated in 1846 by Michigan it has only been since the mid-1970s that energy-poor states have become alarmed by the issue. Their reason for concern has been the unprecedented high rate of severance taxes levied by the new western coal-producing states.

Montana increased its tax rates to 30 per cent in 1975. The rate for Wyoming stands at 17 per cent. Together the two states hold about 60 per cent of the country's low-sulphur coal which electric utilities in the Middle West use heavily. The consuming states are angry at having to pay for energy at rates considerably above free market prices and have lobbied the federal government to limit the rate of severance taxes, particularly when imposed on energy sources recovered from federal lands.

The energy-producing states view the issue differently. Montana which has already had bitter experience of a copper-mining bust has set aside 50 per cent of all severance taxes in a trust fund designed to correct unforeseen environmental damage and broaden the state's economic base. Severance taxes are thus designed to ensure (in the view of producing states) a more even distribution of benefits from energy exploitation between producers and consumers.

Thirty-three states imposed severance taxes on non-renewable energy production in 1981 although 80 per cent of such revenue accrued to five energy-rich states, Texas, Alaska, Louisiana, Oklahoma and New Mexico. Wyoming and Montana ranked eighth and tenth respectively. Texas's total severance tax revenue of $2.2 billion in 1981 came almost totally from a 4.6 per cent tax on petroleum and a 7.5 per cent tax on natural gas.

Natural gas: US looks to Canada and Mexico

The production of natural gas has expanded rapidly in the post-Second World War period to rank as the second major energy source in the United States and the third in Canada supplying 26.9 per cent and 22 per cent respectively of total energy in 1980. However, while reserves and production have steadily increased in Canada, critical shortages have occurred in the United States from the early 1970s, as demand has outstripped supply.

The United States is still by far the world's largest producer and consumer of natural gas, accounting for 34.6 per cent of world production in 1980 with a total of 574 billion cubic metres. Production rose rapidly in the 1950s and 1960s as regions distant from the major areas of production were connected to the expanding pipeline network. By 1960 production reached 361 billion cubic metres (75.5 per cent of world production) but as the lack of new discoveries became critical peak production was reached in 1973 at 641 billion cubic metres (Figure 8.10).

Canadian production in 1980 was 76 billion cubic metres, 5.9 per cent of world production (fifth in world ranking) and well above the level of domestic demand.

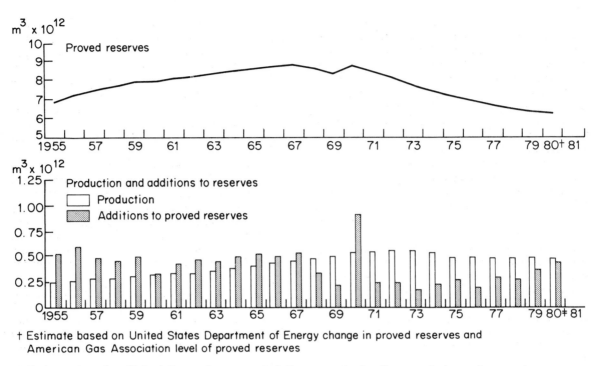

† Estimate based on United States Department of Energy change in proved reserves and
American Gas Association level of proved reserves

‡ Estimate based on United States Department of Energy production figure and change in proved reserves

Fig. 8.10 *US natural gas; reserves, production and additions to reserves 1955–80 (Source: American Gas Association and US Department of Energy)*

Texas and Louisiana dominate US production, accounting for 35.5 per cent and 35 per cent of the 1980 total respectively. Alberta produced 94 per cent of Canadian gas in the same year.

In response to contrasting demand and supply situations exports of natural gas from Canada to the United States have steadily increased. In 1980 21 billion cubic metres of western Canadian gas was sold to California, Mid-western and Great Lakes customers under Canadian government permit agreements. This amounted to over one-quarter of total Canadian production.

Mexico also exports natural gas to the United States. Although the volume of gas from Mexico has been extremely low in the past, recent new discoveries south of the Rio Grande are beginning to change the situation. In 1980 Mexico exported a total of 3 billion cubic metres to the United States.

It seems likely that this movement of gas will increase significantly in the future as the Mexican Petroleum Institute estimate that large surpluses will be available for some time and the United

States is really the only viable market. In total the US imports about 5 per cent of its gas supply, almost all of it from its immediate neighbours.

Like other energy sources, natural gas has not escaped government regulation. Since 1954 the US Federal Power Commission has controlled the price of all gas crossing state boundaries. The result has been that the price of inter-state gas has been kept well below that of intra-state gas. Low prices have greatly encouraged demand but have given little stimulus to the energy companies to invest in further exploration. And thus many energy experts argue that current shortages in the US are artificial rather than real and a result of short-sighted and misguided government policy.

In a belated effort to use the price mechanism to encourage conservation the US government began to deregulate gas prices in 1979 with the introduction of the Natural Gas Policy Act. The process will be complete by 1985.

Rising well-head prices in Canada provided the necessary catalyst for a huge and unprecedented expansion in drilling in Alberta and north-eastern British Columbia. As a result, proven reserves are greater than at any other time in the past, reaching in 1980, 1.6 trillion cubic metres in Alberta alone.

In spite of increasing reserves the Canadian government still maintains a cautious approach to energy exports believing that Canada will use increasing volumes of gas at home, in part to replace costly oil imports into the Maritime Provinces and Quebec. Extension of the existing natural gas pipeline first to Quebec and later to the Maritime Provinces began in late 1980.

The popularity of natural gas in so many markets is due primarily to the fact that it is relatively inexpensive and an environmentally attractive source of power.

However natural gas is extremely difficult to store economically. This creates inelasticity of supply which has led to major shortages in the United States in the 1970s.

Figure 8.4 indicates that the relative contribution of natural gas to US energy is falling and will continue to do so in the coming decades even with the flow of Alaskan gas from the mid or late 1980s. The proposed 7 725 km Alaskan pipeline, although approved by the US and Canadian governments in 1977, remains to be started because of various financial delays.

Gas has also been located in the Mackenzie Delta–Beaufort Sea area and large amounts of natural gas are known to exist in and around the Arctic Islands. Off the eastern coast of Canada there are indications of gas in several locations including Sable Island and the Labrador Shelf. If development is to take place in the Arctic and other frontier areas market prices will have to be high enough to make very expensive delivery systems from these remote areas economically viable.

Offshore development in locations like the Labrador Shelf pose much greater difficulties than in the Gulf of Mexico from which large amounts of gas are already obtained. Deep water, icebergs and pack ice will effectively hinder delivery until the 1990s, that is if the resource is deemed to be large enough for economic exploitation.

The United States especially is also looking to other sources of supply. Liquefied natural gas has made a small contribution since 1968 when supplies arrived in New England from Algeria to help meet peak winter demand.

Gas exists dissolved in salty water in geopressu-

rised water reservoirs, 3600 metres or more below the surface but at present market prices exploitation is not viable. A significant amount of gas also exists in coal seams but extraction might endanger future mining operations and create complex legal difficulties.

In the short term the most promising prospects are in eastern shale and western tight sands. Commercial extraction from both sources is already in operation.

233 000 square km of shale beds lie in the Appalachian Mountain region. The gas trapped in these beds is in rock that is relatively impermeable so that when a well is sunk gas seeps out very slowly over many decades. Methods now in use speed up this process by enlarging fissures in the rock and allowing greater volumes of gas to reach the surface. Similar methods are employed in the western tight sands.

As deregulation progresses and gas prices rise to a truer market value supply will become more and more diverse within the United States. In addition the US will come to rely more heavily on exports from Canada and Mexico in the 1980s and beyond.

Nuclear power: Hiatus after Three Mile Island 2

Nuclear power is one of the most emotive issues in North American life and politics today. The crux of the nuclear debate is that the electric utilities regard the nuclear programme as a safe, clean and the only viable means of coping with the rising pressure of demand, while the opposition lobby view the extension of nuclear power as a serious and unnecessary gamble with the environmental future of the nation.

The depth of involvement of the industrialised nations in the early stages of nuclear power generation was determined largely by their wartime experience in the nuclear field and the level of their domestic energy resources in the immediate postwar period. Compared to the United Kingdom there was no outstanding shortage of fossil fuel in North America and consequently few nuclear power stations were commissioned in the 1950s and early 1960s. But the large expansion in the nuclear programme, started in 1965 and 1966,

Fig. 8.11 Nuclear Power in the United States and Canada 1980

Regional breakdown	On-line (MW)	Under construction (MW)	Total (MW)
New England	4 219 (7)	4 600 (4)	8 819
Middle Atlantic	10 627 (13)	11 396 (11)	22 023
South Atlantic	13 669 (17)	18 830 (18)	32 499
East North Central	10 925 (16)	19 044 (19)	29 969
East South Central	5 209 (5)	19 256 (16)	24 465
West North Central	3 356 (6)	3 450 (3)	6 806
West South Central	1 748 (2)	10 145 (9)	11 893
Mountain	330 (1)	3 810 (3)	4 140
Pacific	4 729 (6)	8 283 (7)	13 012
Ontario	5 248 (10)	2 048 (4)	7 296
Quebec	250 (1)	638 (1)	888
New Brunswick	–	633 (1)	633

(Number of units in brackets).

resulted in a greatly increased generating capacity commissioned in 1969 and 1970, primarily in the United States.

By late 1970 the total installed nuclear generating capacity in the United States equalled that of the United Kingdom at about 5000 MW. In contrast Canada had only two operational nuclear units, one of which was experimental, with a combined capacity of 240 MW. In the 1970s the United States has steadily increased its world lead in terms of installed capacity in spite of the mounting number of problems which have confronted the electric utilities in their bid to 'go nuclear'.

By early 1980 a total of 73 nuclear units were 'on line' in the United States with a combined generating capacity of 55 000 MW. In addition, construction permits had been granted by the Nuclear Regulatory Commission for a further 90 units which would increase the nuclear generating capacity of the United States by 99 000 MW.

Canadian operational nuclear capacity totalled 5 448 MW in early 1980. Ten of the eleven units were located in Ontario with the remaining unit at Gentilly in Quebec. At this time four additional units were under construction in Ontario and one each in Quebec and New Brunswick. Construction of a further eight units in Ontario is planned for completion during the 1980s.

The spatial distribution of 'on-line' and under construction nuclear generating capacity in the United States and Canada is illustrated in Figure 8.11. Significant regional variations are apparent and although the reasons behind these variations are sometimes complex, three dominant causal factors can be discerned: (i) regional demand and rate of increase, (ii) regional availability of fossil fuels and hydro-electric sites and (iii) the power of environmental groups.

The second factor itemised goes a long way to explain Ontario's dominant position in Canadian nuclear power.

In the United States the South Atlantic region stands out clearly as the leader in this field. The region's nuclear programme is geared to a rapid rate of expansion for two important reasons. The South Atlantic contrasts markedly with a number of regions in the United States in that it lacks substantial resources of petroleum and natural gas. Appalachian coal has had limited usage due to the effective price competitiveness of imported petroleum and the difficult problem of meeting federal requirements on sulphur dioxide pollution resulting from the burning of coal. Another impetus to the region's nuclear programme has been the 103 per cent growth in population between 1940 and 1980.

In direct contrast is the rapidly industrialising West South Central region. This region has responded very slowly to the lure of nuclear power because of, until recently, its relative abundance of petroleum and natural gas. Current awareness of

Pickering nuclear power station near Toronto

declining production of these valuable non-renewable resources is indicated by the nine nuclear units which are under construction in the region.

Opposition to the nuclear programme has revolved mainly around the issues of (i) emission of low-level radioactivity; (ii) the chances of a major nuclear accident and the possibilities of sabotage and theft by terrorist groups; (iii) nuclear waste disposal; (iv) thermal pollution; (v) nuclear performance; and (vi) general siting considerations.

In the last two decades the size of nuclear plants has increased very rapidly, with a focus on economies of scale and a reduction in the cost per kilowatt hour. Nuclear units increased in average size from 300 MW in 1962 to 1300 MW in 1977. Opponents argue that the industry has moved too fast in raising the capacity of nuclear units without the necessary backup of field experiences and many utilities are now-rethinking their nuclear strategies.

Nuclear power is under attack in virtually all states and provinces which have adopted or are contemplating adopting a nuclear programme. Opposition groups have fought for and forced referenda in a number of states in the USA although prior to 1979 pro-nuclear forces were successful with referendum victories. However in the aftermath of the Three Mile Island Unit 2 accident at Harrisburg, Pennsylvania, the future of nuclear power in North America is far from certain, particularly in the United States. Nuclear power future growth estimates have been slashed dramatically in recent years. September 1974 was the high point for America's nuclear power industry. At that time there were 239 reactors, totalling more than 237 000 MW capacity either operating, under construction or on order.

In 1980 nuclear power accounted for 11 per cent of electricity generated in the United States and 9 per cent in Canada. In world terms the two countries rank first and fifth respectively in nuclear generation.

Hydro-electric power: A re-assessment?

The role of hydro-electric power exhibits marked contrasts in the United States and Canada. While hydro-electric power is the second most important energy source in Canada, contributing 25.7 per cent to total energy in 1980 its position in the United States is much less significant, accounting for only 4.2 per cent of total energy in the same year. However in absolute terms total hydro capacity in the US is 58 000 MW while Canadian capacity is 37 000 MW.

For hydro-electric power there is a finite limit to development set by physical and climatic considerations which cannot be exceeded unless extremely complex and costly construction and technology is used. Thus once a region has utilised all its available sites it must of necessity look to other sources to satisfy rising demand. This has been the general pattern of development in the United States in the past and as a result the relative contribution of hydro-electricity has steadily declined. The same situation is now being repeated in Canada as the pressure of demand spurs on the development of alternative power sources.

These trends are amply illustrated by the recent history of electricity generation in Canada. In 1960 hydro-electricity was responsible for 93 per cent of all electricity production. By 1977 its share fell to 69.5 per cent with an estimated further drop to 53 per cent in 1990.

In some regions where relief is very subdued hydro-electricity has never, even in the early stages of power development, played an important role. The East North Central region of the United States is perhaps the best example with only 1000 MW of hydro capacity in 1980, a figure which has remained almost unchanged since 1950. By way of comparison the Pacific region, which is by far the most important for hydro-electricity boasts 33 000 MW of hydro capacity. The Federal Energy Regulatory Commission estimates that the US, has an undeveloped capacity of about 110 000 MW, about 60 per cent of which is located in the Pacific division.

In Canada, Quebec is richest in water power resources with over 40 per cent of the national total. The province also has the most developed capacity. Substantial amounts of water power have been developed in all provinces except Prince Edward Island where there are no major rivers. The hydro-electric plant at Churchill Falls in Labrador, with its 5225 MW capacity is the largest single generating plant of any type in the world.

Recent advances in extra-high voltage transmission techniques have given impetus to the development of hydro-electric sites previously considered too remote. After many years of controversy the world's second biggest hydro project opened in October 1979 at James Bay, Quebec. The first phase, due to be completed in 1985, will double Quebec's present electricity capacity. The development comprises five large construction sites strung along the La Grande River on the eastern side of James Bay. It involves the construction of three giant power houses, 33 generators, 80 dykes, 7 dams and 1600 km of road, the diversion of 4 rivers and the creation of 6 lakes.

With the high cost of fossil fuels and nuclear power, hydro power is receiving renewed interest (primarily in the Pacific and New England divisions) particularly the refurbishing and reactivating of retired low-head, low-capacity power dams that were considered, until recently, uneconomical to operate.

In 1980 the United States and Canada ranked first and second in the world respectively in water power consumption, followed by the USSR, Japan and Norway.

Resources for the future

1. Geothermal power

Geothermal energy is the natural heat contained in the earth's crust in the forms of steam, hot water and hot rocks. However, only the former two sources have as yet proved to be technically and commercially viable.

Geothermal reservoirs result from a natural heat transfer circuit within the earth's crust. Ground water percolating down to depths of several kilometres settles in permeable rocks and is heated due to the earth's geothermal gradient which is the rate at which rock temperature rises as the depth below the surface increases. The average value for the earth's crust is $25°-30°C$ per km but values of $80°C$ per km are found at the edges of the tectonic plates. Thus while deposits of hot water and steam occur in many parts of the world they are mostly found in areas of tectonic activity.

In both North America and the world as a whole the use of geothermal energy is relatively insignificant but it may prove to be a most important source in the future. The geothermal heat in the outer 10 km of the earth's crust under the United States alone is estimated at about 1 000 times the heat contained in the total United States coal resources. Although most of this vast store of energy is too diffuse to be exploited economically a reasonable amount is concentrated and is probably recoverable with present day and near future technology.

In the use of geothermal energy to produce electricity the United States leads a group of seven nations (Italy, Mexico, New Zealand, Japan, USSR and Iceland) with a 1979 installed generation capacity of 608 MW. By comparison the largest individual fossil fuel and nuclear power stations have capacities in excess of 1 000 MW.

In the western United States, particularly along the Pacific coast, widespread and intense volcanic activity has occurred during the last few million years and thus the western states hold much promise for geothermal power development.

About 750 000 hectares of land in the western states have now been classified as being within Known Geothermal Resource Areas (KGRAs), with California, Nevada and New Mexico indicated as the leading states.

The production of geothermal electricity in the US and Canada is at present totally confined to The Geysers in Sonoma County, California which began operation in 1960. The plant's twelfth unit came 'on line' in 1979 and exploration for additional geothermal steam more than one and a half kilometres underground is continuing. The potential capacity of the field is estimated at about 2 000 MW when all the planned additional units are completed in the late 1980s. Site development is at present also taking place in the Imperial Valley in southern California and at locations in New Mexico, Utah and Idaho.

In contrast to the dry steam site at the Geysers,

development in the Imperial Valley has concentrated on using underground hot water. The programme has suffered a number of setbacks, namely financial and environmental. Federal assistance has recently been less than anticipated, while the hot water tapped is so briny that for every litre brought to the surface as much as a quarter may consist of salts and solid particles. Apart from the problem of clogging and corroding piping, environmentalists will carefully monitor the disposal of such waste.

Exploration has not been confined to the western states alone. Hot water that can be used for geothermal power has been found in an exploratory well drilled at Crisfield, Maryland, confirming the theory that geothermal energy exists under the Atlantic Coastal Plain.

Little is known about Canada's potential in terms of geothermal energy. The geophysical nature of the western Cordillera makes parts of the area suitable for geothermally heated water. Similar resources may also be found in the deep sedimentary basins of the Great Plains and Western Arctic.

The construction cost of a geothermal plant is only 65–75 per cent of that of a comparable fossil fuel plant. The saving is related to the absence of a boiler and the lack of the related complication of fuel handling and combustion.

Considered against existing alternatives geothermal energy appears extremely attractive because apart from the cost factor the use of natural steam involves very little environmental impact. However a major problem is the location of the resource. Some 75 per cent of presently known resources are on government-owned land, mostly National Parks. Will it be possible for these resources to be used without detracting from the natural beauty of such areas?

Undoubtedly, expansion in the use of geothermal power will not be confined to dry steam and hot water sites, but will eventually also involve the exploitation of hot dry rocks. However earlier forecasts that geothermal energy might produce 5 per cent of US energy by 1985 are now more applicable to the end of the century.

2. Solar energy

Research into the direct use of solar energy has progressed much further in the USA than in

Modules of solar photovoltaic cells being installed at the Lovington Square Shopping Centre in Lovington, New Mexico, in a solar energy research project funded by the US Dept of Energy

Canada due to a combination of latitudinal variations and the greater severity of the energy problem in the USA. The use of solar energy for space heating has achieved a reasonable level of practicality in both countries although costs are still generally higher, especially in Canada, compared to conventional methods. However, it is the generation of electricity through solar energy that is the most important goal for the future.

The latitudinal variations in the receipt of solar radiation are extremely large, with the southwestern United States receiving approximately 80 per cent more radiant energy per year than northern Canada. It has been estimated that 46×10^{18} kilojoules per year of solar energy reach the surface of the United States. Total US consumption of electrical energy could be supplied by 0.15 per cent of this solar energy if it could be used at 10 per cent efficiency.

In spite of the relatively high intensity of solar energy in the southern United States, in terms of power generation sunlight is a diffuse, low density energy source. The most advanced system developed to date to overcome the problem of the collection of solar energy is based on the 'central receiver' concept.

'Solar One', sited near Barstow, California, is the world's largest solar power station. 1818 computer-controlled mirrors (heliostats) follow the sun across the sky focussing its reflection on a boiler (central receiver) mounted on a 73 metre high tower. Each heliostat has a surface area of 49 square metres. Solar One, which cost $140 million can generate 10 MW of power.

The US Department of Energy and a number of electric utilities are also actively engaged in developing the use of solar cells which convert the sun's energy directly into electricity by photovoltaic, thermoelectric and thermionic means. However at present, costs are way above what they have to be in order to compete with nuclear or fossil plants.

A problem with both systems is that peak electrical consumption, summer or winter, comes in the early evening when solar energy is at a very low ebb. Thus without efficient storage solar energy cannot provide for peak load periods. Several techniques for storing solar energy are in various stages of development.

The problem of storage could be by-passed by the use of solar power satellites but it is unlikely that sufficient progress will be made until well beyond the year 2000.

Estimates of the future contribution of solar energy vary widely but it appears unlikely that a figure of more than 10 per cent will be reached by the year 2000.

3. Wind energy

Wind energy conversion systems have been used for centuries but they have been largely disregarded in the last fifty years or so for economic reasons. By 1850 windmills in the United States represented the equivalent of burning more than 10 million tonnes of coal. From 1890 wind driven devices linked to generators started providing electricity on a small scale but such projects were largely abandoned in the wake of much larger scale hydro and fossil fuel generators.

Prior to the 1970s the world's largest wind turbine (1.25 MW) operated between 1941–45 at Grandpa's Knob in Vermont, but damage which occurred in the latter year was never repaired.

However, the changing economics of energy have led to the need to re-examine the possibilities of the large-scale use of wind energy. In 1975 NASA began operating a 100 kW wind generator near Sandusky, Ohio, to be followed by a number of similar projects in other parts of the United States and Canada. In recent years 'wind farms' have been developed whereby a large number of wind turbines are sited together. One facility east of San Francisco will eventually have 300 turbines capable of generating a total of 16 800 kW.

As with any other source of energy, wind power poses a number of problems. Its diffuse nature requires construction of very large units which have a marked visual impact on the landscape. As with solar energy, its intermittent supply requires the development of suitable storage systems unless of course wind turbines are linked to conventional grids and used in conjunction with thermal back-up systems.

An important advantage in North America is that wind movements are at their strongest during the winter months which correspond to the peak demand period for energy supplies. In the frontier areas of northern Canada wind turbines may soon have favourable capital costs competitive with existing diesel-electric systems because of the cost of transporting diesel fuel. However in general capital costs are substantially higher than for conventional plants and thus the widespread adoption of wind energy systems necessitates considerable technological development.

The Wind Energy Systems Act (1980) has initiated an 8 year, $900 million programme to develop cost-effective wind power in the United States.

4. Ocean and tidal power

In North America and worldwide there exists only a limited number of sites where there is both an adequate tidal range and a marginal basin that can be enclosed by a barrage to provide sufficient power from waves. France and the Soviet Union had the only two tidal schemes operational in the early 1980s.

With financial support from the federal government, Nova Scotia is embarking on a tidal power demonstration project on the Bay of Fundy, one of the world's best tidal sites. The 20 MW plant is being built on the Annapolis Basin and is due to come on-stream in mid-1983. The Bay of Fundy has 37 possible power development sites, ranging in size from 50 to 10 000 MW. In theory they could be developed without interfering with each other. A decision on large scale development in the Bay of Fundy is expected by 1985.

The United States Department of Energy is currently researching the possibility of submerging multitudes of gigantic turbines in the Gulf Stream to extract electrical energy from the ocean current. The Department of Energy is also examining the economics of ocean thermal energy conversion (OTEC) which involves the extraction of energy from the oceans, using temperature differences between warm surface water and colder deep water to generate power. Such schemes require a sizeable temperature gradient and therefore the Gulf of Mexico and the Hawaian islands are the most favourable locations.

In fact the world's first at-sea power plant was commissioned in 1979 just off the coast of Hawaii. The 50 kW floating plant, called Mini-OTEC, will use warm surface water and cold subsurface water to vapourise and condense ammonia in a closed system, which, functioning as a heat engine, will power a turbine generator.

The Department of Energy (US) estimates that by the year 2000, OTEC could replace 400 000 barrels of oil a day.

5. Bioconversion

Bioconversion is the general descriptive term used to encompass a number of processes through which organic materials can be converted into useful forms of energy. By 1980 bioconversion made only a minute contribution to energy in North America but it has significant potential for the future.

In the American mid-west alcohol is distilled from surplus crops and blended with gasoline to form 'gasohol'. The mixture of 10 per cent alcohol and 90 per cent gasoline is sold directly to motorists in many of the mid-western states. However, even though production is increasing, gasohol contributed less than 1 per cent to total petrol consumption in 1980.

While bioconversion provides a useful outlet for surplus crop production large scale processing would require a vast area of cropped land to be set aside for energy utilisation. To substitute 10 per cent of the energy currently obtained from petroleum in the United States would require cultivation of an area the size of New Mexico. Large amounts of waste are also generated which would present major environmental problems with a greatly increased scale of operations.

Energy can also be obtained from municipal refuse as well as agricultural and silvicultural wastes.

A number of American cities are now exploiting such sources. In St Louis a waste conversion plant produces dry, shredded fuel from municipal rubbish. It is used as a supplement to pulverised coal in a local power plant. In Los Angeles methane gas is extracted from waste material and used in a

nearby power plant. A number of other schemes are either in operation or under construction in North America.

While it is unlikely that bioconversion will ever become a major contribution to the energy economies of the United States and Canada it does have reasonable potential in providing a useful additional energy source in many areas.

Energy and the environment: A case study of electricity generation in California

The rising tide of environmental awareness in the United States has increasingly focused its attention on the electricity generating industry over the last decade. Heavy criticism has been launched, not only against the nuclear sector, but also against the conventional methods of generation which have been accused of causing unacceptably high levels of atmospheric pollution.

California has consistently ranked as one of the major electricity producing states and is undoubtedly one of the focal points in the environmental debate. Argument has chiefly revolved around the twin issues of power plant location and the means of electricity generation.

These two factors have brought the industry into conflict with the growing array of environmental groups in the state. The contention is that opposition to the utilities plans has not only been the result of pseudo-intellectual awareness of a passing social fad. Rather it has been jolted into action by major locational and organisational changes that have characterised the industry in recent years.

The spatial arrangement of California's generating capacity in 1950 is shown by Figure 8.12. Of the 19 counties (out of a total of 58) situated along the state's 1 726 km coastline only 6 contained any generating capacity. Inland, the Sierra Nevada Mountains were the main area of concentration with others notably clustered in southern California along the valleys of southwesterly draining rivers.

However, from the environmental standpoint it is not only the number and location of power

Moving lineman from tower to tower by helicopter, Ontario

plants that is important but also their type. In 1950, one hundred hydro plants had a combined capacity of 2423.8 MW while the remaining 18 thermal plants combined capacity was 6332 MW. This difference was due to two factors. The thermal plants (oil and gas) were generally of more recent construction when generating technology was at a more advanced stage and also hydro capacity is to a great degree limited by the physical characteristics of the site and the velocity and volume of the river concerned.

Nuclear and geothermal power were not commercially exploited in California in 1950. Coal was not used in thermal power plants at the time due to the state's great distance from the then major coal producing regions. High transport costs meant that coal was not competitive in price with oil and natural gas.

Between 1950 and 1976, total installed capacity not only quadrupled but major changes took place in both the location and type of plant operating. In number, hydro plants were still dominant, ac-

Fig. 8.12 *The location of Californian power plants in 1950*

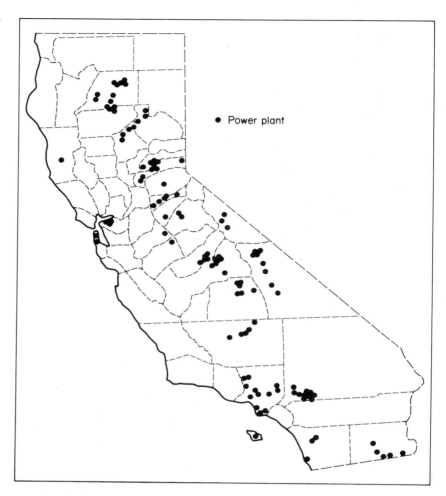

counting for 169 of the 235 operational plants, yet they contributed less than 25 per cent to total capacity. The average capacity of hydro plants increased from 24.2 MW to 48.5 MW between 1950 and 1976 compared to an increase in thermal plants from 351.7 MW to 421.7 MW in the same period. Although the percentage rate of increase for thermal plants was relatively small, in absolute terms it was three times as great.

By 1976 six geothermal plants in the Cloverdale district of Sonoma County were in production along with three nuclear power plants. The state still lacked coal-fired plants although the causal factors behind this absence had changed significantly. The exploitation of large quantities of low-sulphur coal in the nearby mountain states now makes this source an attractive proposition to the California utilities due to the rising cost of im-

ported oil. However air pollution controls in the state are so severe that any proposed coal-fired plant would require the most sophisticated and expensive anti-pollution equipment available. In addition, vociferous environmental groups will be reluctant to allow a precedent to be set by the construction of a coal-fired plant.

Figure 8.13, illustrating the geographical location of all power plants constructed between 1951 and 1976 shows a much more marked cluster distribution, compared to pre-1951 location. In northern and central California further development took place in the Sierra Nevada while in southern California the coastline began to assume a leading role in power plant location. To combat such development, California's long coastline has recently become a restricted area for power plant siting and other construction.

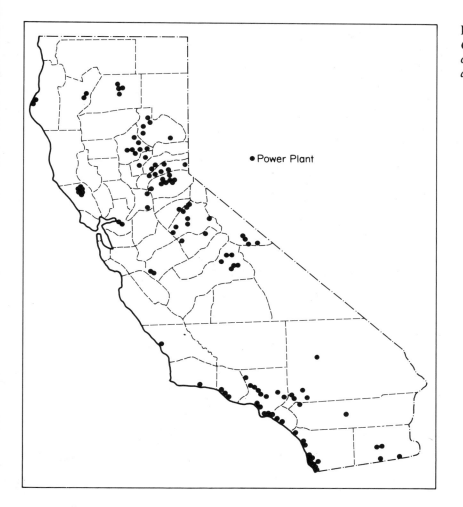

Fig. 8.13 *The location of Californian power plants constructed between 1951 and 1976*

• Power Plant

Analysis of Figures 8.12, 8.13 and 8.14 indicates that there is a marked relationship betweeen population density and electricity generating capacity. From the points mentioned above one might expect that this relationship had become stronger since 1950. However, the extent of this relationship cannot be measured accurately by visual examination of maps alone and suitable statistical analysis is required if meaningful conclusions are sought. Using the Product Moment Correlation Coefficient the relationship between electricity generating capacity and population by county was correlated for 1950, 1960, 1970 and 1976. High correlations were recorded in all cases with a continuous upward trend. The resultant correlation co-efficients were: 0.734 for 1950, 0.862 for 1960, 0.878 for 1970 and 0.884 for 1976

(all results above the 0.1 per cent probability level).

The public's awareness of the environmental effects of power production has obviously been heightened due to both major trends: increasing proximity to urban areas and the rising preponderance of thermal power plants in recent decades. To combat these trends severe restrictions have been imposed by state and regional authorities.

The areas open to power plant development are rapidly declining. Apart from the coastal zone, location in state, regional, county and city parks; wilderness, scenic or natural reserves; areas for wildlife protection, recreation, historic preservation, or natural preservation areas is forbidden unless the utility concerned can prove that there will be no substantial adverse environmental

Fig. **8.14** *California: population density by county*

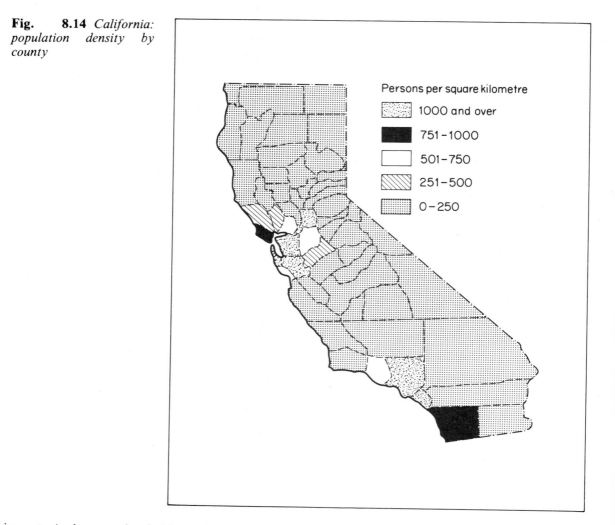

Persons per square kilometre

1000 and over

751–1000

501–750

251–500

0–250

impact. And as much of this land is in public ownership, power plant siting is virtually impossible in these areas.

In addition to the exclusion of coal-fired power stations state law prohibits the burning of oil with more than 0.5 per cent sulphur content and thus Californian utilities are forced to buy the most expensive oil on the world market.

Nuclear power has also come under severe attack in California, resulting in long delays in construction and numerous cancellations. In a survey of nuclear generation in California in 1971 (*Geography*, Nov. 1971) P. F. Mason noted that two plants were operative, one was under construction and a further nine were in the planning stage. Due primarily to intense pressure from

environmental groups resulting in lengthy judicial proceedings and the refusal of permits by regulating bodies the nine planned nuclear units have all since been cancelled. The only addition to operating nuclear capacity has been the Rancho Seco plant located inland in Contra Costa county which came 'on line' in 1975.

However the 2 190 MW two unit Diablo Canyon complex, which Mason noted was in the planning stage, has been completed but is awaiting clearance to commence operation. The $2.3 billion plant has been the longest delayed power plant in the history of electricity generation in the United States. Also, two extra units are under construction at the San Onofre plant, one of the two units operating in 1971.

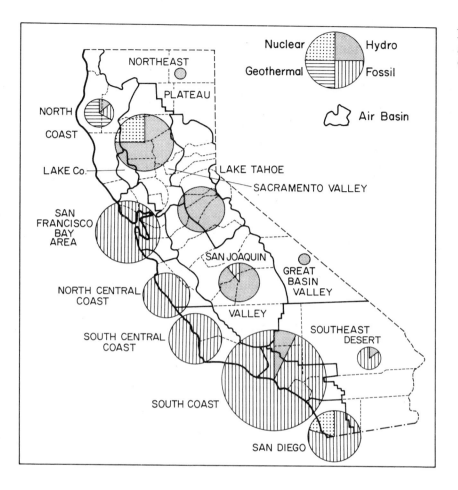

Fig. 8.15 *Power production by source in Californian air basins*

The contribution of thermal power plants to air pollution is debatable. The electric utilities estimate that on average power plants only cause 3 per cent of air pollution compared to the 86 per cent of the motor car. The environmental lobby view the problem more seriously, arguing that the utilities air pollution estimate is much too low and that average pollution levels bear no resemblance to those found around large thermal power plants.

What is clear is that thermal plants are heavily concentrated in areas of high population density where air pollution has reached extremely high levels. The California Air Resources Board has identified five 'critical air basins' where levels of air pollution are well above acceptable standards. The critical air basins (Figure 8.15) are the South Coast, San Diego, San Francisco Bay area, the Sacramento Valley and San Joaquin Valley. The South Coast air basin not only has the greatest installed capacity at 12 232 MW but also the most thermal capacity, accounting for 93.6 per cent of generation in this region.

The environmental costs of energy production then are strongly concentrated in the coastal counties with a marked emphasis in southern California. There seems to be little doubt that in order to cope with increasing demand the electric utilities will want to expand primarily in the more heavily populated regions in order to keep costs to a minimum. It will be interesting to note in future years if the growing array of restrictions placed on the industry will in fact reverse this situation and witness the increasing development of electricity generation in sparsely populated regions.

Non-fuel minerals

The same basic dichotomy between the United States and Canada exists for the non-fuel sector as it does for fuels in that the intense pressure of demand has necessitated rapidly increasing imports into the United States, while Canada remains a very significant net exporter.

Excluding fuels, the remaining range of minerals can be divided into metals and non-metals. Although concentrations of very intense activity are apparent, mining is undoubtedly a truly national industry in both the United States and Canada, affecting to some degree every state and province, with operations stretching from the Atlantic to the Pacific and from the Gulf of Mexico to the inhospitable Arctic.

1. Metallic minerals

The United States: a crisis on the horizon?

The United States is now heavily reliant on foreign sources for the supply of essential metallic minerals as Figure 8.16 indicates. However the mining industry has had to contend with a growing array of problems which have limited investment in many major and potentially significant source regions.

A number of factors have combined to slow down new mineral development in the less developed world. These include rapidly rising costs, new threats to the security of investment and the problems of organising a satisfactory distribution of the risks and benefits among the many differing interests involved.

In the twentieth century the United States steadily strengthened mineral investment abroad, much of which was channelled into areas ruled by the European powers where trading conditions were firmly established in favour of the industrialised nations.

The 1950s and 1960s witnessed the dawning of political independance for numerous parts of the less developed world and during the latter decade the rate of mineral investment paused as the conditions of trade were renegotiated or abruptly altered with resultant hefty cost increases for the industrialised world.

The decreasing attractiveness for investment in the less developed world resulted by the early 1970s in a resurgence of activity in four regions of the non-Communist world, the United States, Canada, Australia and South Africa.

A totally different but equally effective set of obstacles is hindering the exploitation of indigen-

The Faraday uranium mine eastern Ontario near Bancroft

ous resources in North America and causing acute concern about possible future shortages.

Environmental legislation has virtually closed many parts of the United States to mineral exploitation while at the same time heavily raising the cost per unit of extraction as the mining companies comply with stringent new anti-pollution regulations.

The awakening of an environmentally percept-ive populace has greatly restricted access to poten-

Fig. 8.16 Net US imports of selected minerals and metals as per cent of apparent consumption, 1960 to 1980, and by major foreign sources, 1976–1979

[In percent. Figures based on net imports which equal the difference between imports and exports plus or minus government stockpile and industry stock changes]

Mineral	1960	1970	1980 prel.	Rank of major foreign sources 1976–1979
Columbium	100	100	100	Brazil, Canada, Thailand.
Mica (sheet)	94	100	100	India, Brazil, Madagascar.
Strontium	100	100	100	Mexico.
Manganese	89	95	97	South Africa, Gabon, Brazil, France.
Tantalum	94	96	97	Thailand, Canada, Malaysia, Brazil.
Bauxite[1]	74	88	94	Jamaica, Australia, Guinea.
Cobalt	66	98	93	Zaire, Belgium—Luxembourg, Zambia, Finland.
Chromium	85	89	91	South Africa, Philippines, Soviet Union, Turkey.
Platinum group	82	78	87	Rep. of South Africa, Soviet Union, United Kingdom.
Tin	82	81	84	Malaysia, Bolivia, Thailand, Indonesia.
Asbestos	94	83	76	Canada, Rep. of South Africa
Nickel	72	71	73	Canada, Norway, New Caledonia, Dominican Republic.
Potassium	(2)	42	62	Canada, Israel.
Cadmium	13	7	62	Canada, Australia, Mexico, Belgium—Luxembourg.
Zinc	46	54	58	Canada, Spain, Mexico, Honduras.
Tungsten	32	50	54	Canada, Bolivia, Thailand, Rep. of Korea.
Antimony	43	40	53	South Africa, Bolivia, China Mainland, Mexico.
Mercury	25	41	49	Spain, Algeria, Italy, Canada, Yugoslavia.
Titanium[3]	22	24	47	Australia, Canada, Rep. of South Africa.
Selenium	25	11	40	Canada, Japan, Yugoslavia.
Barium	45	45	38	Peru, Ireland, Mexico, Morocco.
Gypsum	35	39	38	Canada, Mexico, Jamaica.
Petroleum[4]	17	22	37	Saudi Arabia, Nigeria, Venezuela, Libya, Algeria.
Gold	56	59	28	Canada, Soviet Union, Switzerland.
Iron ore	18	30	22	Canada, Venezuela, Brazil, Liberia.
Vanadium	(2)	21	15	Rep. of South Africa, Chile, Canada.
Copper	(2)	(2)	14	Canada, Chile, Zambia, Peru.
Iron and steel	(2)	4	13	Japan, Europe, Canada.
Sulphur	(2)	(2)	13	Canada, Mexico.
Natural gas	1	4	5	Canada, Algeria.
Aluminium	(2)	(2)	(2)	Canada, Ghana.
Silver	43	26	(2)	Canada, Mexico, Peru, United Kingdom.

— Represents zero   [1] Includes aluminia   [2] Net exports.   [3] Limenite   [4] Includes crude and products.

tially productive regions, especially those owned by the federal government. Approximately one-third of the total land area of the United States is federally owned. About half of this land is in Alaska while most of the remaining lands are in 11 contiguous western states, which constitute the key mineral belt of the United States (Figure 8.17).

By 1968, 17 per cent of all federal lands had been withdrawn from mining and exploration activities. Withdrawal of land started to accelerate in 1968 and by the late 1970s some three-quarters of all federal land had been closed to mining.

Where reserves are lacking, efforts are being made to substitute one alloy for another or to develop low grade ores. The utilisation of lower grade ores means on the one hand that greater amounts of material have to be moved and extracted for a given unit of metal and on the other hand there is a growing problem of waste disposal.

Another major problem is also emerging. If surface mining is further extended to areas with fragile ecosystems the rehabilitation of land after mining becomes a much more difficult task.

Costs of mineral production have risen significantly due to the increasing requirements for pollution control and because of the long time needed to obtain the necessary permits from various authorities, and have heavily outpaced the general level of inflation.

Economic mineral deposits which constitute only a small fraction of the earth's crust are increasingly difficult to discover in North America. Most of the easily discovered deposits have been developed and thus the industry must explore frontier regions and be prepared to mine to greater depths. Both factors require extremely high levels of investment.

The United States, like several other industrialised nations, is becoming increasingly resource poor and heavily reliant on other nations as

Fig. 8.17 *Mineral belts of the United States (Source: US Bureau of Mines)*

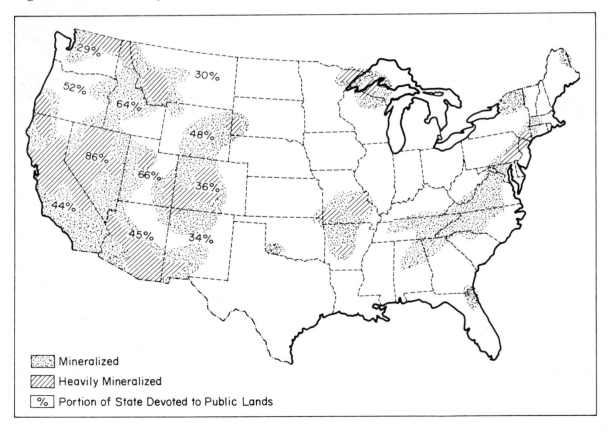

Aerial view of open-pit copper mine, Craigmont, British Columbia

Figure 8.16 indicates. Estimates by the US Bureau of Mines for the remainder of the century show that the position will probably deteriorate further. In projecting the ratios of identified reserves to cumulative demand 1974 to 2000 the Bureau estimates a positive balance for only five out of twenty-one metals.

In 1974 the Council of International Economic Policy submitted a list of critical minerals to the government which are essential to US engineering. Included were the following: aluminium, chromium, platinum, iron ore, nickel, manganese, zinc, tin, titanium, cobalt, tungsten, lead, columbium, vanadium and copper. With the exception of iron ore, lead, vanadium and copper, the United States is currently importing more than half of its requirement.

The greatest anticipated increases are expected to be for columbium, aluminium, vanadium, titanium and tungsten. Annual growth rates for these metals are expected to range from 4.9 per cent for tungsten to 5.6 per cent for columbium.

The demand for columbium rose from 3.9 million lb in 1965 to more than 6 million lb in 1976 with an anticipated increase to 23.6 million lb by the year 2000. This increase is primarily due to columbium's use in HSLA steels, providing steels with improved mechanical properties and higher strength-to-weight ratios. At present the United States is almost totally dependent on imports. Expensive to process, low quality ores occur in Colorado and Utah but apart from the prohibitive cost there is not enough to last more than twenty years.

Vanadium is mainly used as a strengthening agent for a variety of steels. Although consumption grew slowly from 6500 tonnes in 1965 to about 8800 tonnes in 1976, the projected demand is 30 000 tonnes by 2000. More than 40 per cent is presently imported from South Africa and Chile. However the relative role of imports for vanadium has in fact decreased having been at a level of 99 per cent in the mid-1960s. With recent technology 6 per cent vanadium can be recovered from petroleum ash.

The United States produces about 8 per cent of the world's tungsten but consumes 20 per cent. Demand is projected to increase from 15.6 million lbs in 1977 to 48 million lbs in 2000. Almost all indigenous tungsten comes from Pine Creek,

California and Leadville, Colorado. The low grade brines of Searles Lake in California offer future potential if self-sufficiency becomes a positive goal. Over 97 per cent of US cobalt consumption comes from Zaire. The worldwide scarcity of this important mineral has been reflected by its escalating price. The laterites of Oregon and northern California are potential areas of future production as rising world prices make economic production more feasible.

The position regarding chromium is causing considerable concern to US industry as there is no known substitute for chromium in stainless steel. South Africa and Zimbabwe dominate the world chromium market and will continue to do so in the coming decades and thus the uncertain political

Strip mine operations near Utica, Illinois

future of this part of the world is of great concern to the United States. In 1977 the US consumed nearly 25 per cent of world production with more than 90 per cent imported.

The United States is almost totally dependent on imports for manganese. Although indigenous reserves are available they are low grade and not cost-competitive. It seems likely that undersea mining will become an important source of manganese in the future although there are numerous legal and technical difficulties to be overcome when mining in deep international waters.

While being the world's largest copper producer the United States is also its largest consumer, thus necessitating imports. The Mountain States supply almost all of US copper production with Arizona being the main producing state. As with other metals, technological developments have made the use of lower grade ores feasible, thus increasing reserves.

The United States uses larger amounts of iron ore than any other metal and although the best grade ores have been severely depleted the nation has huge identified para- and sub-marginal resources, mainly in low grade Lake Superior ores that require beneficiation and agglomeration. Iron ore is one of the few metals where identified reserves are in excess of estimated cumulative demand to the end of the century.

As a precaution against import discontinuities the United States operates a stockpile of strategic and critical materials. The stockpile goals are based on keeping munitions factories going in a major three year war. However in 1980 the stockpile fell short of its official goals for 37 out of 62 items. In certain instances less than a 90 day supply is available.

In recognition of a possible future strategic materials crisis Congress passed the National Materials and Minerals Policy Research and Development Act in 1980, reaffirming it to be national policy to foster promotion of a strong and stable minerals industry. The decline in smelting capacity is also causing concern. For example,

Fig. 8.18 *Canada: mineral production by commodity and province*

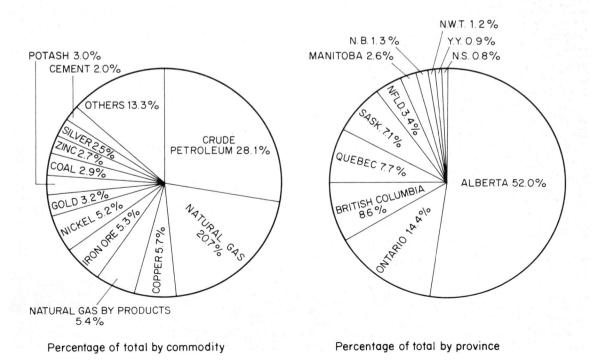

Percentage of total by commodity   Percentage of total by province

in 1969 there were 14 zinc smelters operating in the US, but by 1981 only five were left. On average 70 per cent of US requirements are imported.

Canada: a major world source region

As Figure 8.16 indicates, Canada is a major source region for US imports of metallic minerals. The metals group accounted for 30 per cent of total Canadian mineral value in 1980 and is thus an important factor in the country's balance of payments situation. Copper, iron ore, nickel, gold and zinc together formed three quarters of metal production by value. As Figure 8.18 shows, petroleum and natural gas dominate national mineral production but the total value of leading metals is very significant.

More than half Canada's non-fuel mineral production is exported to over 90 countries throughout the world with metals playing a leading role. Canada is a major world producer of a number of metals. It is first for zinc; second for nickel; third for gold; fourth for copper, lead and aluminium; fifth for silver and sixth for iron ore.

In 1980 total exports of all crude and fabricated minerals were valued at C$ 25.7 billion, made up of 39.5 per cent fuels, 35.6 per cent non-ferrous minerals, 14.4 per cent ferrous minerals and 10.5 per cent non-metallic minerals.

Figure 8.18 also illustrates the provincial breakdown of mineral production, with Alberta responsible for more than half of all production by value. The four western provinces together contribute more than 70 per cent of total mineral value, a prime factor in the economic upsurge of this region in recent times.

Canada produced 19 per cent of world zinc in 1980, mainly in Ontario, Northwest Territories and New Brunswick. Nickel mining is confined to Ontario and Manitoba. The famous Sudbury Basin of Ontario is the largest single source of nickel in the world. Gold, Canada's fourth ranking metal by value, is mined primarily in Ontario and Quebec and on a smaller scale in the Northwest Territories.

With a 1980 copper production of 708 000 tonnes Canada ranks fourth in the world. The major producing areas are in Ontario, British Columbia, Quebec and Manitoba. Copper is frequently associated with other non-ferrous metals such as nickel, zinc, lead and molybdenum.

The Labrador area of Newfoundland is Canada's largest source of iron ore with slightly over half of all production, followed by Quebec, Ontario and British Columbia. National production in 1980 was 50.9 million tonnes.

2. Non-metal minerals

This sector has become of increasing importance in North American mineral production and in the United States now contributes more by value than the metals although the situation is clearly reversed in Canada.

There are a number of significant contrasts between the mining of metals and non-metals. The non-metal group includes a number of structural materials which occur widely over North America such as cement, sand and gravel. In terms of value per tonne such materials are very much lower than the metals and therefore transport becomes a major cost determinant as with any low value, high bulk commodity. Consequently, wherever possible, production is closely allied to the points of consumption. Demand for structural materials is strongly linked with the fortunes of the construction industry and thus tends to dip more sharply than other commodities in periods of recession, as witnessed in the late 1970s and early 1980s.

The phenomenal development of the chemical industry in the post-war period has been a major stimulus to the exploitation of non-metallic minerals such as phosphate, potassium, salts, sulphur and lime. In general these minerals are far more localised than structural materials. For instance the entire US boron production comes from California, while Saskatchewan accounts for all of Canada's potash operations.

Bibliography

Mead, W. J. (1979) 'The performance of government in energy regulations', *American Economic Review*, 69, 2, pp. 352–6.

9
Transport Networks:
The Basis of a Modern Economy

The advanced economies of the United States and Canada are firmly structured around production and trade, the efficiency of both being vitally dependent on transport provision. The development of the continent from the earliest days of colonisation was characterised by an emerging division of labour and production with high levels of specialisation, acting as both a response and a stimulus to the flow of goods and people.

Stated simply, transport is the movement of product or person from a point of origin to a destination. The nature and volume of the product to be moved and the mode of transportation will be influenced by numerous interlinked factors not least of which are the level of technological development, cost competitiveness and the volume of demand. Finance is of course a necessary precondition for such an interaction.

Major investments in transport provision are not usually made unless there is a significant and well defined demand for movement. The early development of the continent, based on harvesting the products of mine, forest and soil progressed with the aid of primitive modes of transport. However the immense wealth of the interior combined with the rapid increase in population provided an overwhelming impetus to link the eastern seaboard and the interior with the new transportation technology emanating from north-west Europe. Although all the available modes of transport have played important roles in the evolution of the human geography of North America it was during the railway era that the major initial exploitation of the continent occurred (Chapter 3).

The railway network which evolved under middle to late nineteenth-century economic conditions has provided a firm foundation for US pre-eminence in the twentieth century. There can be little doubt that without the railway the diffusion of settlement across North America would have been infinitely slower with debatable subsequent repercussions on world history. Since the railway era the transport systems of the continent have undergone major transformations with both the United States and Canada remaining at the forefront of transport technology as transportation is the prerequisite that makes possible all other economic activity.

Recent trends in passenger and freight transportation

The cumulative progression of the various modes of transportation has traced a palimpsest on the North American landscape. This process has witnessed increasing rapidity in recent decades due to major technological advances and the changing cost effectiveness of competing transportation types.

Post-war trends in the United States and Canada have been generally similar although a number of important variations are apparent with regard to both passenger and freight movements. By far the greatest changes concern freight, where the relative importance of the railways has massively declined as a consequence of the developing competitiveness of roads and pipelines. Water transport has maintained its share of the market in recent decades while the movement of freight by air has increased but still only to a very small fraction of the total.

In terms of passenger transportation, post-war changes, while being most significant, have been of a lesser magnitude than freight. This is primarily due to the fact that a major transition had already taken place in the preceding inter-war period with the great surge in motor car ownership. In recent decades the dominance of the motor car has been maintained while the railways have continued their decline. The main development during this latter period has been the tremendous growth of the airways as intercity passenger carriers. Overall, the twentieth century has been a period of competing transport modes as opposed to the railway dominance of the nineteenth century.

Figure 9.1, illustrating recent trends in the United States, clearly shows the demise of the railways as freight carriers. Looking back even further than the period encapsulated by Figure 9.1, in 1916 American railways moved 77 per cent of all intercity freight. At this time, as Stover (1970) states in his major contribution to the subject *The Life and Decline of the American Railroad*, 'The dependence of the national economy upon the railroad was overwhelming.' It must be kept in mind however that the relative decrease in the railway's contribution actually masks an approximate doubling of freight carried between 1916 and 1979 and in spite of the railway's numerous and continuing problems it is still clearly the nation's major freight carrier and is likely to remain so for some time.

The railways have lost the greatest proportion of their markets to truck and pipeline operators. The pipelines, because of their generally lower unit costs, have tended to take their specialist products, oil and gas, out of the competitive reach of the other transport modes, particularly when regular bulk movement is required.

Data for Canadian freight transport is not directly comparable to that for the United States but some differences are clearly apparent.

In Canada the railways have maintained a stronger grip on freight traffic compared to their counterparts in the United States, while pipelines also account for a higher share of movement in Canada although the difference is not great.

While four major carriers are discernable for freight, the private car holds absolute dominance in inter-city passenger transport, accounting for over 80 per cent of movement in both the United States and Canada (Figure 9.2). In the United States, domestic airways now hold almost 14 per cent of inter-city traffic, compared to about 9 per cent in Canada. Another noticeable contrast is

Fig. 9.1 USA Volume of domestic intercity freight traffic 1950–1979

Mode	1950 %	1979 %
Railroads	57.4	35.9
Motor vehicles	15.8	24.3
Inland waterways	14.9	16.2
Oil pipelines	11.8	23.4
Domestic airways	0.03	0.2
Total traffic volume (billions of tonne – km)	1572	3714

Source: Transportation Association of America.

Fig. 9.2 USA Volume of domestic intercity passenger traffic 1950–1979

Mode	1950 %	1979 %
Railroads	6.39	0.8
Private automobiles	86.20	83.4
Bus	5.20	1.7
Inland waterways	0.23	0.3
Domestic airways	1.98	13.8
Total traffic volume (billions of passenger – km)	818	2483

Source: Transportation Association of America.

that the decline in bus and rail passenger transport has been more severe in the United States than its northern neighbour. Overall there has been a trend towards complementarity as termini for different modes have been linked for both passenger and freight transport, with each mode functioning where it is most cost effective.

Regional variations in transport provision

Over a vast continent exhibiting enormous variations in physical and human geography it is only to be expected that there are resultant regional differences in transportation. Such contrasts can be measured by using a variety of criteria but conclusions must be weighed carefully.

A very important aspect of any transport system is its degree of connectivity which is in effect a measure not only of transport provision but also to a certain extent of its efficiency. A simple but reasonably effective measure of connectivity is the Beta Index. The Beta Index measures connectivity by dividing the number of edges (E) or links by the number of vertices (V) or nodes, i.e.,

$$\beta = \frac{E}{V}$$

Results will fall in the range of 0.5 to 3.0 but in practice favour the lower end of the scale.

Figure 9.3 shows the connectivity of the intercity passenger rail network (AMTRAK) and the inter-state highway system for the nine major census divisions of the United States. Where edges cross a divisional boundary the point has been counted as a node because the route (edge) must eventually terminate somewhere. Clearly each census division must be treated as an open rather than a closed system. All junctions have been counted as vertices and for simplicity also, every city has been counted as a single node.

Maps of the AMTRAK and Interstate highway systems appear later in the chapter under the relevant sections.

A reasonably high level of correlation [+0.81 (above the 0.1 per cent probability level)] exists between the two transport networks in terms of regional connectivity, with the East North Central and South Atlantic regions occupying the leading positions in each case while the Mountain and

Fig. 9.3 Regional connectivity of the intercity passenger rail and interstate highway systems. (The Beta Index) 1980

Region	Inter-City Passenger Rail	Inter-State Highway Network
New England	0.88	1.29
Middle Atlantic	0.89	1.32
East North Central	1.09	1.37
West North Central	0.71	1.14
South Atlantic	1.12	1.33
East South Central	0.50	1.09
West South Central	1.00	1.17
Mountain	0.77	1.12
Pacific	0.94	1.14

East South Central regions figure in the last three places under both criteria.

While these examples provide only a limited analysis of regional variations they nevertheless indicate where the major differences lie. A more detailed coverage of regional contrasts follows below where each mode of transport is examined on an individual basis.

Regional variations – a Basic model

The development of the transport system in North America exhibits distinct spatial variations. Such differences can be examined by using a basic model as illustrated by Figure 9.4(a). The reader is invited to apply the model as the chapter unfolds.

The model is concerned with two important dimensions of the transportation factor. The first dimension relates to the maturity of the transport service. A system can be 'mature' in that the basic facilities are in place, offering a high level of service as represented by quality and frequency, or it can be undeveloped with relatively low quality and frequency of service.

The second dimension relates to the degree of competition (inter-modal and intra-modal). The level of competition may vary from high inter-modal competition, with many modes and several carriers for each mode, or high intra-modal competition with basically one mode and several carriers, to the most basic service of one mode and one carrier.

Figure 9.4(b) applies the model to the movement of bulk commodities with reference to Canada. Eastern forest products can be moved by a variety of modes, with rail, truck and water available. Iron ore from Quebec and Labrador is shipped mainly to foreign markets by rail and sea with some potential for intra-modal competition. Arctic resources, located in remote areas where the transport infrastructure is relatively undeveloped and the volumes are still low are often suited to only one mode. The model can be applied to passenger transport with equal validity.

The influence of physical geography

Of course the fundamental question is why such variations occur. The causal factors are multivariate but the major operative influences on the development of transport networks have been the distribution and density of population and the physical environment. The elements of climate, landscape and biogeography have largely governed the peopling of the nation and the resultant demand patterns have subsequently determined the shape of transport networks to an overwhelming extent.

The effect of the physical environment on transport routes has weakened with advances in transport technology but is still a strong one. This inter-relationship differs markedly between the various modes of movement according to their technological limitations and the decree of inertia existing in each system at the present time.

The natural drainage pattern provides the fundamental basis to the network of inland waterways; the extension of the system beyond this basic structure was and still is today dependent on economic and technological factors. Inland waterways are the most 'fixed' of all transport systems.

The railways are the epitome of transport inertia in certain regions with the present network being a remnant from the expansive railway era of the last century. Even modern railways are much more restricted by gradient than road transport and can also be regarded much more as 'fixed' systems. Numerous examples can be found to

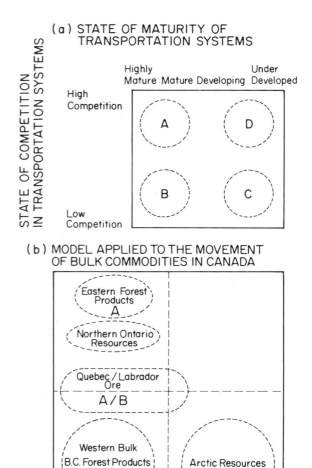

Fig. 9.4 *The maturity of transport systems; a model (Source: Canadian Government Publications)*

illustrate the influence of landscape on rail routes.

The mountain barriers of the Rockies, Sierra Nevada, Cascades and Appalachians have caused severe route contortions where railways have been forced to circumnavigate steep gradients. The routes in these areas are in sharp contrast to those in areas of more subdued landscape.

Major water bodies are also a strong influence on route structure. Chicago's position as the main railway focus in the United States is due largely to the huge obstacle to east-west movement of Lake Michigan protruding southwards into the central lowlands. Chesapeake Bay, untraversed by the railway in the era of that transport mode, remains so today although the Bay is now crossed at its entrance by a road bridge. The problems of bridging the Mississippi in the railway era are clearly evident by the manner in which railway lines follow the river's course with only a limited number of lines crossing this major barrier. Clearly the technology exists to 'straighten' many winding routes but the cost would be prohibitive. Also any such action would isolate the many communities which have developed beside the existing routes.

The road system with its much greater density and ability to overcome steeper gradients has an in-built flexibility which the railway lacks. However, although a number of examples of recent 'straightening' of older routeways can be found, in the mountainous regions of the country road and rail routes tend to follow very similar paths.

The airways provide perhaps the most interesting transport mode in the inter-relationship between population, environment and route structure. While the air lines are almost totally straight-line routes the density of the network is inherently governed by the distribution of population. Although the mountain division has the lowest density of regular flights as it does with roads and railways the actual densities would be much lower were it not for the fact that the function of many of these routes is not simply to link the mountain states to the east but to connect with the more highly populated Pacific states.

The extension of the transport network into areas of sparse population and harsh physical environment will not normally occur unless associated with the exploitation of mineral resources or for strategic reasons. The recent development of the western coalfields has stimulated the greatest realignment of the western railways this century. However the best example of the power of mineral resource location over the transport network is the Trans-Alaskan Pipeline System (TAPS) completed in 1977.

The Northlands: isolation and transportation

The great distances separating communities in the Northlands and the severe environmental conditions prevalent in this vast region have created substantial economic, engineering and maintenance difficulties for transportation development. Firm integration of these lands with the more heavily populated regions to the south has for some time been established policy for American and Canadian governments. Fortunately, the strategic importance of the north along with the potential value of its established and hypothetical mineral resources has improved the economics of greater connectivity.

Immense areas of the Northland are lacking in surface communications. Not one of the eleven railway lines extending into the Northland crosses the Arctic Circle. The most northerly is the Alaska railroad from Seward, terminating at Fairbanks (approx $64\frac{1}{2}°$ N). The railroad was commenced with government funds in 1915 and is the oldest of all the Northland railways. Only five of the other lines, those terminating at Whitehorse, Waterways, Lynn Lake, Churchill and Moosonee were constructed prior to the 1950s. The most recent railway, that to Dease Lake, was not completed until the late 1970s.

Road communications have also improved markedly in the last half century led by three major developments, the Alaskan, MacKenzie and Dempster highways. The Alaska highway, an all-weather gravelled road 2450.5 km long, extends northwest from Dawson Creek, British Columbia to Fairbanks, Alaska. The project was completed during a ten month period in 1942 as an extension of an existing Canadian road between Dawson Creek and Edmonton.

The northern limit of the MacKenzie highway is Yellowknife on the northern shore of the Great Slave Lake. The town, which has a population of over 6000, was founded in 1935 after the discovery of rich deposits of gold.

The most northerly and perhaps the most remarkable of these highway systems is the 721 km Dempster highway which links Dawson, a town of approximately 800 population, to the settlement of Inuvik. An extension of the highway even further north to Tuktoyaktuk is under construction. The $103 million Dempster highway was completed in 1979.

In spite of these most important road and rail extensions the systems are still very basic leaving many communities totally isolated by surface transportation and therefore absolutely dependent on coastal or air services.

The first flight north of $60°$ N took place in 1921

when G. W. Gorman and E. Fullerton flew as far as Fort Simpson. Dickens's flight to Aklavik in the early 1930s, the Yellowknife 'rush' in 1937 and the development of a uranium mine near Fort Radium shortly after, led to the establishment of the first rudimentary air routes. During the Second World War the USAF built a series of airfields across the Arctic to serve as refuelling stops for aircraft being ferried to the USSR. In the late 1950s a series of Distant Early Warning (DEW) radar stations were built across the Northlands to detect aircraft approaching over the Arctic Ocean. An important side effect was to improve air navigation in this huge inhospitable wilderness.

In British Columbia as many as a hundred small fishing and forestry communities were linked only by coastal shipping until local air services were extended.

More than forty communities in the Arctic with a permanent population of between 150 and 900 are having airports built (or rebuilt) under a Canadian government scheme and by the mid-1980s, when the project is due for completion, it is hoped that the quality of air services in the Arctic will have greatly improved.

Short take-off and landing (STOL) aircraft which are capable of landing on water, ice or short unpaved airstrips have been essential in the movement of passengers and goods to isolated communities. In addition, during the period from January to May, air carriers make use of the Arctic ice to operate large aircraft. A 54 tonne plane can land safely on ice 2.13 metres or more thick, so such aircraft as the Boeing 737 or the Lockhead Hercules can fly personnel or supplies directly to sites in the north.

A transportation development matrix can be used to illustrate the extension of air transport in recent decades. Figure 9.5 uses this technique for the Canadian Northland.

The matrix is divided into sectors of 5° latitude × 10° longitude. Each sector is further subdivided to show the number of settlements handling scheduled air services for 1955, 1965 and 1980. Those sectors which had road and /or rail links in 1980 are indicated as such. While the matrix has the mathematical limitation of a reduction in sector area with increasing proximity to the pole (the calculation of a weighting factor can eliminate this) it remains a useful method to employ in such an analysis. The reader is left to examine the trends that can be deduced from the matrix.

Because the cost of air transport is high, advantage is taken of the warmer summer months by using water transport. Since 1930, Canadian Coast Guard icebreakers have been escorting convoys of commercial cargo ships and tankers to Hudson Bay and the Eastern Arctic. Icebreakers based on the Pacific coast perform the same function for Western Arctic communities.

Trains of barges are towed up and down the MacKenzie River bringing supplies to communities along its shores and along the Arctic coast. Further east, barges based in Churchill supply the communities along the Keewatin shore of Hudson Bay.

Fig. 9.5 *The Canadian Northlands: a transport development matrix*

	140°	130°	120°	110°	100°	90°	80°	70°	60°W	Total
75°N										
1980		1	1		1	1	1	1		6
1965										0
1955										0
70°N										
1980	Road 5	3	1	1	2	· 2		2		16
1965	5	2	2	1						10
1955	4	2								6
65°N										
1980	Road Rail 4	Road 4	Road Rail 4		5	1	8	4		30
1965	3	4	5					1		13
1955	3	4	5							12
60°N										
1980	Road Rail	Road Rail 4	Road Rail 5	Rail 7	Rail 5	2	4	3		30
1965		5	4	16	2	1	1	1		30
1955		4	4	13	1					22
55°N										

Water transport on the MacKenzie divides into two sections. The Upper River Region, served by the railway at Waterways, provides service to settlements as far north as Lake Athabasca while the Lower River region, linked by the railway at Hay River, services the Great Slave Lake, Great Bear Lake, a number of harbours on the mainland coast and the islands of the Arctic Ocean.

Climatic conditions greatly restrict movement on the river system. Different sections become navigable between May and July and are closed down again sometime between September and October. Due to low water conditions during the summer, towboats are designed to operate at under 80 cm—the lowest depth of water during the navigation season.

The role of transportation in regional development

Poor transport links have often been cited as a major hindrance to regional economic development. In the past, Appalachia and the South have had their slow growth partially attributed to inadequate transport investment while New England, conscious of its relative isolation, has frequently complained about the economic impact of discriminating rail rates.

Opinions differ markedly among regional economists and planners over the precise contribution of the transport factor to the regional economy. In earlier times, before the spread of the Inter State Highway System in the United States, the development of Canadian highways and the blanket coverage of the continent by air services, some regions suffered from obvious isolation. Post-war improvements have resulted in all regions possessing a reasonable level of transport provision and connectivity. The base level with regard to transport provision in North America is now such that nowhere can the transport factor be identified as the main cause of regional backwardness. However although peripheral regions now have much improved transport provision, if they are distant from the core region(s) then the cost of movement between the two areas will of course be a pertinent factor.

In recent years research has generally found other causes of regional variations such as indus-trial mix, availability of capital and innovative potential to be more significant. In Appalachia the heavy bias of development funding to highways had not gone uncriticised as some commentators have viewed such expenditure as excessive in relation to the region's other needs. M. Strazheim (1972) noted that the wood and timber processing industry, one of the most important industrial groups in the region, switched from rail to truck transport at a much faster rate in Appalachia than elsewhere in the country. This change has led to wood being shipped out of Appalachia for processing as highway improvement has made the economics of exporting raw timber more viable. This is a classic case where limited transport facilities can protect local industry. The improvements in major highways in Appalachia have altered transport costs in a way which has not always been beneficial to the region. However, the general consensus of opinion is that highway development has been of significant help to regional growth.

The cost structure of competing modes of transport is often complex and varies over space and time. Such variations make it extremely difficult to draw long-term conclusions concerning the merits of improvements to particular transport modes.

The transport surface is becoming increasingly homogeneous with the reduction of regional differences in transport provision. Also, there has been a long-term transition in output composition towards higher value goods and services which are less responsive to the transport environment. The consequence of these trends is that the leeway remaining for transport policy in shaping regional development is much reduced and it is important to recognise that in many areas poor transport provision is primarily the result of inadequate demand. Strazheim concludes that 'The weight of current evidence concerning the usefulness of using transport investment or rate regulation as a regional development tool would appear to be on the side of the sceptic'.

Railways in distress

The role of North American railways in both passenger and freight transportation has been steadily undermined in the present century although a combination of historical, geographical

Freight movement through the Canadian Rockies

funding resulting in the development of more sophisticated highway and airway networks.

The economics of railway rates is frequently complex but in general Canadian railways have operated in a more favourable regulatory climate with greater government sympathy. This difference has resulted in Canadian railways giving higher returns on capital which acts as an important stimulus to further investment.

America's shrinking passenger railway network

In 1916, the peak year of American railways in passenger traffic, a total of 56 billion passenger km were logged with a firm monopoly of 98 per cent of all intercity passenger business. However after the First World War a monumental decline in the use of the railways by passengers and freight occurred, the former being by far the more emphatic. By 1966 the number of passenger km carried by the railways had been reduced to 27 billion with passenger trains running on only about one-third of the total rail network. Passenger use declined even further to 16 billion passenger km in 1978.

Although a range of contributory factors can be identified to account for the demise of the railway system, competition from the more flexible road and air networks has been paramount. The motor vehicle dominated the first phase of competition signalled appropriately enough by the establishment of the first federal highway programme in 1916. In the 1920s intercity motor transport soon surpassed traffic by rail and by 1930 was six times as great when 23 million cars were registered in the United States. By 1980 vehicle registrations totalled over 90 million.

The success of the motor vehicle was virtually guaranteed from its inception as it could provide the flexibility and convenience that was glaringly impossible for the railway system. The great dispersal of population created by the automobile further alienated the railway from an increasing proportion of the population and strengthened reliance on motor transport.

The second major phase of competition emerged strongly after the great technical innovations of the American aircraft industry in the Second World War. The scale of the United States in terms of physical size and economic activity has given the airlines with their very competitive rates an

and economic factors has enabled Canadian railways to prove more resistant to competition from other modes of movement than their counterparts in the United States.

Transportation developments have invariably diffused more slowly through Canada than south of the border. In 1850 only 106 km of track existed in the whole country compared to 14 520 km in the United States. Inversely the relative decline of the railways in Canada has been a much more recent phenomenon. Canadian railway passenger traffic peaked in 1967 while in the United States the zenith was reached fitty-one years earlier.

The railway is undoubtedly most competitive over long journeys and average haul distances are significantly greater in Canada. In addition, while severe winter climatic conditions are a hazard to all modes of transport, the railways are less vulnerable to disruption than road haulage. Thus the greater severity of Canadian winters has given the railways a certain competitive advantage in such conditions. An associated variable is that in the United States alternative transportation systems have received proportionately higher federal obvious and increasing advantage over the railways in terms of passenger movement.

Amtrak—passenger rail's last chance?

It has only been since the early 1970s that substantial government involvement with the railways has been apparent and only then to prevent the virtual disappearance of the network from large parts of the country. By 1970 intercity rail passenger traffic had dwindled to only 7 per cent of the total for public carriers with only 450 daily intercity passenger trains remaining in service. Some railways had totally discontinued services while others performed acute surgery on their unprofitable networks. Many large cities such as Dallas found themselves without any passenger train service at all.

In a dramatic bid to halt this downward trend the Rail Passenger Service Act was passed and came into operation on 1 May 1971 creating the first nationwide passenger rail system in the United States. A National Railroad Passenger Corporation known as AMTRAK was established to take over passenger operations on the systems of 22 railway companies.

Amtrak is essentially a contractor buying services from the railways over which it operates, paying costs plus an agreed profit margin to the companies concerned. By joining Amtrak the railway companies had to relinquish all intercity passenger operations. Four major railways remained independent but most were only too eager to rid themselves of their generally unprofitable passenger services.

In the first years of service Amtrak was almost totally dependent on the railway companies, leasing equipment and facilities from them. However a programme of modernisation was quickly put into effect and by 1977 more than three out of four passengers on short distance trains and approximately half of all passengers were riding in new equipment purchased by Amtrak.

While the system has attracted more customers it has required massive federal subsidy, amounting to $3 billion in operating grants between 1971–81. The initial system has been trimmed by amputating the most uneconomic lines.

The passenger rail network operating in early 1980 is shown by Figure 9.6. As well as the Amtrak system the map includes the limited number of

Freight haulage in the Canadian Rockies

lines run by the independent companies.

The connectivity of the Amtrak system is briefly discussed earlier in the chapter where Figure 9.3 indicates that the South Atlantic and East North Central divisions respectively have the most highly developed networks.

Accessibility to passenger train service is due to the interaction of a number of factors. Demand, both at present levels and historically, is of major importance. As new railway construction is extremely costly and difficult environmentally, inertia is a much more significant factor governing the railway network than it is for road or air transport.

The relationship between any region (state or major census division) and its transportation network can be analysed at three levels of interaction: movement within the region, movement between the region concerned and other regions and also movement between external regions whose shortest paths cross the area under examination. This latter point is exemplified by the contrasting position of South and North Dakota.

The states rank 43rd and 44th respectively in

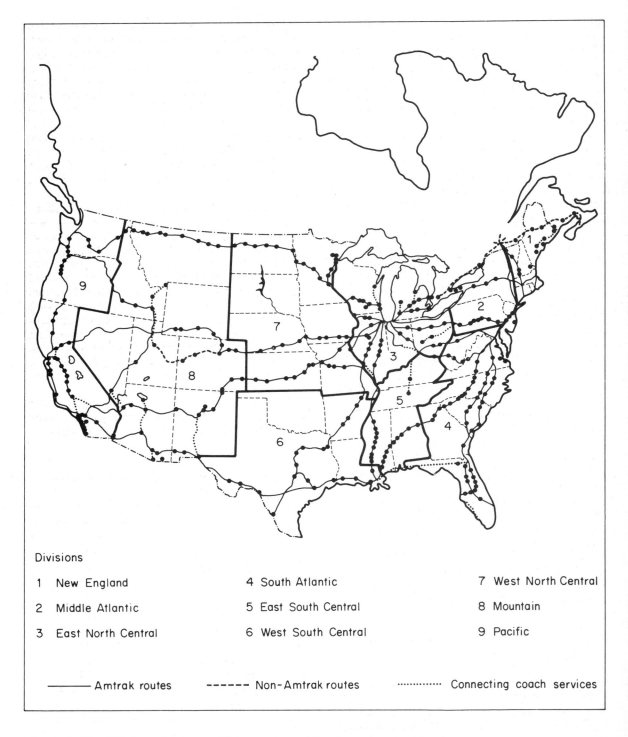

Fig. 9.6 *The US Amtrak system (Source: Amtrak)*

population but while South Dakota has no passenger train service at all the line linking Minneapolis-St Paul to Seattle passes through North Dakota and there are seven passenger stations in the state. South Dakota is one of four states, the others being Maine, New Hampshire and Oklahoma, which have no passenger rail service.

The importance of the spatial interaction between the Pacific coast and the Midwest to the intervening states is indicated by the dominance of east-west routes and the paucity of north to south communications. Four major routes straddle the American West, Minneapolis-St Paul to Seattle, Chicago to San Francisco, Kansas City to Los Angeles and San Antonio to Los Angeles. However there is no direct north-south route through the mountain or Great Plains states.

There are a total of 535 stations on the passenger rail network of the United States. Their regional distribution is shown by Figure 9.7.

Connectivity alone is only a limited measure of accessibility to a transportation service as the frequency of movement must also be considered as there are enormous variations in the number of weekly movements across the United States.

The 734 km Northeast Corridor between Boston and Washington accounts for over 50 per cent of Amtrak's traffic. In contrast to virtually all the remainder of the network Amtrak owns and maintains the Northeast Corridor, which is presently undergoing an extensive rehabilitation and improvement programme that will allow speeds up to 190 km/h.

The section of the Northeast Corridor between New York and Philadelphia with 545 scheduled passenger trains a week is the busiest in the country, followed by the stretch between Philadelphia and Washington with 428 scheduled weekly movements. This situation contrasts markedly with the very low frequences of the routes crossing the American West.

The railways: North America's number one freight carrier

In spite of the emergence of intense competition from other freight movers the railways remain the largest carriers of freight in North America.

The United States retains the biggest operating rail network in the world with nearly 500 com-

panies involved as either 'line-haul' operators that carry freight from origin to destination or 'switching and terminal' companies that run marshalling facilities at the end of lines and operate railway bridges and ferries. In 1979, 46 'Class One' railway companies, those with revenues exceeding $50 million, handled 99 per cent of total railway freight traffic, owned 96 per cent of the track and employed 94 per cent of the workforce. These companies hauled about 1.4 billion tonnes of freight between them with an average haul length of 918 km, compared with 116 km in the United Kingdom.

In Canada the two transcontinental giants, Canadian Pacific and Canadian National railways, dominate railway freight accounting for over 90 per cent of total Canadian railway revenue between them. The basic network of these two large carriers is supplemented by a number of smaller regional companies. Canadian National railways is the larger of the two main systems with 35 420 km of tracks, slightly more than Canadian Pacific's 33 810 km. In the 1960s the Canadian system, unlike that of the United States, was still expanding. By 1979 total track length seemed to have stabilised at around the 97 000 km level with any further large increases unlikely.

Nevertheless in spite of the apparently healthier general position of Canadian railways, their share of domestic freight had declined significantly.

Fig. 9.7 Intercity passenger railway stations in the United States 1980

Region	Number of Stations
South Atlantic	101
East North Central	92
Pacific	72
Mountain	67
Mid Atlantic	62
West North Central	46
New England	36
West South Central	32
East South Central	27
Total	535

Source: Amtrak.

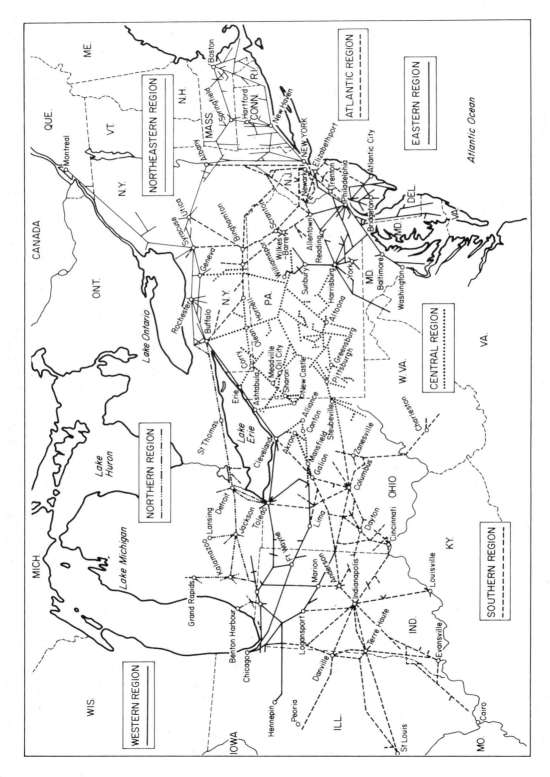

Fig. 9.8 *The Conrail network (Source: Conrail)*

Conrail-a bid to save railway freight in the US manufacturing belt

In the United States the railway's share of intercity freight traffic declined from 77 per cent in 1916 to 37 per cent in 1979. Railway transport is most vulnerable to competition on short and medium haul routes and thus the most profitable railways have tended to be those in the south and in the west. The shorter hauls of the northeast manufacturing belt have suffered from much fiercer competition from the truck, leading to numerous bankruptcies among railway companies and cuts in the overall network.

Five years after the establishment of Amtrak the federal government began its second major excursion into railway operations by restructuring the freight network of the northeast under the Railroad Revitalisation and Regulatory Reform Act of 1976. The Act established the Consolidated Rail Corporation, known as Conrail, by acquiring six bankrupt railways, the Penn Central, Reading, Central of New Jersey, Erie Lackawanna, Lehigh Valley and the Lehigh and Hudson River. Conrail's operational area, shown by Figure 9.8, covers over 27 000 route km in 16 states and in Canada.

As with Amtrak the federal government was forced to intervene under threat of the virtual disintegration of the freight network in the northeast. However, although freight provision in the region has been rationalized, Conrail continues to incur substantial losses largely because it is faced with basically the same difficulties as the six independent companies it replaced. Between 1976 and 1981 Conrail received $3.3 billion in subsidies plus a special $2.1 billion grant to pay for some rail properties in 1976.

A major concern for Conrail is that further decentralisation of manufacturing from the northeast and the trend towards higher value-lower bulk products will further reduce demand for rail freight. Apart from coal the region does not produce in huge quantities the type of commodities which are the lifeblood of railways such as the Burlington Northern and Union Pacific in the west. As a result of relatively short hauls, average tonne km per freight car day and average daily freight car movement tend to be between 20 per cent and 30 per cent less than for the southern and western railways.

Currently about 57 per cent of all automobile industry tonnage is moved by rail with the industry heavily concentrated in the northeast. However this traffic could markedly decrease in the future with further expansion of market-located assembly plants in the south and west.

Unit trains—the railways fight back

The unit train has been the railway's spearhead in the fight to hold on to traditional markets. A unit train continually operates between one origin and one destination. It remains as one unit and almost without exception carries only a single commodity. Loading and unloading facilities are highly mechanised to keep stopping time down to a minimum. A modern unit train can load up as much as 10 000 tonnes in two hours. Such operating procedures have allowed the railways to offer much reduced freight rates.

The prototype of the purpose-built carrier was perhaps the 568 km Quebec North Shore and Labrador, opened in 1954 to connect the ore field at Schefferville with the port of Sept Iles. However it was not until the 1960s that the concept gained significant momentum. Unit trains developed with isolated efforts by individual companies to compete more effectively with barge lines, coal slurry pipelines and mine-mouth power plant siting. The coal companies assisted the emergence of the unit train concept in an effort to halt the loss of coal markets due to changing consumer preference for gas and oil. In the United States unit train systems are responsible for serving more than 50 per cent of all coal-fired power stations. Figure 9.9 gives the operational details for one system, from the Belle Ayr coal mine in Wyoming to the Southwestern Electric Power Company's Flint Creek power plant in Arkansas.

In Canada unit trains are of vital importance in the movement of Alberta coal to the Pacific. At stages in the movement the 8000 tonnes-plus coal trains require eleven 3000 horsepower locomotives to haul them through the Rockies. Each train is equipped with a computer that allows commands to be relayed to unmanned robot locomotives.

As efficiency increased and the scale of unit train operations expanded it became apparent that the unit train could complement other transport modes in North America. Unit trains now frequently link with barges on the Great Lakes and Mississippi River systems. The new $25

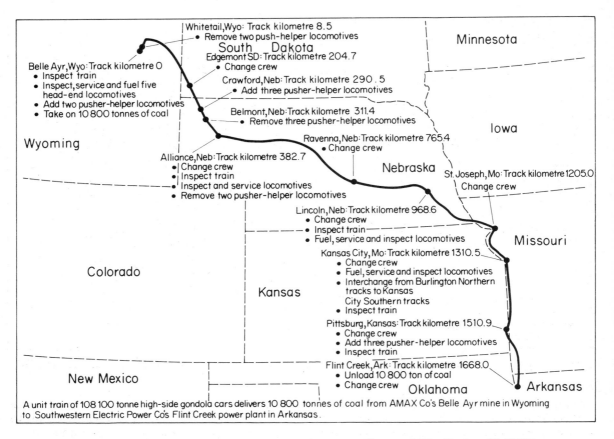

Fig. 9.9 *A unit train system in the American West (Source: Electrical World, Oct 15 1979)*

million Iowa Gateway Terminal at Keotuk on the main channel of the Mississippi River is one of a number of intermodal facilities which have been constructed to handle this growing traffic. The combination of the two transportation modes minimises the cost of moving coal, which is the largest component in the total cost of delivered western coal.

The coal industry has been able to expand its base to western mines which without unit coal trains would not be economically viable.

Highway transportation

Considering the whole spectrum of movement in North America, road transport is indisputably the most essential facility, being of vital importance to the economic, political and social unity of the continent. The motor vehicle has become an indispensible part of North American life with a resultant pattern of land use in both urban and rural environments markedly different from less motorised nations. With motor vehicle registrations currently exceeding 100 million, the continent is the most vehicle-orientated society in the world.

The sophisticated highway network which links the various regions of North America is a relatively recent phenomenon, the emergence of which was dependent upon the construction of the Interstate Highway System and the Trans-Canada Highway.

The outstanding feature of the post-war period has been the great advance in highway design and construction rather than vehicle development for it was only after 1945 that North America began to

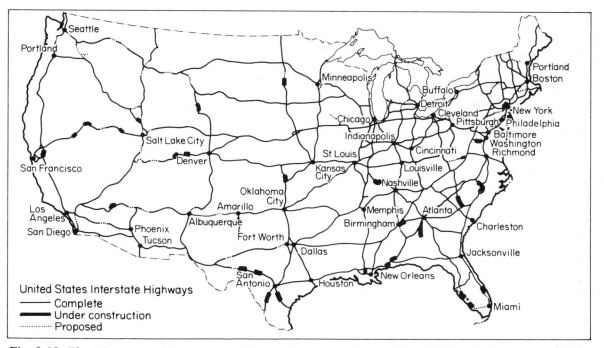

Fig. 9.10 *The US system of interstate and defence highways (Source:* Rand McNally Road Atlas *1980)*

get an effective network of roads built specifically to facilitate the flow of high speed motor traffic.

The importance of fast and efficient inter-regional highways became more and more apparent in the war years and in 1944 the Federal Highway Act was passed authorising 'a national system of Interstate Highways not exceeding 40 000 miles in total extent, so located as to connect by routes as direct as practicable, the principal Metropolitan areas, cities and industrial centres to serve the national defense and to connect at suitable border points with routes of continental importance in the Dominion of Canada and Republic of Mexico.'

The 1944 Act was in fact a declaration of intent and it was the 1956 Federal Aid Highway Act which gave the effective go-ahead for the system to be built, with the federal government paying approximately 90 per cent of the total cost. The Act also added 1600 km to the proposed network. A further 2400 km was designated in 1968. Initially the entire system was expected to be completed by 1971. However by 1980 over 4000 km of essential links were still not open to traffic. Added to the problems of completing the

designated system is the need to bring some 45 000 km of existing Interstate Highway up to current standards of safety and performance.

Although the Interstate system shown by Figure 9.10 accounts for 1.2 per cent of all road mileage in the United States it handles in excess of 20 per cent of total traffic. The greater connectivity of the three north-east divisions and the South Atlantic is designed to handle the higher volumes of traffic flowing on these sections of the system. As might be expected, the ranking of Interstate Highway provision bears a close resemblance to total municipal and rural highway mileage, the regional ranking of which is shown by Figure 9.11.

The high correlation of 0.88 (above the 0.1 per cent probability level) between regional highway mileage and population density illustrates the importance of demand as the prime factor in governing highway provision.

In Canada highway provision again relates strongly to population density although in recent decades much has been done to improve road transport in isolated regions. The most important routeway in Canada is the Trans-Canada Highway, 7535 km in length, which was completed

Fig. 9.11 Municipal and rural highway kilometres per square km 1979

Middle Atlantic	1.58
New England	1.04
East North Central	1.41
South Atlantic	2.20
East South Central	1.05
West North Central	0.94
West South Central	0.72
Pacifc	0.27
Mountain	0.36

in 1962.

Road freight in North America has developed from what used to be almost totally a short haul service to provide a wide range of services over short, medium and long haul routes. As late as 1948 the distance beyond which Canadian railways possessed a cost advantage over road freight was estimated at 56 km. Although certain delivery advantages allowed road freight to compete beyond this range the role of this mode of transportation was essentially a very limited one. In the last few decades hauls of over 1500 km have become common while operations over 3000 or 4000 km are not unusual.

Although the new highway network was not singularly responsible for the huge increase in the volume of road transportation it was the fundamental catalyst. As the railways struggle to maintain their share of the transport market it remains to be seen if road transport will come to dominate freight movement as it did passenger traffic in earlier years.

Inland waterways

Inland waterways make a vital contribution to the movement of freight in North America handling primarily high bulk, low value products. The value to volume ratio of such products, many of which are unprocessed raw materials, frequently makes transport by other modes prohibitive. Water transport allows the movement of large amounts of cargo at one time. Over 40 000 tonnes can be moved in a single tow. In terms of cost, only pipelines can transport products more cheaply but they are suitable only for the movement of a limited number of products.

The cost effectiveness of water transport for bulk movement is illustrated by the long-standing attraction of coastal, lake and major riverside location to heavy industry. Shallow draught units can be easily dropped off at various locations along a waterway with the main tow being sent on its way in a short time. Facilities for berthing barges need not be extensive; the Mississippi River system alone contains 60 inland ports and about 1000 marine terminals.

In a time of concern over energy supply water transport has a distinct advantage. In 1980 a gallon of fuel could move a ton of freight 8 km by air, 80 km by truck, 290 km by rail and 530 km by barge. However like all modes of transport the waterways do suffer from problems. Prominent among these are the freezing conditions in the north and the difficulties caused by high or low water in a number of rivers. Much of the shallow draught navigation system was constructed before World War Two and sections are growing obsolete.

Fig. 9.12 *The St Lawrence Seaway-Great Lakes (Source: Adams, D.K. Mills, S.F. Rodgers, H.B.* An Atlas of North American Affairs, *Methuen, London, 1979)*

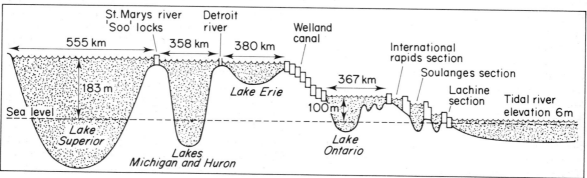

Traffic on the Great Lakes–St Lawrence Seaway overshadows all other inland waterway movement on the continent, practically providing a fourth coastline for both nations although it has not lived up to early expectations. However, the United States does possess a number of other important waterways, especially the Mississippi – Ohio system, which boast considerable annual traffic flows, while in Canada movement by this mode of transport is very limited outside the major system.

The Great Lakes–St Lawrence Seaway system

The Great Lakes form the largest body of fresh water in the world with a combined surface area of 246 050 square km. The area is in addition the world's busiest inland waterway, extending 3768 km from the open sea to Duluth at the western end of Lake Superior.

The routeway in its natural state presented numerous obstacles to movement in the form of rapids, waterfalls and deposition which have been gradually overcome by man. The altitudinal variations between the different lakes and the St Lawrence River are indicated by Figure 9.12.

Man-made alterations to the natural system evolved from 1789 when the first series of small canals were constructed around the rapids at Sault Ste Marie to the most recent and important

Fig. 9.13 Leading Great Lakes-St Lawrence seaway ports – total tonnage handled (million tonnes) 1979

Duluth/Superior	42.8
Chicago	34.5
Toledo	23.4
Detroit	22.3
Conneaut	19.2
Thunder Bay (Can.)	18.3
Cleveland	17.4
Indiana Harbour	16.4
Montreal (Can.)	15.6
Ashtabula	13.0
Quebec (Can.)	12.1
Hamilton (Can.)	12.1

(Canadian figures for 1976).

development of all, the St Lawrence Seaway, a joint United State-Canadian venture opened in 1959. The main components of the project were to improve navigation on the Great Lakes, clear the St Lawrence bottleneck and exploit the river's HEP potential.

The greatest difficulty lay in the section of the St Lawrence between Montreal and Lake Ontario where ancient resistant rocks cross the river's course. Previously this stretch of the river was only navigable for vessels up to 3600 tonnes, making Montreal the effective head of navigation.

The Seaway scheme involved the replacement of the old 4.25 metre deep canals by those of 8.25 metre depth, allowing the passage of vessels up to 22 500 tonnes. Sea-going vessels could now reach any port on the Great Lakes.

The Seaway project has historically been of greater appeal to Canada since negotiations with the United States began in the late nineteenth century. Prior to the 1950s the US response was generally lukewarm. However opinion changed, largely with the realisation of the future importance of Ladrador iron ore to the United States.

A multitude of port facilities are located on both the northern and southern shores of the Great Lakes and along the St Lawrence. The leading ports in terms of tonnage handled are ranked in Figure 9.13. A clear distinction is apparent between the international ports which handle a wide variety of cargo and those like Duluth/Superior which specialise in large volumes covering a narrow range of products.

The major ports along the system are concentrated along the Great Lakes rather than the Seaway with only two Seaway ports, Montreal and Quebec, figuring in the first dozen positions.

The total cargo tonnage handled by the system has steadily increased since the Seaway was opened in 1959. Bulk products dominate traffic with grain and iron ore ranking first and second respectively. Traffic through the Welland canal has increased fivefold by 1980 from 13.1 million tonnes in 1958, a year prior to the opening of the Seaway system.

The bulk of the grain movements originate at the upper Great Lakes terminals from where it is carried by lakers to lower St Lawrence ports for transhipment to ocean vessels. In contrast iron ore movement is predominantly upriver to US and Canadian steelmills located on the Lake shores.

Because most maps are Mercator projections it

is often difficult to realise that some of the ports on the Great Lakes such as Cleveland, Toledo, and Detroit are actually closer to the ports of northwest Europe because of the Great Circle Route, than ports on the Atlantic seaboard. The importance of the Seaway can be recognised when it is considered that while coastal regions are normally the dominating areas of a nation, in North America it is the mid continent that is economically the most important.

Other major waterway systems

The Great Lakes form only a part, albeit a very important one, of the inland waterway network of the United States. While the Great Lakes play a vital role in United States foreign trade a totally different picture emerges when domestic waterborne commerce is considered. For domestic movements, inland waterways, exclusive of the Great Lakes and domestic ocean traffic, account for over 60 per cent of total waterway trade.

The inland waterway system of the United States, at approximately 47 000 km length, is the second largest in the world after that of the Soviet Union (140 000 km).

Traffic is heavily concentrated on a small number of major waterways, primarily the Ohio, Mississippi, Monongahela and the Illinois Waterways.

The Mississippi is navigable from the delta to the Falls of St Anthony in Minneapolis and connects with the Intra-coastal Waterway in the south and with the Great Lakes–St Lawrence Seaway in the north by way of the Illinois Waterway. Channel improvements have facilitated a marked increase in traffic, particularly since the mid-1950s after a long period of decline. High volume goods such as petroleum products, chemicals, sand and gravel and limestone dominate movement. Passage of freight down the upper Mississippi to St Louis takes about 10 days and from St Louis onwards to New Orleans, 5 days. The slower speed in the upper section of the river is due partly to congestion at locks and dams.

The Intra-coastal Waterway (3 950 km long) is partly natural and partly man-made and provides sheltered passage along the US Atlantic coast from Trenton, New Jersey to Key West, Florida and along the Gulf coastline from Brownsville, Texas to the St Mark's River in northwest Florida.

The construction of the Houston Ship Canal (1912–14) has been a major factor in the phenomenal expansion of Houston by making it a deepwater port. The petro-chemical industry is dominant along the canal.

The 845 km New York State Barge Canal connecting the Hudson River to Lake Erie has declined in significance since the Seaway project. The canal has 57 electrically operated locks and can accommodate vessels up to 2000 tons. In recent years pleasure craft have been the largest user of the canal.

Canadian inland waterways, outside the Great Lakes system, are far more restricted with the MacKenzie system described earlier in the chapter being the only one of real significance.

Air transport

The air transport network in North America is the most highly developed in the world and is an essentially important component of the continent's economic well-being. The general affluence of the two nations allows an extremely high per capita usage of air transport to cover the great distances which often separate major cities and make this mode of transport so popular on long haul passenger routes. Air freight has increased significantly in recent decades but is still very limited in volume when compared to the other transport modes. However, many isolated communities in the northlands rely totally on air services for at least part of the year.

In the United States all cities of over 100 000 population and many of a few thousand in less densely-settled areas are linked by regular air services. The airlines, privately owned and operated since their origin in the 1920s, have been aided by the federal government throughout their development by support through the airmail service, direct sponsorship of research and development, purchase of military aircraft and the regulation of the nation's carriers, pilots and air traffic control system.

In 1980, sixty three certificated US air carriers operated 2505 aircraft on domestic and international routes. On the domestic system 200 billion revenue passenger miles were flown. In spite of the profusion of airports the 100 largest accounted for 90 per cent of total passenger traffic.

The 297 million passengers carried amounted to over 80 per cent of all intercity common carrier passenger traffic, a marked increase over the 19 million passengers carried in 1950 when this figure accounted for 14 per cent of domestic intercity common carrier passenger traffic. The airlines' share of intercity passenger traffic rises sharply with increasing distance. In all but a few corridor links in densely populated areas, such as the north-east, intercity air travel at about 300–500 km attracts 10 to 20 per cent of personal travel and at about 800 km from 25 to 50 per cent.

Although air transport continues to gain a larger and larger share of the market the growth of the industry slowed noticeably in the 1970s as Figure 9.14 shows. Tighter economic conditions have restricted demand to well below previously expected levels and increased competition between the airlines to such a degree that many have incurred heavy losses in the effort to maintain their share of the market. The industry logged 5238 million tonne km of domestic freight in 1980, a substantial increase on the 762 million tonne km recorded in 1960. The US aircraft industry is the country's leading exporter after agriculture and is a leading employer totalling over one million jobs. Air transport itself employs nearly 350 000 people.

The major focal points of the intensive US air network are Chicago, New York, Los Angeles, San Francisco, Denver, Dallas–Fort Worth, Atlanta, Washington and Miami, each recording more than 100 000 flight departures per annum.

The highest concentration of movement clearly adheres to the north-east manufacturing belt, the zone of greatest population density.

Whenever cities are closely grouped a traffic shadow effect is often apparent as there is a tendency for the largest city in any cluster of cities to act as a traffic receiving point for the entire cluster. This effect is most marked in the north-

Fig. 9.14 *US domestic air carriers; revenue, distance, passangers 1960–80 (Source: US Corps of Engineers)*

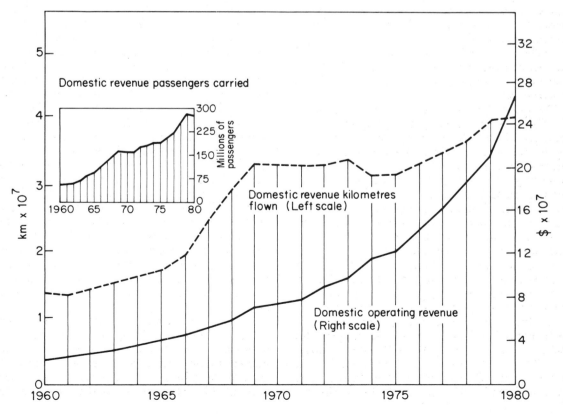

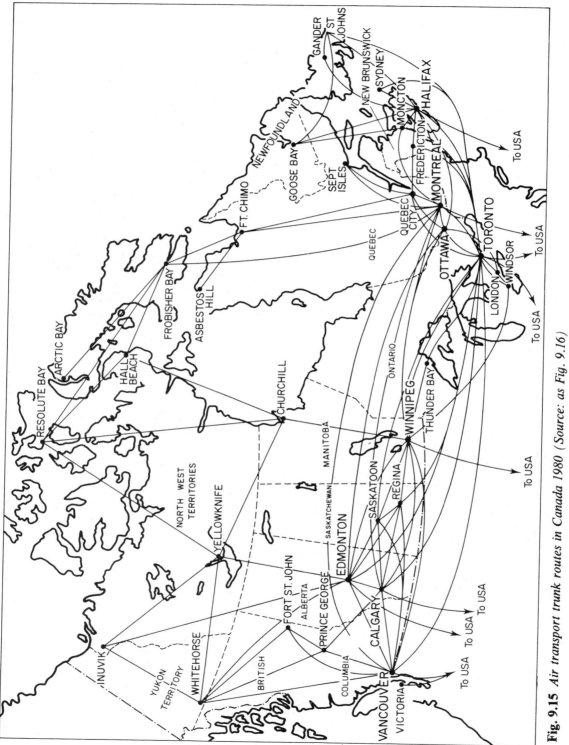

Fig. 9.15 *Air transport trunk routes in Canada 1980 (Source: as Fig. 9.16)*

Fig. 9.16 *Air transport local routes in Canada 1980 (Source: ABC World Airways Guide 1980)*

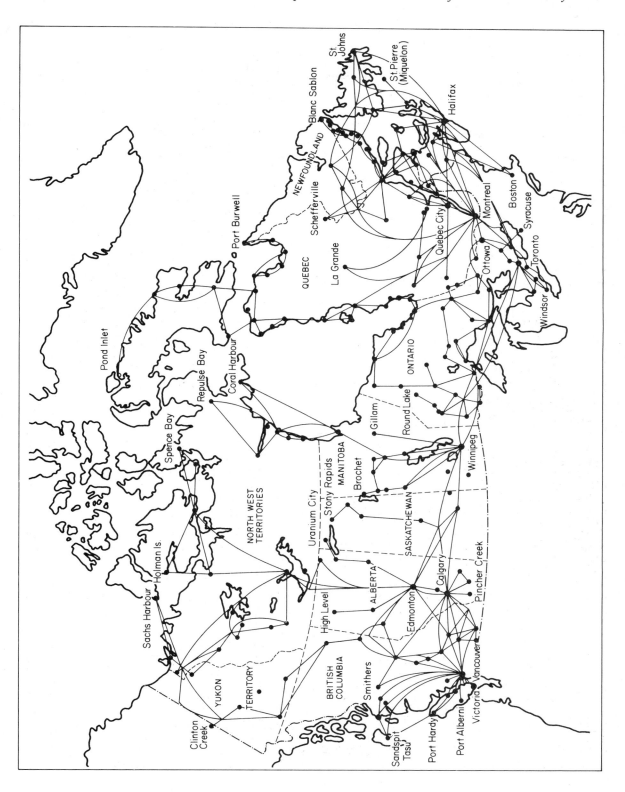

east with New York and Chicago providing clear examples by reason of their fast and frequent air services to and from all parts of the country, plus a range of international connections.

Three distinct levels of service are discernable from the 'first level' of the big scheduled and charter airlines, the 'second level' of regional services, through to the 'third level' small aircraft operators which perform commuter services or link isolated communities.

Commuter services have expanded rapidly in recent years. In 1979 the number of passengers carried by 260 commuter operators of all kinds exceeded 12 million. Commuter airlines in the US already have a fleet of over 1400 aircraft (up to 30 seats) serving over 800 airports. Recently the Federal Aviation Regulations have been amended to permit third level operators to use aircraft of up to 60 seats.

The growth of the commuter service is due to an increasing tendency for people, especially business travellers, to fly rather than drive distances of 150 km or so. In small communities the airport is frequently located within easy reach of the town centre and is thus more accessible than it would be in a large city.

Probably the greatest problem facing air transportation is public opposition to airport expansion and new airport building. Fifteen major US airports will reach saturation by 1985. Major airports which were initially located on the outskirts of metropolitan areas are now hemmed in by later development and thus unable to expand. Some military bases have come under scrutiny for joint use with civilian aircraft and in 1981 ten Air Force airports were operating as joint-use facilities, a trend not generally to the liking of the military.

Figures 9.15 and 9.16 illustrate Canada's scheduled trunk and local routes. Due to Canada's lower population density the network is less complex, especially in the northlands. However, even in relative terms intercity air passenger transport is not as well established as it is in the United States.

The airports at Toronto, Montreal (Mirabel and Dorval) and Vancouver continue to dominate with more than 54 per cent of passenger and 67 per cent of freight traffic. In 1980 Toronto handled over 13 million passengers and 170 000 tonnes of cargo. Montreal was second with 7.5 million passengers and 108 000 tonnes of cargo and Vancouver 3rd with 6.8 million passengers and 68 000 tonnes of cargo.

Air transport and regional development

While the wisdom of investing huge sums of money in transport provision to the detriment of other sectors of the economy is very debatable, the expansion of air services has undoubtedly aided a number of areas to develop their economic base.

Ohio's Airport Development Programme began in 1964 when a survey reported that only 30 of Ohio's 88 counties had runways capable of handling corporate planes and of these only two-thirds could accommodate business jets. The latter airports were mostly located in the larger urban areas.

State planners were anxious to attract additional industry to Ohio to create jobs and increase the tax base. In terms of transportation one noticeable drawback was the lack of airport facilities in many areas. A scheme was designated to develop airports in the state and as a result 62 airports were built or improved. There is now an airport with a lighted, hard surface runway every 40 km or within an average of 530 square km in Ohio. This can be compared to California or Texas with an airport every 2600 square km. In 1970 a survey indicated that the airport development programme was attracting $1 billion in new industrial capital to Ohio and creating 60 000 new jobs with an annual payroll in excess of $250 million. By 1974 it was estimated that these figures had doubled and significantly increased further still by 1980.

Air transport can also be a very important factor in urban development. The city of Atlanta owes much of its post-war growth to its attractive air service facilities. In 1950 Atlanta was about the same size as Birmingham and even smaller than Memphis but the city's early commitment to air transport fostered economic expansion and concomitant urban development. An average of 1450 planes take off and land at Atlanta each day. In 1979 nearly 42 million passengers passed through Hartsfield airport, making it the second busiest airport in the world after Chicago's O'Hare International, which handled approximately 48 million passengers. However the population of Atlanta is only 1.9 million compared with Chicago's 7.7 million.

Mass transit in Toronto

Based on population only, Atlanta could justify about 450 daily flights. Hartsfield's importance is based on the fact that it is the busiest transfer hub in the world. Some seventy per cent of the airport's passengers are there to change planes.

In the post-war years two major airlines, Delta and Eastern evolved a hub and spoke system based on Atlanta whereby relatively small jets shuttle back and forth among cities all over the southeast and Atlanta, where several times a day they cross-connect with one another and with wide-bodied planes which convey passengers to all parts of the United States and abroad. The hub and spoke system evolved because few cities in the southeast could individually generate the traffic to justify long-haul flights. Atlanta was selected as the hub because it boasted the best airport facilities at the time.

Many companies have developed their headquarters or important branch offices in Atlanta because of the high levels of air connectivity and frequency. The city has also become the third largest convention centre in the United States after New York and Chicago.

Urban transportation

While intercity movement has undergone major changes in the post-war period it has been in the large urban areas that the transportation problem has steadily accumulated, epitomised today by traffic congestion and troubled public transport systems.

The extremely high and ever increasing level of car ownership has created enormous terminal and parking problems, with the speed of traffic in many central cities during peak periods frequently as low as 10 to 15 km per hour. The declining use of public transport, to a level well below that in European cities, has gradually accentuated this trend.

Although a limited mileage of urban highways has been constructed, major traffic flows are still often channelled along an outmoded gridiron of streets laid out long before the requirements of a highly motorised society became apparent. The concentration of economic activity in urban areas, characterised by high density construction and inflated land values, has led to a formidable reluctance and in many cases an inability to release more land for transportation corridors. As a result highway standards are frequently in inverse relationship to the needs of traffic with the lowest quality provision being in the zones of highest traffic flow. While the federal government has spent a fortune on the Interstate Highway System the condition of the road network in many urban areas has steadily deteriorated, due primarily to a lack of investment.

The influence of the motor vehicle is nowhere more apparent than in Los Angeles, where the existence of 5 million cars has encouraged the city's suburbs to spread extensively east from the centre into the semi-desert scrubland of San Bernadino county and west to the sea. In North America today there is no urban public transportation system which can be considered a serious competitor with the private car, except for New York where movement and parking conditions are more difficult than in any other city. In the United States in 1980, public transportation of all kinds accounted for only about 5 per cent of all urban trip miles. During the 1960–70 decade while urban car usage increased by 74 per cent in passenger-miles travelled, bus usage decreased by 26 per cent and rail by 8.5 per cent. In the 1970s this downtrend slowed and in some cases was halted but only by a huge input of funds from federal, state and local governments.

The demise of public transportation

Prior to the 1970s transportation planners gener-
ally advocated concentrating expenditure on new highways while largely ignoring the claims of public transport. However, while the construction of the Interstate Highway System proceeded rapidly in rural areas the drastic environmental impact of the system in urban areas became all too apparent as the tougher inner-city links were commenced. A combination of public opposition to urban highway construction and a more enlightened attitude to energy consumption resulted in the revitalisation of public transport gaining a degree of political acceptance unthinkable in previous years. The attitude that public transport should pay its way was abandoned in 1974 when Congress agreed to operating subsidies for transport systems.

To compete with the private car in the large urban areas, public transport must offer as full a range of services as possible. This has been made increasingly difficult by the three problems of collection, delivery and peaking. The number of stops required to make a payload is greatly increased by a dispersed residential population. However more stopping points will increase the overall journey time and subsequently lead to a reduced number of passengers. Low density suburbanisation has caught public transportation in a vicious circle.

Within the downtown areas dispersal of places of work has lengthened that portion of the trip between arrival at the transport terminal and arrival at final destination, which makes the whole journey less attractive in comparison with the direct point-to-point flexibility of the private car.

Often 80 per cent of the volume of traffic is concentrated in about 20 hours of the week, leading to the underutilization of rolling stock and labour for the remainder of the week. The concentration of journeys into narrower bands of time has been a steadily evolving phenomenon.

The lengthening of passenger trips has been a significant factor leading to higher costs. Transit systems have attempted to adapt to decentralization by increasing routes, but with no increase in the total number of miles travelled by buses the expansion of routes had to be at the expense of the frequency of service. In addition, public transport is highly labour intensive making cost reduction difficult.

Such problems have led to the decline of the proportion of operating costs met by revenue in the US public transportation industry from 96 per

Fig. 9.17 The development of rapid transit railways in urban regions 1978 (total track length in brackets)

Operating	Under construction	Planned
Atlanta (35 km)	Baltimore (23 km)	Buffalo (10 km)
Boston (62 km)	Edmonton (7 km)	Calgary (32 km)
Chicago (308 km)		Denver (34 km)
Cleveland (31 km)		Detroit (121 km)
Montreal (30 km)		Los Angeles (n.a.)
New York (885 km)		Miami (22 km)
Philadelphia (39 km)		
San Francisco (14 km)		
Toronto (43 km)		
Washington (160 km)		

Source: 1978 *Railway Statistics.*

cent in 1967 to 53 per cent in 1977.

A recent study of four public transportation systems, the Chicago Transit Authority (CTA), the San Francisco Municipal Railway (MUNI), the Alameda–Contra Costa Transit District (AC Transit) and the Southern California Rapid Transit District (SCRTD) indicated a declining trend in revenue passengers per vehicle mile of service for all four systems. In 1977 AC Transit carried a very low 2.05 passengers per vehicle mile of operations in comparison to SCRTD's 2.15, CTA's 2.70 and MUNI's 4.63. These variations are partly explained by the larger operating areas of ACT and SCRTD which are characterised by relatively low population density.

Rapid transit railways

In a period of rapidly escalating fuel prices and heavy urban traffic congestion the rapid transit railway has gained a new lease of life. Figure 9.17 indicates that apart from the ten systems already operational in 1978 in North America, a further eight were either under construction or in the planning stage. The figures given for those systems in operation are for the final track length of the network and this in some cases includes stretches of track yet to be completed. For example by 1978 only one-third of the projected 160-kilometre Washington Metro was complete. Construction began in 1969 and in March 1976 the first five-station section over a distance of seven kilometres was opened. Completion is set for 1985. The most recent addition to North American rapid transit railways opened in Atlanta in July 1979. Apart from easing traffic flow problems the city is hopeful that the new system will give Atlanta an edge over other southern cities in the competition to attract new business.

While two of the oldest systems, those of New York and Chicago, remain by far the largest it is noticeable that the rapid transit railways under construction or in the planning stage are much more limited in terms of track length.

The New York rapid transit rail system remains by far the largest in North America, and in fact in the world, carrying in excess of 3.5 million passengers daily.

Bibliography

Stover, J. F. (1970) *The Life and Decline of the American Railroad.* New York: Oxford University Press.

Straszheim, M. R. (1972) 'Researching the role of transportation in regional development', *Land Economics*, XLVIII, 3, pp. 212–19.

10

Agriculture

Introduction

North America is one of only a few world regions that can both feed its own population and export large quantities of food abroad. In recent decades the agricultural economies of both the United States and Canada have become increasingly geared to foreign demand.

Measured by most criteria, North American agriculture is the most productive in the world. As Figure 10.1 indicates the region has by far the highest agricultural output per agricultural worker, being in excess of seven times the average for western Europe. Yields per hectare are not generally as high as some more intensively farmed regions such as north-west Europe but the highly mechanized cultivation of large farms results in huge absolute annual production figures which have continually risen due to massive direct investment and considerable expenditure on research and development which has paid handsome dividends.

Agriculture is but one component of the gargantuan North American economic system and in the post-war period the nature of the industry's links with other sectors of the economy has become more complex (Figure 10.2). The expansion of horizontal and vertical integration has spawned the term 'agribusiness' to describe the nature of modern agricultural operations which have to be highly cost effective to remain competitive.

The immense variety of physical environments in North America has allowed a wide array of crops to be grown and livestock kept. Although technological development and the availability of capital has enabled farmers to extend operations into increasingly difficult environments the physical geography of the continent remains a most important influence on agricultural practices.

The role of physical geography must however be kept in perspective. Relief, climate and soil fertility set broad limits as to what can be produced. But overall the physical environment provides only a base which presents the farmer with a varying number of choices. The pattern of agricultural production that has emerged is a result of millions of individual decisions since the initial colonization of the continent whereby each agricultural unit has had to select the nature of production from the options available. It is in such selection that economic factors and more recently government intervention at various levels have become of increasing importance.

While agriculture is in many ways organised in a similar way in the two countries the physical factors of landscape, climate and soil have resulted in profound differences in farm production in the United States and Canada. For this reason the agricultural geography of the two nations is examined in sequence so that important contrasts are not masked in an effort to illustrate areas where they are comparable. An attempt is made at the end of the chapter to give a more detailed insight into location and production in North

Salinas Valley, California, Head lettuce being harvested by field workers are boxed for shipping

American agriculture by the use of three case studies which examine wheat cultivation in the Canadian prairies, cotton production in the US sunbelt and cattle feeding in the United States.

Post-war trends in United States agriculture

Agricultural patterns

Figure 10.3 shows the major agricultural zones of the United States and the marked dichotomy between the eastern and western halves of the country. Although the more intense specialization of the pre-war period has been considerably reduced by progressive diversification in most parts of the United States, broad agricultural regions can still be recognised.

In the upper northeast and north central regions the Hay and Dairying Belt stretches from New England to Minnesota. The cool summers and the long severe winters present sub-optimum conditions for grain cultivation and the emergence of dairying in this region has thus been partly in response to physical limitations on other agricultural practices. Other factors which have encouraged this use of the land were the cultural traditions of the German, Swiss, Scandinavian and Dutch farmers who settled in the western part of the belt and the intense urbanization of the region which presented an enormous market for

Fig. 10.1 Agricultural land, agricultural output per agricultural person and per agricultural worker, world and main regions, 1964–1966, 1969–1971 and 1974–1976

	Agricultural output per agricultural person			Agricultural output per agricultural worker			Agricultural land* (millions of hectares)	
	1964–66	1969–71	1974–76	1964–66	1969–71	1974–76	1970	1976
World	0.19	0.21	0.23	0.46	0.51	0.55	1 459.8	1 488.0
Developed regions . . .	0.91	1.23	1.56	1.94	2.64	3.30	677.9	672.7
Developed market economies.	1.27	1.71	2.17	2.93	3.96	5.00	398.4	394.1
Northern America	5.78	8.22	11.25	14.33	19.52	25.72	234.0	232.0
Western Europe. .	0.84	1.15	1.47	2.02	2.82	3.56	99.9	96.1
Oceania	5.69	6.84	7.67	14.14	16.49	19.28	44.3	46.0
Other developed market economies	0.26	0.36	0.46	0.54	0.74	0.96	20.1	20.0
Eastern Europe and USSR	0.56	0.78	1.00	1.12	1.56	1.96	279.5	278.5
Developing regions. . .	0.09	0.09	0.10	0.21	0.23	0.25	781.8	815.3
Developing market economies.	0.09	0.09	0.10	0.23	0.25	0.26	645.2	674.1
Africa	0.07	0.08	0.08	0.18	0.18	0.19	176.5	182.0
Latin America. . .	0.21	0.23	0.26	0.67	0.75	0.82	133.0	143.6
Western Asia . . .	0.12	0.13	0.14	0.35	0.38	0.44	78.5	81.1
Asia and the Pacific	0.06	0.07	0.07	0.16	0.18	0.19	256.1	266.3
Other developing market economies	0.20	0.20	0.20	0.42	0.42	0.44	1.1	1.1
Asian centrally planned economies . . .	0.09	0.09	0.10	0.16	0.20	0.22	136.6	141.3

Note: The agricultural production estimates on which the above indicators are based are expressed in terms of wheat price equivalents.

* Arable land and land under permanent crops.   *Source:* United Nations.

milk. Milk production dominates in the eastern area while butter and cheese increases in importance farther west. However, even here milk remains the main dairy product close to the major cities. Wisconsin, with 16.8 per cent of US dairy cows in 1980 is the leading producer, having more than double the beasts of New York, the next ranking state.

To the southwest lies the Corn and Livestock Belt, one of the most productive agricultural regions in the world. Corn, the dominant crop, is primarily used as fattening fodder for pigs and cattle and plays a relatively minor role (though a growing one in the 1970s) as a cash crop. Corn requires a growing season of at least 130 days. For the crop to ripen properly high summer temperatures of 21°C or more are necessary along with warm nights. Little corn is grown where the annual precipitation is less than 500 mm or where at least 200 mm does not fall in the three summer months. This region of mixed farming is characterised by a great variety of crops and livestock. Apart from corn, soybeans merit particular mention as the crop has expanded rapidly in the region in recent years.

Iowa and Illinois form the nucleus of corn production, together accounting for over 30 per cent of the planted corn acreage in the country. These two states are also the leaders in soybeans but in the reverse order. In some states such as

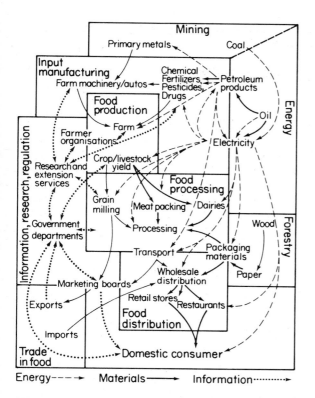

Ohio the acreage under soybeans now exceeds that planted with corn. Corn Belt agriculture is highly mechanized and also uses immense quantities of fertilizers both to maintain and increase yields.

East and southeast of the Corn Belt is a sizeable but irregular area of general farming which can be viewed as a transitional area between the agricultural systems of the Midwest and the South. This zone was known in earlier years as the Corn and Winter Wheat Belt. While both crops are important to the area indicated in Figure 10.3, yields per hectare are generally lower than in the major regions for corn and wheat. Within and bordering this zone are important areas of tobacco cultivation. The major tobacco producing states are North Carolina and Kentucky.

Truck farming or market gardening is not

Fig. 10.2 *Sectors and structural linkages in the Canadian food system (Source:* Atlas of Canadian Agriculture*)*

Fig. 10.3 *Agricultural regions in the United States (Source: Adams, D. K. Mills, S. F. Rodgers, H. B. An Atlas of North American Affairs. Methuen, 1979)*

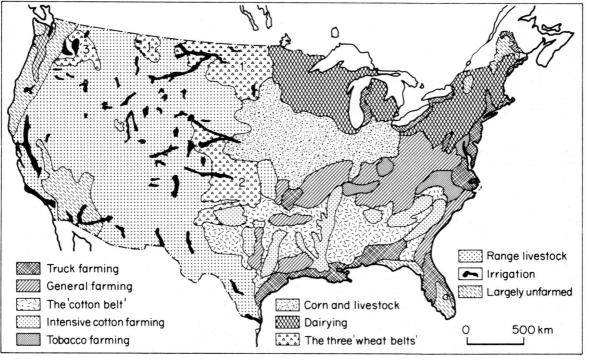

concentrated in one part of the country but occurs in a number of areas where a combination of physical and economic factors makes this type of farming a profitable concern. Regions most noted for truck farming are the north-eastern seaboard, the eastern borders of Lakes Michigan, Erie and Ontario, Florida and the Gulf Coast. The sub-tropical climate of the southern areas allows a range of exotic fruits and vegetables to be grown. Similarly fruit and vegetables are intensively cultivated under irrigation in southern California and in other more restricted areas of the west. California is the leading state for vegetables, accounting for 48 per cent of all US production by value in 1979 and is also the number one state for many fruits.

Along with the Corn and Livestock Belt the Cotton Belt of the south is probably the best known of America's agricultural regions. The staple of the southern economy in the nineteenth century, cotton is now cultivated on a much more limited area which is well below that set aside for the big four crops (Figure 10.4).

Cotton production is now highly mechanized and has undergone a major westward shift in location for reasons which are detailed later in the chapter. Southern agriculture, for so long in a distressed state, has been radically transformed in recent decades with the diffusion of mechanization and diversification. Much less land is farmed and much has reverted to woodland but total agricultural production and farm specialization have greatly increased. In no state is cotton the major source of farm income (Figure 10.5), although it does rank second in Texas, Mississippi and Arizona and third in Louisiana and California. Other major sources of farm receipts are cattle, soybeans, broilers, tobacco, peanuts, rice, eggs, wheat, hogs and dairy produce.

In terms of cropland, wheat dominates on the High Plains, with spring wheat concentrated to the northwest of the Corn and Livestock Belt and the nucleus of winter wheat to the southwest. The westward position of the wheat belts is explained largely by the crop's ability to tolerate drier conditions than the other major grains. North Dakota, the centre of spring wheat production, is the only state in the country, apart from Washington, where wheat is the major source of income. In 1980 the state's production totalled 180 million bushels. However due to far higher yields the winter wheat belt is the major focus of wheat

production in the US and in the same year Kansas and Oklahoma registered 420 million and 195 million bushels respectively. Farther to the west both Washington and Montana are important wheat growing states ranking fourth and sixth in the national league table.

Ranching is overwhelmingly dominant from the drier parts of the High Plains, across the Mountain states into the less favourable agricultural areas of the Pacific divisions. While cattle form the main source of farm income in 14 of the 21 coterminous states west of Illinois it is important to note that the total number of cattle in the eight Mountain states in 1980 was marginally less than the number held by Texas farms.

The extensive cattle ranching of the drylands is interspersed with elongated zones of irrigation farming, frequently straddling major river valleys. Farming in such areas varies widely but cotton, sorghum and alfalfa are of special importance.

Mountainous and arid landscapes present a significant obstacle to agriculture over a large area of the southwest and northwest. In contrast the Pacific coastal lowlands and the linked interior valleys are centres of intense production where the climatic regime is a vital factor influencing the type of farming practised.

As Figure 10.5 indicates, California is clearly the leading state in terms of total farm income. Only Iowa, Texas and Illinois exceeded half of the total farm receipts of the Pacific giant in 1980. The lowest state farm incomes occur in the Mountain states and New England.

Another important measure of agricultural distribution is the percentage of land in farms (Figure 10.6). The centre of the country is again highlighted under this criterion. Of the seven states that have eighty per cent or more of their land area in

Fig. 10.4 Principal crops: area harvested (thousand hectares) 1980

Corn (for grain)	29 568
Wheat	28 674
Soybeans (for beans)	27 461
Hay	24 054
Cotton	5 348
Sorghums (for grain)	5 149

Source: US Statistical Abstract.

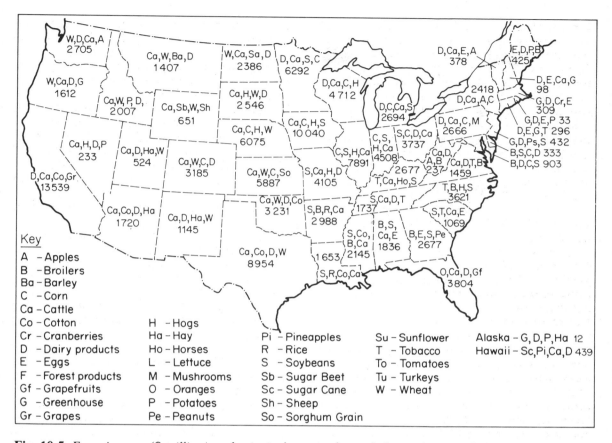

Fig. 10.5 *Farm income ($ million) and principal sources by rank for each state 1980*

farms, five are located in the West North Central division. The East North Central and West South Central also register strongly in this respect. The Atlantic and Pacific states appear peripheral under this yardstick, which masks the intensive nature of production in California, Florida and more limited areas in other states where agricultural land use is restricted by physical conditions, urbanization and other factors.

Increasing mechanization, higher yields, larger farms, less labour

These are the trends which have characterized US agriculture in the post-war decades. Figure 10.7 uses three indexes of farm productivity to illustrate the developing efficiency of farming on a relatively stable area of cropland. Farm output per hour of labour has increased eightfold in the forty year period with very healthy gains also in crop production per hectare and in farm output per unit of total input.

Two hundred years ago there were about 4 million farms in the US with an average size of just over 50 hectares. At the time ninety per cent of the total labour force were employed on the land. At the beginning of 1980 the United States had 2.3 million farms with an average size of 182 hectares, well above the European average, worked by only three per cent of the total labour force. Figure 10.8 illustrates for the 1940–80 period the inverse relationship between the number and size of farms that has helped to transform the country's farming.

Farm size is in itself though a limited measure of

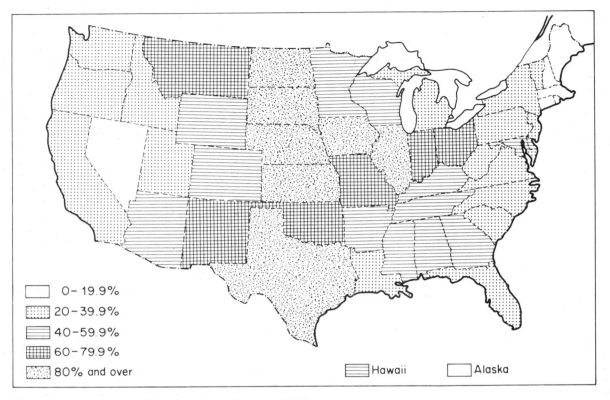

Fig. 10.6 *Percentage of land in farms by state 1979*

agricultural progress as poor quality land is as much an encouragement to large agricultural units as is the desire to achieve economies of scale on much more intensively used land. In 1981 Arizona, Alaska and Wyoming had the largest average farms at 2212, 1619 and 1539 hectares respectively while Massachusetts, New Jersey and Rhode Island were at the bottom of the national league with average farm sizes of 47, 45 and 35 hectares. The leading states according to farm income, California and Iowa, registered averages of 171 and 115 hectares respectively.

The third quarter of the century (1950–75) is frequently referred to as the golden era of agricultural productivity when the composite index of all crop yields more than doubled. In the 1930s grain yields in the US averaged less than 1.5 tonnes per hectare and were similar to those in the third world. This was due to the extensive manner of cultivation. Now US yields average 3.5 tonnes per hectare while yields in the third world have increased only marginally on average.

In the last 50 years chemical inputs have increased by a factor of 15 and are used in such large quantities in many areas that the soil structure is in an extremely fragile condition. One farmer today produces enough food for himself and 65 other people (47 at home and 18 abroad). Productivity gains have slowed recently though. Between 1950 and 1974 productivity in the agricultural sector averaged 1.7 per cent per year but in the following five years dropped to 1.5 per cent with the expectation that it will fall to about 1 per cent per annum at least during the first half of the 1980s. Higher productivity increases after this period will depend on the reaching of further technological thresholds from genetic engineering to the use of microelectronics in farm equipment.

The progressive increase in mechanisation continues to reduce the requirement for agricultural labour to a level unmatched by any other important farming nation of large population. The estimated inventory of US agricultural machinery in 1980 included 4.8 million tractors, 4 million

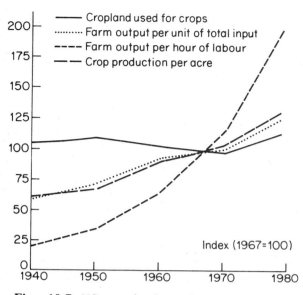

Fig. 10.7 *US cropland productivity 1940–79 (Source: US Dept. of Agriculture)*

Fig. 10.8 *Number of farms and average farm size in the US 1940–80 (Source:* US Statistical Abstract*)*

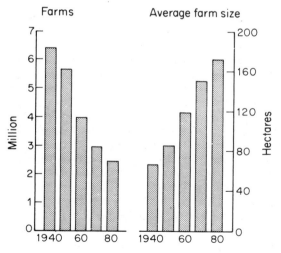

trucks, 669 000 grain combines, 690 000 corn pickers and picker-shellers, 764 000 pick-up balers and 301 000 field forage harvesters. The agricultural machinery industry, one of the most advanced in the world, is constantly seeking to improve established mechanical practices and to introduce machinery into the greatly reduced

number of farming types which still require a substantial labour input. The specialized and intensive vegetable and fruit operations of California and Florida are obvious targets for the industry which will create further problems of farm unemployment.

In 1979 US corn production totalled 195 million tonnes, a new record. In addition the average yield of 269 bushels per hectare exceeded the previous best by eight per cent. A record yield for grain sorghum (156 bushels/hectare) was also achieved and total feed grain production at 232 million tonnes was the highest ever. Sorghum production reached its highest recorded level at 2.27 billion bushels and a 2.14 billion bushel wheat crop tied with the previous best but as the acreage harvested was less a new yield record of 84 bushels/hectare was achieved.

Farm organization: the growth of agribusiness

Although the number of corporate farms (legally defined as a corporation with shares held by more than one person) in the United States rose from 8200 in 1957 to 30 000 in 1979 the family farm remains the cornerstone of agricultural production. In fact the great majority of corporate farms are owned by fewer than ten shareholders suggesting that many are essentially family owned and operated. However, while accounting for only 1 per cent of all farm units in the country, corporate farms are responsible for approximately 15 per cent of total farm receipts.

Corporate farms are on the whole significantly larger than family farms and tend to specialize in both type of production and region of location. Commodities most frequently produced by farming corporations are vegetables, fruit, nursery production and other field crops (particularly sugar cane, sugar beet, potatoes) and beef cattle.

California is the effective headquarters of corporate farming with around one-quarter of all US cash receipts from this type of agricultural organization. Other areas where this type of farming is markedly concentrated are Florida, the Mountain states, the Mississippi delta region and Hawaii. Corporate farming has made very little impact in the northeast and central grain growing regions.

California is where 'agribusiness' is most advanced. The term refers to the developing interest

Rice harvest south of Alexandria, Louisiana

in agriculture of big business such as food retailers, oil, aircraft and insurance companies and the increase in vertical integration in the industry. The status of corporate farming in the state reflects the general land ownership pattern where major corporations own large tracts of private land. Many of the corporate owners came into agriculture almost by accident in that they owned previously marginal lands which are now capable of intensive production due to the extension of water projects in the state. The capital gains to be realised on agricultural investment have also been a powerful incentive.

Vertical integration is exemplified in California by companies such as Del Monte and Safeway, who by developing their farming interests, are now involved in all stages of the food business from initial production to retailing. Controlling the source of supply for an integrated food processing and marketing operation tends to minimise risks and maximise profit opportunities.

Corporate capital has also been attracted into agriculture by the nature of US farm and tax policies which allows substantial tax advantages to such organizations. While the family farm has always been held in the highest esteem by public policymakers, government farm programmes have given an unintended boost to larger farms even though various direct actions have been implemented to aid the smaller family units.

Corporate farming has been criticised by many for driving a wedge into the traditional and sentimental relationship between the farmer and his land and for imposing an unfamiliar social structure on increasing areas of rural America. In a number of midwestern states corporate farming has either been outlawed or sharply restricted.

Despite the increasing share of sales accounted for by corporate farms the family farm is likely to remain the norm for agricultural organization in the US. Compared to many industrial sectors of the economy, economic power in agriculture is relatively diffused whereby the industry is controlled by a large number of individual producers. Some authorities see this position being reversed if the large corporations gain a more sizeable hold over the country's farm sales.

Many large farms are in fact family farms, making the distinction between corporate farm and family farm to some extent rather an academic one. Over the country as a whole six per cent of all farms now account for over half of total farm income. Although the ability of many smaller farm units to stay in business has been surprising, the soaring level of capital requirements continues to squeeze such farmers out of agriculture.

Public policy has encouraged the co-operative concept as a means of enhancing the bargaining power of the average farmers and over 80 per cent of all US farmers belong to one or more of the 7535 farm co-operatives in the country. Farmland Industries is the biggest US co-operative. Its owners are 2300 local co-op associations which are in turn owned by half a million farmers. Alongside Farmland Industries several other co-operatives also rank among the 250 largest industrial corporations in the United States.

As farming has become more competitive, operators have sought to maximize economies of scale. Interestingly a 1980 report by the USDA stated that while agricultural efficiency increases when smaller farms are merged into bigger units, when medium-sized operations are consolidated into large farms there is a very much lower reduction in unit costs of production. The report concludes that 90 per cent of the total economies of scale in agriculture can be captured by family farms. However to gain the remaining 10 per cent the farm has to be greatly increased in size. A wheat-barley farm in the northern plains can attain 90 per cent of the economies of scale at 70 hectares but requires a size of about 600 hectares to achieve total possible economies of scale.

Federal involvement in agriculture

From the initial establishment of the nation the federal government has actively encouraged the development of the agricultural sector of the economy. In the nineteenth century government emphasis was primarily on expanding the agricultural domain but after the frontier could be extended no further federal involvement was centred on productivity and the maintenance of a strong and stable farm sector.

Prior to the early decades of the present century high levels of immigration and steadily rising incomes resulted in an elastic domestic demand for food whereby increasing production was met by concomitant levels of demand. However by the 1920s immigration had slowed markedly and average incomes had risen to such a level that demand for food in the US had become highly inelastic. The standard of living had reached a stage where the majority of the population could buy what they 'wanted' with regard to food so that further income increases would be spent on other products. Production was now frequently higher than demand, causing a fall in market prices and consequently a lower level of farm incomes.

The increasingly precarious position in which farmers found themselves led to direct federal involvement in levels of farm income and production through the Agricultural Adjustment Act of 1933, part of President Roosevelt's 'New Deal'. Since the introduction of this legislation the aims of the government have been to protect farm incomes, maintain relatively stable food prices and control levels of production to relate to domestic and foreign demand for US food. At times of strong demand such as during World War II and the period of postwar construction, the Korean War and the mid and late-1970s farms have maximized production in response to high prices in the world market (and/or from federal price support).

During periods of more limited demand for US farm produce the government has attempted to restrict production of surplus crops by paying farmers to reduce their planted area.

By encouraging production when demand is high and restricting it when demand is depressed the extreme oscillations of farm prices which are likely to result in the absence of such intervention can be minimised. And by guaranteeing farm incomes at a certain level during difficult times, and so reducing bankruptcies to a minimum, stability of production can be maintained.

In reality, however, the situation has not been quite so simple. When farmers have had to restrict their planted area to qualify for federal support programmes they have frequently compensated by retiring their poorest quality land and improving productivity on their remaining areas. Due to such an understandable reaction from the individual farmer, production control has proved to be difficult in practice.

The basic mechanism used to stabilize farm income is the commodity loan (price-support loan) whose level acts as a price floor for farmers. The loans, administered by the Commodity Credit Corporation, permit farmers to borrow from the government at a level pegged to the per-bushel price of whatever crop the farmer offers as collateral. Farmers generally do not market their crops if prices fall below the loan levels; instead they hold them, or default on their loans and let the government keep the collateral.

A variation on the basic price-support loan is the 'farmer-held reserve' programme under which farmers borrow against crops while retaining ownership and managing storage of them. Lending rates, as in 1980, may well be set higher than for basic price-support loans. Farmers in the reserve cannot sell the stored crops for three years unless certain market conditions occur. If a predetermined 'release' market price is reached, farmers may sell their grain and repay their loans; if a higher 'call' price is reached, they must sell.

To provide a supplement for farm income when market prices plummet, Congress in 1973 added target prices to the basic loan system. These prices, calculated on the national average cost of producing a crop, are set above the loan levels. If market prices fail to reach the target-price level, farmers can collect 'deficiency payments', the difference between target prices and loan levels.

Generally the USDA has tried to encourage production of crops in high demand by setting generous support prices and to discourage those in limited demand by establishing less attractive support prices. Thus the pattern of agricultural land use in the United States has been subject to an increasing level of politico-economic influence.

A 'circle sprinkler system' irrigating wheat near Klamath Falls, Oregon

Farmland under attack

Agricultural production in many parts of the United States is being threatened by heavy rates of soil erosion and by competition from other land uses.

The rate of soil erosion per hectare of cropland in the United States averages about 27 tonnes per year and has resulted in a loss of at least one-third of the nation's topsoil. The USDA estimate that soil erosion has reduced yields on one-quarter of all arable land and on sixty per cent of the nation's rangeland. The Soil Conservation Service foresee corn and soybean production falling by thirty per cent over the next fifty years (although both are still rising at present) if the present rate of soil erosion continues.

Inputs of fertilizers have escalated in the postwar period partly in an attempt to offset the effects of soil erosion as well as in the effort to increase yields. About 56 litres of fuel equivalents per hectare is now being used to offset the soil erosion losses on US cropland and such inputs will of necessity have to be expanded in the future.

Increasing concern has been expressed about the effects of high foreign demand for US farm produce in recent years. In response to strong market demand many farmers have abandoned practices such as contour-ploughing and crop rotation and concentrated on maximizing short-term yields. Between 1969 and 1980 the area planted with crops rose from nearly 121 million hectares to approximately 147 million hectares. In the process much land which is particularly vulnerable to erosion has been ploughed up.

An additional and serious consequence of soil erosion is the deposition of sediment in rivers, lakes and reservoirs which is occurring at a rate of about 2.7 billion tonnes a year according to the USDA.

Although federal soil conservation measures were introduced in the 1930s and did a great deal to arrest the most obvious agricultural malpractices, current efforts to combat soil erosion are very limited and considered by most conservationists to be considerably less than adequate.

Prime agricultural land is continually being lost to urbanisation, highway construction, mining, land speculators and other changes of use. Between 1950 and 1980 over 1.2 million hectares of farmland was absorbed by urban development, a trend which is worrying many state governments. Massachusetts, for example, which produces only 15 per cent of its food requirement, views the maintenance of a certain level of farmland, capital investment and agricultural skill as an important aspect of the future development of the state. A food policy report issued by the state in 1976 recommended among other things the limitations of state actions that encroach on farmland, the elimination of unnecessary land use and environmental constraints that interfere with the conduct of farming, public acquisition of development rights to farmland and the assessment of farmland at existing rather than potential use for property tax purposes.

The latter point has been incorporated into legislation by most states in the country. Property taxes are normally set on the market value of land irrespective of how it is used. The market value of farmland in the vicinity of an urban area usually increases considerably as suburbanization approaches and as his land is now worth more on the open market, the amount the farmer has to pay in property tax rises. Such increases may be so high as to impel the farmer to sell out to a property developer or speculator although he had no intention of doing so when his taxes were more manageable. In the 1960s and 1970s a growing number of states allowed farmers to apply for their land to be assessed at its existing use, thus incurring lower property taxes, in return for certain agreements. The California Land Conservation Act of 1965 required farmers to restrict their land to agricultural or related use for a minimum of ten years as a condition of use-value assessment.

However in California the 1965 Act has had only limited success in halting the loss of farmland. Many large landowners who were already committed to remain in agriculture have used the Act to reduce considerably their property taxes.

Although land use zoning has long been a tool of urban land use control it has only filtered through to rural areas relatively recently but will undoubtedly be used by an increasing number of local governments in the future as a method of preventing the loss of agricultural land.

The developing export market

In the 1920s and 1930s the United States was a net importer of agricultural products. The war changed this situation for a while but by 1950 the United States had again moved into deficit in its farm trade. In the 1950s and 1960s the margin between exports and imports was relatively small although generally in favour of the former. However in the 1970s agricultural exports from the United States quadrupled (Figure 10.9) and in fiscal 1980 hit their tenth straight record, exceeding $40 billion. Farm exports are now a major aspect of US trade.

The strength of foreign demand in the last decade has allowed the agricultural sector to behave in a way uncharacteristic of that of the general economy. The United States is by far the largest contributor to the world market in food products and the recent leap in demand for US agricultural produce is the greatest change for the country's agriculture since the introduction of federal support and control programmes during the Depression. The American farmer has become increasingly dependent on unstable foreign demand in comparison to the relative stability of the home market.

The Department of Agriculture estimates that for the early 1980s, three-fifths of the soybean crop, more than half of the wheat and approximately one quarter of all US maize will be sold abroad.

The Soviet Union has been of vital importance to the recent success story of US agriculture and when that country first entered the world grain market in 1972, US grain exports nearly doubled to more than 70 million tonnes to remain at a high level for the rest of the decade. Two-thirds of Soviet arable lands are north of the 49th parallel (i.e. more equivalent to Canada) where extreme cold, devastating crop yields, is likely two out of four years. The need for the Soviet Union to buy heavily on the world market is most likely to continue and as the United States provides about 60 per cent of all feed grains in world markets, trade between the two nations should remain at a high level at least in the near future.

However the willingness of the US government to use the 'food weapon' in a political crisis, such as over Afghanistan, has led the Soviet Union to seek out alternative suppliers as well and not to become too dependent on the US. In 1980 the USSR bought 30 million tonnes of corn and wheat in world markets while China purchased 11 million tonnes. US and Canadian farmers see both countries as major customers again in the 1980s after the large-scale establishment of agricultural trade in the previous decade.

In 1980 total US grain exports jumped to a record 116 million tonnes. The vastness of total production can be illustrated by the facts that Iowa and Illinois grow approximately one-sixth of all world maize and Kansas and North Dakota together produce more wheat than the whole of South America.

Developing reliance on overseas markets has created certain problems for US farmers. When harvests are good elsewhere in the world, particularly in the Soviet Union and China, demand and prices fall to the detriment of American agriculture. At times also a combination of a strong dollar in world money markets and high interest rates can make US produce expensive to purchase for foreign buyers and can act to supress demand. Thus the increasing role of foreign demand has introduced a higher degree of variability into North American agriculture.

Agriculture and rural problems

The drive towards greater efficiency has made US agriculture the most highly mechanised in the world with the result that the agricultural labour requirement has fallen considerably, causing difficulties of varying magnitudes in rural communi-

Fig. 10.9 *Total US agricultural output and exports 1960–80 (Source: US Dept. of Agriculture)*

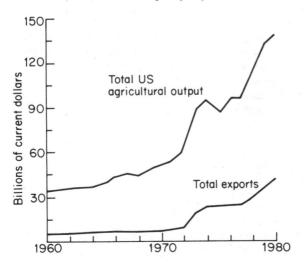

ties. In 1930 the farm population numbered 30.5 million or 24.9 per cent of the total population while farm employment was 12.5 million. Declining annually, the farm population dropped to 23 million in 1950, 15.6 million in 1960, 9.7 million in 1970 and 6.1 million in 1980. In the latter year the farm population accounted for only 2.7 per cent of the total population and actual farm employment was down to 3.5 million.

The relationship between rural distress and agricultural change must be kept in perspective as rural poverty, unemployment and underemployment are a result of the operation of the economy as a whole and cannot be attributed solely to agricultural innovation. Nevertheless the effect of agricultural progress has been a very real one indeed and should not be underrated.

The reducing agricultural labour requirement has had its greatest effect in areas where agriculture is a particularly important part of the local economy and in communities distant from major metropolitan areas where industrial decentralization has had little effect and where commuting to alternative job opportunities is impractical. Such areas have been characterised by high rates of out-migration. The initial lack of job opportunities often sets in motion a downward spiral of rural depopulation (Figure 10.10).

In 1960 three-quarters of the United States 3000 counties, including virtually all the rural and semi-rural counties, were slower-growing low-income places with population increases below the national average if not population losses. These counties covered two-thirds of the total land area but contained only one-third of the population. They were, on the whole, sparsely populated areas having only one fifth of the US population classed as urban. On average these counties lost nearly one per cent of their population each year between 1950 and 1960 and accounted for nearly half of all US families with incomes under $3000 in 1960. They were characterised by over-representation in both the over 65 and under 21 age groups. During the decade a net annual average of one million persons left farms or became nonfarm population. 1500 counties lost population, with the South being the region of major loss (Figure 10.11).

The position changed somewhat in the 1960s when approximately half of the rural and semi-rural counties participated in the general economic expansion of the US economy. Overall rural economic development appeared to be related to the size of urban place within the county with larger towns functioning as either spontaneous or induced growth centres, the latter where funds from economic development programmes were injected into the local economy.

About half of the new jobs created were in manufacturing but the growth of rurally located manufacturing industry in the 1960s was led by industries such as apparel, textiles and forest products, epitomised by the small firm using low skill, low wage labour. Such industries in the mature stage of the product cycle, while providing alternative employment and stemming the rate of out-migration, were not the type to infuse dynamic growth into the areas in which they chose to locate.

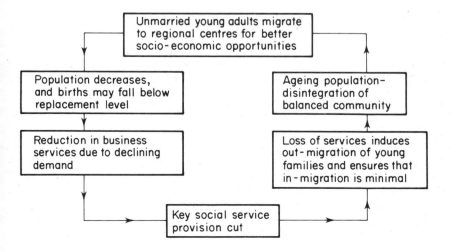

Fig. 10.10 *Model of the downward spiral of rural depopulation*

Wheat harvest on the High Plains near Miami, Texas

The overall effect of the increase in rural manufacturing industry combined with a slower national rate of population growth was that only 1000 counties registered population decline in the 1960s. However a marked shift in the location of rural population loss had occurred with such counties now concentrated in the West North Central division. Nevertheless the South still remained the nucleus of economic distress in terms of low incomes and rural unemployment.

The peak of agriculturally induced out-migration was passed in the 1960s and by the following decade the farm population had reached such a low level that it could no longer influence trends in the total rural population as it had done in the past. Rural population trends are now more influenced by other factors such as employment in the off-farm sectors of agriculture, lumbering, mining, rural manufacturing, retirement zones and general service provision. The 1970s has witnessed a certain swing back to the land as population grew faster outside SMSAs (Standard Metropolitan Statistical Areas) than within them. Nevertheless agricultural mechanization continued to induce strong out-migration in certain regions.

Despite various direct or indirect government programmes aimed at attacking rural poverty considerable problems remain. The lack of working capital, financial reserves and inadequate land of the poor farmer renders him increasingly uncompetitive and forces many off the land, particularly where off-farm supplementary employment is unavailable. Poor nonfarm workers suffer

Fig. 10.11 Farm population by division (thousands)

Division	1940	1950	1960	1970	1980
New England	623	403	232	128	89
Middle Atlantic	1 788	1 388	887	571	354
East North Central	4 638	3 703	2 821	2 053	1 207
West North Central	4 711	3 729	3 015	2 252	1 522
South Atlantic	6 060	4 633	2 838	1 357	744
East South Central	5 283	4 048	2 494	1 329	717
West South Central	5 057	3 215	1 828	1 069	701
Mountain	1 118	859	678	446	310
Pacific	1 270	1 070	842	508	406
Total	30 547	23 048	15 635	9 712	6 051

Source: US Statistical Abstract.

from low and intermittent incomes and most rural poor have little in the way of marketable skills. Underemployment, the use of labour below its full potential in skills, productivity and incomes still presents a considerable problem. Although income differences between farm and nonfarm families as well as between nonmetropolitan and metropolitan households have narrowed, rural America still lags behind the metropolitan counties under virtually all standard socio-economic criteria.

Agriculture in Canada

Regional variations in production

Although the land area of Canada is slightly larger than that of the United States agriculture is restricted to less than eight per cent of the total area and much of this land is only of marginal capability for many field crops. Yet Canada is among the world's foremost producers and exporters of food.

Approximately seventy per cent of Canada lies north of the thermal limit for crop growth and most farms are within 500 km of the US border. Where agriculture is climatically possible adverse relief, soil and drainage conditions impose widespread limitations within three of the major physiographic regions of southern Canada, the Appalachian-Acadian Uplands in the east, the Canadian Shield and the Western Cordillera. The only really continuous areas suitable for agriculture are the Interior Plains or Prairies and the less expansive Great Lakes–St Lawrence Lowland region.

The extent of Canada's agriculturally productive land is illustrated by Figure 10.12 which also indicates the dominant farming type in each region and the great contrast between eastern and western Canada.

In the Atlantic Provinces agriculture is extremely limited by poor soils and terrain and is characterised by extreme fragmentation of holdings, apart from Prince Edward Island, which is sometimes known as the 'Garden of the Gulf'. Agriculture is practised over most of the island and specialises in producing seed-potatoes and breeding pedigree cattle. Elsewhere in these provinces dairying is the main source of income (Figure 10.13) with cattle, hogs, poultry and to a lesser extent fruit and vegetables also of importance. Overall the Atlantic Provinces contain less than two per cent of the total agricultural area of the country.

The central region of Quebec and Ontario is the second largest agricultural region of Canada but most of its farms are confined to the shores of the St Lawrence, the Ottawa Valley and southern Ontario although there are a few isolated agricultural districts farther north. Livestock operations predominate, particularly dairy, beef, hogs and poultry. Corn, mixed grains, winter wheat, oats

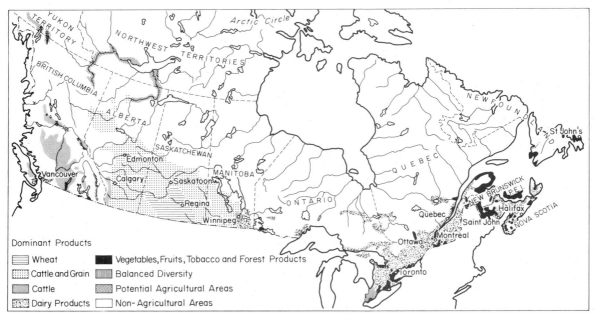

Fig. 10.12 *Agricultural regions in Canada (Source:* Agriculture Canada*)*

Tobacco field in south-western Ontario

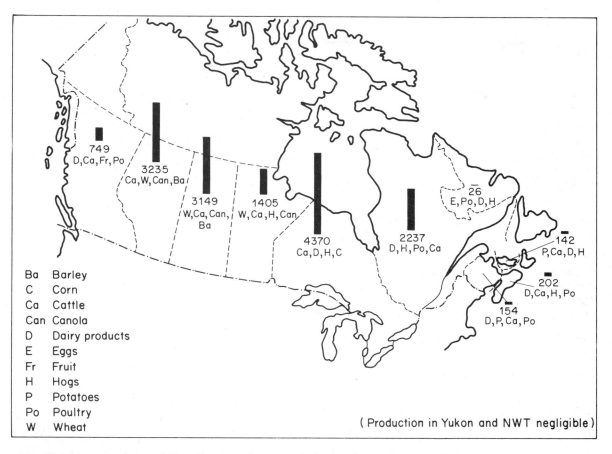

Ba Barley
C Corn
Ca Cattle
Can Canola
D Dairy products
E Eggs
Fr Fruit
H Hogs
P Potatoes
Po Poultry
W Wheat

(Production in Yukon and NWT negligible)

Fig. 10.13 *Farm income (C$ million) and principal sources by rank for each province 1980*

and barley are cultivated for feed. Among the cash crops of the region are soybeans, potatoes, tobacco, fruit and vegetables.

Farms in the central region are considerably smaller than in the extensive farming region of the Prairies, being mainly between 30 and 140 hectares. However the nature of production is generally intensive, being close to urban markets, and while the region contributes only 14.5 per cent of Canadian farmland it was responsible for over 42 per cent of total farm cash receipts in 1980.

The largest of Canada's agricultural regions, with over three-quarters of all farmland, is the Interior Plains in the southern Prairie Provinces, characterized by extensive wheat and cattle farming. Farms average around 200 hectares and are highly mechanized. The climate is particularly suited to the production of high quality hard red

spring wheat and in Saskatchewan wheat sales form almost two-thirds of farm income. Oilseed crops (rapeseed, flax and sunflowers) are becoming increasingly important on the prairies. Seed grain, forage seed, sugar beets and vegetables are cultivated in some areas. The three Prairie Provinces combined account for about half of all Canadian farm sales.

Farmland in British Columbia is extremely restricted by the physical environment with income coming mainly from dairy produce, cattle, fruit and poultry. The Peace River valley in northern Alberta and British Columbia is an anomaly in Canadian agriculture because of its northerly position. The cool climate and short growing season limit agricultural production but are compensated to some extent by long summer days. Grain and forage are the two main crops with livestock operations based on cattle, pigs and poultry.

Physical restrictions

Physical geography has imposed far greater limitations on agriculture in Canada than it has south of the border. In two countries of broadly similar land area the United States possesses more than five times the cropland of its northern neighbour. In addition the United States has a far higher percentage of its cropland in 'optimum' climatic conditions. This means that urban expansion has a more critical effect on scarce prime land in Canada.

One gross assessment of the comparative agro-climatic conditions of cropland has been produced by N.C. Field (Figure 10.14). His analysis generalized thermal conditions as degree months and moisture as the percentage of actual moisture against potential evapotranspiration, to assess the cropland conditions of the United States and Canada. While 81 per cent of US cropland is over the 200 degree month divide according to Field, 98 per cent of Canadian cropland falls below it. The marginality of Canadian cropland is further ex-

emplified by the fact that nearly two-thirds has a greater than 20 per cent moisture deficiency. Field concludes that while 56 per cent of US cropland experiences optimum climatic conditions, the relevant figure for Canada is only 2 per cent.

Figure 10.15 illustrates the distribution of Canadian farmland according to climatic and soil classes. The nation's highest quality farmland is almost entirely located within the 14 counties of south-western Ontario in an area experiencing loss of farmland to urbanization and other competing uses.

Development and change

As in the United States, Canadian agriculture has been characterized by rising levels of mechanization and productivity, increases in size of farm units and a declining labour force.

The farm population, which includes all people living on farms, has been reduced from over three million in 1941 to approximately one million by 1980, a drop from 27 per cent to less than 5 per cent of the total population. The rapid fall in the farm population set in motion a considerable rural to urban migration, particularly in the 1950s and

An aerial view of the quiet, farming community at Blomidan Cape, Nova Scotia

Fig. 10.14 Cropland percentages by thermal and moisture categories

(AM/PE) × 100 (%)	Canada				United States			
	100–199	200–299	300	Total	Degree Months 100–199	200–299	300	Total
90–100	22	2	–	24	8	30	19	57
80–89	10	–	–	10	2	5	2	9
65–79	48	–	–	48	5	7	3	15
0–64	18	–	–	18	4	7	8	19
Total	98	2	–	100	19	49	32	100

1960s. Employment in agriculture now totals only 450 000 and since 1951 over 150 000 farm jobs have been lost in the prairie provinces alone, the region of largest absolute decrease.

The mechanization of Canadian agriculture has progressed rapidly with the number of tractors on farms rising from 400 000 in 1951 to 650 000 in 1980. The greatest use of farm machinery is in areas of larger farms, particularly the prairies and those areas of most intensive cropping in both eastern and western Canada.

The use of fertilizer has risen steadily, particularly with intensively cultivated high value crops such as corn, soybeans, field vegetables and tobacco. Until recently large areas of the extensive wheat and other grain prairie region were cultivated with very limited fertilizer inputs.

Although the number of farms in Canada has declined by about 60 per cent since 1941 the average farm size has more than doubled from 95 to 200 hectares. The trend towards larger units has been most marked in the prairies and the Atlantic provinces. The only areas of Canada with average farm size below 50 hectares are in the extreme

Self-unloading wagon auguring silage into feed trough at steer feeding farm in Middlesex County, Ontario

Fig. 10.15 *Canada: areas in agricultural land resource classes (Source:* Atlas of Canadian Agriculture*)*

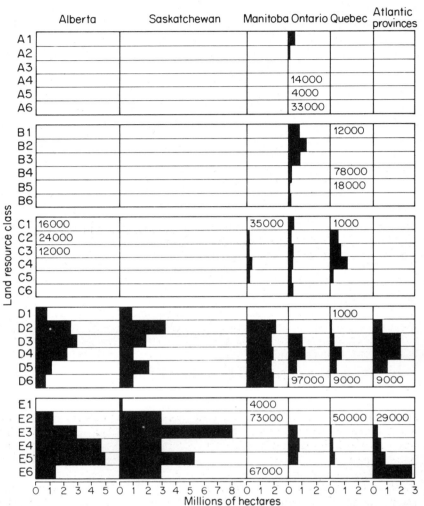

The five climatic zones (A to E) in order of declining quality are based on William's agroclimatic resource index ACRI, which takes into account frost-free season, heat accummulation and moisture deficiencies. The soil capability classes rate soils as follows:

1. No limitations for general field crops
2. Moderate limitations that restrict range of crops or require moderate conservation practices
3. Moderately severe limitations
4. Severe limitations: suitable for only a few crops, or else the yield for a range of crops is low, or high risk of crop failure
5. Perennial forage at best, but improvements feasible
6. Perennial forage, improvements not feasible

Data is not available for British Columbia; estimates for B.C. are 600 000 ha. in classes 1 and 2, 1.4 million ha. in class 3, and 2.6 million in class 4, in various climatic zones

Cattle drive at Douglas Lake Ranch in British Columbia

southern peninsula of Ontario and the Toronto and Greater Vancouver areas where orchard and horticultural holdings and many part-time farms predominate.

Productivity per unit of labour in the agricultural sector now exceeds the average of other sectors of the Canadian economy on both a per person and a per man-hour basis. Yields of all major crops and the produce from livestock have risen considerably in the post-war period, a result of the increased use of agricultural capital, improved inputs and the upgrading of the technical and managerial skills of farm workers, especially owner-operators.

Government intervention and income stabilization

As is the norm in developed countries the Canadian government has intervened in the agricultural market with the express purpose of maintaining a healthy farm sector by ensuring relative stability in farm income and farm prices. The Agricultural Stabilization Act protects farmers against significant market instability by establishing support prices for many products. The Agricultural Stabilization Board which administers the Act supports producers by buying produce at prescribed prices, granting deficiency payments and making direct payments to farmers at a fixed rate.

The creation of marketing boards, particularly the Canadian Wheat Commission, established in the 1930s, and the Canadian Dairy Commission, set up in the late 1960s, has done much to develop the efficiency of the nation's agriculture. The federal government's 'Food Strategy for Canada' stresses the aim of ensuring adequate supplies of safe and nutritious food at prices that are reasonable to both producers and consumers. While the export trade forms an important part of the strategy, Canada has maintained an above average per capita level of food aid to the less developed world.

Canadian agricultural exports amounted to

C\$9.3 billion in 1980, accounting for 12.2 per cent of total exports, while food imports cost the country C\$4 billion. Along with the United States, Canada has increased its positive agricultural trade balance in recent years. Between 30 per cent and 35 per cent of Canada's total agricultural output, including 75 per cent of the wheat crop, is sent abroad. Wheat is easily the country's number one food export with the EEC, Japan and the USSR being the major buyers. Canada is the second largest wheat exporter in the world after the United States.

Canadian barley exports have averaged over three million tonnes in recent years and account for from less than 20 per cent to more than 40 per cent of world trade in this product. In two important oilseed crops, rapeseed and flaxseed, Canada led the export field in the 1970s, supplying up to 60 per cent of total world demand.

Case studies in North American agriculture

1. Wheat cultivation in the Canadian Prairies

Although first planted in 1604 it was not until 1617 that wheat began to be grown seriously in Canada. However the establishment of wheat cultivation on the huge scale that gradually made Canada one of the world's major suppliers awaited the opening up of the western prairies.

The railways were the key to the development of the prairies. As the network extended westward and northward in connectivity more and more land was put under the plough as the agricultural domain spread. By 1876 wheat was being shipped from the prairies to Ontario for seed.

Prairie wheat was early recognised as unusually hard and of outstanding quality for milling. The first wheat shipment from western Canada to Britain, where the expanding population created an ever rising demand for bread, went via the United States in 1877. It began to be shipped by an all-Canada route in 1884, the year after the Canadian Pacific railroad reached what is now Calgary.

The major problem encountered by the early farmers was the short growing season which exceeds 120 days only in the extreme south-east where initial prairie cultivation was concentrated. The first really successful wheat strain to be produced was Red Fife which allowed the westward and northward extension of the wheat growing area from the Manitoba lowland. Shortly after the turn of the century the Marquis strain was developed which ripened a week earlier than Red Fife, allowing wheat cultivation to spread further still. Later developments such as Garnett and Reward combined the characteristics of maturing early with resistance to rust, a fungoid growth.

A constant stream of innovations has gradually changed the agricultural scene in the prairies. The family sized farm has grown from the few acres worked by hand to hundreds of acres easily managed with machines and two or three workers in most cases. Further improved varieties of wheat have reduced the growing season requirement by twenty days compared to the early nineteenth century, while progress in transportation and marketing have combined to make the industry highly efficient.

Ploughing is now virtually obsolete on the prairies as it contributes to soil erosion by making the topsoil susceptible to drifting. Cultivators are designed to cut weed roots an inch or two below the surface without turning the soil. The seed drill plants the wheat in combination with fertilizer in rows 15 to 18 cm apart. A modern combine harvester allows one man to harvest more than 2000 bushels of wheat in one day.

Wheat streak mosaic disease, caused by a virus, can be controlled by cultural practices but recent research indicates that a new variety with resistance to the disease can be produced. New varieties resistant to wheat stem sawfly attack are now cultivated on the prairies. The larvae of the fly develop in the hollow stem of wheat plants and later girdle the stems. The early winds snap the stems and the wheat-bearing heads topple to the ground. New strains produced by the Department of Agriculture have solid stems and greatly reduce the damage that might occur to part of the more than 6.5 million hectares of wheat grown each year.

Red spring wheat is the dominant variety grown in western Canada and is ideally suited to the prevailing climatic conditions. The top grade No. 1 Canada Western Red Spring must have at least 15 per cent protein content.

As important as increasing efficiency and reliability on the farm is the task of transporting the grain to market. The railroad network is vital in this movement. The first country grain elevator in western Canada was built in Manitoba in 1881. Today there is a network of some 5000 elevators, spread across about 2000 railway shipping points from which wheat and other grains are picked up. A standard elevator is a tall wooden structure with a capacity of around 70 000 bushels divided among perhaps 25 separate storage bins. The current trend is to site elevators of increased capacity greater distances apart.

The marketing of prairie wheat, and for that matter barley and oats as well, is controlled by the Canadian Wheat Board which was established in 1935. In order that delivery opportunities are allocated fairly among all farmers a quota system is operated. Each farmer's quota is determined by the area farmed and the crops grown. Quotas are given for oats and barley also. The farmer may use his quota for all three crops or apply it totally to one grain. The quota is administered through a system of delivery permit books.

The Wheat Board operates a system of price pooling which helps to stabilise prices as of course does the price support mechanism. At the time of delivery to the elevator the farmer's wheat is weighed, graded and an initial payment is made by the elevator manager. The full price paid by end customers will not be known until the crop year is over. Then the price received by the Wheat Board for the kind and grade of wheat delivered by the farmer is pooled and the farmer receives a final payment to make up the difference between the pool price and the initial payment.

The movement of grain has to be a precise operation and is organised on a weekly basis by the Wheat Board following a specified routine:
(*i*) The type, quality and quantity of grain required at the central shipping terminals, in Thunder Bay at the head of the Great Lakes, in Vancouver and Prince Rupert on the west coast and in Churchill on Hudson Bay, during the summer shipping season is decided six weeks before delivery.
(*ii*) Elevator managers report weekly on the stocks they are holding.
(*iii*) Shipping instructions are issued on the basis of loading zones. The prairie grain-growing area has been divided into 48 blocks for this purpose.
(*iv*) Grain cars load the wheat (or barley and oats)

and deliver to port where the produce is required to load on ship or to build up inventories in the huge terminal storage elevators.

Canada is the second largest supplier of wheat to world markets after the United States and such trade is a most important part of the prairie province's economies.

Canadian 1980 wheat production is estimated at 19.1 million tonnes, which includes 888 000 tonnes of winter wheat, 1.92 million tonnes of durum wheat and 16.3 million tonnes of red spring and other wheats. With an estimated carryover of 10.6 million tonnes, the Canadian wheat supply for 1980–81 is estimated at 29.7 million tonnes, down more than 2 million tonnes from that of the previous year and the lowest level since 1975–76. Assuming a domestic use of 5.8 million tonnes, there is a balance for exports and ending stocks of 23.9 million tonnes.

In provincial terms, Saskatchewan is Canada's largest producer, 10 million tonnes or more in a reasonable year. Recent decades have witnessed a steady growth in the size of prairie farms while the labour input has continued to fall. The number of active grain farmers in western Canada fell by more than one-third between 1953 and 1980. In addition diversification has occurred and today the region is less reliant on wheat than it used to be, although wheat remains the main source of farm income in the prairies.

2. Cotton production in the US sunbelt

The cultivation of cotton in the United States has undergone a fundamental change in location during the course of the last century. Such a movement illustrates vividly the interaction between physical and economic factors and the developing role of government intervention.

Cotton has been a cash crop in the sunbelt since the earliest days of settlement. Prior to the Civil War it was the stalwart of the southern economy and because of its heavy labour requirements was a prime factor in the pro-slavery attitudes of the southern states. At this time the south-eastern states formed the nucleus of the cotton belt and production was based firmly on the plantation system.

However, even in this early period of cotton, problems began to arise. Cotton, along with the tobacco and maize also grown in the south, was extremely exhausting to the soil. Indiscriminate methods of cultivation led to severe soil erosion in places and heavily declining yields. Cotton is sown widely apart allowing a relatively free flow of water on sloping land which can effectively reduce a weakened topsoil in a relatively short time period in the absence of countervailing measures.

The period following the Civil War witnessed the wholesale destruction of the plantation system. Plantations were fragmented into share-crop units. Share-cropping further aggravated the problems of soil erosion as the tenant farmers strived to obtain the maximum output from land which was not theirs and thought little of the eventual consequences.

Declining yields and the abandonment of some areas by cotton growers hastened the move westward to Texas where large scale units on soils which had not suffered from exhaustive cultivation, allowed more profitable farming. The growth of cotton production in Texas, first on the Black Waxy Prairies in the east but later under irrigation on the High Plains was further encouraged by the ravages of the cotton boll weevil.

The boll weevil moved into the US from Mexico in 1862 and wreaked havoc as it spread eastward, reaching the Atlantic coast in 1921. The boll weevil thrives in moist, humid conditions and is much less of a problem in the drier western regions.

The cultivation of cotton, like all crops, is confined by certain physical requirements. Its northern limit broadly follows the 25°C July isotherm which approximately corresponds with the extent of the 200 day growing season. The southern limit of cotton growing is governed by autumn rainfall in excess of 250mm thus excluding the middle and eastern sections of the Gulf coast plain.

As cotton tolerates a wide variety of soils, and rainfall is nowhere too great within the limits noted above, its longitudinal extent is ruled primarily by lack of water which has been overcome by extensive irrigation. By the 1920s production on the High Plains was slightly above that of the Black Waxy Prairies and not far behind that of the Mississippi Valley. At this time areas farther west accounted for less than 1 per cent of total US cotton production.

The following decades have been characterised by declining acreages, stable production and a significant shift in location further west still into California and Arizona.

The decline of cotton can be traced to the years following the First World War when European customers, trying not to increase their existing debt to the United States, sought their supplies elsewhere. Low prices encouraged farmers to attempt to safeguard their incomes by increasing production, which had the overall effect of further depressing prices. In an attempt to stabilize prices the government restricted the cultivation of cotton to a set acreage, re-examined each year, which is linked to estimated demand. The total cotton area harvested declined from 15.9 million hectares in 1924 to 7.6 million in 1954 and 5.3 million in 1980. However because technological developments have produced higher yielding cotton, the level of production has been relatively stable.

Along with cheaper production in other countries, intense competition from artificial fibres has given impetus to efforts to achieve greater efficiency in cotton cultivation using large units in the most fertile regions. The areas worst affected by soil erosion and those where cotton production was no longer economically viable have rapidly abandoned the crop.

The Black Belt of Alabama, once a renowned cotton area, has suffered severely from soil erosion which has exposed the limestone subsoil in places. In most other parts of the southeast yields have been maintained only by heavy inputs of fertilizer. Although the role of share-cropping and its associated small units has diminished in recent decades, farms remain much smaller in the southeast and less cost effective as they are unable to implement the economies of scale of the larger western units.

Production west of Texas, confined mainly to California and Arizona, has grown rapidly in the post-war period. Contributing only 3.5 per cent of total US cotton production in 1944, the region accounted for 15 per cent of production by 1954, rising to over 40 per cent of the national total in 1980 (Figure 10.16). Undoubtedly this western shift of cotton production would have been on a larger scale but for government intervention. Federal price supports have allowed many inefficient growers in the southeast to remain in business while western growers have had to await the abandonment of acreage allotments held in the southeast before expanding their own units.

Price supports were fixed in relation to the costs of the smaller scale units of the southeast and thus proved highly attractive and a great incentive to western farmers. In the 1970s the amount of total cotton production put under price support varied from a low of 8.5 per cent in 1975 to a high of 31.6 per cent in 1977.

In California the southern part of the San Joaquin valley is the main cotton growing area and here cotton is the dominant crop. Cultivation depends on irrigation and requires a large amount of water in addition to normal precipitation. The low cost of irrigation water, an increasingly controversial issue (Chapter 7), has been a major impetus to this trend. Cotton is also grown in the Imperial Valley. In Arizona production is concentrated along the Salt River downstream of Roosevelt Dam and along the Gila River downstream of Coolidge Dam. Irrigation cultivation is also carried out along the Colorado River downstream of Parker Dam.

As Figure 10.16 indicates, yields in the western region are extremely high due to a combination of good soils, ample irrigation water and the intensive methods of farming. Yields in Texas are by contrast low due mainly to the rather moderate

soils of the High Plains and the extensive nature of the farming practised.

3. Cattle feeding in the United States

Figure 10.17 shows that in the post-war period there has been a marked change in the location of the cattle-feeding industry in the United States. Coupled with this locational shift has been a huge increase in the scale of cattle-feeding units confined mainly to the areas of rapid expansion.

Cattle and calves on feed are animals for the slaughter market being fed a full ration of grain or other concentrates and expected to produce a carcass that will grade 'Good' or better. Traditionally the industry has been heavily concentrated in the mid-western Corn and Livestock Belt with large numbers of cattle brought from the drier plains to the west to be fattened on the vast quantities of grain produced in Iowa and neighbouring states. However the expansion of the cattle-feeding industry on the plains and the

Fig. 10.16 Cotton production in the USA 1949–1980

State	Area harvested (thousands of hectares)				Production (Bales, 480lb net wt)* (thousand)			
	1949	1959	1969	1980	1949	1959	1969	1980
N. Carolina	348	158	67	26	466	322	100	52
S. Carolina	514	229	116	49	554	417	205	77
Georgia	648	265	156	65	604	521	282	86
Tennessee	336	206	162	111	633	660	422	200
Alabama	732	338	221	130	852	718	461	275
Missouri	236	161	123	98	462	508	326	177
Mississippi	1 105	591	480	455	1 487	1 568	1 328	1 143
Arkansas	1 024	526	427	261	1 632	1 544	1 140	444
Louisiana	425	198	170	227	650	492	483	460
Oklahoma	526	253	188	229	610	381	279	205
Texas	4 411	2 570	1 892	2 782	6 040	4 416	2 862	3 345
N. Mexico	125	80	59	51	276	323	157	114
Arizona	162	155	125	255	543	715	634	1 426
California	387	354	285	607	1 268	1 922	1 315	3 109
Total (including others)	11 020	6 107	4 482	5 348	16 128	14 551	10 015	11 122

* Figures for 1949, 1959, 1969 in 500 lb gross wt bales; 480 lb = 217 kg.

Source: US Statistical Abstract.

Fig. 10.17 Cattle and calves on feed by major states 1950–1980 (thousands)

	1950	*1960*	*1970*	*1980*
Ohio	130	194	318	180
Indiana	195	224	356	250
Illinois	532	688	755	460
Michigan	95	130	210	165
Wisconsin	93	121	146	112
Minnesota	294	416	589	390
Iowa	1 020	1 510	2 213	1 390
Missouri	315	298	402	120
S. Dakota	195	247	361	350
Nebraska	420	665	1 477	1 680
Kansas	238	293	892	1 270
Oklahoma	55	69	223	330
Texas	161	239	1 417	1 970
Idaho	78	138	230	260
Colorado	180	385	795	960
N. Mexico	17	54	209	239
Arizona	59	265	510	420
Washington	16	115	155	155
California	196	663	1 031	764
US Total (including others)	4 552	7 206	13 197	12 223

development of breeding and rearing in the mid-west has made this region its own main source of stores.

In 1950 Iowa alone accounted for 22.4 per cent of feed cattle in the United States, followed in rank order by its mid-western neighbour to the east, Illinois, and the adjacent plains states of Nebraska and Kansas. The next three decades witnessed a major shift in the distribution of the industry towards the south and also westward. The following trends can be discerned:

(*i*) the largest increases have been recorded in the middle and southern plains, particularly in Texas, Nebraska, Kansas and Colorado,

(*ii*) a secondary region of expansion in the south-west of the country, especially in California and Arizona,

(*iii*) relatively minor increases in production by comparison in the traditional mid-western region.

The industry has grown most rapidly in Texas. In 1950 Texas was the eleventh ranking cattle-feeding state with 3.5 per cent of the US total, but thirty years later the state was firmly in number one position, accounting for 16.1 per cent of all cattle-feeding in the country. In the latter year Iowa's share of the national total had fallen to 11.4 per cent.

The United States is at the same time the world's largest producer of beef and the world's largest consumer and importer. Two-thirds of the beef produced in the US (and in Canada) is grain fed in contrast to virtually all other beef produced elsewhere in the world where cattle are raised on grassland or marginal cropland.

Consumer demand for grain-fed beef in addition to their greater weight gain in comparison to their grass-fed counterparts has attracted many farmers to 'finish' their animals before marketing by the more costly feeding of grain. Feedlot finishing of cattle by grain feeding results in a carcass with a higher ratio of lean meat to fat, meat which is more tender, has more flavour and which has the desired degree of marbling. Marbling is the little specks of fat interspersed throughout the lean meat that gives the meat much of its flavour. Since grain-fed beef is also more aesthetically appealing than the traditional grass-fed product, all of these factors combine to create a strong consumer demand.

Thus the large number of relatively small scale beef fattening operations found in the Corn and Livestock Belt and the grass fed beef areas have been increasingly challenged by large scale feedlots in the plains and in the southwest. Large-scale feedlots, which were pioneered in California, concentrate great numbers of cattle, fed intensively, on limited acreages. Some feedlots have a capacity in excess of 50 000 head.

The emergence of the major new cattle fattening regions can be attributed to a number of factors. Of prime importance has been the development of hybrid grain sorghum, a high yielding crop which is particularly suited to the semi-arid climate and clay-loam soil found in the southern high plains. In recent years the acreage planted has increased rapidly, much of it under irrigation, particularly in the southern plains. In 1979 Kansas, Texas and Nebraska accounted for 31.5 per cent, 29.8 per cent and 17.8 per cent respectively of total US grain sorghum production. The combination of irrigation and the use of anhydrous ammonia as a fertilizer has dramatically increased yields which have on average trebled although far greater increases have been reached under optimum conditions. Once again, as with cotton, a type of farming has moved west into the area of subsidised irrigation agriculture.

Impetus has also been given to the industry by the availability of relatively low-cost cattle within the region and from the southeast along with the rapid growth of the prosperous Gulf coast market. In terms of the future, the major problem in the southern plains will be the availability of water, where a substantial decline in supply is anticipated in the region south of the Canadian River by the end of the 1980s. In the absence of further scientific development such as the production of feed grains especially adapted to dryland farming methods, cattle feeding is likely to decline in this area.

The industry is, though, likely to increase in importance north of the Canadian River where irrigation water is more abundant. The next decade then may well bring another locational shift with Kansas and Nebraska becoming the clear nucleus of the industry. Feedlot operations in the southwest have expanded in response to the post-war population boom due mainly to rapid in-migration into the region. Both grain supplies and stores are available from the southern plains although local supply has increased in importance recently.

In contrast to the large feedlots characteristic of areas farther west, the corn belt is dominated by thousands of small operations where between 50 and 300 head are usually kept. The industry has grown more modestly in this region, mainly through the expansion of existing units rather than the establishment of new operations. The farms in this region are first and foremost geared to grain production and capital has been injected into this sector in preference to the large initial outlay that would be required to establish new feedlots. The harsher winter climate makes feedlots in this region expensive due to the absolute necessity for sheltered and paved lots. The industrial nature of the region where there are ample opportunities for off-farm employment has also affected investment decisions as large scale beef operations would not allow part time farming to continue.

It seems then that the cattle-feeding industry will continue to be characterised by locational change in response to varying physical and economic factors as it seeks out optimum conditions for production.

11
Fishing and Forestry

Fishing—international trends

In 1946 world production of fish was approximately 20 million tonnes. By the late 1960s the total had risen to about 70 million tonnes, a rate of increase of around 6 per cent per annum. In contrast the 1970s was a decade of stagnation for world fish production as exemplified by the 1980 total of 72.2 million tonnes. However in this period the increase in fishing capacity has been tremendous as more and more nations have looked to the oceans to supplement agricultural production and to satisfy the ever increasing demand for protein.

These trends have heralded a new era of resource management in world fishing epitomised by the unilateral declaration of 200-mile fishing limits in the late 1970s.

Most resource economists would agree that the record of human utilisation of fish stocks has been poor. In the late 1960s a working group estimated that the catch taken from the Northeast and Northwest Atlantic, one of the great fishing areas of the world, could be taken with about 33 per cent less effort than was actually being exerted. The degree of overcapacity was estimated at a needless cost of $100 million a year.

Equally alarming is the fact that the production of fish for direct human consumption has not been increasing over the last twenty-five years. The growth of total fish production in the 1950s and 1960s and the relative stability in the 1970s has

been almost entirely the result of an enormous increase in industrial fish production for meal and oil. The industry has been moving to lower valued species in order to maintain aggregate total production. Coupled with slowly rising demand, this has led to sharp increases in the real price of fish, which in turn has alerted coastal nations adjacent to major fishing grounds to the immense value of food from the sea.

Figure 11.1 illustrates that total catches in 1980 of 3.6 and 1.3 million tonnes ranked the United States and Canada fourth and sixteenth in the world respectively. The supremacy of Japan and the USSR in world commercial fishing is clear to see with the two nations combined totalling 27.5 per cent of world production.

North American fishing grounds

United States commercial fishing is concentrated in four fishing areas as shown by Figure 11.2 but the Atlantic Western Central and the Atlantic Northwest are by far the most important, accounting for 33.5 per cent and 35.7 per cent of United States catch respectively. The Pacific Northeast supplied 18.0 per cent of the total catch and Pacific Eastern Central 10.2 per cent. The combined catch of the Pacific Southeast, Pacific Southwest, Pacific Western Central and Atlantic Eastern Central contributed only 0.7 per cent of US production.

Fig. 11.1 Major fishing nations 1980

World rank	Country	Catch (Tonnes)
1	Japan	10 410 442
2	USSR	9 412 147
3	China	4 240 000
4	USA	3 634 526
5	Chile	2 816 706
6	Peru	2 731 358
7	India	2 423 482
8	Norway	2 398 171
9	Korea	2 091 134
10	Denmark	2 026 836
11	Indonesia	1 853 162
12	Thailand	1 650 000
13	Philippines	1 556 602
14	Iceland	1 514 874
15	Korea, North	1 400 000
16	Canada	1 305 319
World total		72 190 800

Source: FAO *Yearbook of Fishery Statistics*, 1980.

Canadian fishing is far more concentrated, with one fishing area, the Atlantic Northwest, accounting for 86 per cent of the total catch. The only other fishing area of interest to Canada is the Pacific Northeast, supplying 10 per cent of Canadian fish. It should be noted at this point that the data quoted above are for the quantity of landings which in a number of cases differ significantly from the value of landings.

Figure 11.2 shows the combined dominance of the United States and Canada in the Atlantic Northwest and Atlantic Western Central. In the Pacific Northeast and Pacific Eastern Central, Japan and Mexico are respectively the largest producers.

Inland waters, while locally significant in some regions, are currently of limited importance, supplying 1.9 per cent of United States fish and 4.0 per cent of Canadian production. The absolute totals were 69 500 and 53 000 tonnes for the two nations respectively in 1980. In contrast the world leaders in production from inland waters, China and India, registered 1.2 and 0.9 million tonnes.

Industrial concentration

While North America has a huge coastline bordering Pacific, Gulf, Atlantic and Arctic waters there are considerable spatial variations in both the value and volume of landings as well as in the variety of fish caught.

The causal factors determining the varying importance of the fishing industry along the North American coastline are not always easy to

Fig. 11.2 United States and Canadian fishing grounds 1980

Fishing ground	United States (Tonnes)	Canada (Tonnes)	World (Tonnes)
Atlantic Northwest	1 298 798	1 122 059	2 836 674
Atlantic Western Central	1 216 215	—	1 790 512
Atlantic Eastern Central	2 650	—	3 463 723
Pacific Northeast	653 674	130 260	1 954 150
Pacific Eastern Central	369 493	—	2 426 807
Pacific Western Central	3 759	—	5 698 980
Pacific Southeast	13 111	—	6 224 190
Pacific Southwest	7 218	—	369 919
Inland waters (N. America)	69 572	53 000	—
Total	3 634 490	1 305 319	24 764 955

Source: FAO *Yearbook of Fishery Statistics*, 1980.

isolate in detail but three major influences are apparent:

(*i*) proximity to major fishing grounds,
(*ii*) local demand for fish products,
(*iii*) the assessment of investment and employment opportunities in the fishing industry as opposed to competing areas of investment potential and job opportunity.

Figure 11.3 shows the most important states and provinces in the United States and Canada in terms of value of landings. In the United States the Pacific is the dominant region followed by the Atlantic and Gulf regions respectively.

While Alaska is by far the most important state for the value of landings a different picture emerges if the volume of landings is examined. In terms of quantity, Louisiana is the leading state

with 24.4 per cent of the United States total. Alaska and California follow in second and third places. Louisiana's dichotomy between value and volume (8.9 per cent and 24.4 per cent) is due to a very heavy reliance on menhaden, a relatively low value fish. Menhaden accounted for 41.2 per cent of United States landings by volume in 1979, with 66 per cent of the menhaden catch concentrated in the Gulf. Slightly over 98 per cent of menhaden landings were reduced to meal, oil and solubles, the rest being used for bait and for canned pet food.

Of the total United States landings of all fish in 1979, 43.6 per cent was reduced to meal and oil, 36.2 per cent went for human consumption either in a fresh or frozen state and 15.3 per cent was canned for human food. The remainder was either

Fig. 11.3 *Commercial landings and employment in fish processing by region 1978*

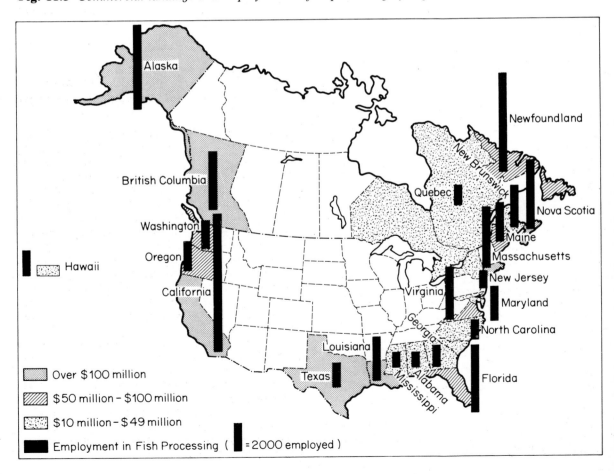

cured for human consumption or used as bait and animal food.

For Canada the Atlantic fishing grounds are dominant both in value and volume but much more so for the latter. In 1980 the Atlantic supplied 86.3 per cent by quantity of Canadian landings amounting to 70 per cent of total marketed value.

Figure 11.3 also indicates employment in fish processing by state and province. Although all coastal regions have some stake in secondary production the Atlantic and Pacific areas are clearly of greater importance than the Gulf. The premier regions for processing are California, Newfoundland, Alaska, Massachusetts, Nova Scotia and Florida.

The United States and Canada differ markedly in the major types of fish caught as illustrated by Figure 11.4. With reference to the value of commercial landings only salmon figures jointly in the leading five for both countries with no correlation in the leading catches by volume.

Commercial fishing is a seasonal occupation with limited numbers being occupied in the industry throughout the year. In the United States, 77 per cent of the catch is landed between May and October inclusive (1979). The Annual Statistical Review of Canadian Fisheries for 1980 indicates that for the three Maritime Provinces of Nova Scotia, New Brunswick and Prince Edward Island only 44.5 per cent of all fishermen gained more than 75 per cent of their income from fishing. 18.1 per cent earned between 26 per cent and 75 per cent of annual income from the industry while 36.4 per cent were below the 26 per cent level. Data for Quebec shows that over 50 per cent of fishermen work in the industry less than five months in the course of a year. In Newfoundland approximately 75 per cent of fishermen are in a similar employment position.

Fig. 11.4(a) United States—Leading fish caught 1979

Fish	Percentage of total by value	Fish	Percentage of total by volume
Shrimp	21.1	Menhaden	41.2
Salmon	18.5	Salmon	8.6
Crabs	12.7	Crabs	7.8
Tuna	7.1	Tuna	5.8
Menhaden	4.9	Shrimp	5.3

Fig. 11.4(b) Canada—Leading fish caught 1980

Fish	Percentage of total by value	Fish	Percentage of total by volume
Cod	21.8	Cod	33.8
Salmon	18.2	Herring	15.7
Lobster	11.6	Small flat fishes	8.5
Herring	10.1	Scallop	5.5
Scallop	9.9	Redfish	4.6

Source: US Dept of Commerce, *Current Fishery Statistics*, 1979 *Annual Statistical Review of Canadian Fisheries*, 1980.

The 200-mile limit—A landmark in resource management

In the latter part of the 1970s the 200-mile fishing limit became the accepted norm in world practice and thus in international law. The contention that open access exploitation of a common property fish stock attracts excessive effort leading to depletion of stocks, is now widely accepted. The objective of and the main justification for increased jurisdiction is that by limiting access and managing effort wisely, coastal states may halt over-exploitation and regenerate net economic benefits. Increasing pressure on the world's resources has greatly enhanced the potential value of the available fish stocks and thus the incentive for coastal states to claim the benefits of exploitation for their own.

The 200-mile limit encompasses most of the world's continental shelves and slopes so that the important demersal stocks that are tied to these shallower areas mostly come under coastal state management.

The extension of United States and Canadian jurisdiction to cover the continental shelf stocks of the Atlantic and Pacific has been of immediate benefit to both nations.

The Canadian government in 1976 developed a comprehensive policy document concerning resource management within the new limits. The country's most extensive fisheries, on the Atlantic coast, have long been in a generally depressed state where the major contributory factor has been the intense escalation of foreign fishing effort leading to resource depletion. Restrictions on foreign fishing operations have been phased in by stages and reasonable quota concessions have been made.

In return for fishing quotas within the Canadian zone, acknowledgement of Canadian authority in setting management rules for stocks straddling or bordering the 200-mile limit has generally been obtained. Other concessions include easy access for Canadian fish products to foreign markets and agreement to land some catches for processing in Canada. Canada is also collecting substantial fees from foreign fishing fleets.

Planned management of fisheries through control of fishing intensity, water quality and manpower resources is vitally important to Canada's efforts to assure optimum future fish harvests. The target for Canadian fisheries is to show noticeable improvement by the early 1980s and to be restored to at least 85 per cent of their peak by 1990.

The United States has adopted similar management policies in its Fishery Conservation Zone (FCZ) although it must be noted that the United States and Canada have come into conflict in the delimitation of boundaries. The greatest dispute concerns where the line should be drawn off Maine, New Brunswick and Nova Scotia. At issue is the rich Georges Bank. Other sectors where agreement has yet to be reached include the Beaufort Sea adjacent to Alaska and the Yukon and Dixon Entrance at the southern end of the Alaskan panhandle.

Revival of a large New England groundfish industry is being promoted, based on the reservation of United States 200-mile stocks for use of the domestic fleet. The principal obstacle remaining to such a development is the importation of cheap Canadian groundfish. As groundfish exports to the United States are the mainstay of Canada's economically vulnerable Atlantic coast fishing industry, the consequences of United States import restrictions could be quite severe.

The importance of the FCZ to the United States is indicated by the fact that in 1979 ninety per cent of total landings were caught within the 200-mile limit. Of the dominant fish landed in the United States only tuna is caught in large quantities outside the FCZ. In 1979 the United States landed 33 per cent of total fish in the FCZ, a marked increase over previous years.

In both the United States and Canada there has been a major change of fisheries management approach within the last few years, particularly the abandonment of the maximum sustainable yield (MSY) concept as the basis for establishing levels of harvest. The pursuit of MSY almost invariably meant low catch rates, relatively small fish, relatively low stock sizes and great variability in supply. There was also a tendency for the target to be exceeded, resulting in stock decline.

Recent attention has focussed on the concept of optimum sustainable yield (OSY). The new policy requires that the catch quotas be established on the basis of economic catching rates with biology setting the limits. For example in Canadian waters the total allowable catch for cod in 1980 was set at 458 000 tonnes compared with an estimate of MSY at 960 000 tonnes. Substantial reductions in stock abundance have occurred throughout the northwest Atlantic as a result of over-exploitation in the late 1960s and early 1970s.

The total allowable level of foreign fishing (TALFF) is that part of the optimum yield that will not be harvested by domestic vessels. For 1979 the United States set a TALFF of 2 102 000 tonnes with 1 205 429 and 540 119 tonnes allocated to Japan and the USSR respectively.

Aquaculture

Aquaculture, the farming of aquatic plants and animals, is an ancient practice recorded in Asia before the time of Christ and common in eastern Europe and south-east Asia in the thirteenth and fourteenth centuries. Aquaculture has emerged in North America in recent decades as a scientific development but is still only in its infancy. In 1975 United States production was 65 000 tonnes out of a world total of 6 million tonnes.

At present aquaculture is more highly developed in other countries where the pressure on resources is greater. Japan increased production from 0.1 million tons in 1971 to 0.5 million tons in 1976. In Israel almost 60 per cent of total fish comes from culture ponds.

Crab cannery, Masset, British Columbia

Aquaculture can make good use of land that is unusable for agriculture as evidenced by the commercial catfish ponds built on poor hilly land in the southeastern United States. The greatest concentration of catfish farming is in the Mississippi River floodplain, again primarily on poor quality land. In Louisiana swampland, crayfish have been successfully farmed simply by building a circular levée and flooding the impoundment after a summer's growth of vegetation. Aquaculture may even form part of a rotation system as in Louisiana where crayfish are rotated with rice.

In the Mississippi floodplain many farms are 100 hectares or more in size with individual ponds of 5–10 hectares. In 1978 catfish farming provided the highest net return for any crop in the state.

Canada may have a surplus supply of some fish products but not those produced through aquaculture. Canada imports trout and oysters from Japan and the United States, but these will increasingly in the future be provided by Canada's domestic aquaculture.

Aquaculture is very much a cottage industry in Canada and can provide a needed instrument of rural development. Although organised in a number of different ways, in general it is privately owned and small scale.

A number of different approaches have been developed in Canada. Notable among these are sea pens, made of net enclosures and placed in coastal bays to provide good water exchanges. Sea pens are used for coho salmon in Alberni Inlet, British Columbia and for rainbow trout in Bras d'Or and for blue fin tuna in St Margaret's Bay, Nova Scotia.

Fish farming as practised widely in Saskatchewan, Alberta and Manitoba makes use of lakes, natural potholes and farm dugouts for keeping trout. Highly intensive factory fish farms have also been developed in eastern Canada to serve the metropolitan markets of Montreal, Toronto and Ottawa. Similar developments have taken place in the United States.

The general increase in the world price of fish has made aquaculture a very attractive proposition in many areas of North America and there seems little doubt that the practice will become increasingly sophisticated as it develops in the coming years.

Newfoundland—A problem region

Some parts of North America still depend to a significant extent on commercial fishing, none more so than the Atlantic Provinces of Canada and Newfoundland in particular where dependence is absolute in many communities.

Newfoundland's strong reliance on the industry is very evident indeed as Figure 11.5 shows. In the province fishing (excluding processing) formed 18.8 per cent of total employment in 1980, by far the highest for any state or province in North America. In absolute terms Newfoundland has over 35 000 fishermen or 40 per cent of the Canadian total. This high level of dependency is also true for the secondary sector of the industry with the province accounting for 35 per cent of all Canadian employment in fish processing.

A more detailed analysis of fishing-dependent communities in the Atlantic region is shown by Figure 11.6, the result of a survey conducted by the Department of Regional Economic Expansion. A more recent analysis is not available but while a certain diversification occurred in the remaining years of the 1970s, dependence on fishing is still very intense.

Specialization here is measured by the Herfindahl Concentration Index, the root-mean of the proportion of employment in each major industrial category in a community. The index has a maximum value of one and a value equal to or greater than 0.30 is taken to indicate a high degree of economic dependence on fishing and fish

Fig. 11.5 Employment in fisheries—Canada 1980

Region	Fishermen (thousands)	Percentage of total employment
Newfoundland	35	18.8
Nova Scotia	11	3.3
New Brunswick	6	2.3
Prince Edward Island	3	6.1
Quebec	6	0.2
Ontario	2	0.05
Prairie Provinces	5	0.3
British Columbia	19	1.6
Canada	87	0.8

Source: Annual Statistical Review of Canadian Fisheries, 1980.

processing. The index in fact underestimates dependence in large communities on account of population size and the correlated size of the service sector and also because it only takes account of direct employment. Nevertheless, in spite of its limitations the technique provides a useful measure of specialization. Newfoundland registered a total of 90 high-dependence communities, more than all the other provinces put together.

In the Atlantic Provinces, household incomes tend to be lower in fishing communities than in the region generally. In Newfoundland the average household income in 1971 was $7200. For communities with some involvement in fishing it was $5600. But for communities in which the fishing industry was the major employer it was $4900. Communities suffering worst from chronically low income were largely those depending on local small-boat fisheries.

In an attempt to alleviate partially this problem the provincial government has implemented a programme of 'centralization' since the 1960s whereby inhabitants of small unviable fishing communities have been encouraged to move to larger settlements. Over a hundred small fishing communities have been abandoned as a result.

The demise of Newfoundland cannot be attributed to fishing alone but the problems of the Atlantic groundfisheries have produced cumulative detrimental effects. Until about 1955 only

Fig. 11.6 The Atlantic Region: fishery-dependent communities

Specialization Index	*Provincial Distribution*					
	Quebec no.	*New Brunswick no.*	*Prince Edward Island no.*	*Nova Scotia no.*	*Newfoundland no.*	*Region no.*
.20–.39	4	14	11	4	31	64
.40–.49	3	3	3	3	25	37
.50–.59	2	1	1	1	20	25
.60–.69	1		1		7	9
.70–.79					6	6
.80–89					1	1
High-dependence communities	10	18	16	8	90	142
All-dependent communities	112	136	94	87	273	702
Total fishing settlements	252	302	207	765	615	2141

Source: DREE.

Canada, the United States and five or six west European countries fished off Canada's Atlantic coast. However fishing intensified continuously from the late 1950s onwards. The groundfish catch more than doubled from 1 260 000 tonnes in 1951 to a peak of 2 829 000 tonnes in 1965. Reduction of stock caused a decline after this date (1 212 000 tonnes in 1980) although there was no comparable reduction in fishing efforts.

Cod is by far the most important fish landed in Newfoundland accounting for 50 per cent by value of all landings in 1980 but the catch is under a quarter what it was in the early 1960s. Figure 11.7 shows the decline in cod landings from the Labrador-Scotia Shelf in the early and mid 1970s. The reversal of this decline has been due primarily to the introduction of the 200-mile fishing limit. Notice the steady recent increase in Canada's share of the total catch. This trend has undoubtedly been of benefit to Newfoundland's fishing industry although great problems do still exist and the province will continue to require a large injection of federal government funds.

The diagram also indicates the projected total allowable catch until 1985 (TAC). This steady increase will be possible due to the new level of resource management now adopted by the Canadian government.

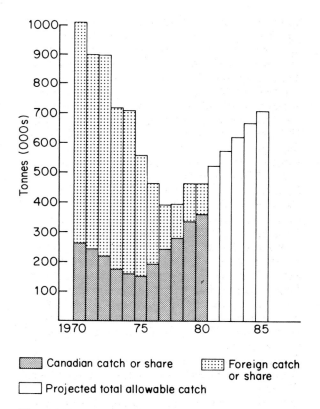

Canadian catch or share   Foreign catch or share

Projected total allowable catch

Fig. 11.7 *Total catches and projected catches of cod on the Labrador-Scotian shelf 1970–85* (*Source*: Statistics Canada)

Forestry

The United States and Canada have a commercial forest resource of about 400 million hectares and as such North America is one of only two areas of the world which have softwood surpluses. The other is Asiatic Russia. The United States and Canada are the world's leading traders in forest products. Canada is the world's largest exporter. The United States ranks second. Together they account for a third of the world's forest product exports.

Due to great physical and climatic contrasts within the continent, North America exhibits enormous variety in its natural vegetation and forest resources. In common with most other developed and many developing regions of the world the forests of North America have been significantly reduced in area as economic development has progressed, with land use patterns evolving at a pace never before witnessed in the world.

Figure 11.8 shows the basic natural vegetation pattern of North America where it can be seen that a general threefold division is apparent between Eastern, Western and Northern forest lands.

Canadian forests

Tundra covers a large part of northern Canada where the intense physiological drought of the winter rather than the low temperature is the limiting factor for tree development. This is an area of permafrost supporting low forms of vegetation such as mosses, lichens, sedges, sporadic grasses along with a few miniature willows, birches and other trees tolerant of a very harsh environment. The tree line generally follows the course of the 10°C July isotherm.

The Boreal forest region comprises the greater

Fig. 11.8 *The natural vegetation of North America (Source: Adams, D. K. Mills, S. F. Rodgers, H. B. An Atlas of North American Affairs, Methuen, London 1979)*

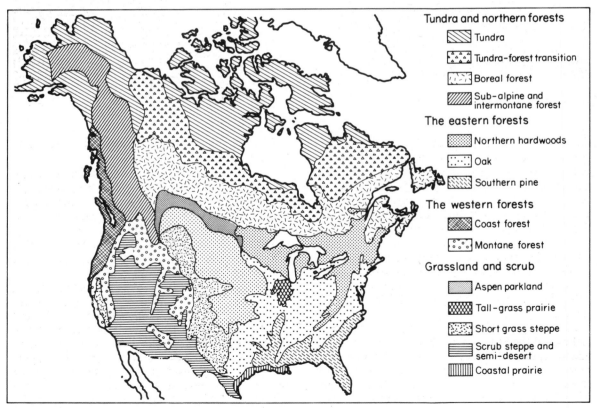

Loading logs, Fort Nelson, British Columbia

part of the forested area of Canada. It forms a continuous belt from Newfoundland and the coast of Labrador westward to the Rocky Mountains and northwest to Alaska. Among the dominant species are spruce, tamarack, balsam fir and various pines and, although the forests are primarily coniferous, there is a general admixture of deciduous trees such as poplar and white birch; these are important in the central and south-central regions, particularly along the edge of the prairie. Towards the north the close forest gives way to an open lichen-woodland which gradually merges into tundra.

Extending inland from the edges of the Great Lakes and the St Lawrence River lies a forest of a mixed nature characterized by white pine, red pine, eastern hemlock and yellow birch. With these are associated certain dominant broad-leaved species common to the deciduous forest including sugar maple, red maple, red oak, basswood and white elm.

A small portion of the deciduous forest, widespread in the United States, extends into south-western Ontario. Here, with the deciduous trees common to the Great Lakes-St Lawrence forest region, are scattered a number of other deciduous species which have their northern limits in this locality such as tulip tree, cucumber tree, blue ash, black oak and pin oak.

Four other forest regions are evident in western and central Canada. The subalpine forest is located on the mountain uplands of Alberta and British Columbia. This is a coniferous forest where the major species are Engelmann spruce, alpine fir and Lodgepole pine. The montane forest region occupies a large part of the interior uplands of British Columbia, as well as a part of the Kootenay Valley and a small area on the east side of the Rocky mountains. Ponderosa pine is a characteristic species of the southern area. Douglas fir is found throughout but more particularly in the central and southern parts. Lodgepole pine and trembling aspen are generally present, the latter particularly well represented in the north-central portions.

The coast forest is essentially coniferous consisting primarily of western red cedar and western hemlock with Sitka spruce abundant in the north and Douglas fir in the south. The Columbia forest closely resembles the coast forest region with western red cedar and western hemlock the characteristic species. Douglas fir is generally distributed throughout the whole forest while western white pine, western larch, grand fir and western yew are found in southern areas.

The Canadian forest inventory shows the dominant position of British Columbia followed by Quebec and Ontario. In every province softwoods are more bountiful than hardwords. In total the Canadian hardwood inventory is not extensive, about 11 per cent of the volume found in the United States. Eighty five per cent of the Canadian maple, beech, yellow birch, oak and other hardwoods are found in Ontario and Quebec, with much of the concentration in southern Ontario.

From an economic viewpoint it is not the total inventory which is important but that part of it which is commercially viable. Figure 11.9, showing lumber production by province, is a prime indicator of industrial production based on Canada's forest resources. The pre-eminent position of British Columbia is overwhelmingly apparent, amounting to almost 64 per cent of the Canadian total.

Ninety per cent of Canada's forest lands are owned by the provinces with only 7 per cent in private ownership. Federal lands are found largely in the Yukon and North-West Territories. However, although restricted in area, private forests in Canada are among the most productive and accessible and supply about 22 per cent of the country's wood production.

Accessibility is vital to economic production. To harvest the immense Canadian forest the industry will have to move farther and farther north and inland from ports in British Columbia and along the St Lawrence River. As this relocation occurs costs will rise rapidly.

Forests in the United States

In the north-eastern United States and continuing into southern Canada is an area of hardwoods such as beech, birch, maple and oak. Except for relatively minor areas and volumes of red alder, oak and aspen in the western states, 95 per cent of the country's hardwood is found in the eastern states.

This area has undergone major exploitation because of the quality of its timber and its relative accessibility. However, while in the last 25 years the area planted with hardwoods has remained about the same, inventory volumes have dramatically increased, by an average of 45 per cent for growing stock and 31 per cent for sawtimber inventories. Each hardwood inventory estimate made by the US Forest Service between 1952 and 1977 has shown not only substantial total increases in volume but also volume increases for each diameter class. Overall in 1977 net cubic metre growing stock volume of eastern hardwoods in the United States increased at the rate of 3.8 per cent while removals were 1.7 per cent. This favourable relationship also exists for eastern softwoods and is projected to continue well into the next century.

On the lighter, sandy soils of the north-east, coniferous species such as red and white spruce, pine and hemlock are found.

The area of hardwoods extends also into the

Fig. 11.9 Canadian production of sawn lumber

	Million metres, board measure 1980	*Percentage*
Nova Scotia	56	1.0
New Brunswick	144	2.5
Quebec	1036	18.1
Ontario	574	10.0
Saskatchewan	49	0.9
Alberta	190	3.3
British Columbia	3651	63.7
Other regions	28	0.5
Total	5728	100.0

Source: Statistics Canada.

southern states. Here the oak is dominant but several species of pine are also common. In parts of Appalachia, below the higher coniferous forest, there are chestnuts and yellow poplars.

In the extreme south-east, pine is the major species present with cypress, oaks, tupelos, cotton-woods and red gums found in the lowest lying areas.

The South is potentially the most important timber resource region in North America with 76 million hectares of commercial forest in a warm and moist climate where pines mature in about 35 years, as against the 60 years it takes a fir or hemlock to reach full growth in the cooler Pacific Northwest. Accordingly large forest product com-panies are turning to the South for most of their current expansion.

The grasslands of the interior lowlands now forming the greatest area of agricultural produc-tion in the world separate the eastern and western forests. The western forests of the United States are essentially conferous with major species being western red cedars, western hemlock and Douglas fir with Sitka spruce being more prominent towards the north. On the drier and frequently higher parts of the Cascades, Sierra Nevada and Rocky Mountains are Ponderosa and Lodgepole Pine of commercial value. In California the forest belt narrows southwards. In this zone the dominant tree is the coast redwood, the world's tallest tree at

over 90 metres high in some cases. In California too is the Sequoia which grows on the western slopes of the Sierra Nevada.

In the west, sawtimber supplies appear to be destined for a major decline as the harvest of old growth goes on. An indication of the importance of the west to the forest products industry is given by Figure 11.10 which shows that the west, the Pacific and Mountain divisions combined, accounted for 56.1 per cent of US lumber production in 1979.

Forestry and resource management

When America was first discovered by Europeans, forests covered more than half the land area that is now the United States. The forests provided both a hindrance to the new settlers, as land had to be cleared for agriculture, and a great economic benefit in the construction of houses and railways as well as for basic fuel. Many forests were depleted more rapidly than they could grow, resulting in stark consequences including soil erosion and the disappearance of wildlife. Various attempts have been made to estimate the size of the original forest. Marion Clawson cites the best estimates of original commercial and non-commercial forest at approximately 350 and 40 million hectares respectively.

Land clearing for agricultural purposes was comparatively small until the mid-nineteenth cen-tury but thereafter progressed very rapidly indeed. The agricultural domain reached a peak in the interwar period but much of the increase after 1900 was in the Great Plains, a largely treeless environment and in irrigated lands (formerly desert). Thus after a sustained decline in forest land from about 1800 onward the forest area stabilised around 1920 and has varied little since.

The general image of America's forest lands changed significantly around the turn of the century. Prior to this time forests were generally perceived as a barrier to development and a hiding place for Indians and wild animals rather than a vitally important national resource. However the federal government, urged on by a small group of enlightened individuals, became increasingly con-cerned over the depletion of forest lands.

After earlier limited legislation aimed at forest protection the US Forest Service was created in 1905 under the leadership of Gifford Pinchot. The Forest Service's brief covered three important

Fig. 11.10 United States lumber production 1979

Division	Total in billions of board metres	Percentage of total
New England	0.30	2.7
Middle Atlantic	0.27	2.4
East North Central	0.43	3.6
West North Central	0.18	1.7
South Atlantic	1.77	15.4
East South Central	1.10	9.6
West South Central	0.98	8.6
Mountain	1.37	11.9
Pacific	5.06	44.2
Total	11.46	100.0

Source: US Statistical Abstract.

areas: to manage the national forests for the public welfare; to cooperate with the states and with owners of private forest to prevent and control fires, plant trees, improve watersheds and fight disease; and to undertake research in forest management, use and protection.

The new agency was given responsibility for 34.4 million hectares which was increased by 1910 to 78.5 million hectares. It was in this period that scientific forest management was initiated after lengthy abuse by timber companies and private settlers. The current National Forest System covers approximately 75.7 million hectares, made up of 155 national forests and 19 national grasslands in 44 states, Puerto Rico and Virgin Island.

A number of estimates suggest that between 1978 and 2000 world wood demand will double, with the greatest increase in volume terms occurring in North America. As the area of forest land is likely to remain relatively stable the levels of forestry and forest management will be by far the most important variables on the supply side in the future.

Although the United States is a large net importer of forest products this is largely a result of the price mechanism rather than a physical inability to produce timber. In fact the United States has a tremendous potential waiting to be harvested. US forests are currently being cut at a rate of 0.4 billion cubic metres per year and growing at a rate of 0.6 billion cubic metres. Some timber economists believe that a total of 1.7 billion cubic metres per year is possible with highly intensive management.

No other country in the world is in a more favourable position to expand its timber production with high quality species of trees, warm climate, relatively low labour costs and an extensive transport network in addition to a formidable industrial division.

Management research has shown that in the southern pine region growth averages 3.1 cubic metres per hectare per year; with fully stocked natural stands, followed by custodial management, growth can average 5.3 cubic metres per hectare per year. With intensive management it can average 10.5 cubic metres. The relative figures for the west coast forests are 3.1, 6.6 and 17.5 cubic metres.

Forest management in Canada has undoubtedly been less intensive than in the United States with a history of argument between the provinces and the timber companies as to who should fund forest management programmes. Some areas are simply running out of trees because of lack of proper management in previous decades. Forestry experts have discovered that one-fifth of the land harvested each year does not, and will not, regenerate on its own.

The Pacific Forest Research Centre in Victoria estimates that 2.7 million hectares in British Columbia, the largest provincial producer of timber are 'not sufficiently restocked'. In Ontario it is estimated that as much as one-third of the yearly 160 000 hectares cut is not being restocked. Quebec has about 2.5 million hectares of poorly regenerated timber while there has been little action to stimulate regeneration in the Atlantic provinces.

Although the provinces and timber companies have begun to tackle such problems on a more comprehensive basis many authorities feel that uncoordinated action in the past may have serious economic repercussions in some regions in later years.

In the future genetic improvement will undoubtedly take over as current methods of forest management reach their peak. Thus the productive potential of North America's forests has hardly begun to be touched.

Running parallel with the development of techniques in forest management has been the increasing efficiency of the forest products industry. Sophisticated machinery in the newest factories has greatly decreased the waste of wood. However there are still many sawmills in North America that recover little more than 40 per cent of the solid wood entering the mill in the form of lumber.

The potential exists in the United States, and Canada as well, to greatly increase timber supply in the future, satisfying not only domestic demand but also selling substantial volumes of timber on the world market.

The economic importance of forest products

1. The United States

The United States trade deficit in timber products tripled in the 1970s, but only a small fraction involved items the United States cannot produce, such as tropical hardwoods. The price mechanism and its historical relationship with industrial capacity is the key factor.

Seventy per cent of imports arrive from Canada. Because of their relatively low price, Canadian forest products have long been attractive to the United States. However in some sectors of the forest products industry such as newsprint, comparative advantage now favours the United States. As this comparative advantage gradually increases industrial capacity, the United States will reduce its dependence on Canadian forest products in the future.

The United States exports less than 15 per cent of its production with the main markets being Western Europe and Japan. In the United States the size of the domestic market alone tends to lead firms to concentrate on sales at home whereas in Canada it is just the reverse. Forest product exports are less than 4 per cent of total US exports and less than 0.3 per cent of GNP.

Imports of timber products into the United States are dominated by hardwood plywood, softwood lumber, and pulp and paper products. Exports of timber products from the United States are led by paper and paperboard, woodpulp, and softwood logs. The export of softwood logs, primarily to Japan, has caused great controversy especially in the Pacific north-west. The woodworking unions and the sawmill owners dislike the growing trade in logs with Japan. The argument is that Japan would buy sawn lumber if unable to buy logs from the United States, thus increasing prosperity in the main wood producing regions.

2. Canada

The forest products industry is the single greatest employer in the country and as such is fundamental to the economic fortunes of the nation. Canada is the world's largest exporter, with approximately two-thirds of production destined for foreign markets. In Canada imports are relatively minor.

The importance of forest products to total Canadian exports rose steadily from 17.8 per cent in 1900 to a massive 30.3 per cent in 1960. However by 1980 this had decreased to 16.3 per cent. Although it is likely that this figure will continue to drop as Canada gradually diversifies its industrial and export base, the forest products industry will undoubtedly remain a cornerstone of the Canadian economy in the future.

In Canada as in the United States, policy is to maximise the value-added aspect of export products, so both countries generally favour export of more highly manufactured goods. Three major product groups comprise Canada's forest producer export portfolio: paper and board, woodpulp, and lumber. Net exports of all other products are relatively small.

As the largest exporter of newsprint, softwood lumber and woodpulp, Canada has gained a substantial share, over a quarter, of world forest products trade.

Total employment related to forest products, direct and indirect, is estimated at one million, or 10 per cent of Canada's work force. The importance of the industry in terms of value added is equally high, representing 15 per cent of the total for all Canadian manufacturing. In addition, forest products manufacture has been a major factor in stimulating the development of other Canadian industries, such as chemicals, machinery, hydro-electric power, engineering and construction.

The newsprint industry: A study in locational change

Newsprint is one of the few sections of the wood processing industry where Canada has an absolute capacity well in excess of that of the United States. However in recent years this difference has been lessened and the faster growth rates of the industry in the United States are projected to continue in the remaining decades of this century. The industry is undergoing a significant locational change in North America similar in many ways to the locational changes in the same industry at the beginning of the twentieth century.

Early in the century newsprint mills moved from New England into southeastern Canada because of the latter region's competitive advantage in forest products. Since that time newsprint has remained overwhelmingly dominant in Canada although significant locational shifts are now occurring.

Despite its relatively small domestic market, Canada has built a world class forest products industry. In 1977 Canadian newsprint represented 38 per cent of total world capacity. In the same year 93 per cent of Canadian newsprint was exported.

North American newsprint capacity totalled 14.2 million tons in 1977 with 10.0 and 4.2 million tons located in Canada and the United States respectively. Limited United States production resulted in approximately 65 per cent of newsprint consumption being imported from Canada. The main market for Canadian production has traditionally been the American 'manufacturing belt' which has a low level of domestic newsprint capacity.

In recent years competitive advantage in the newsprint industry has swung away from southeastern Canada in favour of the southern states of the USA. Between 1957 and 1977 per annum capacity increases in the United States averaged 4.2 per cent as against 2.3 per cent in Canada, with Canada's share of the US market dropping significantly in the intervening period.

As Figure 11.11 shows the South is the clear leader in United States newsprint with 56.6 per cent of capacity in 1977. Texas and Alabama were the most important states with approximately 600 000 and 540 000 tonnes respectively. However in spite of recent development this is well behind Quebec's 4 800 000 tonnes and Ontario's 1 950 000 tonnes.

The interaction of a number of factors has been responsible for the change in competitive advantage. Transportation is one of the largest elements of cost for the industry, ranging between 10 per cent and 40 per cent of the delivered price. In 1978 the average cost of transport for newsprint mills in Quebec was $33 per tonne as compared to $11 per tonne for those in the southern states. This disadvantage is due partly to greater distances from the principal markets and to discriminating freight rates for equal distances.

In the same year, southern newsprint producers with higher productivity and lower wage rates had an advantage of from $7–$12 per tonne over eastern Canada and British Columbia producers.

The cost of wood is the largest component in the Canadian industry, accounting for 30 to 40 per cent of total manufacturing costs. It represents almost half the disadvantage with respect to the southern states. The higher cost in Canada is due to geographic and climatic conditions which result in a lower yield per hectare and relatively slow growth of forest. The greater area to be harvested requires longer access roads, increased transportation costs and remote conditions of work. However an offsetting consideration is that most Canadian forest product companies operate almost exclusively on public land and therefore no investment in land is necessary. In comparison land costs in the South are very high.

A major impetus to the industry's development

Fig. 11.11 *North America; newsprint capacity by region 1977 (tonnes)*

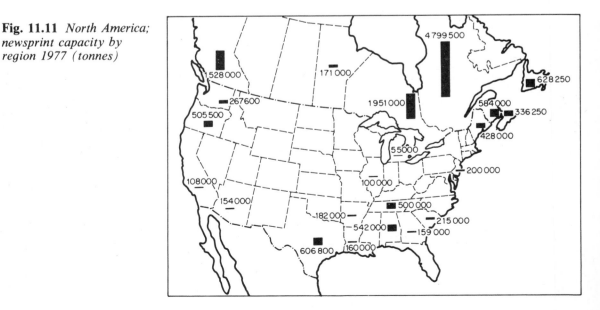

in the South has been technological progress which has allowed the conversion of the long-fibered Southern pine into pulp suitable for newsprint. In addition the South is where the largest growth in the US newspaper publishing industry is occurring.

The combination of all these related variables should result in domestic producers supplying 50 per cent of total United States newsprint requirements by the end of the century.

12
Manufacturing Industry

The affluence of North America has been firmly based on manufacturing industry, the vital catalyst transforming the continent's superlative natural resources into tangible wealth.

Although the industrialization of the United States and Canada has been a relatively recent phenomenon a multitude of changes have evolved in terms of the organization, structure and location of manufacturing industry. The role of this chapter is to analyse and assess the major developments of the post-war period.

While under severe competition in the world market the United States remains the world's premier manufacturing nation, a mantle it assumed shortly before the dawning of the twentieth century. American pre-eminence in this field was at its height in the two decades following the termination of the Second World War but in more recent times higher growth rates in Germany, Japan and other nations have made marked impressions on traditional American markets, both domestic and foreign. Undoubtedly, many of the structural and locational changes that have transpired in North America are a result, either directly or indirectly, of developments in manufacturing industry abroad. Many sectors of industry in the United States particularly in the northeast have undergone extreme trauma in recent years characterized by plant closures and redundancies.

Changes in industry mix are a consequence not only of external competition but also of technological innovation. A new generation of industry has developed, at the forefront of which is the so-called 'electronics complex', whose growth will increasingly affect the very nature of economic activity. The concept of industrial activity is gradually losing the precision it used to have because of the increasingly close links between industry and scientific research and the complementarity of industry and many service activities. North America is undergoing a process of re-industrialisation which will gradually filter through to the rest of the developed world.

However, over the whole industrial spectrum the United States has rapidly lost its monopoly on innovation. In the 1950s the United States was the first to market 82 per cent of all major innovations but by the late 1960s its share had dropped to 55 per cent.

In comparison to the United States, Canada is a lower order industrial nation hampered by a number of factors, particularly the limited size of its domestic market. Canadian manufacturing lacks the diversification and strength of its southern neighbour and the dominant position of US capital investment in the country is a frequent topic of economic debate.

Various measures can be used to assess the importance of manufacturing industry to a country or region. Employment is an index which must be used with care, for North America has led the trend in the industrialised world to a declining ratio of employment in manufacturing industry with corresponding increases in the tertiary and quaternary sectors as illustrated by Figure 12.1.

However in spite of this movement the importance of the manufacturing sector to the general economy of the continent remains unchallenged. While modern regional development may now hinge more heavily on the attraction of tertiary and quaternary activities than on an increase or structural change in manufacturing, a large national economic unit cannot sustain viable tertiary and quaternary sectors without a strong manufacturing foundation.

In common with all industrialised countries, spatial concentration of manufacturing is apparent in North America, but to varying degrees in the United States and Canada. However in the post-war period a distinct decentralisation has occurred. The extent of this diffusion from core to periphery will be examined below, taking account not only of the location of industry itself but also of the spatial distribution of decision-making in manufacturing through the situation of corporate headquarters.

Modern developments in industrial organisation

The organisation of industry has undergone profound changes since the initial establishment of a

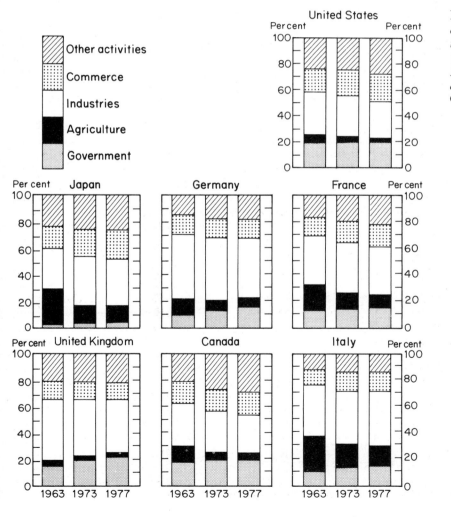

Fig. 12.1 *Distribution of employment in 7 major industrial countries 1977 (Source: Organisation of Economic Cooperation and Development,* **OECD Observer,** *1979)*

manufacturing heartland in the north-eastern United States and south-eastern Canada, which have had an immense influence on the location of industrial activity. A useful typology highlighting the chronology of organisational changes which tend to proceed with national economic development is that of J. R. Lasuen (1969) (Figure 12.2).

Lasuen's typology can be reasonably applied to North America. One could debate at length the actual dates when the two nations individually moved from one stage to another. Space is not available here to embark on such an exercise; suffice it to state without too much fear of contradiction that the United States comfortably reached the final stage in the typology in the early post-war period with similar developments following in Canada from approximately the mid-1960s, although on a smaller scale. Difficulties arise here in attempting to view the two economies in isolation because of the huge level of US investment in Canadian manufacturing.

Nevertheless the pervading trend in the sequence of six stages is one of diversification in terms of all the criteria given, with the crucial relationship between reorganization and location implicitly stated throughout.

US manufacturing has been the industrialized world's standard bearer in effecting economies of scale with clear evidence of increasing numbers of employees working in large plants in the twentieth century, although the position has been relatively stable in recent decades. As Figure 12.3 indicates, in the late 1970s plants of 1000 or more workers accounted for over one-quarter of all US manufacturing jobs. The total number of jobs in the top 500 manufacturing corporations has grown much faster than that of all US manufacturing, primarily because the 500 have been so actively adding to their payrolls by acquisitions.

The size of Canadian manufacturing establishments is smaller due principally to more limited opportunities for economies of scale in Canada.

Employment is of course only a limited measure of scale economies and in highly capitalised industries capital investment and value added in manufacture provide more accurate criteria. Eventually increasing size may become counter-productive due to various factors and the law of diminishing marginal returns becomes operable.

North American firms like those elsewhere in the industrialised world have taken advantage of agglomeration economies resulting in very large concentrations of manufacturing in a relatively small section of the continent (the manufacturing belt). Similar economies to those operable in the manufacturing belt in the late nineteenth and early twentieth centuries have again been effected in the newer manufacturing sub-cores which have developed in more recent times, the most prominent example of which is southern California.

In an effort to minimise costs of production, all firms seek to maximise both internal economies (i.e., economies of scale) and external economies (i.e. agglomeration economies). In the late nineteenth and early twentieth-century reasonably distinct periods of horizontal and vertical integra-

Fig. 12.2 Stages of business development

Stage	Products	Plants	Cities (Location)	Regions (Market)	Processes
1	One product	One plant	One city	One region	One process
2	One product	One plant	One city	One region	Multiprocess (vertical)
3	One product	One plant	One city	Multiregion	Multiprocess (vertical)
4	One product	Multiplant	Multicity	Multiregion	Multiprocess (vertical)
5	Multiproduct	Multiplant	Multicity	Multiregion	Multiprocess (vertical)
6	Multiproduct	Multiplant	Multicity	Multiregion	Multiprocess (vertical-horizontal)

Fig. 12.3(a) Canada: Employment in manufacturing by size of establishment

Size group (Total employed)	1961(%)	1980(%)
Under 5 employed	2.1	1.1
5–9		2.3
10–19	20.0	4.6
20–49		11.2
50–99	12.9	12.3
100–199	14.5	15.9
200–499	19.9	21.8
500–999	12.8	12.9
1000 or more	17.8	18.0

Fig. 12.3(b) US: Employment in manufacturing by size of establishment

Size group (Total employed)	1963(%)	1977(%)
Under 20	7.3	6.5
20–99	18.9	18.8
100–249	16.8	18.0
250–990	26.5	29.1
1000 or more	30.5	27.5

Source: US Statistical Abstract, Statistics Canada.

tion can be identified (Chapter 3). Vertical linkage is effected by the corporate integration of a chain of processes leading to a finished product. The motor industry is a classic example of such linkage. Horizontal linkage is the linking of several firms all involved in the same stage of processing. In the post-war period the process of integration has become increasingly complex with the developing numbers of giant conglomerates.

When examining trends in industrial organization, union membership cannot be ignored. In this respect the United States differs from the majority of its competitors in that union membership is relatively low and declining. In 1955 34 per cent of the US labour force belonged to a trade union. However by 1980 the total had been reduced to approximately 20 per cent. Nevertheless it will be argued below that the geographical distribution of union membership has been a significant factor in industrial location in some manufacturing sectors.

In an attempt to safeguard jobs after companies have given notice of plant closure, the practice of workers buying control of their factories has gained momentum. About 100 ownership transfers of this nature occurred in the 1970s, particularly in the manufacturing belt. The federal government has assisted this process through various schemes.

The structure of North American manufacturing industry

The United States and Canada exhibit distinct differences in the structures of their manufacturing industires with the former fostering a much wider spectrum of activity along with a higher ratio of new heavily capitalised growth industries.

It is apparent when comparing US–Canadian industry mix that Canada's manufacturing specialization is concentrated in the primary manufacturing industries that process natural resources. These sectors still dominate the country's exports. Canada is under-represented in the high growth industries of recent decades, namely professional goods, machinery, plastics, chemicals and electrical machinery and thus has to import heavily in these sectors, indicating a substantial degree of industrial underdevelopment.

Of great prominence in Canadian manufacturing is a group of labour intensive industries such as apparel, footwear, textiles and leather products, utilizing standard production technologies. The less developed world is steadily increasing its hold over these industries, putting high wage competitors like Canada under severe price competition.

Canada's industry mix for the years 1950 and 1980 is illustrated by Figures 12.4 and 12.5. Separate tables appear as a number of changes in statistical enumeration occurred in the intervening period.

While the food and beverages group has maintained the leading position in value terms, paper and allied industry, and transportation equipment

Fig. 12.4 Canada: Manufacturing statistics by industry group 1950

	Gross value of products (C$)	Employees
Food and Beverages	3 029 810 604	16 7664
Iron and steel products	1 524 384 478	164 528
Paper products	1 25 1144 125	77 519
Transportation equipment	1 239 579 727	104 176
Wood products	985 859 493	126 680
Non-ferrous metal products	960 751 814	44 680
Textile products	741 262 685	80 328
Clothing	734 214 334	116 248
Chemicals and allied products	646 870 510	41 475
Products of petroleum and coal	616 126 299	15 177
Electrical apparatus and supplies	580 578 386	60 262
Printing, publishing and allied trades	413 011 915	63 125
Non-metallic mineral products	286 541 363	29 603
Rubber products	239 184 510	21 812
Leather products	210 563 013	32 990
Tobacco and tobacco products	188 330 523	10 322
Miscellaneous industries	169 312 602	27 219

Source: Statistics Canada.

Fig. 12.5 Canada: Manufacturing statistics by industry group 1980

Industry group	Production and related workers	Value added in manufacture (C$ '000)
Food and beverages	158 981	8 470 847
Transportation equipment	137 004	6 141 818
Paper and allied industry	99 071	6 736 951
Primary metals	97 885	5 443 971
Metal fabricating	123 923	5 340 277
Wood products	98 839	3 398 585
Chemical industry	45 603	4 958 372
Electrical products	80 157	3 947 815
Printing and publishing	63 446	3 521 367
Machinery industry	73 086	3 740 316
Non-metallic mineral products	40 775	2 175 289
Clothing	83 452	1 934 217
Textile products	53 490	1 935 361
Rubber and plastics	45 584	1 915 802
Petroleum and coal products	8 277	1 795 559
Furniture and fixtures	42 826	1 202 953
Tobacco products	5 407	558 443
Leather products	21 256	514 170
Knitting mills	18 682	435 137
Miscellaneous manufacturing	48 216	1 792 902
Total – all industries	1346160	65 960 150

Source: Statistics Canada.

industries have moved into second or third places. A major factor contributing to the rapid growth of the transportation equipment sector during this period has been the Automotive Products Trade Agreement (1965) with the United States. The Agreement provides for duty-free trade between Canada and the United States in original-equipment parts and in all but certain specialized types of newly manufactured vehicles. Two other sectors which have also registered very significant advances are the electrical and chemical products industries.

The overall trend in Canadian manufacturing has been a steady relative decline of the traditional staple industries but generally this reduction has been much slower than that witnessed elsewhere in the developed world. Likewise the introduction of new high technology industries has generally been very restrictive.

In the sophisticated and highly complex economy of the United States, old industries constantly decline while new manufacturing emerges. The comparative advantage that the United States has in manufacturing industry is such that industrial change is a much more fluid and less painful process. Figure 12.6 indicates the basic evolution in the structure of US manufacturing industry between 1950 and 1977. As employment

Fig.12.6 U.S. manufacturing statistics by industry group

Industry group	Percentage of total employment in manufacturing		Percentage of total value added by manufacture		Relative capital intensity ratio $\frac{B}{A}$	
	A 1950	1977	B 1950	1977	1950	1977
Food and kindred products	10.10	7.76	11.26	9.58	1.11	1.23
Tobacco products	0.62	0.31	0.89	0.74	1.44	2.39
Textile mill products	8.43	4.47	6.29	2.75	0.75	0.62
Apparel	7.79	6.81	4.65	3.36	0.60	0.49
Lumber and wood products	5.08	3.53	3.53	2.77	0.69	0.78
Furniture and fixtures	2.34	2.37	1.86	1.52	0.79	0.64
Paper and allied products	3.23	3.21	3.83	3.79	1.19	1.18
Printing and publishing	5.16	5.57	5.47	5.47	1.06	0.98
Chemicals and allied products	4.35	4.49	8.06	9.69	1.85	2.16
Petroleum and coal products	1.40	0.75	2.38	2.80	1.70	3.73
Rubber and plastic products	1.61	3.68	1.81	3.37	1.12	0.92
Leather and leather products	2.61	1.24	1.67	0.64	0.64	0.52
Stone, clay, glass products	3.32	3.13	3.50	3.27	1.05	1.04
Primary metal industry	7.64	5.69	8.86	6.42	1.16	1.13
Fabricated metal products	6.69	7.94	6.92	7.78	1.03	0.98
Machinery exc. electrical	9.26	10.63	9.75	11.49	1.05	1.08
Electrical and electronic equipment	5.18	8.80	5.36	8.61	1.03	0.98
Transportation equipment	8.25	9.03	9.52	10.99	1.15	1.22
Instruments and related products	1.53	2.85	1.55	3.21	1.01	1.13
Misc. manufacturing	3.30	2.25	2.82	1.76	0.85	0.78
Administrative and auxiliary	N/A	5.48	N/A	—		

Source: US Statistical Abstract.

data can be misleading as a measure of industrial importance when used in isolation, especially in highly capitalised industries, Figure 12.6 also shows the percentage of total US value added by manufacture for each of the industrial groups classified by the Bureau of the Census. The two indices can be compared to give a relative capital intensity ratio which provides useful information concerning the general level of investment for each industry group.

With regard to employment, the greatest decreases have been incurred by textile mill products, food and kindred products, primary metal products, lumber and wood products, and leather and leather products. All these industrial groups also registered significant decline in their positions in terms of relative value added by manufacture.

Textile mill products again showed the greatest reduction in importance.

The growth industries of the post-war period are equally apparent, the leading sectors being electric and electronic equipment, instruments and related products, transportation equipment and machinery.

The relative capital intensity ratio illustrates a marked dichotomy between those industries which are highly capitalised and those which are labour intensive. The former group is headed by petroleum and coal products, and chemicals and allied products. The labour intensive industries are led by apparel, leather and leather products, textile mill products, and furniture and fixtures. These traditional industries will undoubtedly continue to lose ground to foreign competition which has the considerable advantage of lower wage rates. While such a trend is causing major problems to communities heavily reliant on such manufacturing, on a national scale it is only to be expected as innovative products replace them.

The location of manufacturing industry in North America

Extreme spatial variations are apparent in the distribution of manufacturing industry in North America with the United States and Canada both exhibiting major concentrations within relatively well defined regions although in recent decades a certain decentralisation has occurred albeit to a far greater extent in the United States than Canada.

The United States

Figure 12.7 outlines the geography of manufacturing in the United States using the two criteria of manufacturing employment and value added in manufacturing for the nine major census divisions of the country. The data shows that manufacturing is markedly concentrated in the north-eastern part of the nation, primarily in the Middle Atlantic and East North Central regions. Along with the southern part of New England the region is frequently referred to as the 'manufacturing belt' although it must be noted that much debate has taken place concerning the exact spatial extent of the region.

Together the three divisions accounted for 50.2 per cent of all US manufacturing employment in 1978, a significant decline from the 66.7 per cent recorded in 1950. Regional economic terminology refers to such a dominant area as a 'core region' with the remainder of the country known as the 'periphery'. Where secondary concentrations of manufacturing exist, these may be described as 'sub-cores'.

Whilst all three north-eastern divisions registered relative decreases in terms of both employment and value added, the remaining six divisions all benefited from considerable gains. Figure 12.8 illustrates the changing relationship between core

Fig. 12.7 U.S. Manufacturing statistics by division 1950 and 1978

Region	A Manufacturing employment %		B Value added %		Relative capital intensity ratio $\frac{B}{A}$	
	1950	1978	1950	1978	1950	1978
New England	9.8	7.1	8.3	6.2	0.84	0.87
Middle Atlantic	26.9	18.0	26.2	17.2	0.97	0.96
East North Central	30.0	25.1	33.2	27.2	1.10	1.08
West North Central	5.6	6.7	5.7	7.1	1.01	1.06
South Atlantic	11.1	14.4	9.4	12.5	0.84	0.87
East South Central	4.4	6.7	3.8	6.2	0.86	0.93
West South Central	4.0	7.5	4.3	8.7	1.07	1.16
Mountain	1.1	2.5	1.2	2.4	1.09	0.96
Pacific	7.0	11.9	7.9	12.4	1.12	1.04

Source: US Statistical abstract.

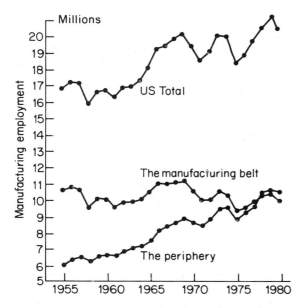

Fig. 12.8 *The changing location of manufacturing employment*

and periphery in the period 1955 and 1980.

Manufacturing 'sub-cores' are not easy to discern from divisional data and such an exercise really demands analysis on a state by state basis. Figure 12.9 shows the value added by manufacture by state in 1977. Seven of the nine states with totals in excess of $20 000 million are within the Manufacturing Belt. These are the states of New York, New Jersey, Pennsylvania, Ohio, Illinois, Michigan and Indiana. Two sub-cores are clearly apparent in the forms of California, which recorded the highest value added in manufacture in the country and Texas which ranked eighth. A weaker sub-core outside the manufacturing belt can also be distinguished, based on North Carolina, Georgia and Tennessee although in this context one must be careful as density shading maps can suggest greater transitions than actually occur in reality. Analysis of the raw data indicates most definitely that North Carolina is a distinct secondary nucleus of manufacturing and while one can debate the status of the other south-

Fig. 12.9 *US value added in manufacturing by state 1977*

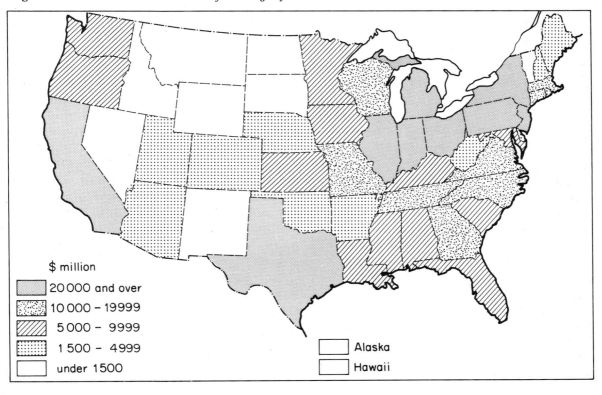

eastern states it is clear that this is a region where manufacturing industry is becoming more and more important.

The situation with regard to manufacturing employment by state is illustrated by Figure 12.10. The general picture is markedly similar to that for value added. California appears clearly as the major sub-core, followed again by Texas and North Carolina.

While it is debateable as to what exactly constitutes a sub-core or secondary manufacturing region the designation of the periphery is relatively easy to determine as evidenced by Figures 12.9 and 12.10.

A relative capital intensity ratio can also be obtained on a divisional basis (as well as by industrial classification) by comparing employment and value added data. Figure 12.7 indicates that the West South Central region, based primarily on Texas, has by far the highest ratio with a nine percentage point increase between 1950 and 1978, a consequence of the very high level of

investment directed to this region in recent decades. The distinct contrast between the West South Central and the other regions of the South, the South Atlantic and East South Central should be noted. Likewise, in the manufacturing belt a marked dichotomy exists between the more highly capitalised East North Central, and the Middle Atlantic and New England divisions.

The manufacturing belt

In spite of decentralisation tendencies in North America the north-eastern manufacturing belt remains the most important industrial nucleus in the world. The term 'manufacturing belt' was first introduced by Sten de Geer (1927) in an article entitled 'The American Manufacturing Belt' published in 1927. De Geer used the term to describe the dominant concentration of industrial activity that had distinctively emerged from the late nineteenth century in the north-eastern region. As

Fig. 12.10 *US manufacturing employment by state 1980*

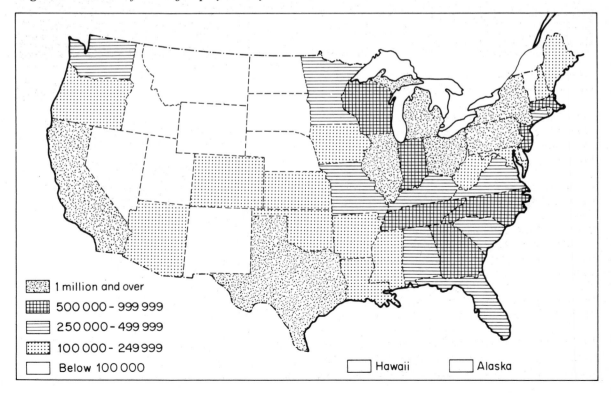

1 million and over
500 000 – 999 999
250 000 – 499 999
100 000 – 249 999
Below 100 000

Hawaii   Alaska

Multi-use of land, agricultural, industrial and residential functions, north of Dyer, Indiana

Fig. 12.11 *The north-east manufacturing belt (Source: Meyer, D. R. Geographical Magazine, June 1980* Industrial Entrepreneurs Make Their Mark*)*

the hegemony of the region has declined the term has been used less frequently and much academic debate has taken place concerning the current validity of the 'manufacturing belt' concept.

There remains another problem – how to delimit the region's boundaries? The area is not one continuous industrial complex but is rather characterised by a number of very large urban regions with a level of manufacturing industry much higher than the national average. Figure 12.11 shows the extent of the belt as seen by David R. Meyer (1980) and the location of the major urban regions of the belt. As Meyer states, 'Some of the largest industrial concentrations in the world sprawl over a 777 000 square kilometre area known as the Manufacturing Belt in which most of the land is occupied by farm and forest'.

For the purposes of statistical analysis in this chapter the limits of the United States part of the manufacturing belt will be taken as the three census divisions of the East North Central, Middle Atlantic and New England.

The development of the manufacturing belt

Manufacturing industry established and increasingly concentrated in this region for a number of identifiable reasons which can be itemised as follows.
1. The Middle Atlantic seaboard was the initial nucleus of population, wealth and economic activity. The equable climate and availability of agricultural land ensured the establishment of permanent settlement.
2. The growth of population through natural increase and immigration from Europe provided both an expanding market and a growing pool of labour. Many immigrants had acquired industrial and entrepreneurial skills in the manufacturing centres of Europe.
3. The abundance of natural resources encouraged capital investment in a wide variety of ventures. The development of the Appalachian and Illinois coalfields and the iron ore fields of the Lake Superior region were of major importance.
4. The Great Lakes waterway system provided a relatively cheap transportation artery for the movement of bulk produce from the northern interior to the seaboard. The situation of the Hudson-Mohawk gap ensured the pre-eminence of New York over other coastal cities.
5. Proximity to the North Atlantic shipping routes, now the busiest oceanic shipping route in the world was most important. Economic development in the region has been highly dependent on international trade.
6. Firms benefited from agglomeration economies and further development took place as companies sought fully to utilise economies of scale.
7. Transportation arteries rapidly developed to all parts of the continent to 'import' raw materials and 'export' manufactured goods.
8. The function of the region as the primary innovation centre of the continent has ensured continued capital investment.
9. The sophistication of the region's infrastructure compared with possible alternative locations meant that decentralisation only occurred due to very strong competititve factors in other regions.

Movement within the manufacturing belt

The combination of the above factors led to the rapid industrialisation of this part of North America and by the turn of the century the United States was out-producing her European rivals with the bulk of production credited to the northeast manufacturing belt. In 1870, 77 per cent of all American manufacturing employment was located within the belt although the region only had 56 per cent of the nation's population a ratio of 1.38. Forty years later the belt had a lower 68 per cent of manufacturing workers but also a lower 48 per cent of total population with a resultant higher ratio of 1.42. The situation remained reasonably stable until the Second World War after which a steady relative decline occurred. By 1969 the belt's share of manufacturing employment was reduced to 56.3 per cent with a further decline to 50 per cent by the late 1970s.

During this time a gradual movement within the manufacturing belt also occurred with the general demise of the Middle Atlantic division in industrial terms in favour of the increasingly dominant East North Central division. By the late 1970s the Middle Atlantic contained only 18 per cent of total US manufacturing workers compared with 24 per cent in 1963 and 34 per cent in 1899. Even though the division's position has declined relatively the East North Central region gained approximately two million manufacturing jobs between 1940 and 1978, far more than any other division, and still accounts for just over one quarter of all manufacturing jobs in the United States.

In comparison to the two major sections of the manufacturing belt the number employed in manufacturing in New England is relatively small. In common with the Middle Atlantic, New

England has undergone a much faster relative decline than the East North Central, the modern day nucleus of the belt.

In 1969 the relative decline in manufacturing that had gradually developed from 1945 became for the first time an absolute decrease in manufacturing jobs, a trend which was maintained throughout the 1970s.

The changing location of manufacturing in the United States

The post-war period in the United States has witnessed a considerable change in the location of manufacturing industry but the migration of firms has accounted for a very small percentage of employment growth in the south and west and a similarly small percentage of employment losses in the north. Births of new firms, terminations of old ones and expansions by existing ones have been the major causes of differential regional employment growth.

Studies at the Southwest Centre for Economic and Community Development have found that locally based firms and new firms, as opposed to external sources, accounted for most of the manufacturing employment growth in the post 1960 period. Such trends signify the ability of the periphery to generate growth internally and a waning of dependence on the industrial core.

R. D. Norton and J. Rees (1979) attribute the core region's manufacturing demise in the 1970s 'to the cumulative effects of a more gradual dispersal of innovative capacity to the south and west', stating that in a reversal of the historical pattern, a growing number of periphery states now tend to specialise in 'rapid-growth' industries while many parts of the core region are dominated by 'slow-growth' sectors. Overall the process of changing manufacturing location can be identified in two broad stages; an earlier stage characterised by the increasing location of slow-growth labour intensive industries outside the manufacturing belt and a more recent period when high technology and heavily capitalised industries have increasingly decided to locate in the south and in the west.

The filter-down process of industrial relocation

The core region has long been vulnerable to the migration of labour intensive manufacturing to lower wage areas of the periphery as exemplified by the historical drift of the textile and shoe industries away from New England and apparel manufacture from New York to the Carolinas. Such a relocation has been referred to as the 'filter-down process' by W. R. Thompson and others.

The filter-down process is based on the notion that corporate organisations respond to changing critical input requirements by altering the geographical location of production to minimise costs and thereby ensure competiveness in a tightening market.

The industrial heartland has historically invented, or at least innovated to a more than proportionate degree and has thus continually benefited from the rapid growth rates characteristic of the early stage of an industry's life cycle (the product cycle), one of exploitation of a new market. The site of production is likely to be the metropolitan area where the firms' main plants and corporate headquarters are located. Figure 12.12, which illustrates the three phases of the product cycle, indicates that in the early phase scientific-engineering skills at a high level and external economies are the prime location factors. As the product cycle moves to the growth and mature stages corresponding changes occur in the prime location factors.

In the growth phase methods of mass production are gradually introduced and the number of firms involved in production generally expands as product information spreads. In this stage management skills are the critical human inputs.

Production technology tends to stabilise in the mature phase. Capital investment remains high and the availability of unskilled and semi-skilled labour becomes a most important location factor. As the industry matures into a replacement market the production process usually becomes rationalised and often routine. The high wage rates of the innovating area quite consistent with the high skills required in the formative stages of the learning process become excessive when the skill requirements decline and the industry, or a section of it, 'filters-down' to the smaller, less industrially sophisticated areas where cheaper labour is available which can now handle the lower skills

Production factors	Product cycle phase		
	early	growth	mature
Management	2	1	3
Scientific engineering knowhow	1	2	3
Unskilled labour	3	2	1
External economies	1	2	3
Capital	3	1ª	1ª

1ª considered to be of equal importance

Fig. 12.12 *Production factors and the stages of the product cycle (Source: Lonsdale, R. E. and Seyler, H. L.* Nonmetropolitan industrialisation, *Winston 1979, Washington DC.)*

required in the manufacture of the product.

The filter-down theory goes a long way towards explaining the southern small-town lament that they get a disproportionate share of slow-growth industries, that is, industries in the mature stage of the product cycle which pay low wages and are characterised by a low rate of job formation. In contrast to the South, the Pacific division is a higher wage manufacturing region which has not proved to be an attractive location for such industry.

The filter-down theory thus highlights differential regional wage rates as an important relocation factor especially in the southern states. Figure 12.13, showing the average hourly earnings of manufacturing production workers by quartiles in 1980, emphasises the regional contrasts that exist. Of the twelve states in the lowest quartile, seven are located in the South. The higher wage rates of the manufacturing belt (outside New England) are clearly evident although a noticeable distinction

Fig. 12.13 *Hourly earnings of manufacturing production workers by state 1980*

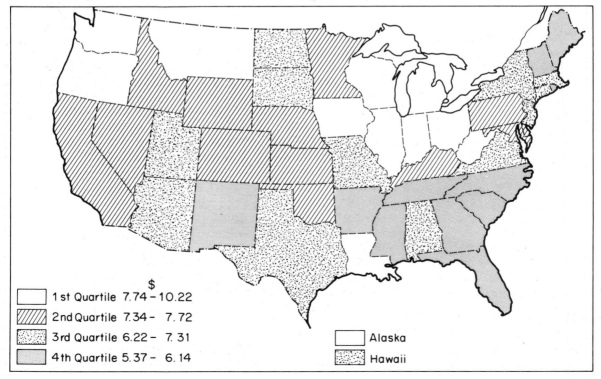

	$
1st Quartile	7.74 – 10.22
2nd Quartile	7.34 – 7.72
3rd Quartile	6.22 – 7.31
4th Quartile	5.37 – 6.14

Alaska

Hawaii

exists between the East North Central division which falls entirely into the first quartile and the Middle Atlantic whose three states average distinctly lower mean hourly production earnings.

However, more detailed analysis of manufacturing wage differentials indicates that wages in the north east may not be so much higher than elsewhere. Adjusted for the skill levels of the workforce, wages in the manufacturing belt are closer to those in the rest of the country than at first might appear. This adjustment is necessary because the industries of the manufacturing belt employ a higher percentage of skilled workers than most other regions. The adjustment is made by looking at what the average regional wage would be if the region had the same percentage of each industry as the nation does.

The higher levels of unionisation and work stoppages in the north east with correspondingly lower levels in the southern states have also been cited by industrialists as important complementary factors in the location decision. Figure 12.14

indicates the average annual percentage of work stoppages for all non-farm workers by state 1966 to 1978. The manufacturing belt states (outside New England) all fall within the first and second quartiles, while the South in general occupies the third and fourth quartiles although there are a few notable exceptions such as Alabama. With regard to union membership, less than 15 per cent of southern workers belong to trade unions. North Carolina registered the lowest relative union membership of any state in 1978 at 6.5 per cent. In comparison the most highly unionised state, New York, recorded a figure of 39.2 per cent.

The diffusion of innovation in manufacturing industry

The manufacturing belt monopolised US technological innovation well into the present century with developments in the machine-tool industry being absolutely crucial to the whole spectrum of

Fig. 12.14 *Annual average work stoppages by state for non-farm workers 1966–78*

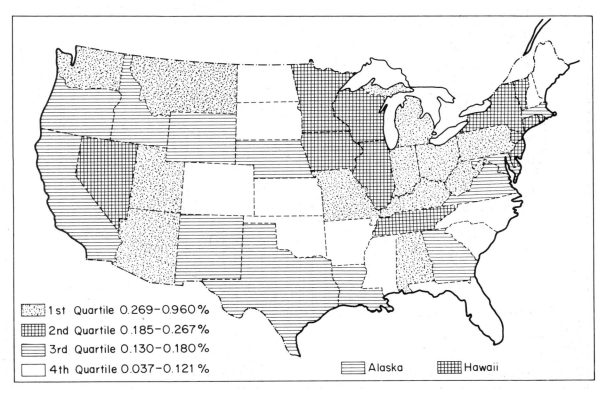

1st Quartile 0.269–0.960%
2nd Quartile 0.185–0.267%
3rd Quartile 0.130–0.180%
4th Quartile 0.037–0.121%

Alaska   Hawaii

manufacturing activity. In regional terms the industry was almost entirely located in the north east giving the region, in the words of Perloff and Wingo (1961) 'the ability to spawn new industries so as to offset the dispersal of its standardised fabricating operations to the periphery'.

Regional economics has isolated industry mix as a vital factor in the overall economic performance of a region. The term 'industry mix' simply refers to the total assortment of industry resident in an area. A region may be said to have a positive mix if it has a bias towards industries with high growth rates and a negative mix if the reverse is true.

Perloff and Wingo in their analysis of the period 1939–54 concluded that most states in the core had a positive industry mix with most periphery states showing negative mix. California proved to be the only major exception and was described as the nation's first 'subnucleation'.

Following Perloff and Wingo's work, Norton and Rees used similar analysis for the periods 1963–72 and 1972–76. Examined in terms of core and periphery, the general dichotomy was maintained for the former period but with respect to both employment and value added, the differences between the two areas had been significantly reduced.

Results for the 1972–76 period showed a negative mix in terms of value added for the core with a counter-balancing positive mix registered by the periphery. This reversal is not apparent from analysis of employment data signifying that a reasonable proportion of the periphery's rapid growth industries are highly capital intensive.

The north east's monopoly on innovation and high growth industries has been broken as new innovating centres have emerged in the south and west. In the same way that the machine-tool industry was the linchpin of manufacturing development in the nineteenth and early twentieth centuries the electronics complex is fast dominating the centre-stage of manufacturing in the latter part of the century. While the manufacturing belt

Fig. 12.15 *Lorenz curve illustrating spatial concentration of U.S. manufacturing employment*

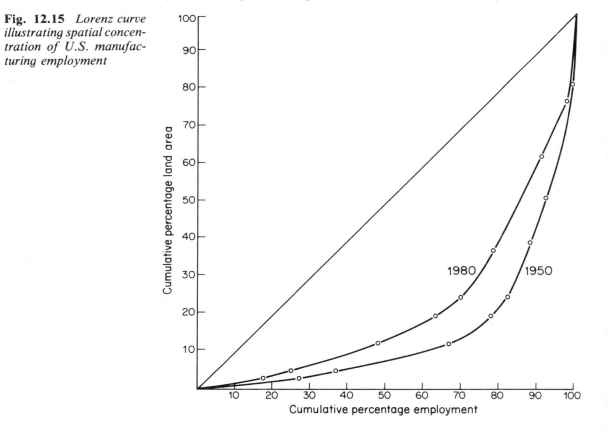

has invested heavily in this sector other parts of the country have as well. Thus while the manufacturing belt remains the nation's manufacturing core its dominance will continue to be weakened as the sub-cores continue to generate a more sophisticated industrial base.

Relocation: an analysis of causal factors

A technique frequently used to illustrate changes in spatial distribution is the Lorenz Curve (Figure 12.15). On the graph cumulative percentage manufacturing employment is plotted against cumulative percentage land area. A curve is drawn through the points plotted. If there were no spatial concentration of manufacturing employment then all the points plotted would lie along a straight line as shown in the diagram. The higher the degree of spatial concentration the greater the curvature away from the straight line.

Curves have been constructed for 1950 and 1980 indicating the extent to which industry has diffused from its earlier concentration. There is little doubt that this trend will continue in the future.

While some of the reasons for the relocation of manufacturing have been briefly mentioned above in examining the general stages of peripheral development, a more comprehensive assessment is undoubtedly necessary. The most important factors may be itemised as follows:

1. The movement of population both to the south and west has greatly expanded the market potential of these regions.
2. The location and exploitation of important raw materials, particularly energy sources, has encouraged investment in associated industries and strengthened the independence of the regions concerned. California and Texas are prime examples of the way in which raw material endowment has had a cumulative effect on industrial development.
3. Federal spending which has become a major factor in regional economic development. A National Journal study for fiscal 1976 calculated that the south and west emerged with surpluses of $12.6 billion and $10.4 billion respectively. In contrast the five Great Lakes states ran a $20.1 billion deficit with Washington, with the Middle Atlantic sustaining a deficit of $12.6 billion.
4. Attraction of lower general costs. Lower real

estate prices, tax and pay scales along with the continuing availability of undeveloped land.
5. Climate; an attraction from a number of viewpoints, (a) lower costs due to longer hours of daylight in winter and lower space-heating requirements, (b) the specific climatic requirements of certain industries—aerospace is the classic example, (c) the general perception of the sunbelt as having a more hospitable climate.
6. Developing infrastructure. Improved national transport networks have decreased unit transport costs and improved accessibility thus reducing the 'isolation' of the periphery. The construction of the Inter-State Highway System has been of immense importance in this respect, bringing easy access to regions poorly served by rail.
7. The development of innovation centres in the south and west, acting as seedbeds for new manufacturing industry.

The advantages of western and southern locations have received extended recognition by industrial corporations in the post-war period and the development of manufacturing in the most well-endowed regions has had spectacular economic effects. Nevertheless the situation must be seen in perspective. Many peripheral areas have changed very little in manufacturing terms and many that have, have attracted only slow-growth industries.

The 'Sunbelt' Concept

The term 'sunbelt' is now in everyday use in the United States although few writers have actually attempted to define its exact meaning and its geographical boundaries. Political analyst K. Phillips, who has been credited with introducing the sunbelt concept in his 1969 book *The Emerging Republican Majority*, saw the region as extending from the East Carolina lowlands, southward around (and excluding) Appalachia, including only the greater Memphis area of Tennessee, skirting the Ozarks and moving west to Oklahoma, and from there westwards further still to California. Some writers have set the northeast border of the sunbelt at Washington DC, while a few have argued for the inclusion of Washington and Oregon (definitely not noted for excessive sunshine). In some cases the concept has been used to refer to a narrower region from Florida westwards to California or alternatively from Florida to Texas. Part of this wide discrepancy in area delimitation is due to the fact that the 'sunbelt' has become a multi-disciplinary term used alternatively to describe political, economic, social and 'geographical' distributions.

It is clear that the general use of the term is to describe areas of warm and hot climate where population growth is above the national average and where general economic expansion, focused on particular growth centres and led by fast growing high technology industries and government employment, is proceeding at a rate significantly above that of the manufacturing belt. There are areas within the region which still compare poorly against the national average under most socio-economic criteria but they generally illustrate some degree of economic expansion in comparison to the aura of stagnation or decline which is evident in many parts of the manufacturing belt. With this fairly loose understanding of the concept it seems reasonable to accept the regional boundaries originally set by Phillips.

The population of Pima County, Arizona which includes Tucson, increased by 51 per cent during the 1970s. The county's largest employer is the University of Arizona, followed by the Davis-Monthan Air Force Base. Eight of the top ten employers are government facilities.

The recent expansion of San Antonio, Texas, is of similar origin. Its modern development began during the Second World War with a substantial military build-up. Today the military employs 29 000 civilians and 41 000 active personnel in the metropolitan area. In contrast the largest private employer, United Services Auto Association (insurance) has a workforce of 5000. Houston, the frequently used media image of the sunbelt, is rather an anomaly in the region in that it has acted as a considerable market for blue collar employment whereas growth elsewhere has been primarily based on white collar occupations.

The so-called Silicon Valley (Santa Clara Valley) in Santa Clara County to the south of San Francisco contains the largest concentration of high technology companies in the US and is burgeoning at such a rate that congestion has become a serious problem. The valley has attracted semiconductor and information processing companies mainly because of the high reputation of Stanford University's engineering department, the perceived high quality of life offered by the location and the initial availability of highly skilled personnel.

In 1980 one study estimated that Silicon Valley was generating one out of every five new jobs in US high technology industries. The resultant sprawling urbanisation reached such a stage that the Sunnyvale city council, with jurisdiction over an important part of the valley, voted a four-month moratorium on all new industrial development in order to study the implications of future growth. Problems relating to housing, traffic, sewage treatment and general environmental quality have caused the greatest concern.

Between 1977 and 1980, 40 000 to 50 000 new industrial jobs were created each year but the housing supply rose by only 12 000 units per annum. The imbalance between housing supply and demand has led to a rapid increase in house prices which in turn has extended the commuting zone as employees seek more affordable accommodation. In 1980 the average commuting distance was 26 km. The region's highway network is creaking under the strain with eight lane highways jammed with bumper to bumper traffic at peak flow periods.

Such problems have resulted in severe recruitment difficulties, particularly of middle management personnel who are now reluctant to move to the valley from outside because of the very high cost of housing. Virtually all electronics companies complain of a shortage of skilled employees along with the equally serious problem of an extremely high turnover rate as the symptoms of growth induce many to seek a less stressful environment elsewhere. Although high technology industry continues to develop in the valley some resident companies are now looking to expand in less congested locations (Fig. 12.16).

Other locational trends in US manufacturing

Locational changes can be recognised at various scales. Apart from the inter-regional changes analysed above significant movements from inner city to suburb and from metropolitan to non-metropolitan areas have occurred.

(I) Suburban decentralization Movement from central to suburban locations has occurred at an increasing level in all major urban areas. An

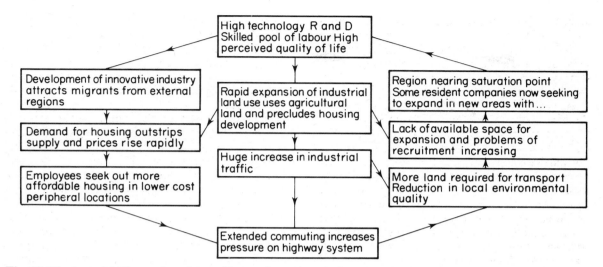

Fig 12.16 *A model illustrating the problems of rapid growth in Santa Clara Valley*

analysis of firm relocation patterns in metropolitan Denver from 1974 to 1976 by C. G. Schmidt identified the following causal factors:

 (i) lack of space due to growth
 (ii) failure to obtain satisfactory lease/rental arrangements or the cancellation of such arrangements
(iii) the unsatisfactory quality of building space
 (iv) deterioration of the inner city region
 (v) a desire to maintain closer contacts with markets, suppliers and labour.

In a study of the Philadelphia region, J. Gruenstein found that the suburban share of the region's jobs rose from 30 per cent in 1948 to 57 per cent in 1975 with many suburban centres offering high levels of services at relatively low cost.

(II) Nonmetropolitan industrialization R. E. Londsdale and H. L. Seyler (1979) regarded the expansion of nonmetropolitan manufacturing as 'a whole new phase in the evolving economic geography of the United States'. Since 1960 nonmetropolitan areas (those outside SMSAs) have accounted for well over half of all new industrial jobs. By 1978 nonmetropolitan areas had 29 per cent of US manufacturing employment, a considerable rise from the 23.5 per cent in 1962. In absolute terms this amounts to approximately six million jobs, substantially more than in agriculture.

The United States has undergone greater non-metropolitan industrialization than any other major industrialized nation due to a combination of both push and pull factors. Labour unionization and wage rates are higher in metropolitan areas giving a certain impetus to nonmetropolitan location. In addition, large US cities have undergone much more social and environmental deterioration than have the large cities of most other developed nations. The high level of personal mobility in the US has also made long distance commuting possible.

Distinct regional differences are evident in this movement. In the period 1962–78 by far the largest gains in nonmetropolitan industrialization occurred in the south, accounting for 53 per cent of the national increase. This expansion took the south's share of nonmetropolitan manufacturing to 46 per cent in the latter year. During the same period the north central region maintained its share at about 30 per cent with 28 per cent of manufacturing employment in this region located outside metropolitan areas. Only 18 per cent of northeastern manufacturing falls into this category and the region's share of such employment fell from 20 per cent to 16 per cent in the period under consideration. The west's share of nonmetropolitan manufacturing employment increased from 6.5 per cent to 8 per cent but in the

Non-metropolitan industrialization in Monmouth County, New Jersey – the Bell Laboratory building

latter year represented only 16 per cent of all manufacturing jobs in the region. Given the physical environment and the geographical distribution of the population, western industry is likely to remain heavily metropolitan in character.

In terms of industrial structure, lumber and wood products, paper and allied products, agricultural chemicals, farm machinery and stone, clay and glass remain the major industrial groups in which employment continues to be most strongly nonmetropolitan.

Clearly the development of manufacturing in nonmetropolitan areas has had a cumulative or multiplier effect on the communities concerned. However some authorities believe that such employment has already reached a peak, possibly as early as 1973. Most employment gains in nonmetropolitan areas since that date have been in sections other than manufacturing.

Contrasting trends in manufacturing: New York and Texas

The varying fortunes of the 'Frostbelt' and the 'Sunbelt' are nowhere better characterised than in New York and Texas, two of the most important states in the USA.

New York fights to maintain its manufacturing sector

New York, like all states in the manufacturing belt, has been affected by a reduction in its manufacturing base. Such losses have not only led to higher unemployment rates, as the emergence of new tertiary jobs has been insufficient to offset industrial reductions, but also to lower tax bases which have fallen to critical levels in some areas. The state government has taken action both in isolation and in co-operation with other north-eastern states to attempt to halt and even reverse this trend.

In 1976 the governors of seven north-eastern states, New York, New Jersey, Pennsylvania, Connecticut, Massachusetts, Vermont and Rhode Island formed the Coalition of North-eastern Governors (CONEG), 'to establish mechanisms to reactivate and rebuild the depressed economy of the Northeast'. The primary aim of this group has been to lobby in Washington DC to redress the current federal expenditures imbalance. In the same year the Northeast-Midwest Congressional Coalition, comprising 204 congressional representatives of sixteen states was established with a similar brief – to redirect a greater level of not only public but also private investment to the region. In conjunction the Northeast-Midwest Research Institute operates to produce evidence of government bias in favour of the south and west.

In spite of recent problems New York has still a powerful manufacturing base. The state itself claims that if it were an independent country it would be the tenth ranking economic power in the world. New York is the second largest manufacturing state in the United States after California, accounting for 7.6 per cent of national manufacturing by value in 1979. The state ranks first in the production of apparel, printing and publishing, leather and leather products, instruments and miscellaneous manufacturing goods. Thirty-five thousand manufacturing firms are located in the state representing 432 out of 450 industrial classifications.

However while New York is still the major industrial state in the manufacturing belt it has declined significantly with regard to both employment and value added. For the latter the state's share of the national total fell from 9.6 per cent in 1967 to 7.6 per cent in 1976.

For a clearer assessment of such trends New York must be examined in the context of the remainder of the manufacturing belt. As Figure 12.17 shows, in the period 1967–80 New York sustained by far the greatest decrease in manufacturing employment both in absolute and percentage terms. Employment in New York fell by a remarkable 24.8 per cent compared to 14.3 per

Fig. 12.17 Industrial employment in the manufacturing belt

State	1967 (000s)	1980 (000s)	Percentage change
MIDDLE ATLANTIC			
New York	1 929	1 451	−24.8
New Jersey	881	783	−11.1
Pennsylvania	1 550	1 328	−14.3
EAST NORTH CENTRAL			
Ohio	1 397	1 268	−9.2
Indiana	710	658	−7.3
Illinois	1 397	1 222	−12.5
Michigan	1 134	1 007	−11.2
Wisconsin	512	560	+9.4
NEW ENGLAND			
Maine	111	113	+1.8
New Hampshire	95	117	+23.2
Vermont	43	51	+18.6
Massachusetts	714	673	−5.7
Rhode Island	122	128	+4.9
Connecticut	478	442	−7.5

cent in the next worst affected state, Pennsylvania. The Middle Atlantic division is clearly shown as the region hardest hit by industrial job losses.

Apart from co-ordinated action with other states New York has adopted various measures of its own to hold on to and attract industry. Since 1977 the state government has enacted radical business tax cuts. Industrialists can now obtain low-interest, long-term financing for job-producing plant expansions through programmes featuring substantial tax credits and exemptions. The state has embarked on ambitious energy and transport plans to ensure that in terms of infrastructure New York does not lag behind alternative locations. The state government has also, in line with many American states, mounted a major advertising campaign both in the United States and abroad in an effort to attract new industry.

New York City's Office of Economic Development (OED) has taken steps to reverse the outflow of business from the city by arranging for some local firms to receive tax abatements and tax exemption industrial development bonds, by assisting firms which are hurt by foreign import competition to obtain federal aid and by reducing the time consumed on local licensing and administrative procedures.

The state has also been gravely concerned with the exodus of corporate headquarters, declining from a total of 140 out of the 500 largest industrial corporations in 1956 to 94 in 1980. Of those present in the state in the latter year, 78 were located in New York City, amounting to 15.6 per cent of the US total. Such a movement has the potential of heavy adverse effects on the city and state economy beyond the direct loss of jobs and tax revenues due to relocation. If these companies sever their links with the city's corporate service firms as well as discontinue their usage of other resources, the effects of the original loss are multiplied several times.

A detailed breakdown of recent changes in New York's industrial structure is given in Figure 12.18. Some encouraging trends are evident such as the greater diversification of manufacturing in 1976 compared to 1960. Of the nine industrial groups that increased their share of value added in manufacturing in the country as a whole, seven of these groups increased their importance in New York state.

Texas expands its manufacturing base

Texas is undoubtedly the most recent large scale growth region in the United States in general economic and manufacturing terms. The state registered the greatest absolute increase in manufacturing employment in the South between 1967 and 1980, an increment large enough for Texas to head the national rankings also. Texas is in a class of its own in the South because of its immense size and wealth. It is the largest of the southern states in area and population and provides a most lucrative market as the fifth ranking state in terms of purchasing power.

Investment in manufacturing in Texas has risen markedly in recent years. At $4768 million in 1976, it was more than double the level in 1966 when measured in constant dollars (1972). Texas led all other states in the amount of manufacturing investment in the period 1974–1976.

The three largest investing industries have been chemicals and allied products, petroleum and coal

Fig. 12.18 % value added in manufacturing by industry group 1960 and 1976

Industry group	New York		Texas	
	1960	1976	1960	1976
Food and kindred products	11.0	7.2	14.0	9.7
Tobacco products	–	–	–	–
Textile mill products	2.7	1.6	0.7	0.4
Apparel	19.6	8.1	2.9	3.2
Lumber and wood products	–	0.6	1.4	1.8
Furniture and fixtures	1.6	1.1	1.2	0.7
Paper and allied products	2.6	2.9	2.2	2.2
Printing and publishing	19.0	13.3	4.1	3.6
Chemicals and allied products	7.0	7.8	23.4	22.6
Petroleum and coal products	–	–	12.2	14.2
Rubber and plastic products	1.0	1.7	1.2	2.1
Leather and leather products	1.8	1.1	–	–
Stone, clay, glass products	1.4	2.5	4.2	3.4
Primary metal industries	1.4	4.1	5.9	3.6
Fabricated metal products	4.5	5.0	4.5	6.7
Machinery excluding electrical	3.0	11.7	7.7	11.6
Electric and electronic equipment	6.5	10.2	4.0	5.3
Transportation equipment	5.4	4.6	9.5	7.3
Instruments and related products	3.9	13.1	0.9	1.3
Miscellaneous manufacturing	7.6	3.4	–	0.3

products, and primary metals. Chemicals and products and petroleum products accounted for 56 per cent of manufacturing investment in the state over the 1972–76 period.

A positive aspect of industrial trends in the state has been the strong growth in manufactures not closely tied to energy resources. In Texas 55 per cent of manufacturing employment is now in durable goods production, in contrast to 45 per cent in 1950. Electronics, fabricated metals, and machinery have been strong growth industries in the state.

Manufacturing industry has been attracted by a wide variety of important resources and good facilities. Strong population growth has been an important stimulus to manufacturers with significant market access costs. In addition low tax rates, comparatively low delivered prices for energy, the availability of non-union labour, favourable weather conditions and other locational factors will continue to give Texas a competitive edge in the plans of many manufacturing industries.

The most important of the state's twenty-five metropolitan areas are Houston (the oil capital), Dallas – Fort Worth, San Antonio and the state capital, Austin. Houston, linked to the Gulf port of Galveston by the Houston Ship Canal, is now the third largest port in the United States. This and other major deep-water facilities have given the state a strong advantage over its inland neighbours.

The relative importance of manufacturing industry to the economy of Texas must be kept in perspective. In 1980 manufacturing employment amounted to only 18 per cent of total non-agricultural employment in the state compared to over 22 per cent in the country as a whole, giving some indication of the strength of other sectors in Texas's economy.

It is important also to note that high growth rates have been a Texas phenomenon for more than a century and have not been confined to the post Second World War period as is sometimes insinuated. The growth of manufacturing employment in the 1970s is more remarkable in its contrast to the situation in the rest of the United States than with respect to the historical trend in Texas.

Canada: Industrial location

Canadian manufacturing is even more spatially concentrated than that of the United States and decentralisation tendencies, although in evidence, are very much weaker. Three broad regional divisions can be recognised (Figure 12.19). The manufacturing core region is based on the Windsor-Toronto region of southern Ontario and the St Lawrence valley region of southern Quebec centred around Montreal. Together the two provinces accounted for 77.9 per cent of national manufacturing employment in 1980, a slight decrease from the 80.2 per cent recorded in 1961.

Fig. 12.19 Canadian manufacturing employment by province

Province	1961 (%)	1980 (%)	Region
Newfoundland	0.78	1.16	Eastern manufacturing periphery
P.E. Island	0.13	0.15	
Nova Scotia	2.04	2.24	
New Brunswick	1.62	1.93	
Quebec	32.94	27.79	Manufacturing core
Ontario	48.07	50.14	
Manitoba	3.05	2.99	Western manufacturing periphery
Saskatchewan	1.00	0.99	
Alberta	2.77	4.01	
British Columbia	7.60	8.58	

Outside the core region eastern and western manufacturing peripheries can be identified although it is patently clear that in all three regions manufacturing industry has agglomerated in the south and avoided the inhospitable areas towards the north for sound economic reasons.

The eastern periphery is of minimal importance in terms of manufacturing with all four provinces totalling only 5.5 per cent of Canadian manufacturing employment. In contrast the four western provinces registered 16.6 per cent of national manufacturing employment as might be expected with their greater population, land area and natural resources.

The Vancouver region of British Columbia is the only significant sub-core that can be realistically identified although this is purely in terms of Canadian manufacturing alone, for there are many city-regions in the United States which are more heavily industrialized but would not be rated manufacturing sub-cores on the scale of American economic activity. In regional economic terminology the Vancouver region was insulated by distance and freight charges from the 'backwash effects' which regions nearer the industrial heartland experienced. Such earlier 'isolation' and the role of the city as the country's major Pacific port proved most important stimuli to manufacturing development. The initial circumstances encouraging manufacturing in this region are very similar to those which existed in Los Angeles, San Francisco and Seattle.

Apart from British Columbia, Alberta is the only other province which increased its percentage of national manufacturing employment between 1961 and 1980. The province's abundant energy resources have attracted both labour and capital which have generated considerable economic growth, particularly in Edmonton and Calgary. These metropolitan areas now rank tenth and eleventh respectively in terms of value added in manufacture by metropolitan area.

The restricted role of Canadian manufacturing

Canada's most formidable economic problem has been the trade deficit in manufactured goods which has persisted in the post-war period. The widening gap between imports and exports of industrial products reached new levels in the 1970s, having a depressive effect on the general economy.

This trade imbalance is partly a consequence of Canada's industrial structure which specialises in primary manufacturing industries processing the country's raw materials. Conversely Canadian industry is underrepresented in the high growth industries of the developed world. As Canadian manufacturing is unable to satisfy domestic demand for such products, importation is necessary. Such industrial underdevelopment has been attributed to a number of factors.

The small size of the domestic market inhibits economies of scale and tends to make unit costs higher in Canada than in the United States. An analysis of variations in firm size in the two countries appears earlier in this chapter.

Canada's highly unionised labour force has increased average manufacturing wages to a level above that of the United States which has to a certain extent undermined Canada's competitive position.

The physical geography of the country has presented substantial obstacles to industrial development. The sheer size of Canada, the great diffusion of markets the majority of which are of very limited size and the harsh conditions of winter have all worked to increase transport costs.

However many economists have cited the high level of foreign control as the most important element restricting the role of Canadian manufacturing. Figure 12.20 gives a detailed breakdown of the levels of foreign ownership in the 300 largest industrial companies in the country.

Fig. 12.20 Foreign ownership in Canadian manufacturing

Company rank	Level of foreign ownership (%)					
	0	1–25	26–50	51–75	76–99	100
1–50	24	6	4	6	4	6
51–100	24	4	3	7	4	8
101–150	25	—	—	6	2	17
151–200	21	3	3	—	2	21
201–250	21	2	—	5	2	20
251–300	24	1	1	5	1	18
Total	139	16	11	29	15	90

Ninety of the largest 300 are under total foreign control with only 139 companies in full Canadian ownership. Foreign control (particularly US investment) is greatest in secondary manufacturing which has a higher technological base and tends to be more heavily capitalised. Such firms have access to sophisticated managerial and professional services from within their multinational organisations. The use of these services accounts for about a quarter of Canada's invisible trade deficit. However the availability of services within the multinational organisation has another detrimental effect on the economy in that it reduces the potential market for domestic service firms. Such trends have significantly limited the quality of Canadian industrial infrastructure.

Another problem related to foreign ownership is the high level of component imports from within multinational enterprises. A consequence of these inter-corporate flows is that firms exert a low level of demand for local industrial inputs. In this way the expansion of local production and the development of new technology that might be expected, given the level of manufacturing in Canada, cannot proceed due to this substitution of intracorporate flows for regional connections.

An additional facet of multinational organisation that has had adverse effects on Canadian manufacturing is the tendency for companies to centralise new technology work in parent plants outside Canada and allocate only routine tasks to Canadian factories. Substantial opportunity costs have developed for Canada as a result of this process.

According to C. Freeman Canadian subsidiaries can be classified as (i) dependent firms which lack R and D facilities and have no involvement in product design and (ii) imitative firms which have adaptive R and D functions but rarely foster substantial innovation.

The actions of foreign controlled firms clearly inhibits the development of Canada's industrial infrastructure and puts a strain on the balance of payments. However such behaviour is quite normal in western economies and has to be viewed alongside the benefits of foreign investment. Government reports have recognised such realities of economic life and have concluded that on balance foreign investment has not been detrimental to the Canadian economy. Such conclusions are partly derived from the knowledge that domestic companies could not possibly replace foreign capital investment.

Energy has recently become a major exception to this viewpoint and Canada now has a firm objective to reduce foreign ownership of energy resources. Another recent trend has been increasing asset acquisition by Canadian companies in the United States, although this remains at a much lower level than reverse ownership relations.

The location of decision-making in manufacturing

The spatial linkage of decision-making centres (corporate headquarters) and major manufacturing plants is a logical requirement for efficient organisation and control although with advances in telecommunications the need for such proximity has been lessened to a certain extent. Such concentration of industry and corporate headquarters is evident in the United States and

Canada and, as with the manufacturing industry itself, agglomeration is far more intense in the latter nation.

As manufacturing has relocated, resulting in a greater regional spread, corporate headquarters have followed suit but to a lesser degree. Certain conclusions may be drawn from this difference in spatial distribution. Undoubtedly the decision-making function in manufacturing remains largely in the north-east because it is advantageous to be situated in the region. Inertia is not as strong an influence on the location of corporate headquarters as it is on manufacturing.

Other explanatory factors are the contribution of branch plants to peripheral expansion and the fact that many firms which have recently located in the south and west do not figure in the largest 500 industrial corporations. In addition there are those companies who manufacture outside the north-east but chose to locate in the region for headquarters' purposes because of its importance in commercial, financial and government terms.

While direct employment in corporate headquarters may in itself be limited their regional economic importance is much more far-reaching with regard to the multiplier potential accruing to such organisations.

Figure 12.21 illustrates the regional distribution of headquarters for the 500 largest industrial corporations in the United States for 1959 and 1980. The data show that although the pre-eminence of the northeast has been weakened it still maintains an overwhelming hold on corporate

Fig. 12.21 Headquarters of 500 largest industrial corporations in US

Division	1959	1980
New England	19	52
Middle Atlantic	214	154
East North Central	148	129
South Atlantic	23	34
East South Central	4	6
West North Central	32	30
West South Central	15	33
Mountain	6	8
Pacific	39	54
Total	500	500

headquarters. New England appears in marked contrast to the other divisions of the northeast with a substantial increase in corporate location due mainly to the expansion of the electronic complex of industries in the region and a significant shift from New York City to Connecticut suburbs.

With relation to specific urban locations the major corporate centres, with their total of headquarters in the largest 500, are New York (80), Chicago (26), Pittsburgh (16), Stamford, Connecticut (15), Los Angeles (12), Houston (11), St Louis (11), Minneapolis-St Paul (11) and Cleveland (9).

Figure 12.22 shows the location of the 300 largest industrial companies in Canada ranked by sales for the 1979–80 year. Concentration is much more intense than in the United States with Toronto and Montreal accounting for just over half of the total. In provincial terms Ontario with 150 corporate headquarters is overwhelmingly dominant, although a marked westward shift is underway. Calgary with 30 large industrial headquarters in 1979–80 boasted only 11 in the previous year. While this is partly accounted for by increased sales by existing energy companies in the city, new location has also been important.

Fig. 12.22 Headquarters of the 300 largest industrial companies in Canada ranked by sales 1979–80

Toronto	101	(33.7%)
Montreal	50	(16.7%)
Calgary	30	(10.0%)
Vancouver	24	(8.0%)
Winnipeg	13	(4.3%)
Hamilton	7	(2.3%)
London	5	(1.7%)
Mississauga	5	(1.7%)
Edmonton	4	(1.3%)
Ottawa	4	(1.3%)
Regina	4	(1.3%)

Bibliography

De Geer, S. (1927) 'The American manufacturing belt', *Geog. Annaler*, IX.

Lasuen, J. R. (1969) 'On growth poles', *Urban Studies*, June, 6, 2, pp. 137–61.

Lonsdale, R. E. and Seyler, H. L. (1979) *Nonmetropolitan Industrialisation*. Washington DC: J. H. Winston & Sons.

Meyer, D. R. (1980) 'Industrial entrepreneurs make their mark', *Geographical Magazine*, June.

Norton, R. D. and Rees, J. (1979) 'The product cycle and the spatial decentralisation of American manufacturing', *Regional Studies*, 13, 2, pp. 141–51.

Perloff, H. and Wingo, L. (1961) 'Natural resource endowment and regional economic growth' in Spengler, J. J. (ed.) *Natural Resources and Economic Growth*. Washington DC: Resources for the Future.

13

Trade and General Economic Trends

Although North America has a vast abundance of natural assets, the sophisticated economic structure that has emerged in the twentieth century could not possibly have developed to the same extent without international trade. Many sectors of the two nations' economies are dependent to a high degree on imports of raw materials or semi-finished products while numerous industries have their fortunes strongly tied to foreign demand.

In the current era of large-scale international transfers of goods, capital and also in some cases labour, no nation on earth is capable of sustaining a high rate of economic growth without trade relations as even the most well endowed world regions lack at least some of the wide spectrum of materials required to satisfy the various demands of modern industry. If any country in the world could survive economic isolation it would be the United States but at a very much lower material level than its citizens now enjoy.

The relationship between economic development and international trade is far from simple. Samuelson in his classic 1939 paper 'The Gains from International Trade' saw trade as allowing every participating country to obtain more of every commodity while performing less of every productive service. But some economists have pointed out that the trade factor alone does not account for economic development. Myrdal (1957) suggests that excessive dependence on trade

may result in a stagnating economy. Meier (1964) presented an intermediate view stating that 'foreign trade may operate as an engine of growth transmission . . . . provided there are latent indigenous forces of development that can be released through trade'.

The aim of this chapter is to examine post-war economic trends and to assess the importance of international trade to the various sectors of the North-American economy.

1. The United States

Post-war economic trends

The United States is still the most economically productive nation in the world but her major competitors, particularly West Germany and Japan, are closing the gap at a rapid pace. As a result the overwhelmingly dominant position held by the United States in the world economy after the Second World War has been steadily lessened in recent decades. This relative loss of position has been apparent, especially since the early 1970s as the United States has experienced high inflation, rising unemployment and balance of payments deficits, problems previously normally attributed to less strong economies.

In 1950 the real gross domestic product per employee in Japan was only 16 per cent of that of the United States while that of West Germany was 40 per cent. In 1973 the average Japanese worker was producing 55 per cent as much as the US norm with West Germany at the 74 per cent level. By 1980 these ratios had increased to 66 per cent and 88 per cent respectively and unless there is a dramatic change in US productivity, West Germany will probably exceed the US in terms of output per worker by the mid to late 1980s, with Japan in close pursuit.

Post-war productivity performance in the United States falls into three reasonably distinct phases:

(i) prior to 1965 output per worker in the private business sector grew by an average of 2.5 per cent per annum,

(ii) 1965–73 when the growth rate fell to 1.6 per cent per annum and

(iii) 1973–80 with an even lower growth rate of 0.8 per cent.

In 1960 the United States accounted for more than a quarter of the manufactured exports of the industrialized nations while supplying 98 per cent of its own domestic market. Since then there has been a marked decline which has been viewed by some American economists as being nothing short of catastrophic. In the 1970s the US lost 23 per cent of its share of the world market, compared with a 16 per cent decline during the 1960s. US manufacturers' share of the domestic market also fell more in the 1970s than in the 1960s, as illustrated by Figure 13.1. The losses of the 1970s are all the more significant as they were accompanied by a 40 per cent depreciation in the value of the dollar which made US exports cheaper and imports more expensive. The decline in the 1970s has been estimated at $125 billion in lost production and two million lost industrial jobs.

While the US had a healthy trade balance in services over the decade, the 1970s saw merchandise trade almost continuously in a state of deficit. At the same time merchandise exports doubled as

Fig. 13.1 Key industries hardest hit in the US market

Domestic market	Ranked by total sales of industry Percent of market		
	1960	1970	1979
Autos	95.9	82.8	79.0
Steel	95.8	85.7	86.0
Apparel	98.2	94.8	90.0
Electrical components	99.5	94.4	79.9
Farm machinery	92.3	92.2	84.7
Industrial inorganic chemicals	98.0	91.5	81.0
Consumer electronics	94.4	68.4	49.4
Footwear	97.7	85.4	62.7
Metal-cutting machine tools	96.7	89.4	73.6
Food processing machinery	97.0	91.9	81.3
Metal-forming machine tools	96.8	93.2	75.4
Textile machinery	93.4	67.1	54.5
Calculating and adding machines	95.0	63.8	56.9

. . . and in the export market

Export market	Ranked by size of US exports Percent of world exports		
	1962	1970	1979
Motor vehicles	22.6	17.5	13.9
Aircraft	70.9	66.5	58.0
Organic chemicals	20.5	25.7	15.0
Telecommunications apparatus	28.5	15.2	14.5
Plastic materials	27.8	17.3	13.0
Machinery and appliances (non-electric)	27.9	24.1	19.6
Medical and pharmaceutical products	27.6	17.5	16.9
Metal-working machinery	32.5	16.8	21.7
Agricultural machinery	40.2	29.6	23.2
Hand or machine tools	20.5	19.1	14.0
Textile and leather machinery	15.5	9.9	6.6
Railways vehicles	34.8	18.4	11.6
Housing fixtures	22.8	12.0	8.1

Source: Business week, 30 June 1980.

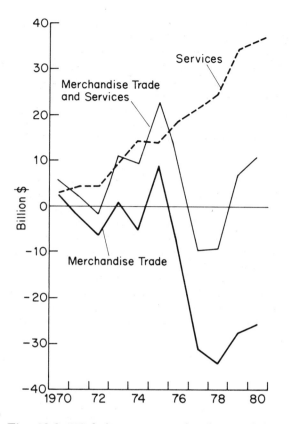

Fig. 13.2 *US balance on merchandise trade and services 1970–80. (Source: US Department of Commerce)*

ates where the increasing proportion of very young and the growing number of women in the labour force, the drop in working hours, reduced opportunities for economies of scale, the rising cost of raw materials, a slower expansion of fixed capital and the legal requirement to increase expenditure on pollution control, have all had an effect. The economist Edward Dennison also notes the importance of other factors such as the slower pace of new industrial innovation, the sharp increase in energy prices, uncertainty and distortions produced by a rising and unstable rate of inflation, tax disincentives and a possible change in the work ethic.

Figure 13.3 uses two standard measures to illustrate how the US and Canada have slipped in relation to their major competitors. In 1979 President Carter's Council of Economic Advisers gave as the two most important reasons for this situation, (i) that business had been reluctant to invest in new capital equipment and (ii) there had been a huge influx of inexperienced and thus less productive young people, women and part-timers into the labour force.

In the same year a study published by the New

a proportion of US manufacturing to about one-fifth, with the result that trends in international trade have a much greater effect on the economy than they did at the beginning of the period (Figure 13.2).

Although numerous explanations have been propounded to account for these trends most economists agree that because the United States was the first to introduce 'best practice' techniques it was only to be expected that other nations would eventually catch up. However few American industrialists thought their competitors would improve so rapidly.

Other contributory factors have also been pinpointed. High among these are changes in the legal and human environment in which business oper-

Fig. 13.3

Growth in real GDP per employed person (% p.a.)

	United States	Canada	Japan	EEC[1] (Big 4)
1950–74	1.93	2.46	7.53	4.29
1974–80	0.86	0.09	4.04	2.49

Growth in output per hour in manufacturing (% p.a.)

	United States	Canada	Japan	EEC[1] (Big 4)
1950–74	2.56	4.15	9.63	4.91
1974–80	1.84	1.66	7.21	3.51

[1] EEC – Only countries included are France, West Germany, Italy and the UK.
Source: US Department of Labor.

Fig. 13.4 Foreign trade of the USA 1980

Domestic exports ($m)	Total	EEC	of which: UK	Canada	LAFTA*	Japan
Food, drink and tobacco	30 407	5 691	716	1 541	4 127	4 506
of which:						
meat and dairy products	1 547	335	51	97	181	412
cereals and products	18 079	1 652	245	178	2 859	2 758
fruit, vegetables and products	2 930	752	139	661	375	356
animal feeding stuffs	2 878	1 697	37	129	205	212
tobacco, unmanufactured	1 334	519	78	26	19	197
Soyabeans	5 883	2 596	121	105	279	1 106
Wood and pulp	5 129	1 217	158	376	360	2 250
Cotton, raw	2 864	208	20	92	1	526
Metalliferous ores and scrap	4 518	1 621	302	546	309	1 066
Coal, coke and briquettes	4 772	1 587	192	884	327	1 319
Petroleum and products	2 833	595	107	951	307	199
Animal and vegetable oils and fats	1 946	240	56	32	357	77
Chemicals	20 740	5 149	751	2 134	4 237	1 964
of which:						
organic chemicals	5 697	1 571	186	527	1 343	590
medical and pharmaceutical products	1 932	693	114	145	210	324
plastics	3 884	837	140	511	743	245
Paper and manufactures	2 831	613	177	397	484	271
Textile yarn, cloth and manufactures	3 632	1 061	334	621	471	111
Iron and steel	3 123	419	157	537	1 089	53
Non-ferrous base metals	2 964	923	159	414	389	605
Metal manufactures	4 205	808	256	956	738	155
Machinery, incl electric	55 570	13 515	3 485	9 531	9 761	2 511
Road motor vehicles and parts	14 590	1 120	229	7 601	2 532	191
Aircraft and parts	12 816	3 765	1 476	707	1 260	1 086
Scientific instruments, etc	6 896	2 365	616	884	740	673
Total, including other items	220 705	53 694	12 694	35 395	32 274	20 790

Other main markets	Saudi Arabia	Rep. of Korea	Taiwan	Australia	Switzerland	China
	5 769	4 685	4 337	4 093	3 781	3 755

* Mexico, Colombia, Venezuela, Ecuador, Peru, Bolivia, Chile, Brazil, Paraguay, Uruguay, Argentina.

Source: The Economist.

York Stock Exchange noted that the buying power of the wages of US workers, adjusted for inflation but before taxes, remained very nearly unchanged in the 1966–78 period. Family income has of course increased as more women have gone out to work, but not the income of heads of households.

America's trading partners

In America's foreign trade with the rest of the world a very distinctive pattern has emerged, indicating trade deficits with Canada, much of Central America, Africa, the Middle East, the Indian sub-continent, Japan and much of southeast Asia. The United States has a trade surplus with the rest of the world.

Figures 13.4 and 13.5 give a detailed breakdown of US trade with her major partners where it can be seen that Canada and Japan are firmly entrenched in the leading positions.

Some important spatial changes have occurred in recent years. For the first time in 1978, US total trade with the countries of eastern Asia (including Australia and New Zealand) exceeded total trade with western Europe. The gap will probably widen because of the high growth rates of many Asian countries, particularly South Korea, Taiwan, Hong Kong and Singapore. The US market is the largest in the world and there is intense competition to supply it. As such it figures as the major export market for many nations whose economic trends are very much linked to the economy of the United States.

However as stated above, the United States has faced increasingly severe competition from the rest of the industrialized world both in the sale of its own goods and in purchasing raw materials. Figure 13.6, which shows the total trade statistics for the main western economies, clearly indicates that West German exports are only marginally behind those of the US although a substantial difference in import totals is evident, a result of West Germany's healthy trade balance.

United States trade in major commodities

The sectorial division of US trade is illustrated by Figures 13.4 and 13.5. While exports cover a wide spectrum, machinery, transport equipment, chemicals and grain (including preparations) are firmly dominant.

The trade balance in machinery is still impressive, reaching a record $22.4 billion in 1980. Yet only the computer industry has maintained its position over the last two decades and the United States may soon have to face intense Japanese competition even in this field. Agricultural machinery is under siege not only in the world market but in the domestic market also. A problem here is that the industry has increasingly concentrated on making big and expensive equipment that is appropriate only to the developed world. The US no longer makes any tractors under 35 horse power and has thus largely excluded itself from growing markets in developing countries.

The textile machinery industry which used to be a strong trade performer for the US has now moved into the deficit category. US manufacturers supplied only 54 per cent of the domestic market in 1979 in contrast to 93 per cent in 1962.

Grain is by far the most variable of the major export categories due primarily to large-scale fluctuations in world harvests. Fig. 13.4 shows that other raw materials are also prominent in the export sector, a fact which sets the US apart from many industrialised countries. Figure 13.7 lists the twenty leading export companies in the United States by value of foreign sales.

Petroleum and petroleum products overshadow all other commodity movements concerning the US, with imports amounting to a massive $76.9 billion in 1980. The sharp rise in petroleum prices has had severe repercussions on the US economy.

The spatial impact of international trade

International trade has had a most profound influence on the spatial development of the United States although the precise extent of its importance would be a very difficult task to ascertain exactly.

The initial accumulation of population, industry and wealth along the northeast seaboard relied heavily on the north Atlantic trade route with Europe and on immigration from that source. This region formed the core from which economic development diffused throughout the country. The present industrial structure of the region is still firmly linked with the export market as Figure

13.8 illustrates. On both an absolute and a relative basis manufactured exports are most important to the northeast although in terms of individual states California with only 3.7 per cent of its employment related to manufactured exports has the largest number of jobs in this category (323 000).

The development of trade with Japan and the rest of Asia proved to be a major stimulus to economic expansion along the Pacific coast, particularly in California. Both coastlines have remained positive attractions for population movements internally and internationally.

According to the Bureau of the Census, ac-

Fig. 13.5 Foreign trade of the USA 1980

Imports ($m)	Total	Canada	EEC	of which: W Germany	Japan	LAFTA*
Food, drink and tobacco	19 945	1 787	2 825	345	310	5 767
of which:						
meat and products	2 580	239	178	–	1	221
fish and products	2 740	564	80	2	225	639
fruit, vegetables and						
products	2 382	81	80	36	39	918
sugar	2 112	1	–	–	–	700
coffee	4 024	–	70	44	–	2 243
Wood and pulp	4 000	3 759	8	–	1	108
Metalliferous ores and scrap	4 072	1 139	179	91	10	620
Petroleum and products	76 936	2 900	2 326	25	23	12 519
Gas	5 274	4 166	20	–	–	663
Chemicals	9 011	2 529	3 560	1 081	756	561
Paper and manufactures	3 697	3 162	154	23	51	91
Textile yarn, cloth and mnfrs	2 677	70	651	96	396	209
Diamonds	2 261	1	722	3	2	21
Iron and steel	8 160	1 035	1 907	624	3 728	318
Precious metals, excl gold	2 450	649	383	23	39	511
Copper	1 510	365	135	75	331	417
Nickel	885	439	61	29	6	–
Aluminium	987	682	93	28	22	10
Tin	786	2	13	–	–	136
Metal manufactures	3 983	621	809	299	1 126	142
Machinery, incl electric	33 148	4 131	8 822	3 761	9 043	2 200
Road motor vehicles and parts	26 745	7 507	5 427	3 964	12 800	315
Aircraft and parts	1 901	509	1 043	50	96	32
Clothing and footwear	9 839	74	1 061	40	238	674
Scientific instruments, etc	2 595	187	677	337	653	119
Total, including other items	252 804	41 995	37 884	12 244	32 961	27 754

Other main suppliers	Saudi Arabia	Nigeria	Libya	Taiwan	Algeria	Indonesia
	13 323	11 316	7 395	7 362	6 881	5 503

* Mexico, Colombia, Venezuela, Ecuador, Peru, Bolivia, Chile, Brazil, Paraguay, Uruguay, Argentina.

Source: The Economist.

Fig. 13.6 Trade and the main western economies 1980

Country	Exports ($m)	Imports ($m)
USA	220 710	253 000
Canada	67 600	62 700
W. Germany	192 900	187 900
Japan	130 400	141 300
France	116 000	134 900
UK	115 100	119 900

Source: IMF

tivities relating to the export of manufactured goods provided 3.5 million jobs in 1976 or 11 per cent of total manufacturing employment. In recent years many US industries have suffered under the impact of increased market penetration by foreign companies. Industries such as iron and steel and motor vehicles in the mature stage of industrial development (as opposed to the innovative and growth stages) have been particularly vulnerable to foreign competition resulting in increasing numbers of plant closures in traditional industrial areas. Low growth rates and huge trade deficits

Fig. 13.7 The leading export companies in the United States

Rank 1980	Company	Products	Exports ($000)	Exports as a percentage of sales %
1	Boeing (Seattle)	Aircraft	5 503 800	58.39
2	General Motors (Detroit)	Automotive vehicles and parts, locomotives	5 287 100	9.16
3	General Electric (Fairfield, Conn.)	Generating equipment, aircraft engines	4 265 000	17.09
4	Ford Motor (Dearborn, Mich.)	Automotive vehicles and parts	3 453 000	9.31
5	Caterpillar Tractor (Peoria, Ill.)	Construction equipment, engines	3 094 000	35.99
6	E.I. du Pont de Nemours (Wilmington, Del.)	Chemicals, fibres, plastics	2 175 000	15.93
7	United Technologies (Hartford)	Aircraft engines, helicopters	2 142 593	17.39
8	McDonnell Douglas (St. Louis)	Aircraft	2 065 800	34.05
9	International Business Machines (Armonk, N. Y.)	Information-handling systems, equipment, and parts	1 615 000	6.16
10	Lockheed (Burbank, Calif.)	Aircraft and related support services	1 358 000	25.17
11	Eastman Kodak (Rochester, N.Y.)	Photographic equipment and supplies	1 357 029	13.94
12	Union Carbide (New York)	Chemicals, plastics	1 240 000	12.41
13	Westinghouse Electric (Pittsburgh)	Generating equipment, defence systems	1 192 000	14.00
14	Weyerhaeuser (Tacoma, Wash.)	Pulp, logs, lumber, wood products	1 140 000	25.13
15	Raytheon (Lexington, Mass.)	Electronic equipment	1 042 000	20.83
16	Monsanto (St. Louis)	Herbicides, textile fibres, speciality chemicals	1 026 400	15.61
17	Dow Chemicals (Midland, Mich.)	Chemicals, plastics, magnesium metal	909 000	8.55
18	International Harvester (Chicago)	Construction and farm equipment, trucks	888 000	14.07
19	Hewlett-Packard (Palo Alto, Calif.)	Electronic equipment	831 000	26.82
20	Archer-Daniels-Midland (Decatur, Ill.)	Soybean meal and oil, wheat, corn	808 941	28.87

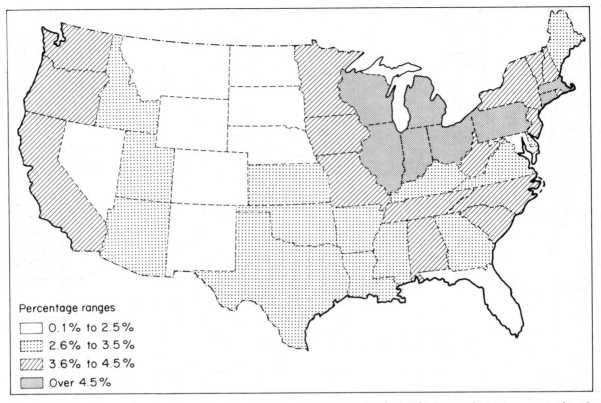

Fig. 13.8 *Employment related to manufacturing exports by state 1976. Shading indicates export-related employment as a percentage of civilian employment. (Source:* Business America, *Nov. 19th 1979)*

have thus had a severe spatial impact in some regions.

Agricultural land use in the United States is extremely dependent on foreign demand as agricultural production is far in excess of domestic requirements. Periods of low foreign demand usually lead to a contraction of the farming area while increased demand invariably results in the extension of the agricultural domain, often to include marginal lands.

The relationship between trade and economic well-being is often complex as international trade may be both beneficial and detrimental to various sectors of a region's or country's economy at the same time. The export of logs from the Pacific northwest is an example which has generated much controversy. While the increasing volume of log exports is undoubtedly providing a significant number of jobs in the region the forest product companies in the area argue that only processed wood should be exported so that the value added

in manufacture would accrue to the region rather than Japan, the principal customer.

2. Canada

The economic development of Canada has been intricately interwoven with the growth of her powerful southern neighbour. In 1980 the United States absorbed 64 per cent of Canadian exports while Canada took 16 per cent of United States exports, indicating the widely divergent levels of mutual reliance between the two countries. Canada is at the same time the United States' major customer and supplier. The strength of economic ties with the United States means that trends in that country have far-reaching consequences for the Canadian economy. However in spite of such strong dependence on the United States, Canada trades with all parts of the world serving an economic base which has considerably diversified in the post-war period to rank as one of the more important industrial economies in the world.

Recent economic trends

Compared to the 1960s, the 1970s and early 1980s were periods of general economic disappointment, a reality faced not only by Canada but also by most of the industrialised world. The Canadian economy, judged in terms of unemployment, price stability and growth, performed well below the levels of the previous decade.

In the 1960s the net balance of payments (trade in goods and services) was consistently negative but the level each year was less than C$1.5 billion and was easily covered by inflows of foreign capital, including substantial direct investment, attracted by favourable investment opportunities in Canada. During the early 1970s this trend continued with in fact a trade surplus for three years in the first half of the decade. Thereafter the situation changed markedly as the country's international competitive position deteriorated under the impact of rising costs and prices and a decline in foreign investment. Between 1972 and 1979 Canada's share of world exports fell from 4.9 per cent to 3.4 per cent.

Figure 13.9 shows that the current account deficit hovered between the C$4 billion and C$5 mark in the latter part of the decade but registered a sharp improvement in 1979.

While the trading account for merchandise remained in surplus apart from a very slight deficit in one year, the position with regard to services (tourist receipts, interest and dividends, shipping and other business services) has grown steadily worse. Tourist receipts have lagged primarily because the great expansion in air travel has given Americans, Canada's main customers for tourism, a wider choice of international travel. The slow growth of receipts from interest and dividends has been related to the good opportunities for investment in Canada that have existed in recent decades and consequently there has not been a strong incentive to invest abroad. The service deficit has also grown sharply because of the higher interest payments on expanded foreign borrowing by the government.

A most significant reason for Canada's large current account deficit has been the relatively sharp increase in labour costs in the 1970s which rose 110 per cent over the course of the decade compared to 80 per cent in the United States. Part of this 30 point difference has been offset in recent years by the devaluation of the Canadian dollar. Yet, measuring Canadian unit labour costs in terms of $US still produces a larger increase over the decade for Canada (87 per cent v. 80 per cent). Such divergence has been particularly important for trade in manufactured products where labour cost is a more significant part of the final price. The deficit in end-products trade increased from $3.4 billion in 1970 to $17.0 billion at the end of the decade.

However, in general Canada has benefited from favourable terms of trade in the 1970s whereby the prices of exports, with their high natural resource content, have risen faster than the price of imports.

The role of staple commodities

The Canadian economy has historically been, and still is to a lesser extent, dominated by staple products such as agricultural products, minerals, fish and forest products. The changing importance of staples to Canadian exports is indicated by Figure 13.10 which does not include minerals because of inconsistent data, therefore underestimating the total position of staple commodities. Forest products are dominant by far, accounting for 16.9 per cent of Canadian exports in 1976.

In 1868, the year after Federation, staples made up 75 per cent of merchandise exports. By 1880 staples had increased to 88 per cent of exports, from which peak they fell to the 70–80 per cent range until the 1930s. A considerable decline

Fig. 13.9 *Canadian balance of payments 1961–80 (Source: Statistics Canada)*

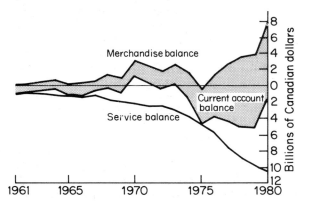

Fig. 13.10 The value of staple products to Canadian exports (C$m)

Year	Total (C$m)	Staples* Total (C$m)	%	Forest products Total (C$m)	%
1868	57.6	43.3	75.2	18.8	32.6
1880	86.1	75.6	87.8	18.0	20.9
1900	183.2	144.1	78.7	32.7	22.7
1930	863.4	632.0	73.2	249.7	28.9
1940	1 178.8	717.9	60.9	348.0	29.5
1950	3 118.4	2 103.9	67.5	1 112.9	35.7
1960	5 255.6	2 734.3	52.0	1 591.9	30.3
1970	16 401.0	5 000.0	30.4	2 865.0	17.5
1976	37 328.5	10 258.3	27.4	6 334.5	16.9

* Staples – agricultural, fish, forestry products. Minerals and petroleum products omitted because of inconsistent data.

was witnessed after 1950.

The so-called 'staple theory' states that variations in the level and prospects for natural resource exports dominate the rate of long-term growth. Watkins (1963), describing the growth path of a staple economy, stated 'Growth is initiated by an increase in demand for a staple export. If the spread effects are potent, as the export sector grows so too will the domestic sectors. The result will be increasing demand for factors (i.e. land, labour, capital). Domestic slack, if it exists at all, will be quickly absorbed, and the continuation of growth will depend on the ability to import scarce factors. If the supply of foreign factors is elastic, the customary tendency for the expansion of one sector, in this case exports, to affect domestic sectors adversely by driving up factor prices is mitigated. This explains the very strong booms that are a feature of growth in staple economies.'

Levitt (1973) sees the role of staples in a different light, suggesting that development of staple industries at present may even be counterproductive, as the currently important staples, forest and mineral products, have weak forward and backward linkages.

Although the Canadian economy can no longer be described as a staple economy, exports of staple goods continue to have a strong influence on Canada's economic growth.

Foreign investment

The limited size of the domestic market has had clear repercussions on the growth potential of Canadian firms and subsequently on the ability to invest. The exploitation of Canada's staple commodities and the utilisation of the nation's human capital has required massive foreign investment, a topic which has stirred a certain degree of controversy among Canadian economists. Sixty per cent of manufacturing industry is foreign controlled as well as 74 per cent of the oil and gas industry, with US companies dominant in both cases.

On the whole there is no evidence of foreign investment causing a balance of payments problem. The Canadian government, after two comprehensive reports (Watkins, 1968; Gray, 1972), has decided that in general foreign investment is beneficial to Canada.

Canada's trading partners

The general export performance of the major western nations in the post-1960 period shows a basic dichotomy between West Germany and Japan whose export penetration has steadily improved and the US, UK and Canada whose share of world markets has declined.

The final destinations of Canadian exports in 1980 are itemised in Figure 13.11. There has been a steady increase in exports to the United States, up from 55.7 per cent of the total in 1960 to 64 per cent in 1980, which is primarily linked to the rise in United States-Canadian automobile trade, a result of the Automotive Products Agreement (APA) between the two countries in 1965. The APA allows cars, trucks and their component parts to move across the border duty free and consequently attracted US motor companies to set up plant in Canada to take advantage of lower employment costs in the industry which in 1979 were 25 per cent lower than in Detroit.

At present Canada produces about 10 per cent of all cars, trucks and buses made in North America. However, while Canada enjoys a surplus of C$1 billion on vehicles it suffers from a C$3.5 billion deficit (1979) in parts. This C$2.5 billion net deficit was approximately half the country's total current account deficit, a gap large enough for Canada to demand an overhaul, in 1980, of the 15-

Fig. 13.11 Canada's trade with main trading partners

Exports, fob	1980 (C$m)	Imports, fob	1980 (C$m)
USA	47 954	USA	48 164
Japan	4 359	Japan	2 782
UK	3 193	Saudi Arabia	2 431
West Germany	1 630	Venezuela	2 165
USSR	1 508	UK	1 960
Netherlands	1 421	West Germany	1 433
Italy	988	France	762
Total exports	75 322	Total imports	68 574

Source: The Economist.

year-old agreement with the United States. Another matter of concern for Canada is that most of the country's auto workers are employed in the assembly of the larger-sized models that are now being phased out. Canada is obviously anxious to avoid unemployment as the motor industry switches to the manufacture of smaller cars.

Vehicles and vehicle parts account for approximately a quarter of Canadian exports to the United States, followed in rank order of importance by metals and minerals, natural gas, softwood lumber and newsprint.

Exports to the UK have steadily decreased on a relative basis because of slow growth in the UK and the latter's membership of the EEC since 1973, resulting in the termination of the preference system enjoyed by Canada and other Commonwealth countries in 1977.

Trade with the founder six members of the EEC has been at a higher level than originally feared due to high growth rates which have largely offset the negative impact of increased tariff barriers. Exports to Japan have grown strongly and in 1973 Japan passed the UK as Canada's second largest market.

China, USSR and eastern Europe have periodically been large markets for Canadian wheat when harvests in those countries have fallen drastically below expectations. In several years in the early 1970s Canadian exports to China accounted for 10 per cent of all Chinese imports.

While Canadian exports have grown appreciably, the country's export penetration in the 1970s in the various main markets has fallen in all cases, causing considerable concern to Canada in view of her rising import bill.

The breakdown of total exports by type is illustrated by Figure 13.12. Manufactured goods account for the highest percentage with motor vehicles and parts dominating this section. Metals

Fig. 13.12 Canadian merchandise trade 1980

Canadian merchandise imports	C$ billions	Percentage of total
Food	4.1	6.0
Crude petroleum	6.9	10.1
Construction material	1.3	1.9
Industrial material	16.9	24.8
Auto and related products	13.4	19.7
Machinery and equipment	16.8	24.7
Other consumer goods	7.0	10.3
Miscellaneous	1.6	2.3
Total	68.2	

Canadian merchandise exports	C$ billions	Percentage of total
Wheat and wheat flour	3.8	5.0
Other agricultural	5.5	7.2
Crude petroleum	2.9	3.8
Natural gas	3.7	4.9
Lumber and plywood	3.6	4.7
Pulp, paper and board	8.8	11.6
Metals and minerals	14.6	19.2
Other fabricated materials	9.1	12.0
Auto and related products	10.8	14.2
Machinery and equipment	6.5	8.5
Other manufactured goods	4.4	5.8
Miscellaneous	2.4	3.1
Total	76.1	

Source: Statistics Canada.

and minerals hold second place with exports covering a wide range of commodities. The figure for natural gas will undoubtedly increase markedly in the coming years as Canada's capacity to satisfy the demands of the US market develops. Forest products and farm and fish products rank third and fourth respectively, both showing a marked relative decline since 1960.

In terms of imports the United States is again Canada's main trading partner, accounting for 70 per cent of the total in 1980. Japan, Saudi Arabia and Venezuela occupied second, third and fourth positions respectively.

In the 1970s Canada changed from being a petroleum surplus to a petroleum deficit nation. This situation has had repercussions not only for Canada but also for the United States, as explained in Chapter 8. In 1980 Canada's net deficit in crude petroleum had risen to C\$4 billion, an important factor in the country's trade balance. The position of Saudi Arabia and Venezuela as Canada's third and fourth largest trade suppliers is due almost entirely to petroleum importation.

Canada has a huge deficit in trade in manufactured end products as the country produces a limited range of industrial goods compared to the larger industrial economies. A small domestic market is a significant limiting factor to economies of scale and thus to Canada's ability to compete in many industrial sectors.

North America and GATT

Every nation has a vested interest in the smooth functioning of international trade and the terms under which such trade operates. In 1947 the General Agreement on Tariffs and Trade (GATT) was signed by twenty-three nations. It laid down a framework for the settlement of trade disputes and the negotiation of mutual reductions in trade barriers. To date six rounds of international trade negotiations have been completed under GATT auspices leading to very significant cuts in tariffs and contributing to an unprecedented expansion of world trade in the post-war period from which North-America has greatly benefited.

The latest round of negotiations began in Tokyo in 1973 with about 100 nations participating and

was concluded in 1979. The 'Tokyo round' was lengthy because it was the first negotiating round to deal not only with tariffs but also with non-tariff barriers to trade. The negotiations were conducted during a period of recession with the forecast that the rate of world economic growth will be lower in the final quarter of the century than between 1950 and 1975.

This downturn, epitomised by rising unemployment, has led a significant body of opinion in the major world markets to advocate selective protection rather than greater liberalisation of trade. Such an attitude has been characteristic of US industries such as steel, textiles and consumer appliances whose domestic market share has been badly hit by foreign competition.

However the US government, although concerned about the problems of individual industries, has been anxious that the obstacles to international trade should be overcome as far as possible with the aim that such action will revitalise world economic growth with resultant benefits accruing to the US economy.

The agreement is certainly a step towards freer trade. Various codes of conduct could prove very important, particularly the one that opens government procurement to foreign supplies. The United States and Japan are currently moving closer to a compromise on one of their central trade disagreements with a bilateral deal which will open the purchasing of Japan's state owned domestic telecommunications monopoly to overseas tenderers.

A code has also been agreed disallowing subsidies that injure another country's trade but GATT recognises the right of poor nations to subsidise exports where there is a development opportunity or a competitive need. It also expects importing countries to prove market injury before they impose countervailing duties. Other codes should prevent trade being obstructed by the procedures of import licensing, the methods of customs valuation or the application of technical, health and safety standards. A significant element in all these agreements is the procedures for the settlement of disputes with GATT committees of one sort or another although most governments will still probably prefer quiet bilateral talks.

The US has been particularly concerned with two aspects of trade in recent years, EEC farm subsidies and the substantial trade deficit with Japan. The EEC has greatly increased its share of the world agricultural export market in which the

US has a most important stake. The federal government attributes EEC success in this field to high farm subsidies and sees such action as unfair competition. More worrying to the US has been its sustained merchandise trade deficit with Japan which is now becoming an increasing source of friction in US-Japanese relations. In American eyes this trade gap is the result of a package of dubious measures undertaken by the Japanese to restrict entry of foreign goods into Japan while maximising its market share abroad.

Canada stands to gain a great deal from GATT. Of the major industrial nations it is the one with the smallest domestic market and thus should benefit significantly from freer trade.

The developing countries have not generally been happy with GATT. A broad complaint is that freer trade among the affluent nations undermines many special preferences which have existed since the colonial era. They see the Tokyo round as not having produced new and specific benefits for the poor.

Ports, trade and economic development

For more than 300 years North American sea and river ports have been the first population centres, the gateways to the hinterland and the focal points of first local and later regional economic development. Ports are an essential component of international trade and economic growth for more than 99 per cent of United States and Canadian two-way foreign trade (excluding US-Canadian trade) is moved by water transport. The future economic development of the continent will be dependent to a significant degree on the ability of North American ports to handle the ever growing volume of foreign trade.

Ports are as important now as they have ever been and in some ways are more so. The United States ranks first in the world in the volume of imports and exports handled and is the world's premier supplier of agricultural commodities and manufactured goods. Foreign trade now accounts for approximately 20 per cent of total United States GNP. As the points of interchange where cargoes are transferred between inland and ocean

carriers, ports are essential components in a vast logistical network.

A US Maritime Administration study estimated that in 1978 the US seaport industry alone directly generated in excess of one million jobs. More than three million jobs in other transportation sectors are dependent on ports. According to Commerce Department estimates the volume of US export/import tonnage will more than double between 1980 and 2000. A huge investment in new port facilities will be required to accommodate such an increase.

A number of ports have been active in promoting overseas sales of products manufactured within their hinterlands. The Massachusetts Port Authority's Small Business Export Program which began in 1977 has attracted much attention and has acted as a blueprint for other port authorities.

In terms of technological advance the most prominent development has been the rapid displacement of the traditional break-bulk cargo ship by large container, roll on-roll off and barge ships in the movement of general cargo. Modern containerships may carry 2200 containers in 20 ft equivalents at speeds in excess of 30 knots. Due to their speed and ability to reduce greatly the time required to load and unload, containerships can do four times the work of a conventional break-bulk ship.

The United States has invested heavily in its seaports to a grand total of $4.8 billion between 1946 and 1978. At many ports well over half the general cargo handled is already containerised and this trend will undoubtedly continue. In 1980 three North American ports were ranked in the world's top ten container ports, with New York first, Long Beach eighth and Oakland tenth. A global container port system is steadily evolving amongst the major trading nations.

Another major recent development in the US port industry has been the rush to expand coal handling facilities. A large number of ports want a greater share of, or want to break into, this potentially lucrative market. At present the ports of Hampton Roads, New Orleans/Baton Rouge, Baltimore and Mobile have 87 per cent of coal handling capacity, but this 'monopoly' will undoubtedly weaken in the future. What is lacking is a nationally coordinated system of expansion to facilitate the growing export of coal and as individual ports compete against each other a

Fig. 13.13 Major United States ports: total foreign commerce 1980

Value ($million)		*Volume (millions short tons)*	
1. New York	44 069	1. Hampton Roads	68 165
2. Houston	22 999	2. Houston	53 503
3. Baltimore	15 313	3. New York	52 743
4. New Orleans	15 183	4. New Orleans	43 791
5. Los Angeles	14 692	5. Baltimore	37 012
6. Long Beach	13 397	6. Baton Rouge	34 569
7. Hampton Roads	13 101	7. Philadelphia	33 278
8. Philadelphia	8 571	8. Beaumont	28 815
9. Oakland	8 459	9. Corpus Christi	25 544
10. Beaumont	6 485	10. Tampa	23 765
11. Baton Rouge	5 826	11. Long Beach	18 598
12. Miami	4 615	12. Port Arthur	16 584

huge excess of capacity may be the eventual result.

Ports can be ranked in a number of ways but the two most significant indices of importance are total tonnage handled and the value of tonnage handled. Figure 13.13 illustrates the ranking of US ports using these criteria. In terms of the value of goods handled New York has almost double the total of its nearest rival. However when the volume of trade is examined the port ranks third behind Hampton Roads and Houston.

Further interesting variations are apparent when the direction of trade is analysed. With regard to imported waterborne commerce New York is overwhelmingly dominant, handling $28 billion of trade compared to $11 billion by Houston, the next ranking port. Yet for exports New York recorded a lesser $16 billion with Houston in second place with a total of almost $12 billion.

North Atlantic ports lost their traditional dominance of total US development expenditure during the 1970s with the Gulf, South Atlantic and Great Lakes groups of ports displaying major relative increases in development expenditure during the period 1973 to 1978 over previous periods.

Forty-two per cent of Canada's international trade is handled by the eight major ports of Halifax, St John, Quebec, Montreal, Toronto, Hamilton, Thunder Bay and Vancouver. In terms of both volume and value of goods handled Montreal and Vancouver are most important. Apart from its position as the country's premier port Montreal is also Canada's number one container port with five modern and efficient container terminals in operation by 1980. Vancouver is the chief Canadian Pacific port and is the major western terminus of railways, highways and airways. In addition the city is the western terminus of the transmontane oil pipeline from Edmonton. Halifax is Canada's principal ice-free Atlantic port and is the eastern terminus of the railway and transcontinental highway systems.

The port of New York and New Jersey: A case study

The port of New York-New Jersey is the busiest in North America, possessing one of the greatest natural harbours in the world. The evolution of the bi-state port complex has been an important component in the region's economic development and of major importance to the nation as a whole. The port is a hub of economic activity with an intricate network of transport and communications linking it to all parts of the continent. However in recent decades the port has reflected the waning economic fortunes of the northeast region as its share of the total waterborne commerce of the United States dwindled from 17.4 per cent in 1948 to less than 10 per cent in 1980.

New York-New Jersey developed as the premier transhipment point of the continent due to a

At the Port of New York-New Jersey, a Japanese ship accepts containers for movement to the Far East

combination of certain natural attributes of both land and sea. The port's advantages of deep water, shelter from the open sea, negligible tidal variation and security from silting and flooding were recognised at an early stage. These factors, combined with control of the Hudson-Mohawk gap, the only lowland route from the mid-Atlantic seaboard to the interior, has given the port a clear comparative advantage over other transhipment points along the seaboard. No less important has been the presence of flat land in the vicinity of the harbour for both industrial and urban development. Being close to such great concentrations of population and economic activity has been a most important causal factor in the port's pre-eminence.

In total the port has 1200 km of water frontage; 740 km in New York and 460 km in New Jersey. The Port District has eight large bays. The principal route through the port is Ambrose Channel,

shown in Figure 13.14. This main channel is maintained at a depth of 13.7 metres below mean sea level and at a width of 610 metres. Numerous other channels of varying widths link all the ports of the bay. The port is able to handle most oceangoing ships, with the exception of very large tankers.

In 1979 the leading general cargo exports were iron and steel scrap, plastic materials, machinery (general), motor vehicles and waste paper while the five major general cargo imports were nonmetallic minerals and slag, sugar, alcoholic beverages, bananas and coffee.

The Port of New York-New Jersey led all US ports in the number of ship calls. A total of 7166 ships, exclusive of naval craft, fishing vessels and seagoing barges came into the port during the year. This total was comprised of 518 autocarriers, 2962 break-bulk vessels, 1587 container ships, 233 passenger vessels and 1866 tankers. Brooklyn docks attracted 1513 of the ships visiting the port and remained its principal terminal for break-bulk vessels.

Fig. 13.14 *New York–New Jersey; Major ocean going channels (Source:* New York Port Handbook *1978)*

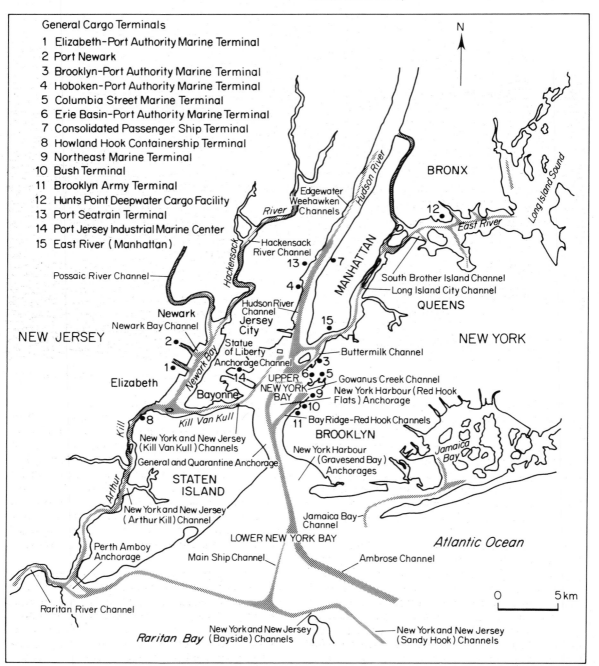

General Cargo Terminals
1 Elizabeth-Port Authority Marine Terminal
2 Port Newark
3 Brooklyn-Port Authority Marine Terminal
4 Hoboken-Port Authority Marine Terminal
5 Columbia Street Marine Terminal
6 Erie Basin-Port Authority Marine Terminal
7 Consolidated Passenger Ship Terminal
8 Howland Hook Containership Terminal
9 Northeast Marine Terminal
10 Bush Terminal
11 Brooklyn Army Terminal
12 Hunts Point Deepwater Cargo Facility
13 Port Seatrain Terminal
14 Port Jersey Industrial Marine Center
15 East River (Manhattan)

The Red Hook Terminal, Brooklyn, the Port of New York and New Jersey's newest container facility

Oceanborne foreign trade passing through the port in 1977 generated $5.1 billion in port industry revenues. This figure is based upon a Port Authority input-output analysis estimate that the movement of every tonne of waterborne cargo in US foreign trade generates, on average, $53 of port industry revenues. The port industry has further indirect or multiplier effects that ripple through the economy from the industries supporting it.

The estimated multiplier for the port industry is 1.6, that is, every dollar of port industry sales generates $1.60 in sales throughout the economy. Thus foreign waterborne cargo passing through the port in 1977 generated at least $8.2 billion in sales throughout the national economy. The same study also estimated that waterborne foreign trade moving through the port created at least 161 000 jobs throughout the country with the greatest concentration within the port region.

The estimated revenue and employment effects per tonne of cargo are greater for New York-New Jersey than for the average US port. At the national level, exports and imports are largely low-value commodities which tend to generate low levels of employment. In the bi-state port, however, cargo is generally high value. In 1977 the average value per long tonne of general cargo passing through the port was $1 844, approximately two and a half times the national average of $729.

As yet the port does not handle coal but the port authority sees coal as a possible area for expansion in the future. A feasibility study has shown that a 18 metre dredged channel could accommodate supercolliers of 200 000 tonnes which would export coal hauled by Conrail from Appalachia.

The port has been at the forefront of modern

handling techniques. The movement to container-isation began in New York-New Jersey when in August 1962 construction began on the first specially designed container port. The port's lead over the country's other container ports is enorm-ous. Containerised cargo handled is at more than two times the level recorded by Long Beach the nation's number two container port.

The Elizabeth Port Authority Marine Terminal, the world's largest container terminal, has more than 1 100 acres of piers, storage and cargo-distribution space and 19 powerful container cranes. Development of such facilities continues, marked particularly by the completion in 1981 of the $20 million Red Hook Container Terminal in the Atlantic Basin section of the Brooklyn water-front with a handling capacity of 25 000 containers a year.

Containerisation has been only one of several techniques–each consisting of some form of pre-loading away from the docks–that have made shipping more capital intensive over the last two decades. One such innovation is LASH shipping, or Lighter Aboard Ship, in which freight ships carry preloaded barges of about 300 tonnes called lighters. Pallet ships where cargo is loaded on portable platforms and roll on–roll off shipping have also greatly increased in use.

In 1979 the US Department of Commerce authorised the opening of a large Foreign Trade Zone at Port Newark and Elizabeth. It is expected that the zone will attract overseas firms to establ-ish assembly and manufacturing which would be a useful boost to the port and the local economy. This is just one way in which the Port Authority is attempting to revitalise sections of the waterfront, many of which have fallen into disuse in the post-1945 period.

Until shortly after World War II the port was a major shipbuilding centre. While many major shipbuilders are currently located on the East Coast, there is only one shipyard in the port with large shipbuilding capabilities–Seatrain, on the site of the old Brooklyn Navy Yard.

The port does suffer from a number of impedi-ments though. Labour and operating costs are generally higher than in competing ports while rail services to some sections of the port are clearly inadequate. The port also suffers navigational hazards arising from the location of old railway bridges which pose a potential obstacle to future growth. In addition rail freight rates for some containerised cargo are higher than for competing ports.

It is likely that the port of New York-New Jersey will still be the premier port in North America in the year 2000 although the major ports on the Gulf and Pacific coasts should significantly narrow the gap with convergence of economic growth between the major regions of the country.

Part 3
Urban North America and the Future

14
Urbanization I: Development and Change

Twentieth-century trends

The North American population is heavily concentrated in urban areas with, for example, one in four Americans living in a city of more than 100 000 persons in 1980. City growth in the present century has largely been a process of suburbanization. Some central renewal has occurred, in fact a substantial amount in some cities, but the greatest change has been in the suburban areas and beyond.

Definitions vary as to what exactly constitutes the metropolitan area. In the United States the Standard Metropolitan Statistical Area (SMSA), which has been defined as 'an integrated economic and social unit with a large population nucleus containing at least one central city with 50 000 inhabitants or more or two cities having contiguous boundaries and a combined population of at least 50 000', is a useful measure. The SMSA includes the county in which the central city is located and adjacent counties that are metropolitan in character. The SMSA does however include substantial rural and semi-rural areas within its boundaries which, some argue, reduces its accuracy as an indicator of urbanisation.

The proportion of the total US population living in SMSAs increased steadily throughout the century although for the 1970–80 period the population grew more rapidly outside the SMSAs than within for the first time. In 1940 SMSAs occupied about 6 per cent of the national land area, containing 52.6 per cent of the population. By 1980 the SMSAs (318 in all) had spread to encompass about 15 per cent of total land area and were the place of residence of over 70 per cent of the population. Although the large metropolitan areas became less attractive in the last decade the population is still urbanizing but increasingly in smaller cities.

Another major change in urban geography in the twentieth century has been that in 1900 most cities were dominantly manufacturing centres. However in most metropolitan areas service functions have become progressively more important with manufacturing accounting for a steadily decreasing proportion of employment. Increasing mobility has enabled the metropolitan areas to supply retail, financial, educational and other services to populations spread over progressively larger areas.

While the level and pace of urbanization in Canada has roughly followed that of the United States there are a number of distinctive differences between Canadian and US cities and therefore it is incorrect to think totally in terms of a North American urban stereotype. Research concerning such contrasts in city development has been limited to date but has focused on a number of important issues which will be discussed below.

The urban Mid-West, Eldora, Iowa

Regional variations

Figure 14.1 illustrates the percentage population in each of the United States living in SMSAs in 1980. Of the sixteen states with more than 80 per cent of total population in SMSAs, ten are located in the 'manufacturing belt'. The remaining states in this category are California, Nevada, Washington, Colorado, Texas and Florida. The role of SMSAs is least in the northern Mountain and Great Plains states, and in northern New England, West Virginia, Mississippi and Arkansas.

Figure 14.2 shows the 1980 rank of the fifty largest American cities, as defined by city political boundaries (as distinct from the larger SMSAs). While the three northeastern divisions contained fourteen of the big fifty, only one of these, Columbus, Ohio, gained population between 1970 and 1980. The lakeside cities of Buffalo, Cleveland and Detroit lost over one-fifth of their populations in the ten year period. While the region was not alone in registering decline in city population it was undoubtedly the focal point of this trend.

Five of the Pacific region's nine cities in the big fifty declined in population. But in this region

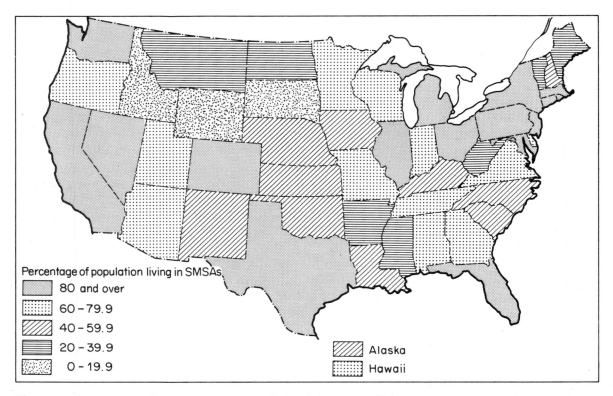

Fig. 14.1 *Percentage of population living in SMSA's by state 1980*

movement to areas outside the city but within the wider urban region has been by far the most important reason whereas in the northeast out-migration from the region as a whole has operated vigorously alongside such inter-urban movement. The greatest contrast to the northeast is provided by the West South Central where seven of the nine cities, led by Houston and Dallas, recorded increases.

The recent urban geography of Canada shows general complementarity with the United States. While data are not perfectly comparable certain observations can be made. Population decline is generally characteristic in the inner zones while, as in the United States, overall growth remains because of the attraction of the new suburbs and fringe. The western cities have been less susceptible to inner metropolitan population decline due to a combination of their more recent history and the economic upsurge in western Canada.

The rivalry between Toronto and Montreal has resulted in a binary pattern of rank-size in Canada

as opposed to the primary pattern exemplified by the United States. While southern and western cities have steadily improved their national rankings in terms of population size a distinctive feature of US urban geography, which is also illustrated in Canada and most other developed countries, is long-term regional rank stability. Along the northeastern seaboard the four largest cities in 1790, New York, Philadelphia, Boston and Baltimore continued to hold the largest urban populations in the region in 1980. Long-term rank stability is however not characteristic of smaller urban areas where a wide variety of influences can rapidly change a town's ranking.

Qualitative as well as quantitative regional contrasts are apparent in the urban geography of North America. While the distinction between the social deprivation of the inner city and the relative affluence of the suburbs is a well documented fact, much recent attention has been directed to overall regional contrasts. D. M. Smith (1979) has shown convincingly that in the United States the quality

Fig. 14.2 The 50 largest cities in the United States

1980 Rank	1980 Population	Change since 1970		1980 Rank	1980 Population	Change since 1970	
1. New York City	7 015 608	Down	11.1 %	26. Kansas City, Mo.	446 562	Down	12.0 %
2. Chicago	2 969 570	Down	11.9 %	27. Nashville	439 599	Up	3.2 %
3. Los Angeles	2 950 010	Up	4.9 %	28. El Paso	424 522	Up	31.7 %
4. Philadelphia	1 680 235	Down	13.8 %	29. Pittsburgh	423 962	Down	18.5 %
5. Houston	1 554 992	Up	26.1 %	30. Atlanta	422 293	Down	14.7 %
6. Detroit	1 192 222	Down	21.3 %	31. Oklahoma City	401 002	Up	8.9 %
7. Dallas	901 450	Up	6.8 %	32. Cincinnati	383 058	Down	15.5 %
8. San Diego	870 006	Up	24.7 %	33. Fort Worth	382 349	Down	2.8 %
9. Baltimore	784 554	Down	13.4 %	34. Minneapolis	370 091	Down	14.8 %
10. San Antonio	783 296	Up	19.7 %	35. Honolulu	365 114	Up	12.4 %
11. Phoenix	781 443	Up	33.7 %	36. Portland, Oreg.	364 891	Down	4.0 %
12. Indianapolis	695 040	Down	7.0 %	37. Buffalo	357 002	Down	22.9 %
13. San Francisco	674 063	Down	5.8 %	38. Long Beach	356 906	Down	0.5 %
14. Memphis	844 838	Up	3.3 %	39. Tulsa	355 500	Up	7.6 %
15. Washington, DC	637 651	Down	15.7 %	40. Toledo	354 265	Down	7.5 %
16. Milwaukee	632 989	Down	11.8 %	41. Austin	343 390	Up	35.4 %
17. San Jose	625 763	Up	36.1 %	42. Oakland	338 721	Down	6.3 %
18. Cleveland	572 532	Down	23.8 %	43. Miami	335 360	Up	0.1 %
19. Boston	582 582	Down	12.2 %	44. Tucson	331 506	Up	26.1 %
20. Columbus, Ohio	561 943	Up	4.1 %	45. Newark, NJ	329 498	Down	13.7 %
21. New Orleans	556 913	Down	6.2 %	46. Albuquerque	328 837	Up	34.5 %
22. Jacksonville	541 269	Up	7.3 %	47. Omaha	312 929	Down	9.8 %
23. Seattle	491 897	Down	7.3 %	48. Charlotte	310 799	Up	28.7 %
24. Denver	489 318	Down	4.9 %	49. Louisville	298 161	Down	17.6 %
25. St Louis	448 640	Down	27.9 %	50. Birmingham	282 068	Down	6.3 %

Source: US Bureau of Census.

of urban life deteriorates quite regularly from northwest to southeast. Smith has mapped data presented by Liu (Figure 14.3) which shows that the worst cities in terms of social well-being are in the south but New York and Philadelphia are also included in this category. The fact that no SMSAs west of the Rockies appear in the bottom two groupings helps to explain the attraction of western urbanisation to frostbelt residents in the post-war period.

By reference to earlier studies, such as that by Thorndike (1939) Smith shows that while there has been a general nationwide improvement in the quality of life, the basic pattern of regional variations remains.

Canadian cities are widely regarded as more 'liveable in' than most US cities and Toronto is often viewed as a model by US planners.

The United States Metropolis

1. An urban transect

A transect across any large metropolitan area clearly exposes the enormous diversification within American society. New York's 'Harlem' or Los Angeles's 'Watts' district blatantly reveal that the ambitions and hopes of many American Blacks and other low status groups have not reached fruition and seemingly have no prospect of doing so in the foreseeable future.

While all large metropolitan areas retain their own individuality the majority do illustrate certain common features which are shown in the generalised transect model of urban land use (Figure 14.4). The model indicates not only the basic land use

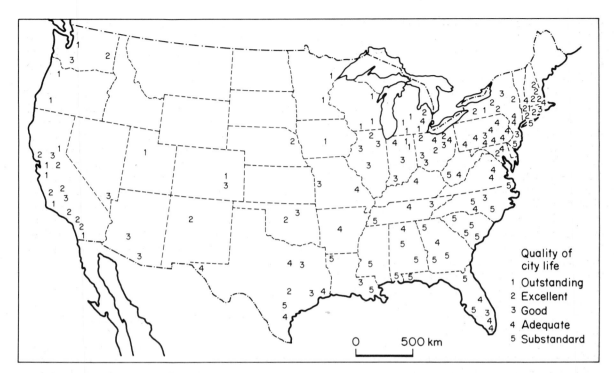

Fig. 14.3 *The quality of urban life in the US (Source: Smith, D. M. Where The Grass is Greener: Living in an Unequal World Penguin, Harmondsworth, 1979 pp. 177)*

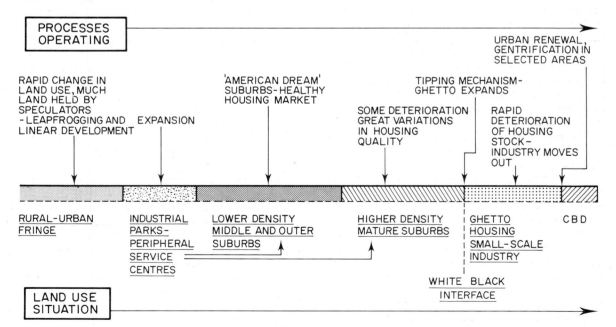

Fig. 14.4 *Transect model of land use in the US metropolis*

changes from centre to periphery but also the fundamental processes at work.

The Central Business District (CBD) of many large metropolitan areas is now distant from the affluent suburban residential areas and has suffered through vigorous competition from outer suburban and out of town shopping centres. 'Downtown', the term frequently applied to the major retail area, has declined significantly as a consequence, and in many cities, particularly in the northeast, deterioration and out-migration of retail establishments is an all too familiar picture.

Small-scale, labour intensive manufacturing has also gradually ebbed away from the CBD as it has from the inner city in general. However the administrative function of the CBD, both public and private, has been strengthened and the area has become more and more the preserve of the white collar worker. Frequently large areas have been cleared and rebuilt under ambitious urban renewal schemes which have given birth to new administrative, educational, cultural and to a lesser extent, residential areas. While such schemes have undoubtedly improved the visual appearance of the areas concerned they have done little for the low income residents. Gentrification is occurring in selected localities in most large cities whereby relatively affluent young and middle-aged suburbanites buy low cost deteriorating properties with potential for renovation on the outskirts of the CBD to be near their place of work and to enjoy the cultural and social benefits of proximity to the central area. Such small areas can quickly become fashionable in a short time period as more and more properties are purchased by the well-to-do. They gradually displace poorer groups as property values and taxes rise.

The inner city is in the main the residence of minority groups living at high densities in frequently deteriorating low-cost housing. Persons of the same nationality or ethnic origin tend to congregate together to form ethnic ghettos which exhibit a high degree of social deprivation. As the population of such groups expands, the ghetto will slowly move outward, usually along selected corridors. Beyond the ethnic ghettos are the mature suburbs, predominantly White, which are at a much higher density than the new suburbs beyond. This region differs widely in terms of housing quality. White areas close to the Black/White interface tend to be in a state of flux and other areas of poor environmental quality and lower prices attract black suburbanization. Much of the region, though, shows marked stability and high environmental quality where residents are determined to retain the advantages of reasonable proximity to the central area.

The lower density outer suburbs have expanded rapidly in recent decades and typify the so-called 'American Dream'. Industrial estates and peripheral service centres have provided new employment locations although many people resident in such areas still commute daily to jobs in the CBD.

The rural-urban fringe is another region in a state of continual flux. The United States lacks the strict planning regulations of the UK and other European countries and much land is held by speculators waiting for substantial returns on their investments as the urbanised area spreads further outwards.

2. The inner city (a) Ethnic ghettos

A simplified model of inner city problems (Figure 14.5) can be used to illustrate the causal factors of deterioration in such areas. The large-scale movement of the White population to the suburbs has created a disturbing duality in American cities as Blacks and other minorities are left in the inner city. In virtually all inner cities the proportion of the population that is White is still falling and ageing. The number of Blacks increased only moderately in the 1970s in most of the big cities and declined in some, but because the White population declined the Blacks are now the majority in Baltimore, New Orleans and Detroit, as well as in Atlanta and the District of Colombia, cities that held that status under the 1970 census. However this out-migration must not be exaggerated and the White population more often than not still accounts for more than 50 per cent of the population contained within official city boundaries. Nevertheless ethnic segregation is generally intense. Virtually every city has its Black area such as Chicago's 'South Side', Detroit's 'Paradise Valley', New York's 'Harlem', Los Angeles's 'Watts' and San Francisco's 'Fillmore'. The out-migration of Blacks has also had an important effect since it results in the abandonment of inner city housing.

Within its wider urban region the City of Los Angeles has more than its fair share of lower

Black and white photograph of colour intra-red view of San Francisco. The Golden Gate Bridge is top centre

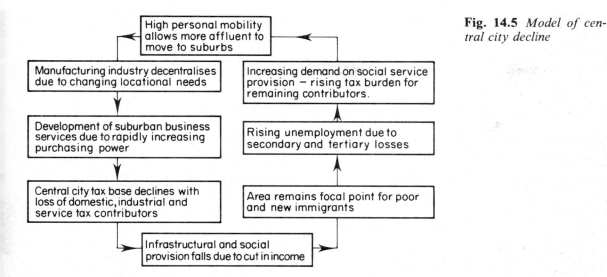

Fig. 14.5 *Model of central city decline*

Boxes in the model:
- High personal mobility allows more affluent to move to suburbs
- Manufacturing industry decentralises due to changing locational needs
- Increasing demand on social service provision – rising tax burden for remaining contributors.
- Development of suburban business services due to rapidly increasing purchasing power
- Rising unemployment due to secondary and tertiary losses
- Central city tax base declines with loss of domestic, industrial and service tax contributors
- Area remains focal point for poor and new immigrants
- Infrastructural and social provision falls due to cut in income

income residents and a high degree of racial segregation is evident. Of the total City population in 1980, 48.3 per cent were classified as White, 17.0 per cent Black and 27.5 per cent Hispanic. Whites comprised 75 per cent or more of the population of 14 of the 35 community plan areas, including 9 of the 14 plan areas of the San Fernando Valley and most of the communities in the western section of the City. Black residents form a majority in only three contiguous community plan areas, Southeast Los Angeles, South Central, and West Adams – Leimert Park – Baldwin Hills (Figure 14.6). Hispanics predominate to the near exclusion of other ethnic groups in the Boyle Heights community and form the majority ethnic group in five plan areas being concentrated primarily in the Central and Harbour Areas. The unshaded areas are separate municipalities such as Beverly Hills, not under the jurisdiction of the City of Los Angeles. The degree of concentration of other ethnic groups can be assessed using Figures 14.7 and 14.8.

Using Spearman's Rank Correlation Co-efficient, the thirty-five areas were ranked in order of highest percentage of White residents and highest median family incomes. A high positive correlation of +0.944 (above the 0.1 per cent probability level) was obtained, indicating the strong relationship between ethnicity and income.

In Los Angeles the proportion of Black and Hispanic households in poverty is twice that of either White or Asian households. The most im-poverished areas are the five contiguous communities of Central City, East and North Central City, Westlake, Boyle Heights, and Southeast Los Angeles. The areas of highest non-White population contain the bulk of the City's older housing stock and have an exceptionally high incidence of overcrowding and inadequate plumbing.

Numerous studies have shown how inner city areas have acted as reception centres for successive waves of immigrants. A pattern of 'invasion' and 'succession' was frequently established whereby, after a period of time, an established ethnic group, having upgraded its economic and social status, would move out to areas of better housing. As this transfer evolved, a new ethnic group would move into the vacating zone (invasion), congregate and steadily become a majority within a relatively well defined sub-area (succession).

The model of invasion and succession certainly applied reasonably well to evolving waves of immigrants from Europe but has a much more restricted relevance to the Black population. While Blacks have concentrated heavily in such inner city zones they have found it extremely difficult to 'break out' to higher quality zones in other parts of the metropolitan area.

In a major contribution to the subject entitled *The Black Ghetto*, Harold M. Rose (1971) has classified Black ghettos on a temporal basis. Defining a ghetto centre as the place of residence of 25 000 or more Blacks (in an urban area of at least 100 000 population), the bulk of whom are

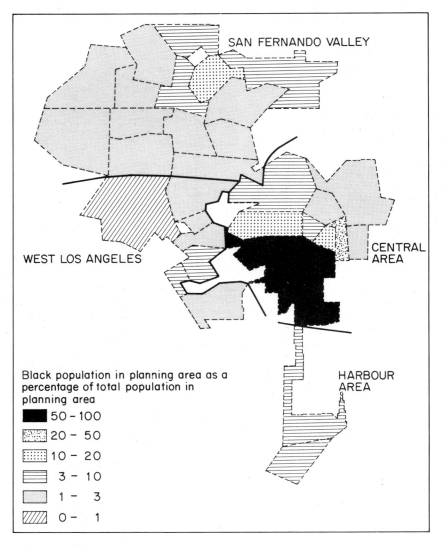

Fig. 14.6 *Distribution of black population in the city of Los Angeles. (Source: Los Angeles City Planning Dept)*

confined to ghetto neighbourhoods, Rose identified first, second and third generation ghetto centres. First generation ghetto centres housed at least 25 000 Blacks prior to 1920, second generation ghetto centres reached such a situation between 1920 and 1950, and third generation centres became so classified after 1950.

First generation ghetto centres are primarily in the south with the remainder in the northeast. The years 1920 and 1950 saw the emergence of more such areas nationwide but by far the greatest

development was in the northeast. Third generation centres also have a wide spread but it is noticeable that most western Black ghettos fall into this category. The latter grouping is the most numerous, indicating the rapid pace of urbanization in the post 1950 period.

Black urbanization has traditionally taken a different form in the south in contrast to other regions. In most southern cities areas were originally allocated for Black residential development with a physical barrier frequently separating Black

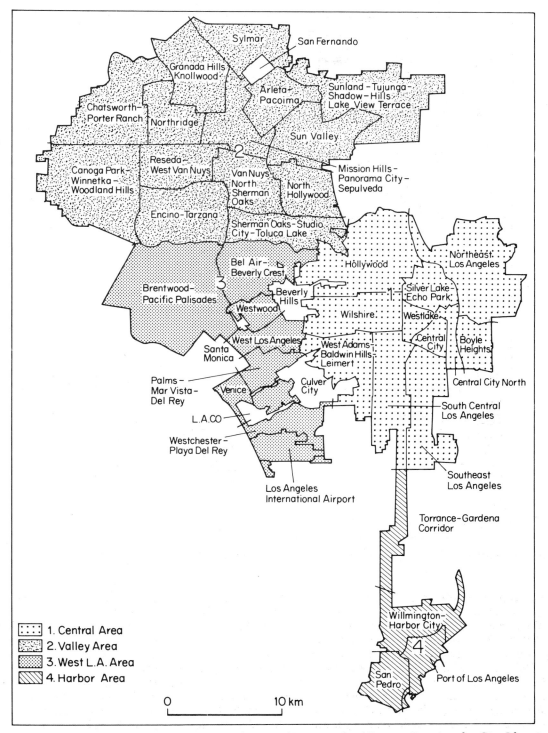

Fig. 14.7 *Community Planning Areas in the city of Los Angeles (Source: Los Angeles City Planning Dept)*

Fig. 14.8 Los Angeles: Ethnic composition of planning areas

Planning Area	White Non Hispanic	Hispanic	Black	Asian Pacific Islander	Native American	Other Non Hispanic	Total
Boyle Heights	2 169	73 618	1 575	3 540	327		81 229
Central City	6 456	12 305	4 680	1 836	318	2	25 597
Hollywood	115 378	39 670	8 719	16 309	920		180 996
N. & E. Central City	1 988	4 428	2 719	3 659	66		12 860
Northeast Los Angeles	54 514	120 261	2 601	19 412	1 491		198 279
S. Central Los Angeles	11 690	52 700	149 952	6 024	786	41	221 193
Silver Lake-Echo Park	21 522	34 927	1 634	18 062	494	11	76 650
Southeast Los Angeles	1 280	52 126	129 067	1 017	462		183 952
W. Adams-Leimert-Baldwin H.	10 784	15 919	115 035	9 110	661	19	151 528
Westlake	15 703	64 487	2 954	8 737	564		92 445
Wilshire	99 345	55 701	32 776	36 458	890	236	225 406
Total Central Area	340 829	526 142	451 712	124 164	6 979	309	1 450 135
Arleta-Pacoima	14 932	40 305	11 489	1 551	658		68 935
Canoga Park-Winnetka-W.H.	114 090	13 253	1 736	4 697	698		134 474
Chatsworth-Porter Ranch	57 745	4 801	1 079	3 870	404		67 899
Encino-Tarzana	60 499	3 854	818	1 392	221	42	66 826
Granada Hills-Knollwood	47 204	4 714	942	2 512	473		55 845
Mission Hills-P.C.-Sepul.	51 735	16 944	3 018	3 842	608		76 147
North Hollywood	65 377	21 192	2 111	3 420	665		92 765
Northridge	44 367	5 859	1 035	2 381	231		53 873
Reseda-West Van Nuys	63 041	9 687	1 273	2 496	538		77 035
Sherman Oaks-Studio City	59 964	3 767	898	1 283	271		66 183
Sun Valley	35 091	20 453	1 220	3 898	524		61 186
Sunland-Tujunga-S.H.-L.T.	34 233	5 341	2 891	1 057	466		43 988
Sylmar	24 632	14 890	1 252	1 035	566		42 375
Van Nuys-No. Sherman Oaks	83 347	19 390	2 409	3 717	659		109 522
Total San Fernando Valley	756 257	184 450	32 171	37 151	6 982	42	10 170 53
Bel Air-Beverly Crest	18 349	731	392	712	17		20 201
Brentwood-Pacific Pal.	49 514	1 800	480	1 705	97		53 596
Palms-Mar Vista-Del Rey	59 639	21 169	3 955	9 565	549		94 877
Venice	23 234	8 759	3 503	802	255		36 553
Westchester-Playa Del Rey	36 078	4 385	1 308	1 778	194		43 743
Westwood	30 451	1 381	541	2 095	56	10	34 534
WLA-Century City-Rancho Pk	48 628	6 725	1 359	5 857	178		62 747
Total West Los Angeles	265 893	44 950	11 538	22 514	1 346	10	346 251

Denver, Colorado

Fig. 14.8 Continued

Planning Area	White Non Hispanic	Hispanic	Black	Asian Pacific Islander	Native American	Other Non Hispanic	Total
San Pedro	36 994	19 082	2 735	2 659	534		62 004
Torrance-Gardena Corridor	11 076	9 935	4 007	4 992	228		30 238
Wilmington-Harbor City	21 410	31 411	2 511	4 517	525		60 374
Total Harbour Area	69 480	60 428	9 253	12 168	1 287		152 616
Final Total	1 432 459	815 970	504 674	195 997	16 594	361	2 966 055

Source: Los Angeles City Planning Department.

from White areas, thereby eliminating the zone of transition which is commonplace in non-southern cities. Clearly, Black suburbanization has to some extent blurred the original intense segregation but it still remains very apparent. Outside the south blacks entered areas previously occupied by whites. In the 1970s the increase in Blacks in southern cities was more pronounced than in most of those in the north. Those Blacks still leaving the farms now tend to settle in southern cities which have prospered in recent years to offer better job opportunities, rather than moving into other regions as they had done in previous decades.

Black suburbanization has progressed most in the first generation ghetto centres while third generation centres such as Milwaukee and Denver have very few Black residents in suburban zones. In the south, however, Blacks are often concentrated in satellite communities which were specially designed as Black housing areas and are thus not a result of the housing market mechanism. Richmond Heights, southwest of Miami, which is over 90 per cent Black, is a classic example of such development.

First and second generation ghetto centres evolved during a period in which residential segregation was sanctioned by law but in the post-war period important legislation has been passed to bring to an end such discrimination. However segregation has been maintained as Whites remain intensely reluctant to share social space with Blacks and other obvious (by colour) minorities. Such attitudes go a long way to explain the 'tipping process' by which the ghetto expands (Figure 14.9). Such a model can be applied to both the private and public housing markets.

D. R. Deskins (1981) notes three stages in ghetto development (Figure 14.10) with each stage characterised by periods of delineation, coalescence and expansion. In a detailed examination of Black residential expansion in Detroit over the last century and a half the three stages of ghetto morphology have been replicated twice, with current trends indicating the likelihood of a third phase.

The changing locational requirements of modern manufacturing industry and its subsequent large scale movement to the urban periphery and beyond has led to a great decline in blue-collar jobs in the inner city resulting particularly in very heavy Black (and other minority) unemployment. Hemmed into the ghetto by social immobility the Black population frequently lacks the physical mobility to gain sufficient access to suburban employment. A number of studies have shown that the journey-to-work distance of black employees has increased significantly in recent years.

Research has also pointed to a low level of 'entrepreneurial heritage' among black Americans. Even in Harlem, the nation's most famous Black community, well over half of all retail outlets are White owned.

Recent trends give virtually no indication that the position of Blacks and other obvious minorities in American society is going to change drastically in the near future. Harold Rose states 'A major overhaul in systems operation is necessary, unless it is agreed that the type of economic system that generates wide-ranging benefits for the vast majority of the nation's citizens is unable to allocate benefits in such a way as to prevent the place of residence of most Black Americans from resembling that of an underdeveloped country.'

(b) Urban renewal

In the 1950s and 1960s urban renewal schemes, often huge in scale, began to alter the face of many US cities. Although redevelopment had occurred previously on a piecemeal scale in all metropolises the new urban renewal schemes were very much larger in scale and were usually attempts at comprehensive redevelopment involving a mixture of different land uses and invariably incorporating substantial high rise commercial construction. This process of 'Manhattanization' was encouraged by substantial federal grants towards clearance. The 1949 federal programme gave renewal agencies the power of eminent domain to condemn and clear slum neighbourhoods, and re-sell the cleared land to private developers at below market price. The twin original aims of renewal were to improve the housing stock and also to upgrade the tax base of the central area in the hope of reversing the spiral of economic and social decline illustrated by Fig. 14.5.

While urban renewal schemes differed widely in size and nature the overall effect in central cities was to demolish old low-cost housing, inner city factories and declining retail centres to make way for quite different functions, in the process greatly increasing the area's vertical profile.

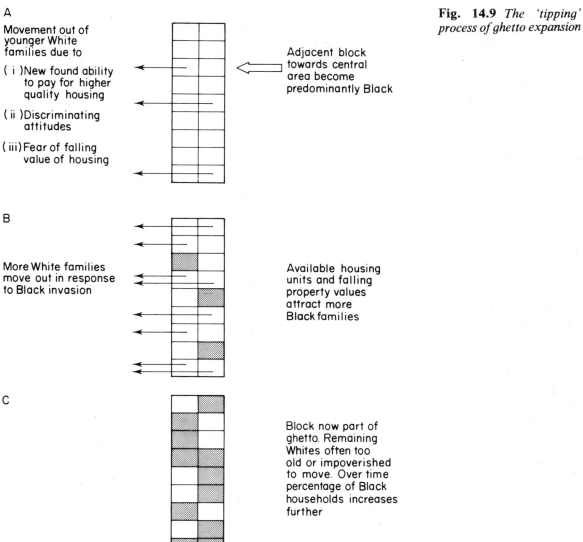

A

Movement out of younger White families due to

(i) New found ability to pay for higher quality housing

(ii) Discriminating attitudes

(iii) Fear of falling value of housing

Adjacent block towards central area become predominantly Black

Fig. 14.9 *The 'tipping' process of ghetto expansion*

B

More White families move out in response to Black invasion

Available housing units and falling property values attract more Black families

C

Block now part of ghetto. Remaining Whites often too old or impoverished to move. Over time percentage of Black households increases further

Houses occupied by Black families

The general result has been to emphasize the trend towards greater specialization in financial business and services in the central area. The now recognized failures of urban renewal were the great loss of low income housing which frequently resulted in greater overcrowding elsewhere in the inner city and also the substantial loss of manufacturing and retailing employment. Boston is a prime example of a large metropolitan area which went through this phase of urban renewal but, having recognized its earlier limitations, has now attempted to gear renewal more positively to the needs and priorities of the inner city population.

The Boston Redevelopment Authority, established in 1957, has been widely accused of quite unnecessary and ruthless clearance of the city's

Phase

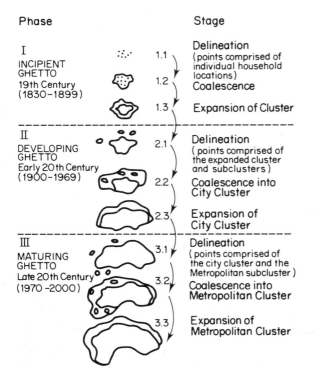

I
INCIPIENT
GHETTO
19th Century
(1830–1899)

1.1
1.2
1.3

II
DEVELOPING
GHETTO
Early 20th Century
(1900–1969)

2.1
2.2
2.3

III
MATURING
GHETTO
Late 20th Century
(1970–2000)

3.1
3.2
3.3

Stage

Delineation
(points comprised of
individual household
locations)
Coalescence

Expansion of Cluster

Delineation
(points comprised of
the expanded cluster
and subclusters)

Coalescence into
City Cluster

Expansion of
City Cluster

Delineation
(points comprised of
the city cluster and the
Metropolitan subcluster)
Coalescence into
Metropolitan Cluster

Expansion of
Metropolitan Cluster

Fig. 14.10 *Phases and stages in ghetto morphology (Source: Deskins Jr, D. R.* Morphogenesis of a Black Ghetto *Urban Geography April–June 1981, Vol 2, No. 2.)*

West End area with great loss of reasonable low cost housing and the destruction of a long established community. Boston's West End, along with clearance areas in a number of other cities, appear to have been selected for renewal not because they exhibited the worst slum conditions but because they offered the best sites for luxury housing.

While Boston has not abandoned the concept of urban renewal, public pressure has resulted in more socially accepted development with architectural styles more in keeping with the city's heritage.

At their worst, renewal schemes have been tagged 'negro clearance' projects where renewal agencies gave very little consideration to the displaced residents. Overall, urban renewal has had very limited success and many argue that urban redevelopment can be undertaken much more efficiently by the private market. The impact of

renewal was also limited from its inception because it was essentially a device for eliminating slums in order to renew the cities rather than a programme for properly rehousing slum dwellers.

Renovation as opposed to clearance and renewal received more attention in the 1970s but overall funding was piecemeal and extremely limited. In 1973 Congress passed the Urban Homesteaders Act which was designed actively to encourage the rehabilitation of properties in run-down inner city areas. In return for the acquisition of properties at nominal purchase prices, residents undertake to upgrade their new homes to meet legislative standards. The advantage to the city is that abandoned and untaxed properties can be transformed into units contributing to the tax base of the city while at the same time stemming the tide of out-migration to the suburbs.

(c) The road to bankruptcy

As Fig. 14.5 indicates at the beginning of this section the inner cities of the United States have all too often been caught in a vicious spiral of distress and the process is still active. A falling tax base in the city is often accompanied by increasing pressure on social and civil services which may eventually lead to acute financial difficulties as experienced by New York, Chicago, Philadelphia, Detroit, Cleveland and other major cities in the late 1970s.

New York's plight was particularly desperate and in 1975 the city approached default and bankruptcy several times with a total publicly-held debt reported to be $14 billion. The federal government at first refused to intervene but as the number of persons on welfare passed the one million mark, financial control measures were enacted and the city was rescued by state, federal and union pension fund aid. Assistance and control measures were renewed in the following years but New York remains in many ways a depressed city of much diminished quality.

A major concern for the city's government is the substantial deterioration of the city's infrastructure, its networks of streets, subways, bridges, tunnels, sewers and power lines. Financial crisis in the 1970s resulted in threadbare maintenance which simply stored up problems for the future. Over the decade the city workforce was cut by 60 000 in an effort to check expenditure.

Downtown Los Angeles

A facility urgently needed in the near future is a third water tunnel. Two tunnels were already in existence but cannot be serviced for fear of damaging them beyond repair. Work on a third tunnel commenced in 1970 but was later halted due to escalating costs and the city's financial troubles. Although work on the project has now resumed it is not due for completion for some years and New York could be faced with a very difficult water supply problem if one of the existing tunnels should cease to operate.

A partial solution to the financial problems of the city as seen by some politicians is to make suburbanites who use the employment, retail, transportation, financial and cultural facilities of the city, pay more towards its upkeep, but under present American law this would be virtually impossible to implement.

However an alternative is open to some cities. Houston has expanded outwards and extended its tax base by annexing unincorporated communities at the urban periphery and has avoided being strangled by its surrounding suburbs. Kansas City, Missouri, and Charlotte, North Carolina have proceeded in a similar manner. Annexation has mainly occurred in the south and in the west as the older cities of the northeast are invariably surrounded by independent municipalities making such expansion impossible. Annexation powers are not confined to central cities though and suburban municipalities have sometimes used this tactic to check the advance of central cities.

Federal aid to urban areas has helped to ease the most immediate financial pressure but many feel that the level of funding is far too low.

3. Spreading suburbs

The expansion of the suburbs has been the most consistent feature of American urban geography in the twentieth century. The first suburbs had developed in the late nineteenth century along the new railroads which radiated from city centres and also with the electric streetcar development from the 1890s onwards. As suburban communities were established along the new lines of communication many cities began to annex their adjacent areas in order to exert political and financial control. Movement to the new suburbs was confined to the middle class and wealthier families who could afford to utilise the greater mobility

that new technology had made available.

There was also a decentralization from central cities as companies fled from the union control which was being established in close-knit communities. For example the Pullman Company moved from central Chicago to a suburb where it set up what was virtually a company town. Steel companies also moved out of Chicago across the state border to Gary (Indiana) and from Pittsburgh to Youngstown for similar reasons.

The process of suburbanization at this stage also resulted in early zoning regulations whereby those wishing to buy land and build in townships and counties outside the central city were subjected to regulations which were frequently designed to preserve the community for the well-to-do. Similar attitudes were behind the reactions against further annexations of territory by central cities, since the outlying areas did not wish to pay taxes towards the upkeep of expensive central city facilities.

In the 1920s there was an important phase of new suburban building around American cities. This continued earlier trends but on a larger scale and was carried out largely by the construction of small housing estates near public transport lines. This period came to an end in the 1930s when the Depression reduced construction to an all-time low. Likewise, in the early 1940s there was limited residential development since resources were overwhelmingly channelled into the war effort.

However after the war there was a tremendous demand for new housing and in the following decade a major phase of suburban construction ensued, greatly encouraged by federal government guarantees for low-interest mortgages with low deposits, income tax concessions for house buyers and further finance to extend the road system. A notable feature of this period of suburbanization was that it was not specifically related to the major transportation lines which had governed most of previous development. During these years the interstitial areas were progressively infilled and later construction spread gradually outwards.

There was little resistance by many local jurisdictions since new housing increased the tax base and areas which were zoned for farmland were frequently turned over to housing development without undue complication. Zoning also had the effect of creating 'house-only' or 'commerce-only' zones, separating home from workplace even further.

By the mid-1950s vast numbers of Americans were separated from their workplaces and from retail centres, resulting in long journeys to work, to shop and to entertainment for those who had moved out to the suburbs. In response to this spatial imbalance the mid-1950s witnessed a substantial construction phase of new shopping centres, industrial estates and administrative complexes being established in peripheral locations. Such development was not entirely new but had generally been very small scale beforehand.

The decentralization of manufacturing, retailing and administration had two important effects. It now meant that many more of those who lived in the new suburbs could also find employment in these areas but conversely this process took many irreplaceable jobs from the inner city to locations difficult to reach by the less affluent. Transport systems had not been designed to distribute people from the central areas to suburban employment opportunities, instead they focused on concentrating workers in the city centre.

The extension of urban areas has generally continued unabated in recent decades in the absence of strict planning regulations which are in use in most other developed countries. Three basic forms of sprawl can be identified:
(i) peripheral accretion, where new housing estates are constructed on the edge of the built-up area;
(ii) linear development, with construction along main highways and feeder roads;
(iii) leap-frogging, where intervening tracts of land are left vacant. At its extreme this process has been sometimes termed 'urban splatter'.

Suburban expansion in the United States has been at a much lower density than in western Europe and has consequently had a much greater impact on the landscape. In the 1945–75 period Phoenix, Arizona spread from 44 square km in area with 45 000 people to cover 642 sq km and house 750 000 people. Figure 14.11 shows the outward extension of Minneapolis-St Paul between 1950 and 1970 and also serves the purpose of illustrating spatial differences between central city, built-up area and SMSA.

Commuting zones have extended significantly as urban workers have sought homes farther from the central city. Figure 14.12 shows the changing commuting pattern for Cedar Rapids and for Los Angeles between 1960 and 1970. The commuter zone has expanded for both cities although commuting has in fact decreased in certain parts of the inner zone. Reverse commuting has also developed in response to the decentralization of commercial and industrial functions.

The selective use of zoning powers remains an important influence on suburban development today. R. J. Johnston (1981) notes two basic types of suburb, the exclusive suburb and the mixed land use suburb, which he classifies according to the use of such powers. The former is usually a very affluent small political unit which is invariably zoned only for residential development. Its exclusiveness is preserved primarily by using density controls where minimum building lots may be set at say two acres, thus allowing entry to only the very affluent. Zoning regulations usually also forbid the construction of apartment blocks which might attract lower income residents.

The mixed land use suburbs tend to be the preserve of those in the middle income range where commercial and industrial use is frequently encouraged to increase the local tax base.

The overall effect of zoning in both types of area is to restrict population growth in outer urban regions while acting as a barrier to social and physical mobility to those of lower income. It has been argued that such restrictions prevent several million people from living in the suburbs of New York rather than in the City.

Suburban freeway corridors

The suburban freeways that encircle the large metropolises of the United States have become new focal points for industrial and commercial development in recent years, often to the detriment of the CBD. In Atlanta the 'Perimeter' Highway has succeeded Peachtree Street in the provision of high order functions for many of the city's population. Similar developments can be witnessed along the 'Loop' in Houston, the Tri-State and Northwest tollways near O'Hare airport in Chicago, and along many southern Californian freeways, as well as in numerous other metropolitan areas.

T. J. Baerwald (1978) has examined the evolution of commercial and industrial development along a seven mile stretch of Interstate Highway 494 south of Minneapolis which is the largest and most highly developed suburban freeway corridor in the Minneapolis – St Paul metropolitan area

Fig. 14.11 *Urban expansion of Minneapolis–St Paul 1950–70 (Source: Hart, J. K.* Urban Encroachment on Rural Areas *Geographical Review, Jan 1976, Vol 66, No. 1, pp 1–17)*

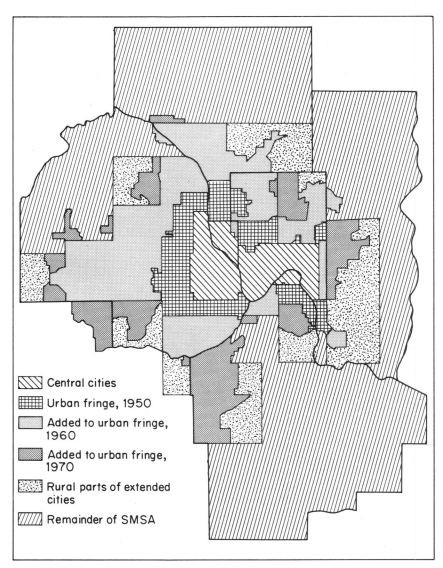

Central cities

Urban fringe, 1950

Added to urban fringe, 1960

Added to urban fringe, 1970

Rural parts of extended cities

Remainder of SMSA

(Figure 14.13). The 494 corridor has become the third 'downtown' in the Twin Cities area in the last thirty years.

The interchange of a major radial route with the circumferential freeway has become the most prestigious commercial location and the highest-order shopping centre and other retailers, dependent on high visibility, have occupied land within a half-mile radius. By the late 1960s, the corridor's land use pattern was basically set with only minor changes thereafter.

Circumferential freeways have generally ex-perienced the most intensive corridor development because they contain a wide variety of sites of approximately equal accessibility from elsewhere in the metropolitan area whereas radial freeways are orientated towards a smaller sector of the metropolitan hinterland.

4. The rural–urban fringe

The rural-urban fringe is the boundary zone where urban and non-urban land meet and is an area of

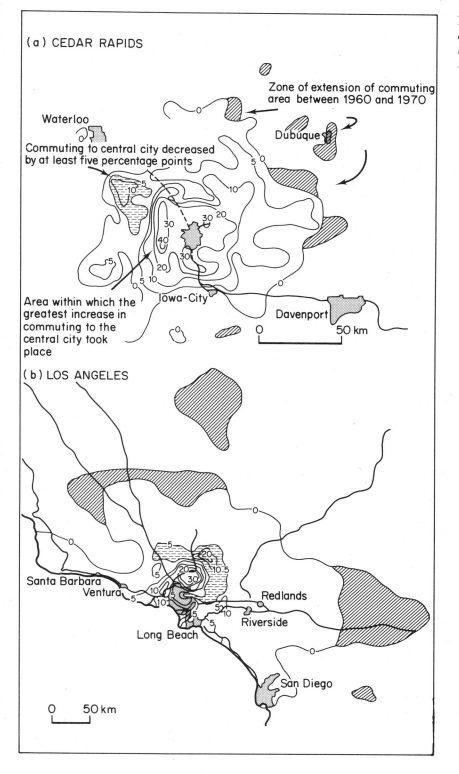

Fig. 14.12 *Cedar Rapids and Los Angeles; Changes in commuting to the central city 1960–70*

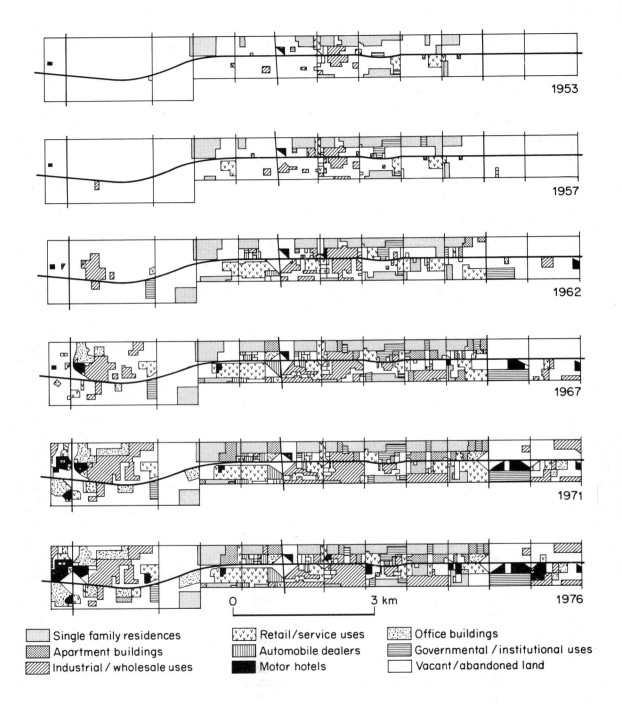

Fig. 14.13 *Development of a suburban freeway corridor (Source: Baerwald, T. J.* The Emergence of a New Downtown *The Geographical Review, 1978, Vol LXVIII, pp. 308–318)*

transition from agriculture and other rural activities to urban use. The exact size and nature of the area undergoing such transition has been the centre of much recent research, the more conclusive observations of which are illustrated by Figure 14.14. In general the size of the fringe area is dependent on the size of the overall metropolitan area and the effect of nearby and competing metropolitan areas.

As land values can change so rapidly in fringe areas speculators frequently hold much of the undeveloped land with the ownership and character of land frequently beginning to change more than twenty years before the area is actually built over. In a study of the rural-urban fringe of six metropolitan areas in the United States and Canada (Atlanta, Buffalo, Boston, Calgary, Sacramento and Toronto). H. J. Brown *et al.* found that investors and property developers own a much larger fraction of fringe land where development pressures are strong than where such pressures are moderate or weak. A marked change

Fig. 14.14 *A model of the North American rural-urban fringe*

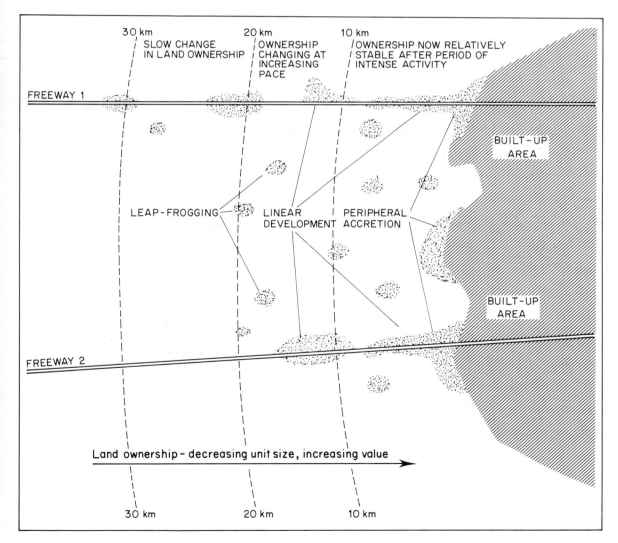

Black and white photograph of colour infra-red view of Washington DC taken from an altitude of over 50 000 feet

in ownership land size with distance from the built-up area was also noted. In US rural areas over 30 km from the urban boundary more than one-third of the land is held in parcels larger than 80 hectares. In contrast, in fringe areas where urban encroachment is taking place, fewer than 10 per cent of land parcels are larger than 80 hectares.

Stricter controls on subdividing land parcels around Canadian cities has generally reduced the role and pace of land speculation while the higher quality of the Canadian inner city has resulted in a weaker impetus for suburban expansion.

The Canadian City

While there are many similarities between Canadian and US cities certain distinctions are apparent that undermine the North American urban stereotype that is sometimes presented. Such contrasts are a product of historical evolution whereby urbanization in Canada has been subject to different property laws, financial systems, government, immigration experiences and a host of other factors which combine to mould the human landscape.

Although research concerning Canadian/United States urban comparisons has been limited a number of recent papers, mainly of Canadian origin, have stressed that fundamental differences are clearly evident.

The disturbing problems of the US inner city have only a limited applicability to Canada. A national inner-city study based on the 1971 census identified neighbourhoods in decline as only one category in a four-fold classification (Figure 14.15). Declining areas are characterised by continuous and worsening physical deterioration, outmigration, lack of community organisation and rising social pressures. Prominent among the causal factors resulting in neighbourhood decline are (i) a weak economic base which encourages out-migration and fails to attract new investment, a process evident in several inner city areas in Winnipeg; (ii) poor original construction where neighbourhoods remain the preserve of low income groups. There is little incentive for renters or owners to upgrade properties so deterioration escalates, particularly where local industry decentralises. Exemplification is provided by the Montreal neighbourhoods of Saint-Henri and

Pointe Saint-Charles; (iii) the threat of redevelopment which discourages investment, apart from that by speculators. The Milton Park area of Montreal underwent noticeable residential deterioration after the announcement of a large private redevelopment project in the area.
(iv) transition to other uses where non-residential uses are becoming of increasing importance such as in Centre-Sud in Montreal.

Canada's earlier response to urban decline was to follow the United States example and concentrate on urban renewal programmes but in the wake of fierce criticism this approach has been gradually abandoned. In its place the 1973 amendments to the National Housing Act introduced two new programmes, the Neighbourhood Improvement Program (NIP) and the Residential Rehabilitation Assistance Program (RRAP). The emphasis is now firmly on preservation and improvement of existing neighbourhoods rather than clearance and replacement by new functions.

Stable inner-city neighbourhoods usually have the firm basis of a sound housing stock. Such neighbourhoods can differ markedly, from upper class enclaves such as Westmount in Montreal, to traditional working class communities like Hochelaga in the same city.

Revitalisation tends to be concentrated in a few select inner city areas which become fashionable over a short period of time. Evident mainly in rapidly growing cities it usually involves the influx of young professional people into working class neighbourhoods to gain proximity to the CBD. Known as 'gentrification' in the USA, this process has been termed 'whitepainting' in Toronto and other Canadian cities. The New Edinburgh area of Ottawa shows the hallmarks of this trend.

Large scale redevelopment is also most likely to occur in rapidly growing cities where there is an intense demand for accommodation. Such action invariably involves the replacement of traditional housing by moderate to high rise apartment and office blocks as in St James Town and South Parkdale in Toronto.

While the inner city has tended to act as a reception centre for immigrants, and non-Whites are more likely to be found in the inner city as opposed to the suburbs, Canadian cities fortunately lack the vast ethnic ghettos that are characteristic of the large US metropolis. Race does not appear to be a primary factor affecting residential selection and neighbourhood change to

Fig. 14.15 Zones in the Canadian inner city

	1. Decline	2. Stability	3. Revitalization	4. Massive redevelopment
Population	Continuing loss of population	No significant losses or gains	Little change	Gain in populat
Socio-economic status	Decreasing	Stable	Increasing	Increasing
Family status	Increasing proportion of non-family units and elderly	Maintenance of population mix	Maintenance of population mix	Loss of families, gain of singles, young couples
Ethnicity	Varies—can be influx of deprived ethnic group or breaking down of traditional community	Sometimes strong ethnic community	Sometimes loss of ethnic groups	Seldom importa
Community organizations	Poorly organized, unstable	Varies	Increasingly well organized	Usually unorganized
Physical conditions	Worsening	Stable	Improving	Improved housi possible environ ment problems
Housing/land costs	Increasing much less than metro average	Increasing at same rate as metro average	Increasing more rapidly than metro average	Increasing more rapidly than me average
Tenure	Increasing tenancy	Varies, but often high ownership	Little change	Tenancy
Non—residential functions	Loss of commercial-industrial functions with no replacement	Maintaining a mix of functions	Maintaining a mix of functions	Losing some co mercial function but gaining othe
Pressure for redevelopment	Low	Low	Strong, but controlled	High

Source: R. McLemore, C. Aass, P. Keilhofer, *The Changing Canadian Inner City.*

the extent it is in the United States and the well documented 'white flight to the suburbs' has no parallel in Canada.

In the 1960s when central city population loss was widespread in the US the phenomenon affected only a very small number of Canadian cities. However in the 1970s a much larger number of Canadian cities recorded central city population decline, pointing to the fact that while urban evolution appears to be similar in sequence in this respect, it lags a decade or so behind the US urban experience.

In spite of this recent record of population loss in central cities in Canada, residential vacancy rates run at a very low level and there is little evidence of the high rates of property abandonment which characterise many of the lowest grade residential areas in the US city.

Comprehensive data is lacking but the CBD in Canada has very much remained a viable entity in terms of retailing and has not illustrated the effects of intense competition from peripheral retail centres which has been the case in a number of large metropolitan areas in the US. J. Mercer (1979) points to the recent establishment of major department stores in traditional CBDs and the sizeable investment in underground shopping malls which abound in large Canadian downtowns, following the example set by Montreal. The 'City Below' in Montreal has its component parts linked by Metro, giving access to major department stores, hundreds of specialist shops, hotels, cinemas, the Stock Exchange, art galleries, a concert hall, theatres and dozens of office buildings.

Overall the aura of deterioration and financial crisis has not affected the Canadian metropolis to the same extent as its US counterpart. One obvious reason for this, apart from the issues discussed above, is the geography of local government. The central city in Canada contains a higher proportion of the total urban population and dualism (the sharp contrast between poor inner city residents and affluent suburbanites) is nowhere near as clear cut, with a much gentler income profile across the metropolitan area as a whole. Consequently the Canadian city has a more viable tax base and has a greater degree of planning flexibility.

Suburban contrasts are also apparent between the two countries, with the Canadian metropolitan area exhibiting both a lesser degree of urban sprawl and greater control over the form that such growth takes. Personal mobility in Canada is high but significantly below the level of the United States. The per capita ownership of cars is lower, freeways mileage is generally less and public transport systems are more heavily used north of the border. In addition stricter land use controls have restricted peripheral development to a much greater extent. Canada has been more concerned than the US about the loss of prime rural land to urbanization because of its more restricted endowment of such high quality land. Of course greater apparent satisfaction with inner city life in Canada has resulted in a more subdued demand for such new development on the rural-urban fringe.

While suburban office development has boomed due to a number of other reasons as well, the sizeable gap between downtown and suburban rents has been a major factor (Figure 14.16). Vacancy rates are increasing in many US cities with the appearance of a growing number of environmentally attractive and less expensive alternatives to the new downtown office towers. As yet the Canadian CBD does not appear to have suffered in the same way but as the cost factor continues to widen this may not be the case in the not too distant future.

As in the United States there are widespread regional contrasts, with western metropolitan

Fig.14.16 Suburban and Downtown office rents

City	1981 rent (C$ per sq metre) Downtown	Suburbs	Monthly savings* per employee in suburbs (C$)
Montreal	2.8	1.4	250
Toronto	3.7	1.3	433
Calgary	2.4	1.5	167
Edmonton	2.0	1.2	150
Boston	3.3	2.0	250
Chicago	3.3	1.7	283
Seattle	2.2	2.0	50
Houston	3.1	2.2	150

* Assumes 20 square metres per employee.

areas in Canada illustrating the vibrant expansion that is underway in the American west and along the Gulf Coast, although in general there has been a greater degree of infill in inner areas prior to spread on the margins. Calgary shows all the signs of rapid recent growth where the cost of an average house or apartment more than doubled to over C$100 000 between 1976 and 1979. Homes in new suburban areas are considerably more expensive. The city now sprawls over 440 square kilometres, with the population increasing from 370 000 to 550 000 in the same three-year period due primarily to a very high rate of in-migration. The metropolitan population is expected to reach one million by the turn of the century.

As a result of the country's considerably lower population, urban areas occupy a much more restricted land area in Canada compared to the United States but due to the harsh physical environment of the north the location of large settlements is much more concentrated than south of the border.

Place of work data, available for the first time from the 1971 census, has enabled the zones of attraction, based on the spatial relationship between the place of residence and place of work, to be mapped and a hierarchy recognised (Figure 14.17). The zones of attraction are designated primary, secondary or tertiary depending on their influence or 'pull' with regard to employment. Toronto, Montreal, Winnipeg and Vancouver are primary poles; Halifax, Windsor, Sudbury,

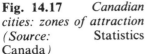

Fig. 14.17 *Canadian cities: zones of attraction (Source:* Statistics Canada*)*

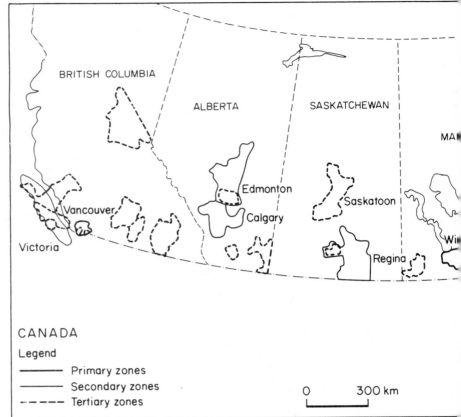

Ottawa, Calgary and Edmonton are prominent among the secondary poles while St John's, Saint John, Shawinigan and Brantford are examples of tertiary poles.

Megalopolis

The term 'megalopolis, was first coined by Jean Gottman in 1961 to describe the almost continuous stretch of urban and suburban landscapes along the northeastern seaboard of the United States from southern New Hampshire to northern Virginia. No other region in the country illustrated such an extent of urban decentralization and coalescence and Gottman felt that the terms 'city' and 'conurbanation' were no longer adequate to describe the stage of urbanization reached here.

The region was regarded as unique not just because of its size but also because of the intense interaction between the various centres. Gottman saw the seaboard megalopolis as 'a very large polynuclear urbanized system endowed with enough continuity and internal interconnections that it can be considered a system in itself.' Within megalopolis (Figure 14.18) lie five of the largest metropolitan areas in the nation, Boston, New York, Philadelphia, Baltimore and Washington, interspersed with a host of smaller cities and towns. Over forty million people, almost one-fifth of the total US population live in this region. Despite the decentralization of economic growth to the south and west the region remains the 'main street' of the nation, providing the whole of the United States with so many essential services. Megalopolis is indisputably the political, economic, social and cultural centre of the nation and although its rate of growth has fallen behind the

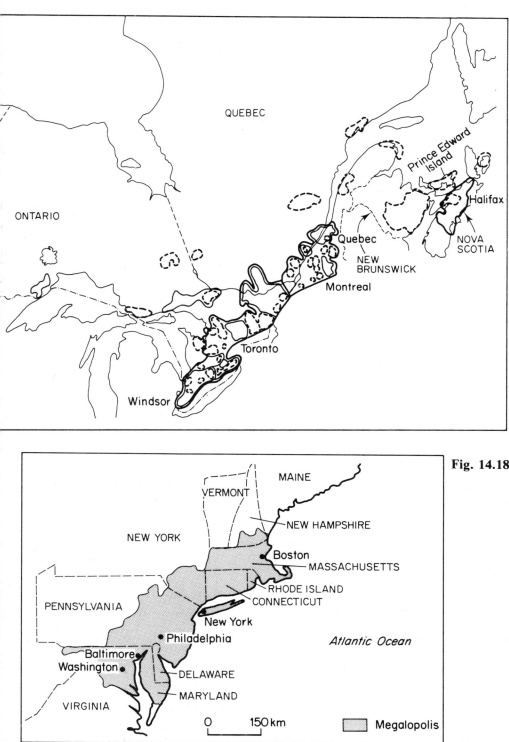

Fig. 14.18 *Megalopolis.*

cities of the sunbelt the urbanized area continues to expand.

Sizeable tracts of woodland and farmland remain but the loose and numerous scattering of buildings indicates the influence of the cities over the entire region and most of the farmers in the region have additional sources of income apart from agriculture.

The concept of megalopolis has not gone unchallenged. Some authorities deny its very existence as a phenomenon and much debate has occurred about the term's applicability to other regions in the United States and worldwide.

The heavily urbanised Great Lakes region between Chicago and Pittsburg, sometimes known as 'Chipitts', and the San Francisco–San Diego ('Sansan') region of central and southern California have also had the term 'megalopolis' applied to them by some writers. However most authorities agree that while urban growth in these regions is very extensive it is far from the size and the degree of complexity evident along the northeastern seaboard.

In California the eventual formation of a megalopolis is extremely debatable. While the northern and southern zones of the 1000 km axis have sprawled over vast areas the central zone is as yet unaffected by big city development. In the central 350 km between the two major urban poles there is no settlement along or near the coast with a population above 40 000. Although the rate of population growth over the last two decades in this region has been much faster than in the state as a whole the topography of this part of California and the growing concern among residents about the effects of rapid growth will be powerful counterweights to intense urbanization.

Bibliography

Baerwald, T. J. (1978) 'The emergence of a new downtown', *The Geographical Review*, LXVIII, pp. 308–18.

Deskins, D. R. Jr (1981) 'Morphogenesis of a Black Ghetto', *Urban Geography*, April–June, 2, 2.

Gottman, J. (1961) *Megalopolis*. Cambridge, Mass.: MIT Press.

Johnston, R. J. (1981) 'The political element in suburbia: a key influence on the urban geography of the United States, *Geography*, November.

Mercer, J. (1979) 'On continentalism, distinctiveness and comparative urban geography: Canadian and American cities', *Canadian Geographer*, 23.

Rose, H. M. (1971) *The Black Ghetto: A Spatial Behavioral Perspective*. New York: McGraw-Hill.

Smith, D. M. (1979) *Where the Grass is Greener: Living in an Unequal World*. Harmondsworth: Penguin Books.

15

Urbanization II: Case Studies and the Future

As one of the most highly urbanized regions of the world the North American continent presents a vast array of urban settlements all unique in their own way. However comprehensive coverage of the different sizes and types of towns and cities is clearly beyond the scope of this text where the confines of space allow only limited case study analysis.

The major metropolises of Toronto and Chicago have been selected to illustrate the dominant processes evident in the urban geography of large cities in the United States and Canada. Both cities are huge and complex urban systems undergoing continual transition and the studies presented here offer only a brief insight into some of the more important geographical processes at work.

Different aspects of large city development have been highlighted in each case study in an effort to avoid repetition and to acquaint the reader with as many of the ongoing trends as possible in these major conurbations.

Toronto: City and region

Toronto, with a Census Metropolitan Area (CMA) population of 2.8 million (1976) is marginally the largest city in Canada ahead of Montreal.

Located on the northwestern side of Lake Ontario and functioning as the provincial capital, it is a port of entry and an important commercial, financial, and industrial centre as well as the banking and stock-exchange centre of the nation. Toronto's importance as a port has increased significantly since the opening of the St Lawrence Seaway in 1959.

Demographic evolution

While Toronto exhibits its own distinct individuality the city does illustrate many trends which are characteristic of Canadian cities as a whole and to a lesser extent of urban areas in the United States.

Toronto's population and the built-up area have expanded rapidly throughout the century as illustrated by Figure 15.1, which also shows the development of Montreal and Vancouver, Canada's next two largest cities. This spatial diffusion of the urbanized area has been accompanied by major demographic changes which have in recent decades led to a considerable decline in the population of the inner city and a huge increase in the numbers living in new suburban and fringe areas.

Figure 15.2 shows the results of such intra-urban population changes between 1961 and 1976 for Canada's three largest metropolitan areas. The

Downtown Toronto

average change for the twenty-three largest metropolitan areas in the country during the same period was −24.8 per cent in the Central Area, −15.1 per cent in the Mature Suburbs and +106.2 per cent in the New Suburbs and Fringe. The thriving western metropolises, such as Vancouver, have generally recorded lower inner city losses due to tremendous recent economic expansion.

The area covered by the Toronto Census Metropolitan Area is shown by Figure 15.3, along with the boundary of the City of Toronto and the wider Toronto Region which includes the regional municipalities of Durham, York, Peel and Halton. It should be noted that the City of Toronto and Metropolitan Toronto do not coincide exactly with the subdivision used in Figure 15.2 (i.e.

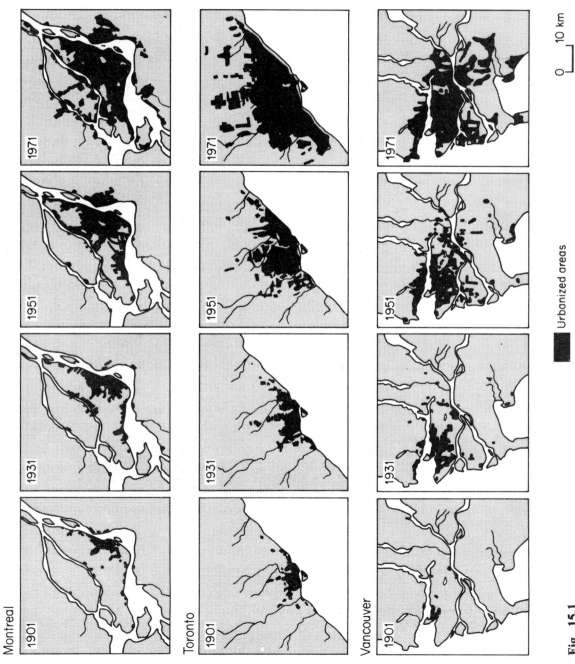

Montreal
1901 1931 1951 1971

Toronto
1901 1931 1951 1971

Vancouver
1901 1931 1951 1971

0 10 km

■ Urbanized areas

Fig. 15.1

Fig. 15.2 Population by zone: Canada's three largest cities

	Total population 1976 (000s)	Population change 1961 to 76 (%)	Distribution of total metropolitan area population 1961 % 1976	
			1961	1976
Toronto				
Central area	111.2	−12.5	7.0	4.0
Mature suburbs	778.2	−7.5	46.1	27.7
New suburbs and fringe	1 913.6	123.5	46.9	68.3
TOTAL CMA	2 803.0	53.6	100.0	100.0
Montreal				
Central area	104.8	−38.3	8.1	3.7
Mature suburbs	596.7	−22.8	36.6	21.3
New suburbs and fringe	2 101.2	80.0	55.3	75.0
TOTAL CMA	2 802.7	32.9	100.0	100.0
Vancouver				
Central area	69.0	9.6	8.0	5.9
Mature suburbs	344.2	−1.5	44.2	29.5
New suburbs and fringe	753.1	99.3	47.8	64.6
TOTAL CMA	1 166.4	47.6	100.0	100.0

Central Area, Mature Suburbs and New Suburbs and Fringe).

The population of the City of Toronto decreased from 713 000 in 1971 to 633 000 in 1976, the largest decrease in the City's history. For Metropolitan Toronto, the Census reported only slight growth, less than 35 000. For years the City's population had hovered around the 700 000 mark while the rest of Metropolitan Toronto had grown rapidly. The 1976 Census indicated a distinct change in this trend.

Comprehensive demographic analysis shows that movements of population between areas within the Region are closely related to stages in the life cycle, with the available housing stock being a major determinant of where people live at various periods in their life. A broad concentric zone pattern tends to form in Toronto (Figure 15.4). Young adults frequently choose housing closest to the CBD while older families occupy the next ring out. Middle aged families are more likely to reside at a greater distance from the central area and farther out still, in the newest suburban areas, young families dominate. This simplified model applies particularly well to a rapidly growing metropolis like Toronto where an invasion and succession process evolves over time.

In the periods 1961–66 and 1966–71 the City of Toronto registered net migration gains for only three of the standard age groups, 15–19, 20–24 and 25–29 and between 1971 and 1976 a net gain was recorded only in the 20–24 group. Net losses occurred in all other age groups with particularly large losses for adults at peak family formation age (30–40 years) and for children under the age of fifteen.

Recent trends for Metropolitan Toronto have illustrated increasing similarity after an earlier period of marked contrast. Between 1961–66 Metropolitan Toronto experienced net gains in almost all the standard age groups. However between 1966–71 gains were more restricted and were little more than negligible except in the 15–34 age range, with the greatest rise by far in the 20–24 group. By 1976 Metropolitan Toronto's migration profile began to closely resemble that of the City in the 1960s with large net losses of adults and young children and net gains restricted entirely to the 15–24 age range.

In contrast to the City and Metropolitan

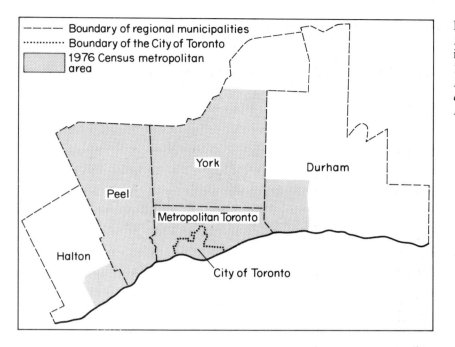

Fig. 15.3 *The Toronto Region (Source:* Toronto in Transition *City of Toronto Planning and Development Dept Policy and Research Division, April 1980, p. 7)*

Toronto the rest of the Toronto Region grew rapidly during this period with gains in all age groups. Between 1971 and 1976, 52 per cent of population growth in the outer part of the Toronto Region was due to outmigration from Metropolitan Toronto with most of the migration losses from the inner zone a consequence mainly of the relocation of households with children to family housing being constructed in the outer region.

The City of Toronto contains a much higher percentage of rented and small unit accommodation than the outer regions which, along with the stimulus of employment and the social attraction of the central area, has attracted young adults to this area. Over 90 per cent of the housing units built in the City in the 1970s were in the form of apartments. Between 1961 and 1976 the number of one and two person households in the City almost trebled.

In the rest of Metropolitan Toronto population is also lost as family households, which settled in the inner suburbs in the 1950s and 1960s, mature and children leave to form their own households in outer areas where the bulk of new housing is located.

The degree of ethnic concentration in Toronto as in most Canadian cities is markedly less than in

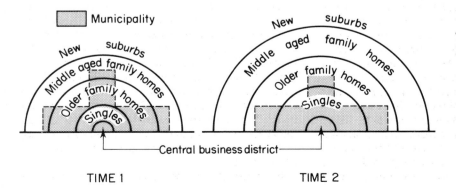

Fig. 15.4 *Changing social structure in a growing city (Source:* Toronto in Transition *City of Toronto Planning and Development Dept. Policy and Research Division, April 1980, pp. 21)*

Fig. 15.5 *Toronto: percentage population with mother tongue other than English 1976 (Source: Toronto Planning Atlas p. 29)*

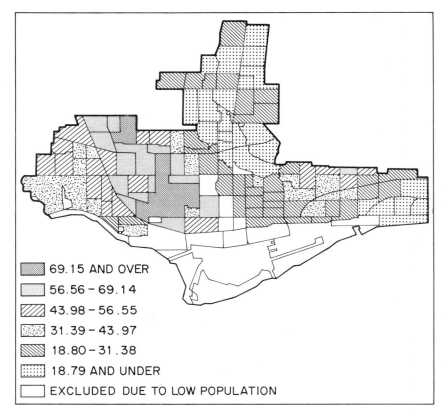

69.15 AND OVER

56.56 – 69.14

43.98 – 56.55

31.39 – 43.97

18.80 – 31.38

18.79 AND UNDER

EXCLUDED DUE TO LOW POPULATION

American cities and decreased considerably in the 1970s. In 1971, one in six of City residents was a recent immigrant compared to one in eleven in the rest of Metropolitan Toronto. However by 1976 the proportion had fallen to one in twelve for both the City and the Metropolitan area as a whole.

The City of Toronto appears to be losing its traditional role as 'the' immigrant reception centre of the Toronto Region. Clearly, more and more immigrants are locating directly in suburban areas, particularly in apartment complexes. This may to an extent reflect less of a need by new arrivals to concentrate in ethnic neighbourhoods (most of recent immigrants speak English and are well educated) but is more likely a result of the limited availability of rented homes and the increased cost of housing in the City. In addition, earlier immigrants, having established themselves in the wider community, frequently decide to move outwards to better quality housing. The suburbanization of the Italian-speaking population provided a classic example of this trend in the 1970s.

Nevertheless as Figure 15.5 indicates, within the City persons whose mother tongue is other than English are noticeably concentrated in the western sector. The largest groups by mother tongue in the City are English (61 per cent), Italian (7.7 per cent), Portuguese (6.9 per cent), Chinese and Japanese (3.3 per cent) and Greek (2.5 per cent).

Although Toronto's inner city does not illustrate urban decay and social deprivation on the scale of the larger US metropolitan area, its poorer areas are nevertheless clearly evident and are located mainly in the central area. Perception of the functioning city obviously appears differently to many inner city and suburban residents as has been exemplified with regard to the city's income flows (Figure 15.6). In recent years gentrification has occurred in small selected areas of Toronto as reasonably affluent young families have bought up property in socially strategic areas within the inner city and carried out extensive renovation.

1. Suburban view of Toronto's income flows

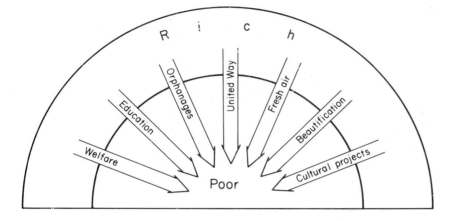

Fig. **15.6** *Contrasting views of Toronto's income flows (Source: Bunge, W. W. and Bordessa, R)*

2. Inner city view of Toronto's income flows

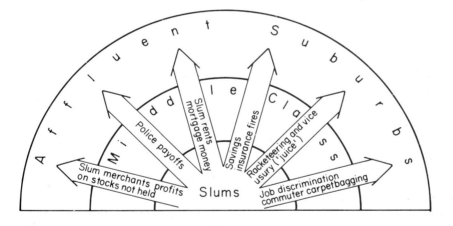

Land use

While the appearance of the City, particularly its vertical profile in the central area, has undergone very noticeable change in the 1960s and 1970s, the overall division of land use has not altered a great deal. In 1976 42 per cent of City land use was classed as residential, 14 per cent as commercial, office and institutional, 15 per cent as storage and industrial, 7 per cent as utilities and transportation and 22 per cent as open space or vacant. The greatest changes since 1961 were registered by industry which fell from 10 per cent to 8 per cent and open space which increased from 15 per cent to 18 per cent.

The overall land use figures indicate a slight increase in office use but fail to convey the huge expansion in office space (mainly through vertical development) that has occurred in recent decades. Between 1965 and 1980 the total amount of office space in the City almost doubled with most development concentrated in the Central Core (Figure 15.7). As of 1 January 1981 over five million square feet of new office space was under construction in this area.

The number of persons employed in the City has

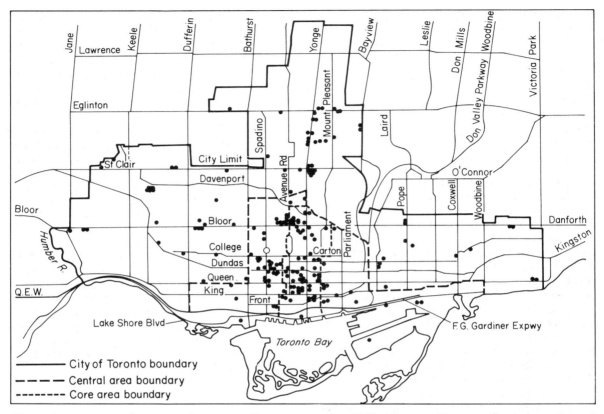

Fig. 15.7 *Toronto; location of current office construction 1979 (Source:* Toronto Statistics, *City of Toronto Planning and Development Dept, April 1981)*

continued to rise steadily but most of this growth has been accounted for by the office sector (Figure 15.8), a trend common to most North American metropolises.

In the years from 1966 to 1975 manufacturing employment declined at an annual average of 2942 jobs due to the decentralization of manufacturing industry to suburban locations and to structural changes in the economy. The major manufacturing employers in the city are food and beverages (20 per cent), clothing (16 per cent), printing (15 per cent), metals (7 per cent) and chemicals (6 per cent). In common with virtually all other North American metropolitan areas unemployment rates are significantly higher in the central area and mature suburbs than further out.

Over half of all persons working in the City reside outside its boundaries with the result that over 250 000 commute into the City of Toronto from surrounding municipalities every day. As there is also reverse commuting, which has been a developing North American phenomenon, the City has a lower net daily commuter flow of approximately 170 000.

In spite of strong decentralization tendencies in population, manufacturing and to a lesser extent retailing, Toronto's CBD remains a vibrant and very much a viable entity and does not appear to have suffered unduly from spatial diffusion unlike many US cities.

Future trends and the necessity of regional planning

Recent population projections estimate that the population of the Toronto Region will increase from 3.18 million in 1976 to 3.55 million in 1986 and 3.87 million in 2001. Undoubtedly growth will occur unevenly over the region with heavily in-

Fig. 15.8 City employment

	1970 %	1976 %
Office	38.1	45.2
Retail	10.0	9.3
Industrial/warehouse	25.0	21.1
Other	26.9	24.4

creasing demand for certain services creating intense pressure in areas of expansion, while some areas will be faced with the often under-estimated problem of declining demand. If resources are to be efficiently allocated, with organized growth generating further economic expansion, comprehensive regional planning is vital. While larger scale planning has developed considerably in recent times much remains to be done in the future.

Population movements can have a tremendous effect on public spending. For example in education where a rising population in the outer suburbs has made new school building necessary, falling rolls and school closures in parts of Metropolitan Toronto illustrate the reverse effect.

The rising cost of transportation is beginning to dampen demand for housing in outer suburban locations as demand appears to be switching to more central locations. If the housing industry responds directly by increasing residential development within Metropolitan Toronto the number of new housing units required in the fringe municipalities will be reduced considerably below earlier projections.

The Joint Metro/TTC Transit Policy Committee estimates that Metropolitan Toronto currently has an infrastructure in place (i.e. sewers, water, roads, transit) capable of supplying a population of three million, approximately one million more than currently within the area. The additional housing stock requirement could only be made available by substantial infilling and redevelopment. The Committee has recommended that area municipalities within Metropolitan Toronto review zoning policies and official plans to encourage the development of higher density housing in order to achieve a better utilization of the infrastructure already in place.

Within the Region jobs have decentralized at a slower pace than population with a resultant increase in the average journey to work. Development at the fringe of the urban area is frequently at densities much too low to be effectively served by public transport and decisions over the region concerning the future quality of roads and public transport have to be made if mobility levels are to be maintained and hopefully increased.

All administrative regions compete in the ambition to enhance their tax bases. Both the City and Metropolitan Toronto have recently embarked upon programmes which will actively promote economic growth within the respective areas. However similar efforts by the regional municipalities (Durham, York, Peel and Halton) have placed the two sub-regions in the position of competing against each other for a share of the limited economic growth anticipated in the Toronto Region. In the near future subcentres within Metropolitan Toronto would seem to have a greater chance of success than those in the outer region as most of the necessary infrastructure is already in place. However such unstructured competition becomes in reality a 'no-win' situation which can be resolved only by comprehensive regional planning.

Chicago: A major urban system

With an SMSA population of over seven million Chicago is the third largest metropolitan area in the United States and the socio-economic centre of the dynamic mid-western region of the nation. Throughout the city's evolution its strategic location at the southwestern tip of Lake Michigan has made transportation the overwhelmingly dominant factor in Chicago's development.

After the initial establishment of a trading post at the mouth of the Chicago River in the 1770s, Chicago was platted in 1829, grid system fashion at the northern end of a planned canal to link Lake Michigan with the Mississippi River. Chicago quickly became the key focal point for transcontinental communications, a characteristic it has maintained to the present day. By 1856 the city was the hub for ten trunk rail routes and its economy expanded with increasing rapidity as

Fig. 15.9 *The concentric zone model of Chicago's urban ecology (Source: Berry, Brian, J. L. et al Chicago: Transformations of an Urban Systems, p. 45, Ballinger, Cambridge, Massachusetts, 1976)*

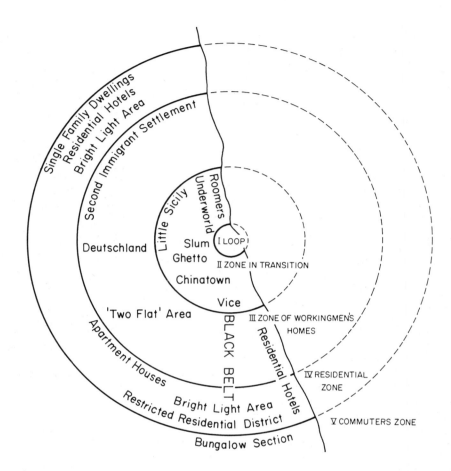

more and more freight of great diversity was handled by Chicago companies.

The disastrous fire of 1871 which made one-third of the city's population homeless soon allowed large-scale redevelopment to proceed and provide a firm basis for the expansion of the modern city. Chicago developed both vertically and horizontally at what at times seemed like an alarming rate, due in no small way to the city's role as a centre of architectural innovation. The Chicago 'school' of architecture pioneered the steel-frame skyscraper, the garden suburb and the planned satellite city.

Suburban spread was facilitated first by the horse-drawn omnibus and later by cable cars, electric lines, commuter railroads, elevated and subway trains and of course the automobile. The 'Loop', an elevated rail line opened in 1897, encircled a massive and diverse central business district.

The processes of 'invasion' and 'succession' noted in the previous chapter were first recognised in Chicago by Burgess *et al.* (Figure 15.9) who formulated the classic concentric zone model of urban residential development. The inner city acted as a reception centre for wave upon wave of immigrants from Europe, who, once they were established economically and culturally, sought out better quality housing, usually at greater distance from the CBD. The blacks, many of whom were brought north as strikebreakers, encountered both racial prejudice and job-related enmity and were unable to match the socio-economic progress of other groups. As a result they remained within their initial environment establishing 'Black Chicago' which has been sometimes termed 'a city within a city'.

Congestion at the centre necessitated new locations for industry, made possible by considerable development of the transport system. Of immense importance was the construction of a succession of circumferential railroads, particularly the Chicago Outer Belt Line that formed an arc approximately 55 km from the central area. Industrial satellite towns, such as Joliet, Aurora, Elgin and Waukegan, were established where important radial routes crossed the Outer Belt line.

The spatial structure of Chicago owes much to planning, primarily of a piecemeal nature in the nineteenth century but markedly more integrated in the present century. The 1909 Chicago Plan produced by Daniel H. Burnham became an important guideline for city policies until the Second World War. Lasting attributes to the Plan are a monumental civic centre, a lakefront preserved in a belt of continuous parks and beaches, a greenbelt of forest preserves encircling the built-up area in Cook County, streets and landscaped boulevards and an east-west highway stretching outwards from the city centre.

The automobile encouraged an unprecedented suburban expansion in the first quarter of the century followed by a period of stagnation due to the Great Depression and the Second World War. The end of hostilities heralded a new era of expansion with the Chicago metropolis at the forefront of many of the trends that have transformed metropolitan America in recent decades. Chicago has the world's tallest building, Sears Tower, and two others in the top five, the First National and the John Hancock and is undoubtedly one of the major administrative, cultural, educational and industrial centres in the continent.

In the post-war period decentralization has been the key process operating in the Chicago urban system. In 1960 the City of Chicago contained 57 per cent of the 6.22 million people within the six-county metropolitan area. By 1977 the City recorded only 42 per cent of the increased 7.04 million in the wider urban region.

The manufacturing base of the Chicago economy has declined, particularly within the City where tertiary employment has not expanded fast enough to make up the deficit. The overall result has been a considerable decline in the City's tax base. Total public spending in Chicago (The City) doubled to $10 billion between 1970 and 1978 but the City's income only rose by 58 per cent. Federal

The Central Business District, Chicago, with Lake Michigan in the background

funds have had to make up the shortfall. In 1970 the federal government spent 2.5 times more money in the City than City Hall did; by 1978 it was spending 4.3 times more.

In terms of employment Chicago fared better than many northern cities in the 1970s and between 1970 and 1976 actually registered a net increase of 60 000 jobs. However this was derived from a net gain of 260 000 jobs in the outer metropolitan region and a net loss of 200 000 jobs within the City itself. The City's share of employment for the whole metropolitan region fell from 68 per cent in 1960 to less than 50 per cent in 1978. In the 1970s 6 of the 7 sub-areas of the City lost jobs, the only exception being the city centre which contains tremendous wealth. This can be viewed as a case of too much economic development being concentrated in too small an area.

Industry has increasingly located in organised industrial parks which provide a complete range of essential services to the manufacturer. There are now in excess of 350 industrial parks within an 8 county area of northeastern Illinois and northwestern Indiana. The movement of manufacturing industry to the outer metropolitan area has greatly increased the degree of reverse commuting while the spreading suburbs have led to an increase in the average journey to work.

City Hall has attempted to attract employment back to the central city. Prominent among such efforts has been the designation of two economic redevelopment areas lying at the core of the old South Side and West Side ghettos, the Stockyards Redevelopment Area (1967) and the Midwest Impact Area (1970). It has been estimated that these two schemes could eventually create 40 000 direct jobs.

To cater for the diffusion of population over a wider and wider region, regional shopping centres, which first appeared in Chicago in the early 1950s, have steadily increased in number. Now 15 major regional shopping centres (Figure 15.10) as well as over 100 smaller plaza-type centres serve the metropolitan region. The concept of the recreational shopping park has emerged in the early

1960s and 1970s whereby indoor shopping centres are offering a competing array of amenities aimed at developing the recreational and entertainment aspects of the shopping trip.

The number of daily shoppers in the CBD has declined precipitously since 1945 and as expected has adversely affected retail sales. In response the retail giants have invested more and more heavily in the outer metropolitan area. However as the retail function of the CBD has decreased in importance office space has rapidly increased as financial and administrative functions have gained an even firmer hold on the sub-region.

Residential decentralisation involving mainly middle class whites has resulted in the sharp contrast between the inner and outer metropolitan area typical of virtually all large US cities. Within the City itself Whites account for 43 per cent of the population and Blacks and Hispanics 42 per cent and 15 per cent respectively. Approximately 85 per cent of metropolitan area Blacks in Chicago reside

Fig. 15.10 *Location of major planned regional shopping centres in Chicago. (Source: Berry, Brian, J. L. et al* Chicago: Transformations of an Urban System, *p. 45, Ballinger, Cambridge, Massachusetts, 1976)*

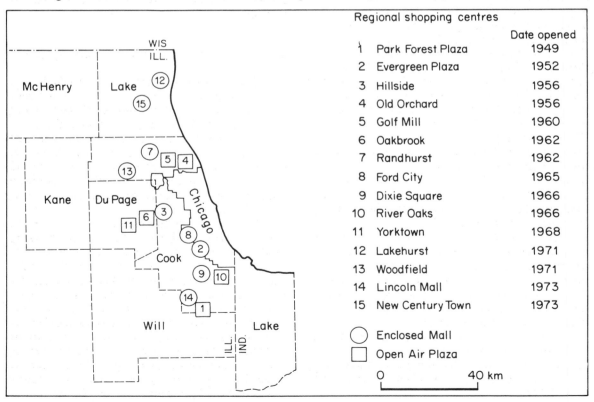

Regional shopping centres

		Date opened
1	Park Forest Plaza	1949
2	Evergreen Plaza	1952
3	Hillside	1956
4	Old Orchard	1956
5	Golf Mill	1960
6	Oakbrook	1962
7	Randhurst	1962
8	Ford City	1965
9	Dixie Square	1966
10	River Oaks	1966
11	Yorktown	1968
12	Lakehurst	1971
13	Woodfield	1971
14	Lincoln Mall	1973
15	New Century Town	1973

○ Enclosed Mall

□ Open Air Plaza

0   40 km

The Atrium Mall at Water Tower Place in Chicago's Magnificent Mile. The seven-storey mall houses two major department stores, many boutiques and speciality shops

within the City boundaries. Many poorer Black residents live in public housing constructed in the 1950s as part of huge urban renewal projects but now vilified as 'vertical ghettos'. The Robert Taylor Homes in the South Side district is the largest public housing project in the country, extending for 25 blocks and housing 75 000 people. Far worse poverty exists in the West Side with burned-out buildings and abandoned factories stretching for miles. Roosevelt Road, extending west from downtown out to the city limits, was the urban riot corridor in the 1960s. Recently gentrification has occurred in selected areas as young Whites have upgraded the housing stock, but, in perspective, total numbers are rather small. A test for the City is when the children of these young professionals reach school age. In the past the poor reputation of the City's school system has often impelled families who would otherwise stay to move to the suburbs.

B. Berry *et al.* (1976) note that events in the intervening decades have destroyed Burgess's concentric zones (Figure 15.9) and argues convincingly that it is easier to understand the social dynamics of the central city in recent times in terms of five zones of racial change. The zones illustrated by Figure 15.11 are:

1. The 1960 Ghetto: communities that were over 50 per cent Black in 1960;
2. The 1970 Ghetto Extension: communities that became over 50 per cent Black between 1960 and 1970;

3. The Ghettoizing Zone: communities that were between 10 and 50 per cent Black in 1970.
4. The Contiguous Zone: communities under 10 per cent Black in 1970 contiguous to Black communities; some Spanish and some White;
5. The Outlying White Zone: the remaining communities, refuges for other minority groups mainly from eastern and southern Europe, dominantly catholic.

Berry observes that for the white population the contrasting spatial distribution of the WASPs (White, Anglo-Saxon, Protestants) in the newer outer suburbs and the catholics in the older suburban areas, is very noticeable indeed.

Micro-regions are every bit as evident in the suburbs as they are in the inner city. As Berry states 'An increasingly fine-grained set of community distinctions has emerged, each catering to a particular group with a particular lifestyle by offering housing types, physical design and a package of environmental amenities that convey a particular image.' The relationship between suburban location and stages in the life cycle, highlighted in the Toronto study, are also broadly true for Chicago.

Transport and the major urban system

The city is served by three scheduled flight airports, O'Hare International, Midway and Meigs Field. In 1978 over 50 million people flew to and from Chicago via the airport system. The combined total was over 12 million more than the total passengers handled by any other city in the world. O'Hare has been the busiest airport in the world since 1961 when it took over the title from Midway Airport. The 1978 traffic for the three airports is illustrated by Figure 15.12.

O'Hare is one of the major employers in the Chicago region, with over 33 000 people working at the airport. A total of 26 major carriers, 7 commuter airlines, 5 supplemental carriers and 3 cargo carriers operate out of O'Hare on a regular basis. The ascendency of O'Hare has left only a minor role for Midway although there have been attempts to revive the latter. Non-scheduled activity accounts for 90 per cent of total operations at Meigs Field. Being only five minutes travelling distance from the loop, Chicago's business centre, Meigs Field is extremely convenient for company jets and it has been estimated that 94 per cent of

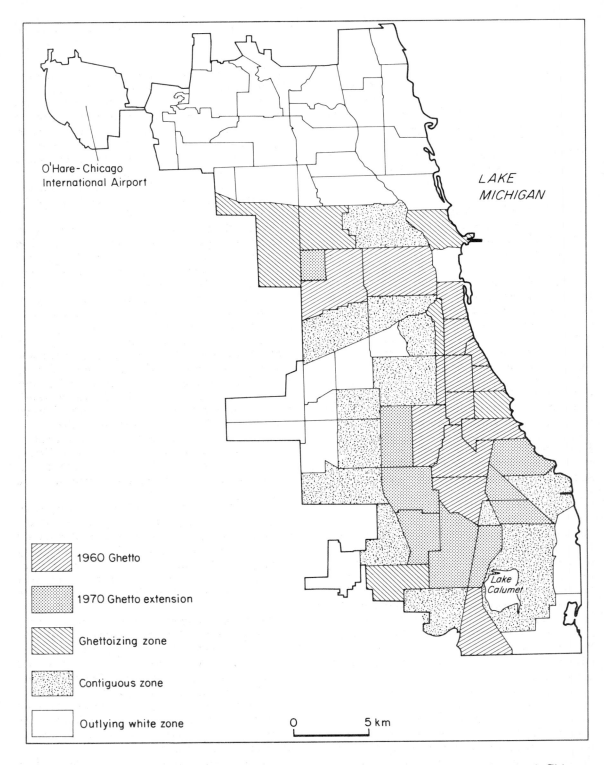

O'Hare–Chicago
International Airport

*LAKE
MICHIGAN*

Lake
Calumet

1960 Ghetto

1970 Ghetto extension

Ghettoizing zone

Contiguous zone

Outlying white zone

0   5 km

Fig. 15.11 *Chicago's five racial zones of the 1960s (Source: Berry, Brian J. L. et al Chicago: Transformations of an Urban System, p. 54, Ballinger, Cambridge, Massachusetts, 1976)*

Fig. 15.12

	Air Operations	Passengers	Air Cargo (tonnes)
O'Hare	760 606	49 151 449	928 935
Midway	176 094	726 352	22
Meigs Field	80 456	430 590	33

the traffic at Meigs Field is business traffic.

Chicago's location at the southern extremity of Lake Michigan quickly established it as a gateway between the northeast and the west, first for the railways and later for the spreading highway system. While the northeast corridor has the highest frequency of movement for railway passenger traffic, Chicago is the pre-eminent route centre, being the focal point of eleven routes. In terms of both connectivity and volume of traffic Chicago remains the most important railway freight centre in the country.

Eight Interstate highway routes focus on Chicago and its surroundings, providing efficient and rapid road links to all parts of the United States. The concentration of routes on Chicago goes a long way to explaining the primacy of the East North Central in terms of the regional connectivity of the Interstate highway network. Such centrality in time, cost and distance has been a most important factor in the economic growth of both city and wider region.

Chicago is the eleventh most important port in the United States and the first on the Great Lakes. Domestic movements dominate as the port fails to register in the first thirty in terms of foreign waterborne commerce. Chicago is the only Great Lakes port with direct water connection, via the Illinois Waterway, to the Mississippi River system. The Lakefront Iroquois Terminus, a 79 hectare facility, is being developed to provide the Port of Chicago with the most modern and efficient container handling operation on the Great Lakes.

To fulfil its role as a dynamic regional node the city is as dependent on its internal transport structure as it is on external links.

Major highways, commuter railway lines and the rapid transit system are of vital importance to the socio-economic base of the city. Such links have been essential in extending the daily urban system of the city which is illustrated by Figure 15.13. New expressways, financed largely by the federal government under the National Interstate Defence and Highway networks have opened huge areas to suburban development. Car ownership per household in the outer metropolitan area is approximately double that of the central city.

The Chicago Transit Authority runs the second largest public transport system in North America after New York City. Weekday rides total approximately 2.5 million. In 1978 the total for the year was more than 660 million rides.

On the 307 km rapid transit system more than 2400 train trips are made each weekday. The Authority has a fleet of 1100 rapid transit cars which operate on six routes connecting a total of 140 stations. The area served by rapid transit comprises the 570 square km of the City of Chicago plus 36 nearby suburbs with a total population in excess of four million.

The Chicago Transit Authority also operates 2 400 buses over 138 routes totalling 3 500 route kilometres and even in the late night and early morning hours more than 50 per cent of the bus routes provide a service. With the rapid transit system also operating in the 'small hours' Chicago is one of the few cities in the world that has a transit service around the clock. A major extension of the rapid transit to connect with O'Hare airport is underway. This two track extension is being constructed in the central reservation of the Kennedy expressway.

Eighty-two per cent of all rail passengers in Chicago travel to or from the city centre with the private car extending an overwhelming dominance for other trips. Even with Chicago's relatively strong public transport system the average number of trips is only 80 to 90 per head per year as compared with 200–300 in large European cities.

The original gridiron street pattern has been gradually overlain by new systems, particularly the freeway network radiating from the city centre. While the development of freeways has eased problems of congestion, environmental groups have become fervently opposed to further extensions. In fact some planners have advocated the complete banning of motor traffic from the central area compensated for by massive investment in public transport.

The future of Chicago and other large cities rests heavily on the viability of its transport systems. However as networks extend the costs of

Fig.   15.13 *Chicago's daily urban system (Source: Berry, Brian, J. L. et al Chicago: Transformations of an Urban Systems, p. 14, Ballinger, Cambridge, Massachusetts, 1976)*

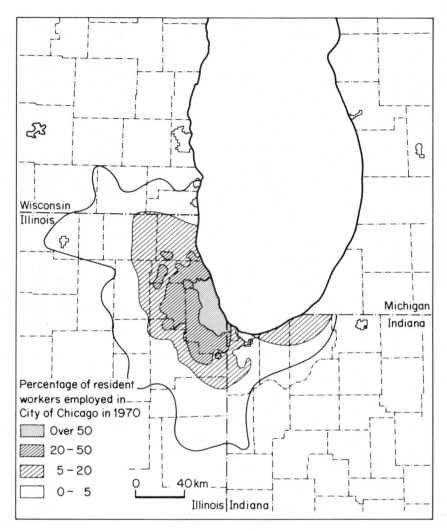

repair and maintenance increase and public transport losses continue to escalate. With movement clearly seen as the vital base for all economic interaction transportation planning has emerged as a vital component of the city's future development.

Urbanization and the future

Most recent predictions of the future see North America as becoming an increasingly complex society. The dominant theme is one of progressive economic development and material advancement. However, although present trends do point to such development the expected picture could be drastically changed by any number of possible occurrences such as major international warfare, a catastrophic and sustained decline in world trade or a turnaround in the political ideology of the continent. Thus the assumption of continuing economic progress facilitating the expansion of the spatial system is but one alternative, albeit the one which most North Americans would like to take, for the future.

Perhaps the most common factor among serious predictions of the future is that they invariably seem gross exaggerations at the time of forecasting but eventually prove to underestimate the intervening rate of progress. Brain Berry (1970) emphasises the fact that man normally undervalues the pace and capacity of change, pointing to the past predictions of H. G. Wells and R. Vaughan which in many respects materialised well before the expected time.

The geography of the future will be founded upon the existing spatial structure, from trends which have already begun and from developments which are yet to be recognised. The movement towards the dispersion of daily urban systems will undoubtedly continue while the intervening low accessibility areas, the 'inter-urban periphery' will gradually recede in area. Improved transportation and reductions in the working week will allow journeys to work over longer distances (although rising transport costs may halt this at times) while reverse commuting and cross-metropolitan journeys will increase in importance. The trend towards the multi-nuclei metropolis is already clearly underway.

The process of urbanization in the United States by the year AD 2000 will, according to H. Kahn and A. Weiner (1967) result in at least three huge megalopolises, Boswash (Boston-Washington), Chipitts (Chicago-Pittsburgh) and Sansan (San Francisco-San Diego), which should contain more than half of the country's population.

Berry feels that such forecasts are probably too conservative and miss what J. J. Servan-Schreiber (1969) has called the essence of the American challenge, 'the compression of time and space in a way that was inconceivable even ten years ago'. Berry sees the United States moving into an era of 'telemobility' and from mechanical into electronic environments whereby present geographical concepts such as distance-decay, gravity models and heartland-hinterland relationships will be outdated. Under such conditions the diffusion of information will be almost completely independent of distance. As Berry states 'Traditionally we have moved the body to the experience; increasingly we will move the experience to the body'.

But as Berry sees man as underestimating the pace of change some would see him as possibly overreacting to recent trends. The generation of new wealth is very much linked to the constant supply and efficient utilization of natural resources. While improvements in the latter have unmistakably been achieved, the 1970s has made

The Boston and Merrimack River area as photographed from the Skylab space station in Earth orbit

North Americans all too aware of the relationship between their relative opulence and natural resource availability.

The effect of natural resources motivating the extension of settlement into increasingly harsh environments such as the North Slope of Alaska and the Arctic Islands is likely to continue. Advanced technology will make habitation of such areas more tolerable. Developing communications will more firmly link such resource frontiers with the economic cores of the continent.

Coastal regions may well undergo yet another surge of comparative advantage in comparison to many inland locations as the exploitation of mineral resources in territorial waters gains momentum. If such development reaches the stage that some authorities predict then a strong new impetus to coastal industry and residential location will occur.

Urbanization and commensurate economic growth is likely to continue for some time to be faster in the US sunbelt and in western Canada in comparison to the traditional heartland areas of both countries. In addition the tremendous recent population growth rates of sparsely peopled areas such as Colorado and Nevada seems likely to continue as the more affluent seek out less crowded environments. Such 'quality of life' regions will act as a strong counterweight to areas of prime economic activity. However certain 'limiting factors' cannot be ignored. In the western United States the problem of water supply is already a serious one in many areas and much greater numbers could not be adequately accommodated unless supply can be significantly raised.

While successive census reports indicate that the number of persons below the poverty line has declined, the dualism exhibited by the large metropolises has become more and more pronounced. Opinions vary sharply as to whether such great inequality will be perpetuated while most hope for the eventual 'unification' of the city. Unfortunately the weight of opinion is firmly on the side of the sceptic.

Population growth is of course a key variable in the future of urbanization but it continues to be notoriously difficult to predict with any high degree of accuracy. What is apparent is that personal space is an important part of the American Dream and as average living standards increase, this greater affluence will be translated into more low density suburban housing. Such a process will of course have a much lesser effect in lower population density Canada.

However, even if the higher population projections are fulfilled it must be remembered that North America is a relatively sparsely populated continent and even with a considerable extension of low density suburbanization vast areas will remain lowly populated.

As the scale and complexity of urbanization multiplies the necessity for more comprehensive and future-orientated planning becomes more and more apparent. With magnification of scale the consequences of miscalculation will become greater and thus a structured flexibility and capacity for change must be an indispensible part of urban planning in the coming decades. The difficulties currently presented to large-scale planning by the multiplicity of local government units will have to be surmounted if sufficient progress is to be made in this field. The United States continues to lag behind Canada in this respect.

Extension of the spatial structure is expensive and is not a once in a lifetime cost. Large sections of the Interstate Highway Network commenced in the late 1950s require substantial and expensive repair. The costs of maintaining the present spatial structure are only just being realised and could prove to be a prime obstacle to its future enlargement.

Abler, Adams and Gould (1971) see as a major challenge to the future the ability to design and construct an urbanized system that is psychologically viable as well as physically habitable. Stress is a disease of modern living but does it necessarily have to remain so in the future? Whether or not Constantine Doxiadis's 'Ecumenopolis', a universal city which will consist of the entire habitable area of the earth, will ever evolve is very debatable. It has been estimated by some that such a possibility could occur within the next fifty to seventy-five years. Nevertheless whatever the size or quality of life in the future, planning is the key to making the best of the conditions prevailing. In such a world the geographer can play a most important role.

Bibliography

Alber, R., Adams, J. S. and Gould, P. (1971) *Spatial Organisation: The Geographer's View of the World.* Englewood Cliffs, N. J.: Prentice-Hall.

Berry, B. J. L. (1970) 'The geography of the United States in the year 2000', *Transactions of the Institute of British Geographers*, November, 51, pp. 21–53.

Berry, B. J. L. *et al.* (1976) *Chicago: Transformations of an Urban System.* Cambridge, Mass.: Ballinger.

Kahn, H. and Weiner, A. J. (1967) 'The next thirty-three years: a framework for speculation, *Daedalus*, 96, pp. 705–32.

Servan-Schreiber, J. J. (1969) *The American Challenge.* Harmondsworth: Penguin Books.

Index